Fundamentals of Advertising Research

Fourth Edition

Alan D. Fletcher
Louisiana State University

Thomas A. Bowers
University of North Carolina

Wadsworth Publishing Company
Belmont, California
A Division of Wadsworth, Inc.

Communications Editor: Kris Clerkin
Editorial Assistant: Nancy Spellman
Production Management: Mary Douglas
Print Buyer: Randy Hurst
Design: Kevin Pruessner
Copy Editor: Elizabeth Judd
Compositor: Thompson Type
Cover: Vargas/Williams/Design

1984, 1979 editions published by John Wiley & Sons and Grid Publishing Co.

Printed in the United States of America

1 2 3 4 5 6 7 8 9 10 — 95 94 93 92 91

Library of Congress Cataloging-in-Publication Data
Fletcher, Alan D.
    Fundamentals of advertising research / Alan D. Fletcher, Thomas A. Bowers. — 4th ed.
        p.   cm.
    Includes bibliographical references and index.
    ISBN 0-534-14778-X
    1. Advertising — Research.   I. Bowers, Thomas A.   II. Title.
HF5814.F57   1990
659.1'072 — dc20   90-46828
                                                              CIP

Contents

9   Experiments   145

10   Data Processing and Analysis   160

11   Writing the Research Report   189

16   Audience Research: Print   293

17   Other Syndicated Research   310

Part Four   The Outlook for Advertising Research   337

18   Looking Ahead   338

· · · · · · · ·

· · · · · · · ·

· · · · · · · ·

Preface

Previous editions of *Fundamentals of Advertising Research* have been used in undergraduate courses in advertising research, advertising management, advertising campaigns, public relations, and marketing research. In some courses, it has been used as the sole textbook; in others, it has been the primary textbook, supplemented by small introductory paperback books on statistical methods. In some courses it has been the unifying resource, supplemented by numerous journal articles and heavy use of outside assignments. Although the textbook was originally written for undergraduate advertising students, it has been used at the graduate level as well. Faculty members have used previous editions in courses in mass communication research, advertising research, public relations research, and marketing research. The primary use of this text at the graduate level has been as a supplementary source of information about research techniques and descriptions of major advertising research suppliers.

Changes in the Fourth Edition

In the advertising research business, companies come and go, and their services change from one year to the next. That is why the major changes for this fourth edition are in Part Three: Syndicated Research Sources. By the time you read this, there will have been new alliances, mergers, and closures, and some ongoing companies will have added new services and revised existing ones. Most of the companies included in Part Three are well established and well known in the industry.

In other parts of the book, we have added or modified conceptual material while trying to preserve the book's most commonly identified strengths — its practical approach and straightforward style.

Chapter 2 gives improved coverage of psychographic or lifestyle research such as VALS. We have also added material on the development of single-source data on media usage and purchasing decisions. In Chapter 4 we have deleted some secondary research sources and added new ones, giving special attention to electronic databases. And we have added a short chapter on qualitative research methods.

In several early chapters we have included short cases for analysis. They are designed to provide examples of situations in which research has potentially important applications.

The chapters in Part Three have been rewritten to include new sources and updated samples of existing sources. For each research service, we provide brief descriptions of the research method used, the types of reports offered, and instruction on how to read the reports. We have placed emphasis on the concepts that are reported and have minimized technical detail. In the last chapter we have revised the discussion about future developments in advertising research.

A Message to Students

It is clear that most students in advertising and marketing research courses have no intention of becoming research professionals. Yet they recognize that throughout their careers, they will be using research supplied by someone else. They realize the importance of being able to differentiate good from bad research. That is one reason that the best advertising and marketing programs typically include a research course as a requirement for all students.

Many students approach a research course with some apprehension. In under-graduate advertising programs that do not require a research course, some students avoid it altogether. Don't be afraid; *Fundamentals of Advertising Research* is written largely in nontechnical language and is intended to be readable. According to student evaluations of previous editions, a major strength was readability. "It's not threaten-ing." This readability has not changed in the fourth edition. Upon completing the introductory research course, many students have commented that it wasn't as difficult as they had expected. There's nothing mysterious about research; good research uses lots of common sense. If you feel intimidated, don't be.

••• **Acknowledgments**

We wish to thank several colleagues who reviewed one or more editions of this book and made recommendations for additions and other changes. These reviewers include Arnold M. Barban, University of Alabama; Donald Jugenheimer, Fairleigh-Dickinson University; Timothy Bengston, University of Kansas; Conrad R. Hill, University of Rhode Island; Leonard J. Hooper, University of Florida; William Miller, Ohio University; Joseph Pisani, University of Florida; Richard Tino, University of Bridgeport; Donald Vance, University of Miami; Wei-Ma Lee, University of Texas–Austin; and Tsan-Kuo Chang, Cleveland State University.

Alan D. Fletcher
Thomas A. Bowers
August 1990

PART ONE

The Nature of Research

Advertising research is becoming increasingly important as manufacturers face more uncertainty and risk in advertising and other aspects of their business. They are encountering increased competition from other manufacturers in their product categories. Many competing brands are very similar to each other, and it is difficult to promote differences. For that and other reasons, the majority of new products or brands introduced each year are unsuccessful.

Retailing, especially in the food industry, has changed with the introduction of scanning machines that read product codes at the checkout counter. Advertising media have changed dramatically, too. Consumers have many more media alternatives to choose from, and advertisers face a bewildering choice of options in which to advertise. Media costs have risen while economic conditions have forced many advertisers to reduce advertising expenditures.

The consuming public has changed in many ways, too. Older age segments are growing in size. Lifestyles are also changing, and consumers are becoming more concerned about the quality of life and about their health and the environment.

As uncertainties increase, advertisers face greater risk and have to rely more on research to guide their decisions. Advertising research can answer questions about the nature of the market, appropriate advertising strategies, message effectiveness, and media audiences.

But advertising research cannot answer all questions. Properly conducted, it can reduce uncertainty by narrowing the range of alternative decisions. It must also be conducted at a reasonable cost; in some cases the costs of research outweigh the benefits. In other words, advertising research may not always be the answer.

In this section, we examine the uses and limitations of advertising research and place it in the perspective of an advertiser's decision-making process. Chapter 1 explores the need for advertising research in more detail, discusses the role of intuition, stresses the importance of relating costs to benefits of research, compares advertising and marketing research, and explains some categories of research: applied, basic, methodological, descriptive, exploratory, and explanatory. Chapter 2 describes how advertising research is used at different stages of the advertising process, including target market definition, positioning, pretesting, posttesting, and audience research. It also discusses how needs for advertising research may vary according to the product's stage in its life cycle. ■

CHAPTER 1

The Role of Advertising Research

- When an airline introduced a nonstop flight from Charlotte to London, the airline's advertising director had to decide how to divide the advertising effort between advertisements for business travelers and advertisements for pleasure travelers.
- That advertising director also had to decide whether to advertise all year or to schedule advertisements in blocks of several weeks' duration throughout the year or just during peak periods.
- Later, the airline's advertising agency had to choose between four possible creative strategies aimed at the pleasure travel segment. The creative director preferred one, the account manager preferred another, the media director thought another best fit the media plan, and several others preferred a fourth strategy.

These three decision areas are typical in the advertising of almost any product or service. In each case, people had to make decisions under conditions of uncertainty and risk. In each case, advertising research guided that decision making by suggesting that certain alternatives were better than others.

The airline's ongoing marketing research showed the relative importance of different segments of the market for air travel. The advertising director used that research to ascertain what percentage of overseas travelers are on business trips and what percentage are on pleasure trips. Data showed frequency of trips by people in each market segment. Data also showed who flies first class and who flies tourist class. The director's strategy called for allocating advertising dollars according to the relative importance of each market segment. In other words, research helped to reduce uncertainty and risk.

To determine the scheduling of advertisements, the advertising director looked at data on boardings and on travel planning. Seasonal data on boardings showed peaks and valleys in the popularity of the airline's Charlotte-to-London service. The director identified times when business persons and tourists took trips to London, and advertisements aimed at each segment were scheduled differently. Again, research reduced uncertainty and risk.

In determining which creative strategy to propose to the client, the agency's account manager authorized a pretest of the four strategies. The manager found that two strategies appeared most appropriate for the overall advertising campaign. One, a simple, factual approach, tested best for the business market. The other, which used pleasant imagery of a visit to London, tested best for the tourist trade. Again, research was used to reduce uncertainty and risk.

Case 1.1 describes how Sterling Motors and its agency, AC&R Advertising of New York, used research to position Sterling cars with advertising and to select an appropriate creative strategy. Advertising research showed that Americans liked the car's interior and that they associated the car with excellent road-handling performance, and those findings led to the car's positioning. Research about possible creative strategies told the company and its agency that a James Bond theme would do well with consumers.

••• The Growing Need for Research

In today's complex and diversified marketplace, advertisers face conditions of greatly increased uncertainty and risk. Gone are the days of the relatively simple marketplace where merchants dealt with small numbers of consumers and could easily respond to the needs of their customers. Gone are the days when merchants could make adjustments in product and pricing on relatively short notice in response to comments by customers. The relationship between producer and consumer could be close, and communication was simple.

Gone, too, is the sometimes unassailable position of the tradesman or other marketer. Before mass production, producers could sell all they could make. Producers had relatively few direct competitors. And customers may have had little choice but to accept products because there weren't many others from which to choose.

An Example of How Research Contributes to Advertising Decisions

AC&R Advertising, a New York agency, relied on research when it developed advertising strategy for Sterling Motor Cars, manufacturers of a British luxury import car.

The agency research department began by conducting 31 focus group interviews to find out what consumers thought of British people, British cars in general, and Sterling in particular. The focus groups turned up potentially useful ideas, but the agency wanted to know if findings from the focus groups were true of the population as a whole, so it followed the focus groups with studies of several hundred people.

The studies showed that Americans liked the Sterling's interior and that they associated the car with excellent road-handling performance. That gave the agency an idea for positioning the Sterling.

Creative research was next, and AC&R pretested two strategy ideas with groups of consumers. One tried to take advantage of Americans' positive feelings toward the British and featured references to Winston Churchill, Britain's wartime prime minister. Research results suggested it would not be a good strategy because many Americans did not know who Churchill was. Research also indicated that the second strategy to be tested—associating the car with British grace under pressure—was also a bad idea because not enough people were familiar with the car.

A third creative strategy did show promise when tested. Research subjects were shown a picture of the car (no words) while they listened to the theme song from James Bond movies. The research results showed that people associated the car with James Bond, so the agency secured the rights to use the Bond theme music in its commercials.

The careful attention to research paid off; consumer awareness of the Sterling increased by 70 percent in the cities in which the advertising appeared.

Randall Rothenberg, "AC&R Keeps the Faith in Research," *New York Times*, Nov. 17, 1989, p. 47(Y).

• • •

Compared with the marketplace of today, early merchants had little incentive to respond to customer wants, unless it was convenient to do so.

Today's marketplace is vastly more complex and impersonal. A product may be assembled on two or more continents before being shipped to a retail store. Competition within product categories has increased enormously. More than 28,000 brands of different products are now available in the United States.[1] That means keen competition for producers and almost bewildering choices for consumers, because many of the brands are virtually indistinguishable from each other. Much of that increased competition, of course, has resulted from foreign imports.

Consumers are also bombarded with a bewildering array of new products or changed products. In 1988, packaged goods manufacturers introduced more than

10,500 new products, and most were extensions of existing brands or products. General Foods alone accounted for 137 new products, followed by Kraft with 116 and H. J. Heinz with 106.[2]

Relationships have also changed between producers and sellers. The use of electronic scanners at supermarkets has changed the control of information and the balance of power between producers and retailers. Store managers now have almost instant data about brand sales in their stores; they know which brands are selling well and which are languishing on store shelves. And they have access to that information before producers do. Before scanners, producers were usually the first to know about brand sales, which they learned from slow and cumbersome research.

One result of the change has been an increase in the amount of spending on coupons, premiums, point-of-purchase displays, meetings and trade shows, and other sales promotion activities because they produce fast and measurable results at the checkout counter — results that satisfy retailers. In 1988, manufacturers spent $124.5 million on sales promotion and only $67 million on media advertising. Sales promotion expenditures increased 7.5 percent over 1987, and advertising expenditures increased 6.8 percent. In the 1980s, sales promotion expenditures grew at an average annual rate of 13 percent, compared to 10 percent for advertising.[3]

The media scene has changed greatly, too, for both advertisers and consumers. More than 50 percent of all households now subscribe to cable television, and the average number of television channels available for the typical household increased from eight in 1975 to twenty-eight in 1986.[4] Videocassette recorders are now used in more than 60 percent of all households, and they add to viewer choices. More than 75 percent of households have remote control devices on their VCRs or television sets, and more than half of them change channels during programs. Viewers use those remote control devices to switch channels easily; some report they watch up to three programs simultaneously.[5]

Consumers also have greater choice when they face a magazine rack. New magazines are being added constantly while others fail and disappear. In 1988, publishers introduced 491 new magazines, an increase over 477 in 1987 and 372 in 1986. However, only about two out of ten new magazines can be expected to survive after four years.[6] Advertisers face a similar complexity when they have to choose magazines for advertising schedules: In addition to the large number of magazine titles, more than 300 magazines have geographic or demographic editions. More than 130 have split-run capabilities, and there are nearly 250 metropolitan, regional, and state magazines.[7]

Consumers themselves have also changed, adding to the complexity faced by producers and retailers. More than 60 percent of all households have two wage earners, and that has added to consumer spending power and changed shopping and purchasing behavior. Partly because of that increased income and partly because of the two wage earners, families are going outside the home for a growing number of their meals. The age composition of the population is changing, too, most noticeably in the older segments. And changing consumer attitudes and lifestyles, particularly about health, nutrition, and the environment, have had an impact on purchasing behavior.

With all of those developments and the resulting uncertainty and risk, advertising research has become increasingly important for decision makers. Research can help to reduce the uncertainties about how to advertise products in the face of tremendous competition, how to appeal to consumers with different lifestyles, or how to select media in the face of the great number of consumer media choices. Unfortunately, however, some advertisers have responded to the increasing uncertainties by reducing advertising expenditures (including research) in cost-cutting moves. That is short-sighted because those companies should be devoting greater—not less—emphasis to advertising in the face of competition and uncertain times.

What Research Can't Do: The Role of Intuition in Decision Making

Unfortunately, advertising decision makers sometimes associate magical quali-ties with research. That behavior is exemplified with statements like "Numbers don't lie" or "Our steady growth figures show that . . ." On occasion, those decision makers may request research when research will not be able to provide the answers they want. Or, they may call for research to provide obvious answers or answers that are needed merely to lend support to decisions that have already been made.

The point is that advertising research can help lead to a decision by eliminating some courses of action, but sooner or later someone must make a decision. Graphically, here is what must happen. Without research, many decision options may present themselves. One does not necessarily know which option is most appropriate in that situation.

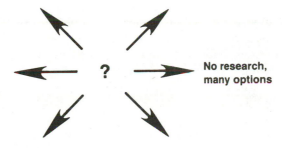

No research, many options

If you conduct good research, you can eliminate some of the potential solutions. The field is narrowed.

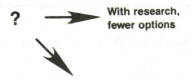

With research, fewer options

At this point, experience and intuition come into play.

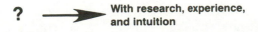

With research, experience, and intuition

Advertising managers have broadly different views about the value of advertising research. In some large firms, research sometimes assumes major proportions, such as in some of the opinion surveys conducted on a national scale or expensive test-market experiments that involve numerous cities. In other cases, advertisers do not believe they can afford research; they prefer to place all their budget in paid media rather than to use some of it to study the effectiveness of what they are doing.

Effective research is valuable, and undoubtedly many executives could have made more informed decisions if they had used research findings. Yet research may not always be justified. If a decision must be made quickly, time may preclude a research effort. Perhaps most important, the research may be too expensive to justify. When you try to assess whether a research project is too expensive, you must think beyond just the total cost; you must also think of the benefits you will derive. In other words, you must balance the benefits and the costs of the research.

• • • Relating Costs and Benefits of Research

Advertising managers and research directors must look at the cost-benefit ratio of the proposed research. In other words, they must anticipate the value of the information they will get from the research — its value in reducing risk and uncertainty. They must assess whether that information will add anything to what they already know. Then they must balance that perceived value of research against its anticipated cost.

At the very least, the cost-benefit ratio should be one-to-one. That is, the benefits from the research should at least equal the cost of the research. If that is not the case, the research probably should not be undertaken. Another option is to reduce the scope of the research to reduce costs. Instead of using a simple random sample, you might use a convenience sample. Interviewing a simple random sample is much more costly than interviewing a convenience sample, and the extra benefits of the random sample may not equal the added costs. Although a large-scale survey of a representative sample might be an excellent way to learn consumers' opinions about a product, a less expensive focus group study of eight or ten consumers might be just as useful, especially when you consider the great expense of the large-scale survey.

• • • Marketing Research and Advertising Research

How does advertising research differ from marketing research? The differences are not always clear, and marketing research can sometimes be useful for advertising decisions (as in the example at the beginning of this chapter of the data about airline passengers' reasons for trips), just as advertising research can sometimes be useful for marketing decisions. Nevertheless, there are some differences that you should understand.

Advertising is one of several activities subsumed under the rubric of marketing. You are probably familiar with the "Four P's" of marketing: product, price, promotion, and place (distribution). Some people would add a fifth: people. Advertising is a part of promotion, along with sales promotion and personal selling.

• • • Marketing Research

Included in marketing research are product development research, in which producers ascertain the need for new products or product improvements as well as how consumers use existing products. Product distribution and product sales research are also important marketing research activities. Product sales can be measured by store audits or by scanners that read the universal product code symbol (UPC) on packages.

To conduct store audits, research companies select a representative sample of food or drug stores and periodically visit the stores to measure the number of product units sold. Earlier in this chapter, we alluded to the fact that information garnered from store audits was paid for and used primarily by manufacturers to gauge brand sales and share of market. That gave them greater knowledge about brand sales than store managers had and gave manufacturers the balance of power. The store scanners are installed by store managers, who are the primary users of the resulting data. Now they have control of the information and the balance of power. They can see results more quickly, especially the results of sales promotion activities like coupons or price reductions. Advertising results are not as quickly or as easily seen, and this fact has led store managers to demand that manufacturers spend more for sales promotion, which usually means less for advertising.

Consumer behavior research is another important part of marketing research. It includes research about how consumers seek and use information (including advertising) as they make purchase decisions. It also includes research about how consumers make brand choices and includes measures of brand loyalty, the tendency to purchase the same brand time after time. In addition, consumer behavior research explores the perceptions that consumers have about various products and brands.

Other marketing research studies focus on ways to motivate salespeople and to make personal selling more effective. Some studies are concerned with market segmentation, perceptions of price and quality, and methodological research, such as ways to increase responses to mail questionnaires.

Advertising research, on the other hand, focuses on gathering information that will help to reduce uncertainty and risk associated with advertising—as opposed to marketing—decisions. That information includes consumer attitudes toward products, consumer reactions to different advertising strategies and messages, information about competitors' advertising expenditures, and information about media audiences.

• • • Applied, Basic, and Methodological Research

Advertising research can fulfill various roles, with varying emphasis on the immediacy of applicability. The most common roles of advertising research are applied, basic, or methodological.

• • • Applied Research

Most advertising research is applied; that is, it is designed to have direct applicability to the decision-making process. Applied advertising research is usually designed to identify problems that require decisions, such as market analyses, market descriptions, competitive analyses, or situation analyses. Some research is designed to evaluate the effectiveness of different advertising approaches, media weights, different premiums, and other relatively short-term problems.

Much applied research is product-specific or even brand-specific; that is, results of such studies are valid only in the immediate situation—that particular brand at that particular time. Generalizing the results to other products or brands can be risky. For example, a concept for a humorous television commercial may test well for a low-priced car but may be ineffective for an expensive car. You would not want to conduct a study of humorous advertisements for the manufacturer of a low-priced car and use the results for a manufacturer of a high-priced car.

Applied research is usually *proprietary* research, meaning it is paid for by one company. Because the research results are designed to give that company an edge over its competition, the company will carefully guard the results and will not release them outside the company.

• • • Basic Research

The purpose of basic research, also sometimes referred to as theoretical research, is to discover principles by which advertisements and general strategies and schedules can be constructed. Usually the results of these studies can be generalized to other situations and can therefore be useful to a number of firms. For example, Case 1.2 describes a basic research study that compared the effectiveness of two different kinds of celebrity endorsements. The conclusions from that study—that two-sided endorsements are more effective than one-sided ones—could be applicable in many situations.

Another example of basic research is research on frequency of exposure, which is the number of times a person is exposed to the messages of an advertising campaign. The purpose of such research is to learn the optimum number of media insertions of an advertisement the advertiser should schedule to reach prospective customers a given number of times. The results would be valuable to a number of advertisers, not just one or a few.

Much basic research is significant in the long run, but when compared with day-to-day research, it may not answer "right now" questions that require immediate answers. That is the reason most advertisers and advertising agencies do not conduct basic research. It is hard to justify financially in the short run, and many advertisers believe they have enough to worry about with day-to-day research without having to worry about more basic questions. If they do give attention to that kind of research, it will be by reading publications such as the *Journal of Advertising*, the *Journal of Advertising Research*, the *Journal of Marketing*, and others.

An Example of Basic Research

Advertisers use well-known celebrities to attract attention to their advertisements and to create credibility for their claims. Research has shown that consumers find celebrities to be attractive and well liked but not always credible.

This study used an experiment to test the effectiveness of two types of celebrity endorsements: one-sided and two-sided. In one-sided endorsements, celebrities say only positive things about the brand or service; in two-sided endorsements, they suggest some mildly negative things and then counter them with positive statements. Based on their review of earlier research, the authors of this study concluded that two-sided endorsements would be more effective than one-sided ones. They stated that conclusion in the form of three hypotheses or predictions to be tested. (1) Subjects would rate advertisements with two-sided endorsements as more credible and effective than those with one-sided endorsements. (2) Two-sided endorsements would lead to more positive evaluations of the ad sponsor than one-sided endorsements. (3) Two-sided endorsements would lead to higher levels of purchase intention than one-sided ones.

Advertised Service The researchers selected an actual management consulting firm as the subject of their test ads. It was a relatively new company in the Los Angeles area. When the experiment was conducted, the company had not yet done any advertising.

Subjects Subjects for this experiment were 52 executives of small- to medium-sized businesses in the Los Angeles area that might be potential customers of the consulting firm. Using actual business executives resulted in more validity for the study's results; it made the results more real and easier to generalize the results to similar decision makers.

Advertisements The researchers did some preliminary research among 20 undergraduate business majors and 10 business executives and selected actor Leonard Nimoy as the endorser for the consulting firm. In the one-sided version, Nimoy said only positive things about the client and said he used the company in his business. The two-sided version was identical, except for the addition of a statement acknowledging that the consulting firm was not well known. The two ads were identical in layout and all other respects.

Procedure Researchers visited the subjects in their offices after calling and setting up appointments. Subjects were told they were to serve as judges for an advertising competition. The researchers had previously assigned each subject to one of two groups (one-sided and two-sided). Subjects looked at the appropriate ad for two minutes and then answered several questions about it.

Variables The dependent variables were advertisement evaluation, sponsor evaluation, and purchase intention. The advertisement evaluation was operation-

(continued)

ally defined as the subject's rating of the ad on seven-point scales measuring credibility and effectiveness. Sponsor evaluation was measured on a seven-point scale ranging from poor quality of service to excellent quality of service. Purchase intention was measured on a seven-point scale from not inclined to purchase to strongly inclined.

The independent variable was termed "sidedness" and was manipulated by creating the two experimental groups. Half the subjects saw the one-sided version, and half saw the two-sided version. The researchers calculated the average (mean) ratings on the dependent variables and compared the means of the experimental groups.

Results Ratings from the two-sided group were higher than from the one-sided group on all three measures—advertisement evaluation, sponsor evaluation, and purchase intention. That suggested support for the hypotheses, but the researchers performed statistical tests to confirm that the results were due to real differences and not just to chance occurrences. All statistical tests showed a very low probability that the results were due to chance, so the researchers concluded that two-sided celebrity endorsements are more effective than one-sided ones. They suggested, however, a need for additional research, especially to test one-sided and two-sided approaches for a variety of products and with noncelebrity endorsers.

Michael A. Kamins, Meribeth J. Brand, Stuart A. Hoeke, and John C. Moe, "Two-Sided Versus One-Sided Celebrity Endorsements: The Impact on Advertising Effectiveness and Credibility," *Journal of Advertising*, Vol. 18, No. 2, 1989, pp. 4–10.

• • • Methodological Research

The purpose of methodological research, which is research about research methods, is to discover new and better ways of conducting research and to enhance its value to advertising practitioners. As consumers are increasingly subjected to questionnaires, interviews, and other forms of research, they become less willing to respond. Consumers may also become increasingly sophisticated about research and may think they know answers that will please interviewers. Methodological researchers try to develop techniques to minimize such problems and generate more accurate data.

Case 1.3 is an example of a methodological research study; it compared the accuracy of different ways to measure people listening to car radios and concluded that different methods of recording station listening did not produce significantly different results. Other studies have been conducted to learn ways to stimulate high return rates in mail questionnaire research. For example, some research has tested whether an incentive, such as one dollar or five dollars, should be offered to persuade recipients of a questionnaire to answer the questions and return the questionnaire in the mail. Other research has tested the effectiveness of follow-up letters to persons who don't respond within a specified time.

An Example of Methodological Research

Audience measurement methodology has received a lot of attention from advertising researchers. In this study, Abernethy, a professor at Auburn University, tested a new measurement methodology and compared it to more traditional methods. His purpose was to test the accuracy of diary measures.

Radio audiences are measured by diaries that are maintained by listeners for one week at a time. Ideally, researchers hope that listeners will update their diaries as they listen to the radio. Practically, most diary keepers probably update their diaries only once a day or even less frequently by trying to remember when they listened to the radio and what stations they listened to. Listening to the radio in a car presents special problems because listeners cannot fill out their diaries while listening and because they are likely to switch stations frequently while driving.

Avery measured car radio listening three ways over a three-month period. One was a questionnaire in which his subjects estimated the percentage of their total radio listening for individual stations and for dayparts. They completed this questionnaire at the beginning and at the end of the study period. The data it provided (stations and dayparts) revealed "average" listening behavior. The second method was a traditional diary that subjects maintained for a week to provide data for one week of self-reported behavior. The third method was unique: Abernethy asked subjects to use a battery-operated tape recorder in their cars to record what they listened to. Abernethy later played the tapes and listened for station call letters to measure the amount of time subjects listened to different stations and dayparts. That gave Abernethy data for actual behavior and not self-reported data.

He looked at data from the three different methods to see the percentage of listening for individual stations and dayparts. He compared those percentages to see how closely they paralleled each other. He did find differences. Here, for example, are the listener percentages for the top-rated station:

From the tape	21 percent
From the diary	25 percent
1st questionnaire	19 percent
2nd questionnaire	17 percent

Similar differences were reported for other stations, but calculations of the Chi-square statistic led Abernethy to conclude that the differences were not statistically significant. He surmised that some of the differences, particularly between the first and second questionnaires, were probably caused by real differences in listening. In other words, people don't listen to the same stations week after week.

You should read the article in its entirety for a fuller discussion of the methodology and the conclusions.

Avery Mark Abernethy, "The Accuracy of Diary Measures of Car Radio Audiences: An Initial Assessment," *Journal of Advertising*, Vol. 18, No. 3, 1989, pp. 33–39.

• • •

An Example of Descriptive Research

Many studies have used a descriptive research technique called content analysis to assess the extent to which members of minority groups appear in advertisements. Such studies have been prompted by a feeling that minority groups have generally been underrepresented as characters in advertisements and that society as a whole would benefit if minorities had greater presence in advertisements.

Method Content analysis is a systematic study of television commercials, print ads, and other printed and video materials. Researchers count the incidence of certain words, themes, or even types of people. The researchers in this study recorded prime time television programming on the ABC, CBS, and NBC television networks for seven consecutive days in the fall of 1984. Three different people (coders) then carefully analyzed the content of all commercials appearing during that time.

The coders categorized more than 900 commercials that featured live models. The categories of analysis included (1) the frequency of appearance by African-American or Hispanic characters, (2) the perceived importance of African-Americans or Hispanics in the commercials, and (3) the type of product advertised. An important part of content analysis research is to make sure that coders are using the same definitions and are interpreting those definitions in a uniform manner. Researchers using content analysis therefore have to measure for intercoder reliability, or the extent of agreement among coders for the same materials. To do that, the researcher[5] in this study asked all three coders to look at a small sample of the same commercials and asked them to categorize them.

Descriptive, Exploratory, and Explanatory Research

In different situations, applied, basic, and methodological research can be done for one or more of three purposes: descriptive, exploratory, or explanatory.[8] In other words, basic research might be descriptive, exploratory, or explanatory. Or, methodological research might be explanatory and exploratory. Of course, any particular advertising research project might be undertaken for more than one of the purposes.

Descriptive Research

As the term implies, descriptive research is a report or a depiction of a situation. It typically does not try to explain any of the findings; nor does the researcher usually begin with any predictions (hypotheses) to test. Many advertising research surveys are examples of descriptive research. Measures of media audiences, such as those done by Nielsen Media Research or Simmons Market Research Bureau, are examples of descriptive research. So are studies of companies' advertising expenditures. Case 1.4

• • •

is an example of a descriptive research project that measured the appearance of African-American and Hispanic characters in television commercials. It found that Hispanics appeared in only six percent of all commercials and that they were generally in roles that were considered to be unimportant to the commercial. The study also found that research coders from particular ethnic groups are more aware of the nuances of their particular subculture and are more likely to recognize members of their own ethnic group. This latter finding has important implications for methodological research as well.

• • • Exploratory Research

Exploratory research is often the first step in a program of research on a major topic. You might want to do an exploratory study for one of three reasons. First, you might want to satisfy your curiosity about a particular topic or to attempt to discover the relationships among a number of advertising variables. Second, you might be considering a more elaborate study but feel it is prudent to conduct a smaller-scale study to see if the larger scale is feasible. Third — and this is related to the second

An Example of Exploratory Research

The Acquired Immune Deficiency Syndrome (AIDS) epidemic has captured worldwide attention and concern. It has raised public awareness of safe-sex practices and has broken down many former barriers to the advertising of condoms as a way to prevent the spread of AIDS. The purpose of this study was to explore consumers' attitudes toward AIDS (AIDS anxiety) and their attitudes toward advertisements for condoms.

The author reviewed related research on consumer anxiety and the use of fear appeals in advertising. He observed that prior to the AIDS epidemic, condom ads were generally limited to men's magazines and used appeals that focused on pleasure. Now, however, condom advertisements are found in many media vehicles and use anxiety or fear appeals about the possible dangers of AIDS virus transmission through heterosexual contact. He formulated three hypotheses for this study: (1) persons who have high anxiety levels about AIDS will have more positive attitudes toward condom advertisements than will persons with lower anxiety; (2) persons with more sexual partners will have more positive attitudes toward condom advertisements than will persons with lower numbers of sexual partners; and (3) high-anxiety persons will have more positive attitudes toward condom ads with moderate-fear appeals than toward ads with high-fear or nonfear appeals.

Subjects The subjects for this experiment were male and female college students. That was appropriate for this kind of exploratory study, especially because they come from a segment of society that is likely to have more sexual

reason — you might want to do an exploratory study to refine your research methods before you tackle the more elaborate and more expensive study.[9]

An exploratory study may involve a very small sample, even so small that one might not consider the investigation a "study." For example, you might want to find commonalities among a small number of award-winning magazine advertisements. You might need only ten to twenty such advertisements to determine if they share characteristics that deserve additional study. In applied research, an example of an exploratory study might be a series of focus group interviews in which you would try to draw out from a small group of people their feelings about a product, a product category, or some other topic germane to the advertising of a client's product.

Exploratory research in the methodological area could involve a pretest of a new questionnaire format with only a few respondents. The purpose would be to learn whether a different format has potential for generating improved response rates. Knowledge gained in that pretest could lead to a larger study to determine effects of different formats.

Case 5.1 is an example of exploratory research that examined the relationship between subjects' anxiety about AIDS and their evaluation of condom advertisements. Among other things, the study's findings indicated that persons with high anxiety levels about AIDS and sexually active persons have more positive attitudes toward condom advertisements.

contacts than other segments. When subjects came to participate in the experiment, they were automatically assigned to one of two experimental groups: low-anxiety or high-anxiety.

Procedure Subjects in the low-anxiety group were asked to read a document that claimed that fears about AIDS were illogical because of the low statistical probability of contacting the disease through heterosexual contact. Subjects in the high-anxiety condition read a document that claimed that people stood a relatively high probability of contacting the disease and that portrayed AIDS as a gruesome way to die. The author had earlier pretested this manipulation and concluded that it generated the two levels of anxiety he was seeking.

After reading the documents, subjects completed questionnaires that measured their attitudes toward a series of condom advertisements and toward specific brands. The individual ads used different levels of fear appeal. The high-fear appeal emphasized the sure death faced by AIDS victims. The moderate-fear appeal merely suggested that casual sex was a "risky business." The nonfear appeal mentioned only pleasure and not the threat of AIDS. Subjects were also asked to tell the number of sexual partners they had the previous year.

Results The ratings of the advertisements and brands generally supported the hypotheses, although not all of the differences in ratings were statistically significant.

Ronald Paul Hill, "An Exploration of the Relationship Between AIDS-Related Anxiety and the Evaluation of Condom Advertisements," *Journal of Advertising*, Vol. 17, No. 4, 1988, pp. 35–42.

• • •

• • • Explanatory Research

As the name suggests, explanatory research is undertaken to try explain events or phenomena, such as the relationship between the sidedness and persuasive power of celebrity endorsements explored in Case 1.2 (basic research). Explanatory research goes beyond description and attempts to explain how and why certain things happen. When they conduct explanatory research, researchers usually start with *hypotheses* about expected relationships among variables, and the purpose of the research is to provide support for the hypotheses. In the example in Case 1.2, the researchers' review of related research led them to hypothesize that two-sided endorsements would be more persuasive than one-sided ones; the data from their experiment supported their hypotheses.

Because you will be trying to prove explanations in explanatory research, it is important that you control all variables as much as possible. The researchers in Case 1.2 controlled the advertisement variable by making the one-sided and two-sided advertisements identical except for the sidedness. They controlled for possible differences among their subjects by randomly assigning them to one of the two experimental groups. The controls over the advertisements and the subjects meant that any differences in the dependent variables (ratings of the advertisements) were most likely due to the difference (sidedness) between the two messages.

Summary

Properly conducted, advertising research can help advertising decision makers reduce risks and uncertainties associated with the outcomes of their decisions. The need for research is growing, not diminishing. Advertising decision makers face intense marketplace competition from several competitors with many brands. They also face intense demands from retailers, who insist on quick sales and high profitability. It has become more difficult to sell and advertise products to consumers, whose characteristics and lifestyles are more diverse and changing.

Advertising decision makers should not pay blind allegiance to research because research is not always an appropriate response to conditions of risk or uncertainty. Advertising research can help to reduce alternative courses of action by eliminating the most risky; the final decision must still be made largely on the basis of the decision maker's intuition. Before embarking on a research project, researchers and advertising decision makers must assess the perceived benefits and the costs of the proposed research.

Advertising research is related to marketing research, but they are not the same thing. Marketing research focuses on the product, price, sales promotion, personal selling, distribution, and consumer behavior. Advertising research focuses on the meaning of products to consumers, research for creative strategies and executions, media audiences, and competitors' advertising expenditures.

One way to categorize advertising research is applied, basic, and methodological. Applied research is product- or brand-specific and is conducted to find answers to immediate and practical problems, such as an evaluation of different creative executions. Most applied research is also proprietary, meaning it is available to and used only by the company that paid for it. Basic research is undertaken to discover general principles that may apply to many situations; it is not product- or brand-specific. Methodological research helps researchers improve their research by testing different ways of conducting research.

Applied, basic, and methodological research can be undertaken for different purposes. Descriptive research is a report or a depiction of a situation; it does not attempt to explain relationships among variables. Exploratory research is often undertaken as a preliminary step toward larger and more elaborate research studies. It can be used to test tentative ideas about relationships among variables or to test the feasibility of more elaborate research. Explanatory research attempts to explain how and why certain phenomena occur.

Notes

1. Michael Schudson, *Advertising, the Uneasy Persuasion: Its Dubious Impact on American Society* (New York: Basic Books, 1986), 107.
2. Rebecca Fannin, "Where Are the New Brands?", *Marketing and Media Decisions*, July 1989, p. 24.

3. Russ Bowman, "Dollars Up But Cooling Down," *Marketing and Media Decisions*, July 1989, p. 124.
4. Neil Hickey, "Decade of Change, Decade of Choice," *TV Guide*, Dec. 9, 1989, p. 29.
5. Peter Ainslie, "Confronting a Nation of Grazers," *Channels*, September 1988, pp. 54–62.
6. Steve Damiano, "Checking Out Magazines," *Marketing and Media Decisions*, June 1989, p. 20.
7. Judann Dagnoli and Scott Donaton, "Reynolds to Pare Magazine Ads," *Advertising Age*, Nov. 27, 1989, p. 1.
8. Earl Babbie, *The Practice of Social Research*, 5th ed. (Belmont, Calif.: Wadsworth, 1989), 80–82.
9. Babbie, *Practice of Social Research*, p. 80.

••• Self-Test Questions

1. Discuss the changes in marketing, media, and consumers that have significantly increased the importance of and need for advertising research.
2. Discuss how the use of electronic scanners at supermarkets has changed the relationship between manufacturers and retailers, particularly with regard to research.
3. What is the primary use of advertising research by decision makers? How should they combine such research with experience and intuition?
4. Explain why it is important for decision makers and advertising researchers to consider the costs and benefits of research. Test your understanding of the principle of cost-benefit analysis by describing a hypothetical example in which the analysis would suggest that the research would not be worthwhile.
5. How does advertising research differ from marketing research?
6. Discuss the differences among applied, basic, and methodological research. Briefly outline a research project for each of those types.
7. Examine a recent issue of the *Journal of Advertising* or the *Journal of Advertising Research* and see if you can categorize studies as descriptive, exploratory, or explanatory.

••• Suggestions for Additional Reading

Babbie, E. *The Practice of Social Research*, 5th ed. Belmont, Calif.: Wadsworth, 1989.
Boyd, H., Jr., R. Westfall, and S. S. Stasch. *Marketing Research*, 7th ed. Homewood, Ill.: Irwin, 1989.
Bradley, U. (ed.). *Applied Marketing and Social Research*, 2nd ed. New York: Wiley, 1987.
Chisnall, P. M., *Marketing Research*, 3rd ed. New York: McGraw-Hill, 1986.
Churchill, G., Jr. *Basic Marketing Research*. Chicago: Dryden Press, 1988.
Luck, D. J., and others. *Marketing Research*, 7th ed. Englewood Cliffs, N.J.: Prentice-Hall, 1987.
Tull, D. S., and D. I. Hawkins. *Marketing Research: Measurement and Method*, 4th ed. New York: Macmillan, 1987.
Zikmund, W. G. *Exploring Marketing Research*, 3rd ed. Chicago: Dryden Press, 1988.

CHAPTER 2

The Subject Matter of Advertising Research

From a manager's viewpoint, the best way to think of advertising research is as a continuing, ongoing process. If research is to contribute most effectively to success in the marketplace, you should not think of it as something to do only in an emergency.

Primary research is original research with fresh data obtained for one's own purposes. Research using data collected by government agencies, trade associations, trade publications, and numerous other sources is *secondary* research. Much of the data uncovered in secondary research were originally gathered for a variety of reasons but happened to be applicable to an advertiser's specific problem.

It is also useful to identify advertising research as *customized* or *syndicated*. Customized research is that which is done for a specific advertiser or agency. It can be done by that advertiser or agency, or it can be supplied by an independent research company. Customized research is usually primary research.

The distinguishing characteristic of syndicated research is that it is paid for and used by numerous advertisers and agencies. Independent research organizations conduct the research and sell the data to clients willing to subscribe to the service and pay for the data.

But what shall we study about our advertising campaign? Where can research play a role that will help imaginative people be creative with a purpose and with the desired effect? What kinds of research will enable media people to allocate hard-to-come-by advertising dollars so that money can have its greatest effect? What research will help us make the overall promotional effort efficient?

All these questions call for practical answers and, therefore, applied research. Depending on one's view, this research can be grouped into six major categories: target market research, competitive activity research, positioning research, pretest message research, posttest message research, and audience research.

• • • Target Market Research

Nowhere is it more obvious that advertising is a marketing function than in the process of identifying target markets for advertising campaigns. A target market consists of the people who are likely to buy or use the product or service, particularly those who are identified as heavy users.

Target market research seeks to learn three things about people: their level of product usage, their important identifying characteristics, and their media usage patterns. Researchers must learn how often people buy or use products and the amount they use. They learn this by asking a rather simple question:

"How many glasses of _____ does your family use in a week?"

You can also learn this by asking consumers to keep diaries or records of their product purchases for a specified time. Data gathered in this manner are used to categorize consumers on a continuum from heavy users to light or nonusers. Heavy users are naturally important because they may constitute a small portion of the population but account for a large portion of total product consumption.

• • • Demographics

Demographics are the identifying characteristics that we use to describe persons in the target market. Several demographic variables are usually used to describe typical buyers or users of a product or service: age, gender, occupation, income,

education, race, and family size. Geographic labels may also be applied to users: census region, metropolitan or nonmetropolitan area, and county size. The advantage of using demographic variables is that they are relatively easy to obtain and verify. The researcher can easily identify the gender of respondents, and respondents themselves are usually capable of indicating their age group, income range, level of education, race, family size, and place of residence. (Although it's true that many people are reluctant to tell an interviewer their precise age or income, they are usually willing to specify a range of age or income, as in 18 to 24 or $20,000 to $24,999.)

These descriptions, although conceptually simple and relatively easy to determine, are not always adequate. For example, just because a male is between 18 and 34 years of age, has a high school education, and is a blue-collar worker, he is not necessarily a potential customer of a particular brand of cigarettes, although studies may indicate that he should be. Rather, the important factor may be that he is motivated by a desire for status or that he is action oriented.

. . . Psychographics

Consequently, target market research and other types of advertising research can also examine psychological variables that may affect how people feel about products and that might help to predict product purchase. The term *psychographics* is used to denote a technique of segmenting consumers on the basis of their attitudes and other psychological characteristics. One of the pioneer psychographic researchers, Emmanuel Demby, defined psychographics:

> The use of psychological, sociological, and anthropological factors, such as benefits desired (from the behavior being studied), self-concept, and lifestyle (or serving style) to determine how the market is segmented by the propensity of groups within the market — and their reasons — to make a particular decision about a product, person, ideology, or otherwise hold an attitude or use a medium.[1]

One problem with psychographic research is that researchers have to rely on consumers' own descriptions of their psychological characteristics or attitudes. For example, some early psychographic studies asked the following kind of question:

> "On a scale of from one to five, with one being most impulsive and five being least impulsive, how impulsive would you say you are?"

A major problem with that kind of question is the fact that the word *impulsive* will mean different things to different people, so that each person will be answering a different question. By contrast, an income range of between $10,000 and $14,999 means the same thing to most respondents.

The best-known practical application of psychographic research, the *VALS 2™ Segmentation System*, has been developed by the Values and Lifestyles Program at a company called SRI International. It has developed a typology of consumer types that is illustrated in Figure 2.1. The typology is based on two dimensions. The horizontal dimension, going from left to right, is based on consumers' self-orientation. It reflects

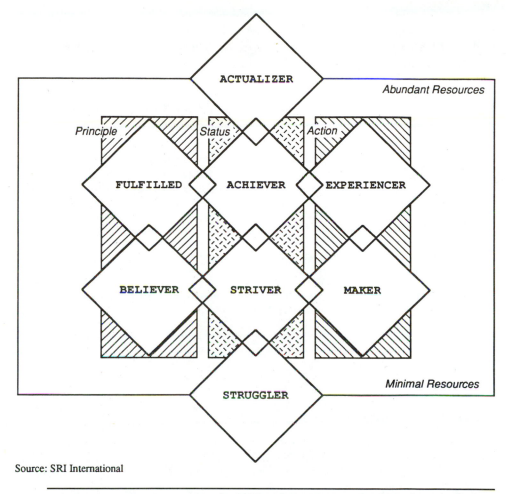

Source: SRI International

Figure 2.1 The VALS 2™ Segmentation System. *Source:* SRI International. Reprinted by permission.

the fact that people buy products and seek experiences in accordance with their self-defined image. *Principle-oriented* consumers are guided by their own beliefs or tenets rather than by the beliefs of others. *Status-oriented* consumers are shaped by a desire to win the approval of others and to live a lifestyle that reflects their status. *Action-oriented* consumers want physical or social activity, and they want to experience life. They like to act on their environment, either with constructive activity at home or risk-taking through adventure.

The vertical dimension of the VALS 2™ typology is based on the resources available to consumers. It ranges from *abundant* (top) to *minimal* (bottom). Resources in this case encompass more than just money; they also include psychological, physical, and other material assets that consumers possess.

SRI has developed a lengthy questionnaire that can be administered to consumers. Answers to the questions are used to categorize consumers into one of the eight VALS 2™ segments illustrated in Figure 2.1. The fact that the categories overlap signifies that they are related: Experiencers are somewhat like Achievers and Makers, and so on.

Consumers in each segment share distinctive attitudes toward products and services and exhibit similar consumer behavior patterns. Briefly, here is how SRI describes consumers in each segment:

Actualizers. Successful, sophisticated, active, take-charge people. High self-esteem, abundant resources. Established and emerging leaders. Open to change. Continue to seek challenges. Rich and diverse lives. As consumers, they have a desire for the finer things in life.

Fulfilleds. Mature, satisfied, comfortable, reflective. Well-educated, professional, well-informed, content, calm, open-minded, self-assured. Conservative and practical as consumers. Concerned about functionality, value, and durability.

Believers. Conservative, conventional, strong attachments to traditional institutions. Modest income and education. Deeply rooted moral codes, established routines. Conservative and predictable consumers. Favor American products and established brands.

Achievers. Successful, work-oriented, in control of their lives. Predictable, stable, committed to family. Conventional, politically conservative, respectful of authority and the status quo. Favor established products that reflect their success.

Strivers. Seek motivation, self-definition, and approval from others. Unsure of themselves, low on resources. Very oriented toward approval of others. Easily bored and impulsive. Seek possessions that emulate others with more resources.

Experiencers. Young, vital, impulsive, rebellious. Seek variety, excitement, the off-beat, and the risky. Uninformed, politically uncommitted. Disdainful of authority and conformity. Physically active. As consumers, they spend much of their income on clothing, fast food, music, and movies.

Makers. Practical, traditional, politically conservative, suspicious of new ideas, respectful of authority. Unimpressed by physical possessions, except for practical things.

Strugglers. Chronically poor, ill-educated, low-skilled. Aging, concerned about health, despairing, passive. Concerned about meeting immediate needs, security, and safety. Cautious consumers, loyal to favorite brands.[2]

Advertisers who wish to use psychographic research such as VALS 2™ can pay a company to collect data from a sample of product users and determine the types (psychographic segments) most likely to use the product. That kind of knowledge can help the advertiser create advertising that appeals to those segments. It is less useful in selecting media, because not much is known about psychographic profiles of media vehicle audiences.

Case 2.1 is an example of how Timex Corporation used psychographic research to define its target audience, design packages, develop creative strategy, and select media.

How Timex Used Psychographics
for Its Healthcheck Products

Faced with a decreasing demand for its traditional watch products, Timex Corporation has entered the home health care market with products such as digital thermometers, scales, and blood pressure monitors sold under the Healthcheck brand name. Timex used VALS psychographic research to shape target audience definition, packaging, creative strategy, and media selection. Although SRI International, which created the VALS concept, has revised its psychographic typology into VALS 2™, the Timex story is an excellent example of how psychographic research can be used.

Timex was dissatisfied with the traditional demographic information it had about potential users of its health care products, so it contracted with SRI to do VALS research. That research identified two types of consumers (psychographic segments) that seemed most likely to purchase such products: societally conscious individuals and achievers. They tended to have higher levels of education and more concern for health.

That kind of knowledge about its likely customers helped Timex to design packages for its product. Rather than using traditional packaging that emphasized illustrations of the products, Timex developed packages that featured the consumers' lifestyles and emphasized the products' benefits. Even the clothing on the models on the packages was carefully selected to appeal to the societally conscious and achiever groups.

The psychographic research also helped Timex to select a theme for its advertising. After research indicated problems with three other headline and theme ideas, Timex settled on "Technology where it does the most good." Creative executions for individual ads were also influenced by the VALS typology. The models, their clothing, and the settings for the ads all reflected the lifestyles of the two groups.

Timex and its agency, J. Walter Thompson, also used the VALS research to shape its media strategy. Because it knew that achievers and societally conscious types tend to watch news programs but not much else on television, Timex decided to place its advertising on early and late news shows.

Timex's efforts were successful; its brands quickly become leaders in their respective categories. While it may be debatable to say that the VALS research was primarily responsible, it certainly did contribute to the company's success.

Source: "Timex and VALS Engineer a Psychographic Product Launch," *Ad Forum*, September 1984, pp. 12–14.

• • •

. . . Media Usage

Target market research seeks another kind of information about consumers: their media usage. Researchers try to find out the media that people are exposed to and at what levels. This can be as simple as asking respondents to tell what newspapers they read or what radio stations they listen to (without seeking the extent of reading or listening). Or more elaborate research might ask respondents to keep media diaries for one or more weeks.

Once researchers have accumulated this kind of information about consumers, advertising planners can define and identify the best prospects for the product (target market with demographic, geographic, and psychographic labels), and media planners can select the media most likely to deliver the appropriate advertising message.

Target market research is normally conducted with surveys of samples of consumers and is more likely to be syndicated than customized. Simmons Market Research Bureau (SMRB) and Mediamark Research, Inc., described in Chapter 16 as audience research companies, also gather and syndicate data about product usage, identifying characteristics, and media exposure. It is also possible for advertisers and agencies to do their own target market research on a much smaller scale, particularly a survey of store customers. For example, age, income, and occupation information is usually required on applications for charge accounts, and that information can be used to develop a profile of the store's charge account customers.

• • • Competitive Activity Research

Target market research and competitive activity research are sometimes referred to as *situation analysis research* because the information describes the situation in which the advertising decisions will be made — the background, so to speak. Results of this kind of research enable an advertising planner to paint a picture of the situation: who the product users are and what the competition is doing.

The purpose of competitive activity research is to learn how much money competitors spend on advertising and what media they use. In a less formal sense, competitive activity research may also be concerned with competitors' creative strategies and executions. Once advertising planners know the media that competitors are using, they can select either the same media or different media to avoid confrontation. Knowing how much money competitors spend also helps advertising planners determine their own appropriation levels.

Competitive activity research is usually syndicated research because of the extensive effort required. All media vehicles must be monitored, and all advertisements must be identified by brand and company. Then someone must estimate the cost of advertisements and total expenditures. The primary sources of such syndicated research data — including Broadcast Advertisers Reports, Leading National Advertisers, and Radio Expenditure Reports — are discussed in more detail in Chapter 17.

Can advertisers and agencies do their own competitive activity research? They can — but only on a very limited basis because of the great effort and expense involved. Those performing the research would need to make sure they were monitoring all media vehicles that competitors might use during all times that competitors might use them. They would need estimates of what the advertisements cost, and they would need to compile all the data into a report. Even some suppliers of syndicated data use samples of media vehicles and samples of time periods because they cannot possibly assemble and analyze data for all vehicles and all time periods. This kind of research is practical for agencies and advertisers to do only when there are one or two major competitors in a limited geographic area. Even then, it will probably be necessary to limit the research to the media vehicles most likely to be used and to short periods of time.

Of course, if you are trying to learn something about competitors' creative strategies, a much less rigorous approach is called for. In fact, mere casual observation of media might be appropriate.

... Positioning Research

Product positioning is a very important part of the marketing and advertising process. The positioning concept has become well known and widespread primarily through the writings of Al Ries and Jack Trout. They say that product positioning does not really involve what manufacturers do to a product. Rather, it is concerned with what advertisers do to the minds of consumers — to take their existing attitudes and to "retie the connections" that exist between consumers and brand names.[3] They cite the example of Seven-Up, which learned through positioning research that consumers categorized soft drinks as cola drinks and noncola drinks. The company then changed its advertising (but not the product) and positioned Seven-Up as a noncola drink instead of just another soft drink.

The purpose of positioning research is to find what consumers think of existing products, proposed new products, and competing products. It asks consumers what benefits they seek, how they use the product, or how they might use a new product. Advertising strategists can use the research findings to position products with advertising.

For example, a toothpaste manufacturer might learn through positioning research that a significant percentage of toothpaste users consider pleasing taste to be the most important aspect of toothpaste. That manufacturer could use advertising to emphasize the brand's taste — to appeal specifically to the segment of consumers who think taste is important.

By its nature, positioning research is brand-specific, meaning it is conducted to learn about one brand. Consequently, it is almost always customized research — conducted by agencies and advertisers or by research companies that do it for them. Surveys can be used, although focus groups are often sufficient and are more widely used than surveys. The important requirement is to conduct the research among people who already use the product or who are likely to use it, and to get them to talk freely about the product. Another benefit of positioning research is that it can give an advertiser good ideas for strategies and executions of individual advertisements, sometimes even employing words used or suggested by research subjects.

Pretest Message Research

Many advertisers use research to test the effectiveness of advertisements before spending money to place them in the media. The usual method is to show several proposed advertisements to a group of consumers and to measure their responses to the advertisements. Researchers might be interested in knowing what the advertising copy means to consumers, or what the consumers learn or can recall from the advertisements, or what they like about the illustration or copy. Researchers sometimes use finished versions of the advertisements in the tests, although the test advertisements are more likely to be rough or unfinished versions to save the costs of producing advertisements that will not be used in the campaign.

Pretesting can be done in different ways. A focus group of potential users of the product talking about the proposed advertisements can be especially valuable. The evaluations in the users' own words can be much richer and more detailed than quantitative data about the percentage of subjects who liked one particular version.

At a more elaborate level, researchers can measure consumers' physical responses to proposed advertisements by using mechanical devices. Eye-movement cameras can identify the first spot that readers focus on when they look at a print advertisement and can then show how their eyes move through the advertisement. That can indicate whether an illustration designed to capture reader attention works better than the headline in the same advertisement. Pupillometers measure pupil dilation as subjects view print or televised advertisements and can show their involuntary reactions. Brain wave scanners can show brain wave activity as research subjects look at advertisements and can indicate the amount and type of attention and processing the subjects are giving to the advertisements. Similar reactions can be inferred from devices that measure galvanic skin response, including perspiration.

Proposed television commercials are sometimes tested by showing them to consumers individually or in small groups. That kind of research can be done with a television set and a videocassette recorder in almost any location — especially in shopping malls, where there is a ready supply of consumers. A common procedure is to begin by asking consumers to indicate their brand preferences and purchase intentions for a particular product category. Researchers then show the consumers some commercials, including the one being tested. The test commercials are sometimes, but not always, shown in the middle of some kind of television program. Researchers measure attitudes and purchase intentions after showing the commercials, and any changes in those attitudes and intentions are assumed to be caused in part by the commercials. By comparing results from two or more test commercials, researchers can determine which is most effective.

In other forms of pretest message research, researchers place test advertisements in actual magazines or television programs. After subjects have had an opportunity to see or read the advertisements under normal conditions, researchers question them about what they saw and remembered from the test advertisements.

Agencies and advertisers can conduct focus group research to pretest their advertisements, but mechanical measurements, experiments, and field testing normally require the facilities and expertise of special research companies. It is customized research because it is normally done for only one client. Even though a research company might conduct pretest research studies for more than one client at a time, the results would be available only to the appropriate individual clients.

••• Posttest Message Research

The distinction between pretesting and posttesting may not always be apparent. At some point in the advertising process, advertisers must commit themselves to a full-scale campaign in the media. Testing done after that point is technically posttesting, even though the methods may be the same as those used in pretesting. The purpose of posttesting often is to determine whether the ads that proved effective (according to a specific definition) in pretests with small groups under artificial conditions are as effective under normal conditions. That companies often do both pretesting and posttesting exemplifies the continuing nature of advertising research.

Some posttest research evaluates individual ads by asking subjects if they read the ad when it first appeared or by measuring how much they can remember from the ads they have read or seen. Other posttest research tries to evaluate the effects of campaigns (several ads) by measuring memory or awareness of advertising slogans. The preferred approach is to measure awareness before the campaign and during its run. Differences in awareness can be assumed to result from the advertising campaign.

Posttest research is normally done with fairly large groups of readers or viewers. Several companies that do pre- and posttest message research are discussed in Chapter 13 and 14. In addition, Chapter 12 has a section on some of the problems of message research.

••• Audience Research

Audience research seeks information about the size and composition of audiences of media vehicles. Advertising planners use this information to select appropriate vehicles for advertising messages. Audience size is important, of course, but so is the makeup of the audience — the kind of people who watch, read, or listen. Audience research is also used after key segments of an advertising campaign have ended to verify that advertisements reached the desired audience.

Audience research is conducted by surveying large numbers of people and asking them to report their media usage. It is also done by auditing circulation data supplied by publishers. Because of the large number of media vehicles involved and because of the need to interview large numbers of people or to audit several hundred publications, syndication is the only economical way to conduct audience research. Companies that supply audience research, including Audit Bureau of Circulations, Mediamark Research, Inc., Simmons Market Research Bureau, Arbitron, and Nielsen, are described in Chapters 15 and 16.

An Example of Research Application

Here, then, is a hypothetical example of how research might be used in the planning and execution of an advertising campaign for a product. This example is not meant to suggest that research is used that way in all advertising campaigns — or that it should be. Neither is it meant to suggest that advertising research always takes place in the order listed.

1. Target market research locates heavy users of the product — a proportionately small group that accounts for a disproportionate share of product consumption. Research identifies pertinent demographic, geographic, and psychographic characteristics and media exposure patterns of the heavy users. The information is useful for creative strategy (you must know whom you are talking to before you can decide what to say) and media strategy.
2. Competitive activity research identifies advertising expenditures and media used by competitors. This helps to set an advertising expenditure level and to select media needed to reach users of competing brands.
3. Positioning research reveals the product characteristics that consumers find most important. This information is useful for strategically positioning the product against competitors.
4. Pretest message research suggests which ads are likely to have the greatest impact on consumers — in accordance with communication goals of the advertising. It helps to reduce the risks and uncertainty of deciding which creative executions are best.
5. Audience research tells which media vehicles have the largest concentrations of heavy users and aids in the selection of appropriate vehicles. After the advertising appears, subsequent audience research can estimate the number of people who saw the vehicle in which the advertising appeared.
6. Posttest message research indicates the success of individual advertisements and of the advertising campaign by measuring recall or recognition of the advertising as well as awareness of slogans. This helps to determine whether the advertising should be changed.

The Relationship Between Message and Audience Research

Because of the nature of advertising, some advertising research is difficult to categorize as message research or audience research. Some of it crosses between the two types. The continuum between advertising medium distribution and sales response runs through both areas, as shown in Figure 2.2.

The model in Figure 2.2 shows six points on a continuum, starting with superficial evaluations and ending with the most rigorous evaluations. It is divided into two parts, "prospects" and "nonprospects." It shows that most advertising campaigns will reach both types of people despite the effort to reach only the prospects. In a well-

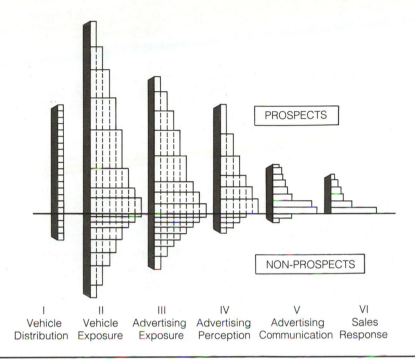

Figure 2.2 A model for evaluating advertising. Reprinted from *Toward Better Media Comparisons*. Copyright 1961, by the Advertising Research Foundation. Used by permission.

designed advertising plan, the prospect section of the model should be much larger than the nonprospect section. The blocks that form each bar in the model are symbolic of the number of units, whether they be copies, people, exposures, or sales of the product.

Point VI is the most desired level of advertising research—trying to learn the effect of the advertising on product sales. That is very difficult to determine because so many other marketing and nonmarketing factors affect product sales. However, the answer can be found by controlling for all factors except advertising. One method is to use different advertising strategies in different test cities—as long as the cities and marketing strategies are similar. Differences in sales levels at the end of the test are assumed to be caused by differences in the advertising. This kind of research takes a considerable amount of time and money, so advertisers frequently compromise and settle for research conducted at Point V.

Point V research tests how well the advertising communicated, so researchers usually try to measure awareness of advertising themes and slogans (campaigns) or memory of specific ads. The link between Point V and Point VI is the assumption that the advertising cannot have any effect on sales unless it communicates. Broadcast recall research (especially the kind that measures the specific information that viewers can recall) is an example of this kind of research. Again, the time and money required for Point V research often lead advertisers to compromise and to rely on research conducted at Point IV.

Point IV research is concerned with how many people perceived the advertisements. In actual practice, it is usually difficult to measure perception as distinct from communication. Perception is more than exposure but less than communication. Exposure means that the person faces the advertising message with open eyes; perception implies that the person makes some connection with the message; communication implies that some meaning is transferred from the message to the person. The connection between Point IV and Point V is that an advertising message cannot communicate unless it is perceived. Because of the difficulty of measuring perception and communication of advertising, advertisers sometimes compromise and settle for Point III research.

Point III research tries to measure the number of people who were exposed to the advertising. The link between Point III and Point IV is that a person cannot perceive an ad without being exposed to it. Much exposure is assumed without being measured because it is difficult to measure exposure to ads as distinct from exposure to a program or publication. Nielsen and Arbitron ratings tell how many people saw the program but not how many saw an advertisement on the program. Of course, program exposure is a theoretical limit on all ad exposure: Only those who see the program can see the ad. These difficulties lead advertisers to rely more on Point II research than on Point III research.

Point II research is probably the most common—at least if measured by the amount of money spent on it. Point II research measures audiences of media that carry the advertising. All broadcast audience measurement is at this level, and so is total audience measurement for publications (all people who see the publication—including those who do not buy their own copy).

Point I research is primarily measurement of publication circulation, as exemplified by the Audit Bureau of Circulations or Business Publications Audit of Circulation.

(Target market research, competitive activity research, pretest message audience, and audience research are not depicted in Figure 2.2.)

Advertising Research and the Product Life Cycle

Another useful way to conceptualize different types and purposes of advertising research is to consider the different kinds of research that are appropriate at different stages in a product's life cycle or history. Table 2.2 outlines stages in the product life cycle and the kinds of research that are needed at each stage.

At the conception stage, before the product is even fully developed, researchers want to know how consumers feel about existing products, whether there are any consumer needs that are not being met, and how many people are likely to buy the product being considered. Research at that phase is needed to test the feasibility (production and marketing) of the new product idea. Motivation research is specifically concerned with determining consumer motivations or desires and how those motivations can be fulfilled with products.

In the preintroduction phase, which includes all activities from the time of new product conception to the beginning of its introduction, the company wants to know if

Table 2.2 The Relationship Between Marketing Research and the Product Life Cycle

Phase of Marketing Life to Be Analyzed	Some of the Questions to Be Asked	Some Research Techniques to Answer the Questions
CONCEPTION (Before the new product is actually developed.)	How many and what kinds of people are likely to buy the product? How satisfied are customers with brands now on the market? What customer needs and desires exist that are not now being met?	concept testing consumer attitude surveys motivation research
PREINTRODUCTION (Everything that happens from the time it is decided to develop the product until just prior to full-scale marketing.)	How will customers like the product when they actually use it? What selling points do we use to get people to buy the product? What will be the growth in sales for the product? How much will have to be spent in advertising and promotion to obtain sales at a profitable level?	product use tests packaging tests group interviews test marketing advertising weight testing
INTRODUCTION (The product is brought to market scale.)	How well is the product doing in the market? How long will it take before it turns in a profit? What can be done to accelerate the product's growth?	store audits customer attitude surveys repeat buying surveys advertising weight surveys motivation research
GROWTH (The product is at the peak of its sales life.)	How well is the product doing in the market? How can profits be maximized? How can competition be headed off?	store audits customer attitude surveys advertising cutback tests tests of new campaigns (in test markets) promotion tests
MATURITY (The product's sales have passed peak and have stabilized.)	How can product sales be maintained and expanded? (By getting new customers, revising the product, or creating new uses for the existing product?)	product use for revised product forms package tests customer attitude surveys advertising weight tests tests of new campaigns

Source: B. Jaffe, "Some Important Things I Believe a Young Account Representative Should Know About Market Research." New York: American Association of Advertising Agencies, 1965. Used by permission.

consumers will actually use and like the product being considered. It also wants to know the selling points that will appeal to consumers and how much advertising and promotion it will take to make the product successful. Advertising weight testing can be conducted in test market cities to determine appropriate levels and combinations of advertising for the new product.

In the introduction phase, when the product is brought to market, decision makers need to know how well the product is doing (sales) and the prospects for profit. Store audits are conducted by examining store records to ascertain the number of units of the product that are sold. Repeat buying surveys determine the extent to which consumers buy a particular brand more than once.

In the growth phase, when the product is at the peak of its sales, the company wants to know how to maximize profits (perhaps by reducing advertising) and how it can meet the challenge of the competition. Advertising cutback tests attempt to assess the feasibility of reducing advertising expenditures without serious effects on sales. Promotion tests measure the impact of coupons, premiums, price reductions, and other sales promotion activities.

In the maturity phase, when the product's sales have leveled off or are declining, researchers seek to learn how sales can be expanded, perhaps by changing the product, suggesting new uses for the existing product, or by getting new customers. Researchers test consumer reactions to proposed changes in the product, proposed changes in packaging, or new advertising campaigns.

. . . The J. Walter Thompson Planning Cycle

Another way to conceptualize the role of research at various stages of the advertising process is described in a recent book by John Philip Jones about his years of experience at the J. Walter Thompson advertising agency. Jones describes Thompson's Planning Cycle concept, which includes five phases, each denoted by a question.

1. Where are we?
2. Why are we there?
3. Where could we be?
4. How could we get there?
5. Are we getting there?

In the first two stages, researchers are concerned primarily with the situation analysis. Research is designed to assess the brand's current position and the reasons for that position. Both quantitative and qualitative research (demographic and psychographic) can be useful in devising advertising strategy.

Jones says focus groups can be particularly useful in providing research information needed at the third and fourth phases — determining strategies for making the brand's advertising more successful. In-depth comments from potential consumers suggest potentially fruitful strategies as well as approaches that might not work so well. Measures of brand sales and market shares are needed at the fifth stage to assess how well the strategy is working.[4]

Summary

Advertising research defies neat categorization or compartmentalization. Depending on the situation, advertising research is used in a wide variety of ways for a variety of purposes. It can be primary or secondary, and it can be customized or syndicated. This chapter described advertising research from different perspectives to show that different techniques can be used to discover the same information and that the same information or techniques can be used for different purposes — depending on the situation and information needs.

The first perspective illustrated how advertising research is needed at different stages of the advertising process. Target market research can tell advertisers important data (demographics and psychographics) about characteristics of people who use their products. Competitive activity research provides advertisers with data about advertising expenditures and media strategies of their competitors. Positioning research can tell advertising decision makers information about consumer attitudes toward their product and can suggest ways to use advertising to relate the product to consumers' needs and attitudes. Pretest message research can reduce risk and uncertainty by suggesting creative strategies and executions that seem to be effective at conveying the desired message. Posttest message research provides data about the advertisements' performance in the real conditions of the actual marketplace. Audience research provides data about the people (number and characteristics) who read or see advertising vehicles and can reduce uncertainty and risk about appropriate ways to deliver advertising to customers.

Another perspective offered in this chapter was the product life cycle and the kinds of research needed at various stages: conception, preintroduction, introduction, growth, and maturity.

Notes

1. Emmanual H. Demby, "Psychographics Revisited: The Birth of a Technique," *Marketing News*, Jan. 2, 1989, p. 21.
2. Values and Lifestyles Program, Descriptive Materials for the VALS 2™ Segmentation System, SRI International, Menlo Park, Calif., 1989.
3. Al Ries and Jack Trout, *Positioning: The Battle for Your Mind* (New York: Warner Books, 1986).
4. John Philip Jones, *Does It Pay to Advertise? Case Studies Illustrating Successful Brand Advertising* (Lexington, Mass.: Lexington Books, 1989), 8–16.

Self-Test Questions

1. Test your understanding of the research process by outlining the research you might consider for an advertising campaign for a telephone fascimile machine.

2. Repeat the process in Question 1, but this time think of your client as a local retailer. Specifically consider how you would conduct the various types of research.
3. Discuss the research needs of a well-known company that decides to enter the telephone fascimile field. What kind of advertising research might be appropriate — in terms of the product's stage in its life cycle?
4. Discuss the reasons why a media researcher would investigate competitive media expenditures.
5. Discuss the differences among primary, secondary, customized, and syndicated research. In what situations might you use each of these?
6. Compare and contrast demographics and psychographics. Under what conditions might one or the other be preferred?
7. Compare and contrast the three consumer self-orientation categories in the VALS 2™ system: principle-oriented, status-oriented, and action-oriented.
8. In which of the eight VALS 2™ categories would you place yourself or your family?

• • • Suggestions for Additional Reading

Demby, E. H. "Psychographics Revisited: The Birth of a Technique." *Marketing News*, 23 (1989), 22.
Dimingo, E. "The Fine Art of Positioning." *Journal of Business Strategy*, 9 (1988), 34–38.
Friedman, R., and V. P. Lessig. "Psychological Meaning of Products and Product Positioning." *Journal of Product Innovation Management*, 4 (1987), 265–273.
Graham, J. "New VALS 2 Takes Psychological Route." *Advertising Age*, Feb. 13, 1989, p. 24.
Jones, J. P. *Does It Pay to Advertise? Case Studies Illustrating Successful Brand Advertising*. Lexington, Mass.: Lexington Books, 1989.
"Product Positioning: A Crucial Marketing Strategy." *Small Business Report*, 13 (1988), 18–22.
Riche, M. F. "Psychographics for the 1990s." *American Demographics*, 11 (1989), 24–31, 53–54.
Ries, A., and J. Trout. *Positioning: The Battle For Your Mind*. rev. ed. New York: McGraw-Hill, 1986.

Conducting Advertising Research

The principles of conducting advertising research are not unique. Advertising researchers use the scientific method as a guide in their search for accurate information and in their analysis of that information. Researchers in this field, however, often find it necessary to strike a balance between the ideals of the scientific method and the practicalities of time and expense.

Part Two describes the application of social science research methods to advertising problems. Chapter 3 presents the need for proper planning for good research. Chapter 4 provides direction on the conduct of secondary research, a building block that provides a sound foundation for primary research. Chapter 5 discusses the uses of probability and nonprobability samples, including appropriate sample size and methods for selecting samples. Chapter 6 explains the important process of writing questions and constructing questionnaires, which are widely used in advertising research. Chapter 7 describes survey techniques that are commonly used for gathering data. Chapter 8 covers so-called qualitative techniques of gathering data, such as focus groups. For research that goes beyond simple surveys, Chapter 9 covers experimental techniques. Chapter 10 deals with processing and analyzing research data. And, finally, Chapter 11 discusses the important phase of writing the research report. ■

CHAPTER 3

Strategic Planning for Research

A dvertising research cannot be done haphazardly; you must plan it carefully. You must have a specific reason for doing it, a specific goal. And you must have a plan for achieving that goal. Otherwise, you will be like Alice from *Alice in Wonderland*.

'Would you tell me, please, which way I ought to go from here?'
'That depends a good deal on where you want to get to,' said the Cat.
'I don't much care where,' said Alice.
'Then it doesn't matter which way you go,' said the Cat.
'— so long as I get *somewhere*,' Alice added as an explanation.
'Oh, you're sure to do that,' said the Cat, 'if you only walk long enough.'[1]

Unfortunately, advertising researchers are usually not able to walk long enough, because we must produce results quickly and efficiently. If we don't have an objective, we will probably strike out in some random direction without much chance of success.

Because every dollar spent on advertising research is one less dollar that could be spent on media buys or on advertising production (or is one less dollar of profit), research must be done carefully and efficiently. *Strategic planning for research* enhances the likelihood of conducting useful research efficiently and correctly. The process involves five stages:

1. Research problem analysis
2. Research objectives
3. Research strategy
4. Research tactics
5. Research evaluation

You should not just jump into a research project (conducting a focus group interview, survey, or experiment, for example) without carefully thinking through the entire process. Before you begin, you should prepare a *written research proposal* that discusses the research problem analysis, research objectives, and research strategy in detail. The proposal should tell your management and the client exactly what you plan to do. Preparing the proposal will also be good for you because it will force you to organize your thinking and planning. That should minimize false starts and mistakes.

Research Problem Analysis

A very important early step in analyzing the research problem is to ascertain that advertising research is actually needed in the situation. An initial question—"Is this an advertising problem?"—should not be shrugged off as being too obvious. The problem faced by an advertising decision maker may be deeper than it appears; it may be a management or a marketing problem. Testing a television commercial may seem to be an immediate task, but the real problem may be whether television should be used at all. At an even more basic level, the appropriate question may be whether personal selling might be more appropriate than advertising.

Defining the Research Problem

You must determine what kind of research information is needed. You must define the research problem and ascertain the kinds of questions that your research is supposed to answer. Research is conducted to help decision makers reduce uncertainty and risk associated with their decisions, so the need for research information is influenced by the kind of decisions that have to be made and the kind of data needed for those decisions. That means it is important for you to talk to decision makers to ensure that you know the kind of decisions they are making and the type of data they need.

It is possible that you could do a well-conceived and well-executed research project but still provide essentially worthless data because you were unclear about the exact kind of decision the data were needed for. For example, an advertising manager might want to know which of two advertisements does a better job of *teaching specific sales points* to consumers. If you were to conduct a research study that measured consumers' *attitudes toward the brand and the advertisement*, your research would be off-target because it would not provide the kind of data the manager needed. Such a study would not have much value.

In your early discussions with persons who need the research, you should ask them to state the *research question*. In other words, what decision are they making and what do they need to know? The answers will determine the type of research needed. For example, if they are thinking about positioning strategy and want to know how consumers feel about the product and how they use it, one or two focus group interviews may be appropriate. If they want to test the relative effectiveness of two different magazine advertisements with different audiences, a more controlled study such as an experiment may be better. If they want to know the extent of consumer awareness of the brand, a larger-scale survey might be in order.

Although the responsibility for defining the advertising problem more properly rests with advertising managers than with advertising researchers, researchers should be involved in discussions that lead to the problem's definition. Astute researchers should ask questions about what they are expected to do. Call it skepticism or, more positively, healthy skepticism; it is a wise way to stick to the essential task — producing accurate answers to appropriate questions.

・・・ Research Costs

You obviously must give careful consideration to the cost of the proposed research before you begin so your manager and client have a good idea of what it will cost and so they can approve the project. Thinking through the entire research project, defining the advertising problem and the advertising research problem, and carefully planning all stages of the research process will help you estimate and control research costs.

You must consider data gathering costs. If you plan to use a mail questionnaire, for example, you need to include printing and postage costs in the estimate. Telephone toll charges and interviewer payments have to be considered. Subjects may have to be compensated for participating in mail or telephone surveys or in experiments. Some experiments may require the purchase of special equipment.

Data analysis and report preparation costs are also important. You may have to pay to convert questionnaire responses to a form needed for computer analysis. You may need to purchase a computer and software to do the analysis; otherwise, you will have to pay for time on other computers. You must also include the cost of preparing and distributing a written report of your research.

Once you have established the research questions and estimated the cost of finding the answers to those questions, you will have to decide if the benefits of the answers are worth the cost of getting them. You should not necessarily assume that the research will be worth the effort. The cost may be far in excess of the benefits of the research; in that case, you or the client may decide to forego the research. You may also have to decide to scale down the scope of the proposed research, such as by using shorter interviews or reducing the size of the sample. You must be careful, however, that you do not harm the validity or reliability of the research by cutting corners too much. In some instances, it may be worse to waste money by conducting shoddy research than to not conduct the research at all.

· · · Secondary Research

The research problem analysis should also include secondary research — a review of information and research results already available. Some of that information will be held by the agency, company, or client. You can also do secondary research in a company, public, or university library. The literature of marketing and advertising research is rich in studies that can be helpful as you seek solutions to a current problem. An article in a periodical such as *Advertising Age* or in a journal such as the *Journal of Advertising*, the *Journal of Advertising Research*, the *Journal of Marketing*, or the *Journal of Marketing Research* could save you considerable time and money. The research problem in the articles may not exactly parallel the one you are investigating, but it may be close enough to be useful. Chapter 4 explains the process and sources of secondary research in detail.

You may incur some expenses for the secondary research, including the cost of your time (and that of other researchers). You may also have to pay the cost of searching online electronic databases for relevant information and for references to earlier studies. However, as Chapter 4 explains, using such database searches will almost always be cost efficient because of the time saved by doing such searches.

· · · Research Objectives

A clear understanding of the advertising problem — and an accurate definition of the research problem — ought to suggest the objective of the research. This is to gather the data needed to help management make the right decision to alleviate or solve the problem. Just as an advertising plan should be based on definite goals, an advertising research plan must also have well-defined goals.

Because the goal of advertising research is often to determine whether or not advertising objectives have been achieved, the advertising goals must be clear. If management is not clear about its advertising objectives, researchers will have a difficult time determining whether the objectives have been met. If researchers are involved in setting advertising goals — and they should be — they can help to ensure that the advertising goals are well defined.

Advertising goals can relate to many aspects of the advertising effort. It is prudent to think about advertising goals in a structured way.

. . . DAGMAR

A classic discussion of a structured approach to setting advertising objectives can be found in Colley's *Defining Advertising Goals for Measured Advertising Results,* known as DAGMAR.[2] Colley developed an extensive list of questions advertisers can use to define the objectives of an advertising campaign. For example, one question asks, "To what extent does the advertising aim at closing an immediate sale?" The possible answers are as follows: (1) perform the complete selling function, (2) close sales for prospects already partly sold through previous advertising efforts, (3) tie in with some special buying event, and (4) stimulate impulse sales. Advertising managers using the DAGMAR approach would rate the importance of each of these objectives on a six-point scale of importance.

Table 3.1 shows the general DAGMAR areas and specific objectives for each area. Using this or a similar approach to the delineation of advertising objectives, advertising managers and researchers can more efficiently identify questions for research and can suggest the research approaches that might be used.

For example, statement 7 suggests that one goal of an advertising campaign could be to increase brand awareness. The research to determine the success of this goal would require that the objective be stated in quantifiable terms: "The goal of the advertising campaign is to increase Brand A's top-of-mind awareness from 0 percent to 15 percent in one year." For the purpose of this research, top-of-mind awareness would be defined as "naming Brand A first when asked to name brands in the relevant product category." Because this is a new product, awareness would be zero when the campaign begins. At the conclusion of one year, a research study could measure top-of-mind awareness and indicate whether the advertising campaign had achieved its objective.

To take another example, statement 37 suggests that another goal of advertising could be to tell consumers where to go to purchase Brand A. The researcher could do a study before the campaign begins (called a baseline study) to learn how many people know where to buy Brand A. Another study — asking the same questions — at the end of the campaign would reveal how well the campaign had achieved its objective.

The Colley book and similar approaches to defining advertising objectives emphasize the importance of knowing where you are going and what you are trying to do if you are to know whether or not you have succeeded. Without specified advertising goals, it is difficult to know what to measure. In the same vein, without specified advertising goals, it is difficult and perhaps impossible to interpret the results of research that *was* conducted.

. . . Other Advertising Goals

A word of caution is in order. Advertising goals must be realistic and must be limited to the kinds of tasks that advertising can reasonably be expected to do. It would not be reasonable, for example, to state an *advertising goal* as follows: to increase the brand's share of market from 6 percent to 10 percent by the end of the campaign. Share of market has to do with brand *sales*, and other factors besides advertising affect sales. So it could be unrealistic to use brand sales or share of market as a test of advertising effectiveness.

Table 3.1 "Which of These Fifty-Two Advertising Tasks Are Important in Your Business?"

To what extent does the advertising aim at closing an immediate sale?

	SCALE OF IMPORTANCE					
	Not Important			Very Important		
	0	1	2	3	4	5
1. Perform the complete selling function (take the product through all the necessary steps toward a sale)						
2. Close sales to prospects already partly sold through past advertising efforts ("Ask for the order" or "clincher" advertising)						
3. Announce a special reason for "buying now" (price, premium, etc.)						
4. *Remind* people to buy						
5. Tie in with some special buying event						
6. Stimulate impulse sales						
OTHER TASKS:						

Does the advertising aim at near-term sales by moving the prospect, step by step, closer to a sale (so that when confronted with a buying situation the customer will ask for, reach for, or accept the advertised brand)?

	SCALE OF IMPORTANCE					
	Not Important			Very Important		
	0	1	2	3	4	5
7. Create awareness of existence of product or brand						
8. Create "brand image" or favorable emotional disposition toward the brand						
9. Implant information or attitude regarding benefits and superior features of brand						
10. Combat or offset competitive claims						
11. Correct false impressions, misinformation, and other obstacles to sales						
12. Build familiarity and easy recognition of package or trademark						
OTHER TASKS:						

Table 3.1 (continued)

Does the advertising aim at building a "long-range consumer franchise"?

	SCALE OF IMPORTANCE					
	Not Important			Very Important		
	0	1	2	3	4	5
13. Build confidence in company and brand which is expected to pay off in years to come						
14. Build customer demand which places company in stronger position in relation to its distribution (Not at the "mercy of the market-place")						
15. Place advertiser in position to select preferred distributors and dealers						
16. Secure universal distribution						

	SCALE OF IMPORTANCE					
	Not Important			Very Important		
	0	1	2	3	4	5
17. Establish a "reputation platform" for launching new brands or product lines						
18. Establish brand recognition and acceptance which will enable the company to open up new markets (geographic, price, age, sex)						
OTHER TASKS: _____ _____						

Table 3.1 (continued)

Specifically, how can advertising contribute toward increased sales?

	SCALE OF IMPORTANCE					
	Not Important				Very Important	
	0	1	2	3	4	5
19. Hold present customers against the inroads of competition?						
20. Convert competitive users to advertiser's brand?						
21. Cause people to specify advertiser's brand instead of asking for product by generic name?						
22. Convert non-users of the product type to users of product and brand?						
23. Make steady customers out of occasional or sporadic customers?						

	SCALE OF IMPORTANCE					
	Not Important				Very Important	
	0	1	2	3	4	5
Increase consumption among *present users* by:						
24. Advertising new uses of the product?						
25. Persuading customers to buy larger sizes or multiple units?						
26. Reminding users to buy?						
27. Encouraging greater frequency or quantity of use?						
OTHER TASKS:						

Table 3.1 (continued)

Does the advertising aim at some specific step which leads to a sale?

	SCALE OF IMPORTANCE					
	Not Important				Very Important	
	0	1	2	3	4	5
28. Persuade prospect to write for descriptive literature, return a coupon, enter a contest						
29. Persuade prospect to visit a showroom, ask for a demonstration						
30. Induce prospect to sample the product (trial offer)						

OTHER TASKS:

_____

_____

How important are "supplementary benefits" of end-use advertising?

	SCALE OF IMPORTANCE					
	Not Important				Very Important	
	0	1	2	3	4	5
31. Aid salesmen in opening new accounts						
32. Aid salesmen in getting larger orders from wholesalers and retailers						
33. Aid salesmen in getting preferred display space						
34. Give salesmen an entree						
35. Build morale of company sales force						
36. Impress the trade (causing recommendation to their customers and favorable treatment to salesmen)						

OTHER TASKS:

_____

_____

Table 3.1 (continued)

Is it a task of advertising to impart information needed to consummate sales and build customer satisfaction?

	SCALE OF IMPORTANCE					
	Not Important			Very Important		
	0	1	2	3	4	5
37. "Where to buy it" advertising						
38. "How to use it" advertising						
39. New models, features, package						
40. New prices						
41. Special terms, trade-in offers, etc.						
42. New policies (guarantees, etc.)						
OTHER TASKS: _____						
_____						

To what extent does the advertising aim at building confidence and good will for the corporation among:

	SCALE OF IMPORTANCE					
	Not Important			Very Important		
	0	1	2	3	4	5
43. Customers and potential customers?						
44. The trade (distributors, dealers, retail sales people)?						
45. Employees and potential employees?						
46. The financial community?						
47. The public at large?						
OTHER TASKS: _____						
_____						

Table 3.1 (continued)

Specifically what kind of images does the company wish to build?

	SCALE OF IMPORTANCE				
	Not Important			Very Important	
	0	1	2	3	4	5

48. Product quality, dependability

49. Service

50. Family resemblance of diversified products

51. Corporate citizenship

52. Growth, progressiveness, technical leadership

OTHER TASKS:

Source: R. H. Colley, *Defining Advertising Goals for Measured Advertising Results* (New York: Association of National Advertisers, Inc., 1961), 62–68. Reprinted by permission.

Advertising research might be conducted for other reasons, but all the purposes are tied to providing managers with information for making better decisions. For example, some research might be done to suggest creative concepts or themes for the advertising campaign. Other research may be done to test different media strategies. The research may not indicate a single, best answer because that is often a matter for the manager's judgment. However, properly planned and conducted research can help managers eliminate many of the riskier solutions to a problem.

Regardless of what they are, advertising research goals should be in writing and should be agreed upon by researchers and managers before the research begins. Here are some examples of research goals:

- To measure changes in top-of-mind awareness of Brand A from January 1 to July 1
- To compare recall scores for Commercial A and Commercial B
- To compare consumer comprehension of Print Ad C and Print Ad D
- To identify consumer perceptions of Brand X that might suggest strong advertising themes
- To compare the abilities of Headline A and Headline B to attract reader attention

Research Strategy

If you have defined an advertising problem properly, that definition should suggest an appropriate objective. In turn, the objectives should suggest appropriate *research strategies*, the general approaches to designing the study to gather the appropriate data. It should be a logical progression from one stage to the next. In the research strategy stage, you need to determine the kind of research you will need to answer your questions or to fulfill your research goals. You must be certain that your strategy will enable you to meet your research objective. Several decisions are involved at this stage.

Defining Variables

Variables are the factors you will study in your research. An *independent variable* is one you manipulate or change to learn what will happen to a *dependent variable*. Advertisements or advertising strategies are examples of typical independent variables. Dependent variables can include brand awareness, advertising slogan awareness, advertising recall, or brand preference. We usually assume that changes in an independent variable will cause or be associated with changes in a dependent variable.

For example, you might design a study to compare the effect of a media strategy that calls for three television commercials per week with one that calls for seven commercials per week. You might select one or two cities in which to try the three-commercial strategy and other cities in which to use the seven-commercial strategy.

At the conclusion of the study, you would compare brand awareness in the two markets. In that study, the strategy would be the independent variable because you would control (manipulate) the number of commercials per city. Brand awareness would be the dependent variable, and you would expect awareness to be different because of the effect of the independent variable.

You might sometimes use *classification variables* to categorize persons (or even things) you are studying and to examine differences between groups. For example, in a study of the recall of a magazine advertisement, you might want to compare recall scores between men and women. Many surveys routinely include questions about demographics or even psychographics to enable researchers to make comparisons.

In some studies, researchers want to find out how changes in an independent variable might cause or be associated with changes in one or more dependent variables. Such research might be motivated by a desire to answer a question of "What happens if I use a four-color ad as opposed to a black and white ad?" In other studies, however, researchers make predictions about what will happen to a dependent variable if the independent variable is changed. Such formal predictions are called *hypotheses* and are more likely to be found in research conducted by academics. For example, in Case 1.2, the researchers hypothesized that two-sided celebrity endorsements would be more effective than one-sided ones. The resulting data supported the hypothesis.

• • • Operational Definitions and Measurement

The study comparing a three-commercial per week strategy to a seven-commercial one sounds simple, and it is in a sense. However, it is not as simple as it seems. For example, what do you mean by *brand awareness*, and how will you measure it? Such a question suggests that you must define variables carefully and precisely. Trying to evaluate the effectiveness of a magazine advertisement is meaningless unless you define precisely what *effective* means and explain how you will measure it. *Effective* could mean the ability to get people to read most of the advertisement. It could also mean getting readers to respond to a coupon offer. It could also mean increasing readers' knowledge of the brand's benefits. Each of those definitions would require a different research strategy.

It is essential, therefore, that you establish *operational definitions* and *measurements* for your variables. An operational definition is a specific, carefully delineated and measurable definition of an independent or dependent variable. It is a definition that is custom-made for the particular research project. In the media strategy example, you would operationally define the independent variable (media strategy) as either three commercials per week or as seven commercials per week. You would operationally define the dependent variable as the percentage of respondents who list that brand name first when they are told the name of the product category.

That definition also suggests the way you will measure the variable: You will read respondents the name of the product category, count the number of times that each brand is mentioned first, and calculate the percentage who name the tested brand first. In such a case, you are assuming that the first brand named is the one that is most important to the respondents, or at least the one that is foremost in their minds.

As you think about ways to measure variables, you must consider the amount of precision you will need in the answers to the research question that prompted the study. If the question asks what kind of uses potential users might suggest for a new product, you will be interested in the variety and richness of their feelings and not be so concerned about being precise in measuring their attitudes. Hence, you might ask subjective, open-ended questions in a focus group interview and not worry about counting or tabulating the answers. On the other hand, if the research question asks whether advertisement A has more memorability than advertisement B, you need more precision in your operational definition and measurement. You must have an operational definition of memorability and a precise way to measure and compare it.

You must also think about how you will analyze and present your results. As Chapter 10 suggests, you should think about how the tables and charts of your results will look even before you begin the research. Doing that should help you to define your variables and measurements.

Case 1.2 describes an experiment that tested the effectiveness of two-sided versus one-sided celebrity endorsements. The researchers termed the independent variable *sidedness*; they created one magazine advertisement that featured a celebrity presenting only the positive aspects of the advertised service and another advertisement that featured the same celebrity presenting both positive and negative aspects of the service. The researchers had three dependent variables: advertisement evaluation, sponsor evaluation, and purchase intention. The advertisement evaluation was operationally defined as the subject's rating of the ad on seven-point scales measuring credibility and effectiveness. Sponsor evaluation was measured on a seven-point scale ranging from *poor quality of service* to *excellent quality of service*. Purchase intention was measured on a seven-point scale ranging from *not inclined to purchase* to *strongly inclined*. Each subject saw either the one-sided or the two-sided advertisement and rated the ad on the various scales. The researchers calculated a mean for each of the scales.

• • • Validity and Reliability of Measures

As you consider your operational definitions and measurements, you must keep two very important concepts in mind: validity and reliability. *Validity* is concerned with the question of whether the measurement is accurate or whether it reflects reality. This is sometimes referred to as *external validity*. Sometimes, laboratory experiments in advertising research are so artificial (especially when you ask subjects to pay close attention to a television commercial) that they bear little resemblance to the reality of television viewing. Hence, you might question the validity of that research, saying essentially that real life is too different from the laboratory setting. What you must be careful about is the generalizability of your research findings to the real world. In other words, you want to be able to say that the findings of your research study are true of the real world as well. If you have used valid definitions and measures, you should be able to say that with a considerable degree of confidence.

Look back at Case 1.2, the one that tested the effectiveness of one-sided versus two-sided celebrity endorsements. Think about some procedures the researchers *could* have used and how those procedures might have affected the validity or generalizability of their research. Suppose, for example, that the management consulting company in the advertisements had been a large and well-known company. The subjects' prior knowledge of that company might have affected their responses to the advertising and reduced the validity of the study. If the researchers had used college students as subjects instead of business executives, the research would not have had nearly as much external validity because college students are not in a position to evaluate such services and advertisements.

You might recall that the subjects were shown the independent variable ads (either a one-sided one or a two-sided one) in their offices. They were given the advertisements, asked to look at them, and then asked to evaluate the advertisements on several seven-point scales. That is not the way that most people see and process advertisements, so the procedure raises questions about external validity. You might also question whether rating scales can measure effectiveness, whatever that means.

You should be aware of the fact that researchers often have to use procedures and measures that are practical but not ideal. It is true that the advertisement exposure and evaluation in Case 1.2 was not realistic or ideal, but it would have been extremely difficult for the researchers to conduct their study by relying on procedures that were more natural. They had to control the exposure — to make sure that some subjects saw the one-sided advertisements and that the others saw the two-sided version. If they could somehow have put these two versions into actual copies of a magazine and then telephoned subjects until they found some who could remember having seen the ads, it would have been more valid but extremely costly.

Think also about Case 1.5. That was the study of the relationship between anxiety about AIDS and reactions to condom advertisements. Like many research studies, both in advertising research and in other fields, it used college students as subjects. However, the researchers make a strong case for the validity of that procedure because college-age persons are likely to be more sexually active than other groups and are hence more likely to be concerned about AIDS.

You may also recall that the researchers manipulated the independent variable (anxiety about AIDS) by showing subjects documents that were designed to create low-anxiety or high-anxiety feelings. The subjects read the documents and then read print advertisements for condoms. Again, that is not at all like the real world, but it was necessary to give the researchers the kind of controls that were essential in their research. That is a problem with experimental research, in fact, because researchers have to deal with the conflict between controlling variables and risking external validity because of artificial conditions and procedures.

Another type of validity to consider is *face validity*. If we say that a research study has face validity, we mean that its results are logical or predictable. Look back at Case 1.4, the one that used content analysis to measure the presence of minorities in television commercials. If the results had suggested that Hispanics were present in more than 50 percent of all commercials, that would have been counter to what we intuitively think is true. The study would have been suspect because it lacked face validity.

Predictive validity can also be important in some kinds of research or measurement. If we say that a measurement device has predictive validity, we mean that the results we get by using it can be verified by comparing them to some other measure. Suppose you devised a rating scale that you thought would predict how well an advertisement would generate telephone inquiries about a product. You would like to perfect such a rating device so copywriters could evaluate advertisements before they appear. If you used the scale to select advertisements that you believed would generate high levels of response, and if actual trials proved you right, you could say that your rating scale had predictive validity.

Here's another way to think about predictive validity. Colleges often use high school grade-point averages and Scholastic Aptitude Test (SAT) scores to guide their admissions decisions. They usually justify that practice by saying that those grades and scores do a good job of predicting success in college. In other words, they are saying that their past experience with those measures suggests they have predictive validity. Or think about the grade you will get in your advertising research course, or even the grade you expect to get on your final examination. (Examination grades and course grades are a type of measurement.) Do you think that students who get higher grades will be more successful as advertising researchers than those who get lower grades? Will that be consistently true? In other words, what is the predictive validity of those grades?

What can you do to improve the validity of your research? For one thing, you should carefully think through your operational definitions, measurements, and procedures to try to make them as realistic as possible. You should sacrifice reality only when you can justify it in terms of control of variables. Justifying it in terms of expense may be dangerous; the lack of validity may make the entire study worthless and a waste of money.

Reliability

Reliability is concerned with whether the same research procedures, if repeated in similar circumstances, would give approximately the same results each time. Reliability is not the same thing as accuracy or precision, however. A research procedure can be highly reliable, meaning it will produce the same results time after time, but it could still be inaccurate.

Look again at Case 1.4, which used content analysis to study the presence of minority persons in television commercials. In that study, research workers (coders) had to view more than 900 television commercials and make decisions about the frequency of African-American or Hispanic characters, the importance of those characters in the commercials, and the type of product advertised. The persons conducting the research had to be reasonably sure that their research assistants were all using the same criteria to make the coding decisions — in other words, that they were reliable. To measure intercoder reliability, the researchers asked all coders to categorize a small sample of the same commercials. The researchers then calculated the percentage of times the coders agreed. The percentages of agreement on the three dimensions varied from 77 percent to 90 percent, which is generally considered acceptable for that kind of research.

You should be able to understand how a procedure such as the one just described could produce a *reliable yet inaccurate measure*. In that study, the researchers had to prepare written instructions that told coders how to determine the presence of Hispanic characters in the ad, using clues such as skin color, names, or speech patterns. Theoretically, such instructions could be so clear and so precise that most coders would agree most of the time. However, if the instructions were wrong, the coding could be inaccurate while still being reliable.

In fact, the researchers in Case 1.4 did additional research that dramatically suggested that kind of reliability problem. They hired three new coders — a Hispanic, an African-American, and an Anglo — to code all the commercials that had previously been identified as having Hispanic or African-American characters. The Hispanic coder identified a larger number of commercials with Hispanic characters — and in more important roles — than the African-American and Anglo coder did. Likewise, the African-American coder counted a greater number of commercials with African-American characters playing more important roles than either the Hispanic or Anglo coder. The results suggest that coders from particular ethnic groups are more aware of the nuances of their particular subculture and are more likely to recognize persons from their own ethnic group.

Reliability problems can affect research in other ways besides content analysis coding. Any time you use interviewers, you have to be concerned about the reliability of their work. In most surveys that employ interviewers, it is very important that each question be asked the same way by all interviewers. Otherwise, it is risky to lump all the responses together.

You also have to make sure that interviewers talk to the respondents they are supposed to contact rather than using their friends or making up the answers. You can gauge the reliability in several ways. Many research companies that do large-scale telephone interviewing conduct the interviews from special facilities in which several interviewers make calls simultaneously. Those special facilities usually have the capability to permit a supervisor (or a client) to listen unobtrusively as interviewers make their calls. If you hire interviewers to make calls from such a facility, you should monitor calls by all interviewers.

If you hire interviewers to conduct interviews at subjects' homes or places of business, you will probably assign them the names of persons that you have carefully chosen in your sampling process. You will need to make sure, then, that the right people are interviewed. You also want to make sure that interviewers are not simply making up fictitious answers. To check on that, you should select a sample of the interviewed respondents and call them to verify that they were in fact interviewed.

You can do other things to improve the reliability of your research. In many instances, you will be asking respondents questions, either in surveys, focus group interviews, or even experiments. You should take great care in developing those questions and should pretest them with a small group of people before you start the actual interviews. You must also take great care to train interviewers to ask the questions in the way you want them asked.

In addition, you should be careful about asking questions that are difficult for respondents to answer. That might be true, for example, in the case of psychographic studies that ask people to categorize themselves on such dimensions as creativity, assertiveness, or compulsiveness. It might also be a problem in studies that ask re-

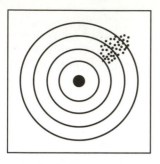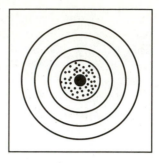

| Reliable but not valid | Valid but not reliable | Valid and reliable |

Figure 3.1 An Analogy to Validity and Reliability

Source: Earl Babbie, *The Practice of Social Research*, 5th ed. (Belmont, Calif.: Wadsworth, 1989), 126.

spondents to tell you about their previous week's television viewing or to tell you the many grocery items they purchased.

If you are having trouble distinguishing between validity and reliability, consider this statement from one of the leading textbooks about social science research describing the bull's-eyes in Figure 3.1:

> If you can think of measurement as analogous to hitting the bull's-eye on a target, you'll see that reliability looks like a "tight pattern," regardless of where it hits, since reliability is a function of consistency. Validity, on the other hand, is a function of the shots being arranged around the bull's-eye. The failure of reliability in the figure can be seen as a random error; the failure of validity is a systematic error.[3]

... Designing a Sample

When you do a survey (and other kinds of research), you will rarely, if ever, base it on a census or measure of the entire population or target audience. Instead, you will probably design an appropriate sample of the larger group and generalize from those sample results to draw conclusions about the larger population. You will need to match the sampling design with the objective of the research study. Chapter 5 explains the sampling process in more detail.

... Designing a Questionnaire

Regardless of whether you are doing a survey, an experiment, or a focus group interview, you will almost always have to ask people questions to give you data about the effect of the variables you are manipulating and measuring. The wording of individual questions and the order in which you ask them can influence the results, so you need to give much care and thought to writing the questionnaire.

You must also think about the purpose of each question. You will have to think about how the answers to each question will be used. You will have to decide if you need numerical or verbal answers. That will depend on how you plan to use the data. Chapter 6 explains questionnaire design.

... Planning Data Collection

Another part of the research strategy is to determine the appropriate way to collect the data you need. That decision will be greatly influenced by the objective of the research. You might elect to do a survey, which is particularly appropriate to analyze larger groups. For other kinds of research objectives, an experiment or a focus group interview might be more appropriate. You will want to choose the most cost-efficient way to gather the data you need. There is no point in wasting money to gather data you will not need. Chapter 7 (surveys), Chapter 8 (qualitative methods), and Chapter 9 (experiments) describe common data gathering techniques in more detail.

... Pretesting

Careful researchers always pretest their questionnaires and data collection methods. Pretests are a good way to identify confusing or embarrassing questions and to realize that some questions might yield unusable data. You should conduct a pretest with a small sample of the same kind of people who will be in your actual study. Use enough subjects to yield sufficient data for a crude analysis of the pretest data. Don't treat the pretest lightly; put as much thought into it as you can. Such care will increase the likelihood that you will discover problems. Clients who are paying for your research have a legitimate right to expect you to conduct *and report* results of a pretest.

Research Tactics

In the tactics phase of the research, you carry out or execute the strategies you have already selected. It goes without saying that the tactics you use must follow from your strategies — which follow from the objectives — which follow from the situation analysis.

... Data Collection

This is what people often think about when they envision research. Data collection requires the same care as other stages of the process. Unless you are doing a very small study, you will almost certainly hire interviewers or other assistants to help you gather data. You will have to plan a way to supervise interviewers and to ensure quality control in data collection. You will have to establish written procedures to ensure uniformity in the way questions are asked or in the way that experiments are conducted. You will have to make careful arrangements for focus group interviews. A well-planned project can be ruined by poor fieldwork.

... Tabulation and Analysis

After you collect the data, you must tabulate and analyze them. You must plan for this *before* you collect the data. You will have to think about how you will tabulate, present, and analyze your data. It will be too late to make changes once you start to conduct experiments or interviews.

... Reporting Results

You will have to report your results to clients, management, and other researchers. Researchers know that the best way to ensure that management will use the results most effectively is to make those results as easy as possible to read and understand. The findings must be spelled out clearly and simply, and the significance of the findings must be made readily apparent.

... Research Evaluation

After you have devoted weeks or months to planning a study, conducting it, and reporting the results, you will be tempted to want to forget that study as soon as possible and to move on to the next project. However, it is important to look back carefully at the research study and to evaluate how well it was done. That kind of analysis can give you valuable insights about future research studies. In many ways, research ought to be thought of as a circular process, and evaluation, the "last" stage in the process, ought to be considered a turning point leading to the next research.

An obvious area to examine, of course, is the cost of doing the research. You should estimate the cost of the research before you conduct the study, and you should keep careful records of expenses as the research is carried out. Comparing your estimates with the actual expenses will improve your accuracy in estimates of future research projects.

It would also be wise to have some follow-up discussions with the client or the user of the research. You should ascertain if your study provided answers to the research questions that prompted the project. You may also want to find out how the research was used. Researchers too often give their report to the client and then do not bother to see how useful the research was and how future research could be improved.

When you analyze your procedures and results, you should think carefully about reliability and validity. Do your measures of reliability indicate that reliability could have been improved? Did your checking of interviewer work suggest that training was inadequate and that validity was a problem? If you did a laboratory experiment, were the procedures so artificial that they severely weakened external validity? If your evaluation reveals serious problems, it will be too late to correct them in that current study, but you can improve them in future studies.

Research Ethics

We must note that we have been speaking of properly conducted research. That is, *research* here means scientifically controlled investigation and analysis. We have not been concerned with findings that only purportedly resulted from research. A poorly conceived or poorly executed study may be worse than no study at all because it might not pay for itself and could result in a grossly inappropriate decision. Fraudulent research, or research with predetermined results (done to prove a point), is less than worthless.

Here is an example of a researcher who was tempted to slant data for a client but refused to do so. The researcher received a call from the advertising manager of the local newspaper. The manager was alarmed to observe that local automobile dealers were shifting advertising dollars from the newspaper to local television stations. He believed that the dealers' advertising agencies were recommending the change to pick up larger media commissions.

"This is going to have to stop," the manager said. "I've got to have some sort of study that will explain accurately why the dealers are moving to television and why it would be in their interests to stay in my newspaper. If we can show them that most car buyers rely on newspapers more than on television, maybe we can get them back."

The woman who was proprietor of a research firm wanted very much to please her new client. She thought her chances were good because she was convinced the newspaper would come out ahead of local television in the study. Over the next two months, she conducted the study. Unfortunately, the results of the study did not show newspapers as clearly superior to television. Ahead, yes, but not by much.

"I can report the findings honestly and objectively," the researcher thought, "or I can pull out only the data that will support the advertising manager's hopes that newspapers are better than television for promoting new car sales. . . . If I'm honest and objective, I will know that I've done my best for my client, yet he may be so unhappy with the results that he won't come back to me in the future. If I manipulate the data to make things look better, he'll be delighted, but I won't have given him what he really needs to know. I wonder which way I should go."

In this case, the researcher decided to report the data in as unbiased a manner as possible.

In another case, a researcher decided *not* to make an honest report. He owned an advertising agency that had just landed a new account, a bank in a small town nearby. Although the bank was small, it stood a good chance of growing rapidly and becoming an increasingly profitable account for the agency.

Naturally, agency management wanted to hold on to the new account for as long as possible. So management decided that a baseline (benchmark) survey, to show townspeople's perceptions of and attitudes toward the bank, would be in order. If a baseline survey conducted immediately upon acquiring the account could be followed a year later by a similar study, the agency would be able to show the client the benefit obtained through using the agency's services.

In the excitement and urgency to conduct the surveys, the agency produced data that were largely worthless and misleading. Worthless, that is, except from the agency's standpoint; the purpose of the surveys was to make the agency look good, not to learn the actual perceptions and attitudes of the local residents.

Here is how the advertising agency conducted its "research":

1. The baseline survey was conducted via telephone interviews with the bank's customers. The interviewers were instructed to "probe deeply when a customer gives an unfavorable response to the questions about the quality and range of services" offered by the bank. Some questions were designed to evoke neutral or negative responses.

2. In the later survey, the telephone interviewers were instructed to "probe after all *favorable* responses to questions about the quality and range of services." Several questions used in the initial study were rephrased to elicit favorable answers — to exaggerate the positive attitudes toward the bank.

The "don't know" and "no response" answers were omitted from the final tabulations wherever including those responses reflected badly on the results of the advertising campaign the agency had been conducting for the bank.

The result of the two "research" projects was a before-after report that was given to the bank's advertising director. The report informed him of the outstanding improvements the agency had produced in the public's attitudes toward the bank and its services.

The advertising director asked no questions about the method by which the data were collected and analyzed. After reading the report, he was pleased at having selected the advertising agency personally. The agency had met its objectives.

Some research may be misleading, although the investigator's motivations were good. Things can go wrong, as in the case of the researcher looking at sales of his client's brand of cat food. He learned accidentally that one of his client's managers had done a favor for one grocer by giving him a new point-of-purchase display and a larger than usual supply of the product. Since the sales study was being conducted in a limited local area, such unusual treatment of a single retailer would have contaminated the study. If the researcher had not learned of the manager's action, the test could have produced misleading results.

The preceding discussion strongly suggests the importance of ethical principles and behavior by researchers. As you plan and conduct a research project, you should always be guided by the highest ethical principles. Advertising researchers have important ethical obligations to their subjects and their clients. Clients also have ethical obligations to their researchers.

... Treatment of Subjects

It should go without saying that nothing in your research procedures can be physically or emotionally harmful or threatening to your subjects. Experimental procedures must not expose them to any physical danger, mental stress, or embarrassment. In an experiment, you should explain to subjects what you will be doing—but you can disguise the purpose of the procedures.

For example, you should explain to subjects that you are going to use a pupillometer to measure their eye pupil dilation as they view magazine ads—but you are not obligated to tell them that the purpose of the procedure is to see how they react to the use of attractive models in the ads. In fact, you should not tell them the purpose, because that will almost certainly affect their response and contaminate the data. After the experiment, you may explain your purposes. However, you should make sure that these subjects will not reveal your purpose to other subjects who have not yet participated in your experiment.

In experiments involving mechanical devices such as pupillometers or eye movement cameras, have someone use the equipment on you so you can experience what subjects will experience. Reassure subjects that the equipment will not harm them.

... Anonymity

If you seek any information from subjects—in experiments or surveys—you must take steps to ensure that their responses will never be publicly associated with them. You must assure subjects of this anonymity before you ask the questions. It should not be necessary for you to write a subject's name on a questionnaire; subjects should always be treated as numbers on questionnaires. Sure, that sounds impersonal, but that is what you must be. And even though you can trust yourself, remember that other people may be assisting you in the research.

In mail surveys, it is sometimes tempting to try to put an identifying number on questionnaires or return envelopes so you can keep track of the people who have returned them. That will allow you to send follow-up notices to those who have not responded without the expense of sending follow-up letters to all of the original subjects. It is difficult to do this without compromising the respondents' anonymity, and the possible reduced costs are probably not worth causing subjects to become suspicious about the number or code on the questionnaire.

In telephone surveys, subjects may be curious about how you got their name. When you use a telephone directory as a basis for a sample, you should record only the numbers and not the names. You and your interviewers can legitimately tell respondents that their telephone numbers were randomly selected from the telephone directory and that you do not know what their name is. You should not have any reason for asking their name in the interview. You may write the telephone number, but not a name, on the questionnaire.

What can you say to someone with an unlisted telephone number? You can explain that you used a selection procedure that used randomly generated telephone numbers, thus explaining why people with unlisted numbers could be included.

... Revealing the Client

What do you say to respondents who are persistent in learning the purpose of the research and the identity of the company or individual paying for it? You should not reveal the purpose or identity before the interview, because such knowledge by respondents will almost certainly contaminate their responses. If subjects persist in their questions about these issues, you should probably thank them for their time, apologize for the inconvenience, and end the interview. The information you get, if you get any, will not be worth the antagonism. You could explain the purpose of the research after the interview, but there is a chance that this information could be passed on to others whom you might call later.

... Honesty Is the Best Policy

You have an obligation to be honest with subjects and clients throughout the research process. Much of this will be reflected in the research report. It goes without saying, of course, that you did exactly what your report says you did. It is unethical to cover up mistakes or omissions in your procedures.

Methods
Your report should describe your research design in detail. Describe exactly how subjects were selected and explain any possible biases that might have resulted from your sample selection procedures. If your data analysis suggests that you had one or more improperly worded questions or some other form of questionnaire bias, you should report that honestly.

Giving Due Credit
If you use someone else's ideas or methods, report that fact. In research, there is nothing wrong with doing things the way others have done them. That practice is called replication, and it is perfectly acceptable. But don't claim someone else's ideas as being your original ideas.

Reporting Results
We should not have to mention that it is reprehensible to make up data that were not collected or to falsify results. It can happen because it is difficult to monitor what a researcher does. A researcher can report results that supposedly came from five hundred telephone interviews, and the only substantiation of that fact is the researcher's word.

Some companies that pay to have interviews conducted use a verification procedure. The company doing the interviews will provide a list of names and addresses of people interviewed, but without associating the names with questionnaires. The company paying for the research can contact, by telephone or mail, the people who were interviewed and verify that the interviews were in fact conducted. That may be an unnecessary step in most research studies, but if you are getting paid to conduct interviews, you should be prepared, or even offer, to provide names and addresses for such a verification. If you are paying for the interviews, you should have no hesitation about asking for such verification. Completed questionnaires and other records of the research should be retained for several years in case of questions about their content. However, those records should be retained in a way that ensures the anonymity of respondents.

Errors of Omission

It may be tempting at times to omit certain details in a research report — perhaps because you realize that the client (or your firm's management) may not want to hear those details. In some research studies, management's biases may be obvious: They want research results to justify a decision they have already made or are about to make. You might think it would be acceptable to omit such data, and you might rationalize this to yourself by saying that omitting some details is not nearly as bad as deliberately misrepresenting facts. Neither is acceptable, and certainly not omission of facts. As a researcher, you have an ethical responsibility to make a full report of all facts, regardless of the consequences. Likewise, your interpretation of results must be honest. Do not report just what the client wants to hear.

• • • Summary

Strategic planning for advertising research will help you to avoid costly mistakes and will help you to do more cost-efficient research by limiting your efforts to the tasks that must be done. It is useful to think of stages in the research process. You should begin with a careful analysis of the research situation that should lead to a definition of the research problem or a statement of the research question. The situation analysis should also include a careful estimate of the cost of the research and a consideration of whether the research benefits will outweigh the costs. Secondary research should be part of the situation analysis.

A research study should have an objective, and the statement of the research question should suggest the appropriate objective. The objective of many studies is to help to determine if the objectives of the advertising campaign have been accomplished, so it is important that the stated advertising objectives be appropriate to advertising and be quantifiable.

The research objective, in turn, should suggest the appropriate research strategy, including operational definitions and measures of the independent and dependent variables, the appropriate data collection technique, sample, and questionnaire. You must also give careful consideration to the problems of validity and reliability.

Research tactics involve the actual research (collecting and analyzing data) and reporting the results. The final stage — evaluation — is also an important bridge between the just-completed study and future ones. Researchers must also be concerned about ethical behavior toward subjects and clients.

••• Notes

1. Lewis Carroll, *Alice's Adventures in Wonderland* (New York: Random House, 1965), 71–72.
2. R. H. Colley, *Defining Advertising Goals for Measured Advertising Results* (New York: Association of National Advertisers, 1961).
3. Earl Babbie, *The Practice of Social Research*, 5th ed. (Belmont, Calif.: Wadsworth, 1989), 125.

••• Self-Test Questions

1. Outline a research proposal for an advertising research project for a retailer in your community who caters especially to college students. Include a discussion of the research problem or question as well as the factors that would have to be considered to estimate the cost of the research.
2. Outline a research proposal for an experiment to test the effect of the use of a color versus a black and white ad in a campus newspaper. Identify the independent and dependent variables and discuss your operational definitions and measurements.
3. What kind of secondary research might you do for the project in Question 2?
4. What kind of data analysis and data tables would be needed in the experimental study mentioned in Question 2?
5. Discuss how DAGMAR or a similar concept is important to advertising research.
6. Discuss the external validity problems you might have with the experiment mentioned in Question 2. What could you do to minimize those problems?
7. Distinguish between face validity and predictive validity.
8. Discuss some of the reliability problems you might face in a study that utilized several interviewers. What could you do to minimize those problems?
9. Discuss the possible ethical concerns that might arise in a research study similar to the one mentioned in Question 1.

••• Suggestions for Additional Reading

Babbie, E. *The Practice of Social Research*. 5th ed. Belmont, Calif.: Wadsworth, 1989.
Colley, R. H. *Defining Advertising Goals for Measured Advertising Results*. New York: Association of National Advertisers, 1961.

Stempel, G. H., III, and B. H. Westley. *Research Methods in Mass Communication*. 2nd ed. Englewood Cliffs, N.J.: Prentice-Hall, 1989.

Zaltman, G., and C. Moorman. "The Importance of Personal Trust in the Use of Research." *Journal of Advertising Research*, 28 (October–November 1988), 16–24.

Zaltman, G., and C. Moorman. "The Management and Use of Advertising Research." *Journal of Advertising Research*, 28 (December 1988–January 1989): 11–18.

CHAPTER 4

Secondary Research

- Suppose you wanted to conduct a survey of advertising directors at U.S. daily newspapers. Where could you find names and addresses of those directors?
- Suppose you were planning a test market campaign and needed to know the number of households in Richmond, Va., with annual incomes greater than $50,000. Where could you find that information?
- Suppose you were preparing a campaign for a personal computer and wanted statistics about the number of households that have personal computers as well as some magazine articles about how families use computers. Where could you find that information?
- Suppose you were a media planner preparing a spot radio campaign and needed to know the estimated cost for radio advertising in the Fort Wayne, Ind., market. Where is such information available?
- Suppose you were working for a client in the farm machinery industry and needed information about forecasts for that industry. Where could you find those forecasts?
- Suppose you wanted a job as a copywriter and wanted to write to creative

directors at large agencies in Atlanta. Where could you get the names and addresses as well as the number of employees at each agency?

- Suppose you also wanted to know something about the personal backgrounds of those creative directors. Where could you find it?
- Suppose your advertising director wanted to join the Association of National Advertisers. Where could you find the address of the association?
- Where could you find coverage maps of television stations?
- Suppose you wanted to advertise resort vacation packages to Canadians. Where could you find the names and advertising rates of Canadian newspapers?

These are a few examples of questions that advertisers and advertising researchers must frequently answer. Those questions could be answered through primary research, by seeking information from original sources. For example, you could write to the agency creative directors and ask them for their biographies. Or you could call radio stations in Fort Wayne to ask them their rates. Or you could browse through consumer and business magazines to look for articles about how families use computers.

However, such questions can probably be answered more easily, quickly, and economically through secondary research—in published material in libraries. Such secondary research can eliminate or reduce the need for primary research. At the least, it should help you to narrow the scope of your inquiry and to avoid problems and errors experienced by earlier researchers who asked similar questions.

Therefore, an early step in any research project, even primary research, should be exhaustive secondary research. It is important to plan your secondary research and to execute that plan carefully and completely. You will waste time and overlook important sources if you do not carefully organize your search for secondary information.

You should begin by precisely defining the question or problem you are investigating. If you take that precaution, it will be easier to seek appropriate sources of secondary data. Next, you should list all the sources you think might be useful. As you begin to examine those published sources, you will probably uncover other sources that appear to be useful. You should add them to your list and not conclude your secondary research until you have thoroughly examined all the sources on your list. Don't trust your memory; it is important to keep careful written records about sources you have consulted and ones you need to consult.

You will do your research in public, university, or private company libraries, and you will find the assistance of trained reference librarians to be extremely useful. They are experts who know what resources are readily available and how to locate some that are not.

• • • Electronic Databases

Secondary research has been dramatically altered in recent years by the introduction of electronic databases. In such databases, information is stored electronically and is easily available to researchers using personal computers. Storing data electronically makes it easier for researchers to search vast numbers of sources in a very short time for particular subjects. Compilers and suppliers of such databases can also update them more easily and more frequently than they could with printed databases.

Before electronic databases, researchers had to look at printed lists of sources in books. For example, if you wanted to search for newspaper articles about advertising agency mergers, you would have to look at separate indexes for several newspapers. Each volume of those printed indexes might cover only a year or a shorter period of time, so you would have to look laboriously through several volumes for the same newspaper and repeat that effort for other newspapers. In addition, you would have to leaf through each volume to look under several different topic headings that might have articles about agency mergers. (For example, you would have to look at headings for the names of individual agencies as well as the general topic of agency mergers.) The listings you would find would give you the title of the article and the date of publication but nothing about the content; you would then have to find bound or microfilmed copies of the actual newspaper and look for the articles to learn if they were relevant to your research. If a listing seemed to be useful, you would have to write it out for future reference.

Now you can use a computer software program to search a single electronic database that includes several years of articles for several newspapers. You can specify that the program look for all articles with certain words (such as "agency mergers" or "Saatchi and Saatchi") in the title or in the text of the article. In a matter of seconds or minutes, the software program will provide you with a list of several articles pertinent to the topic. In addition to information about the newspaper name and date of publication, article citations can also include a brief summary or the complete text of the article. Furthermore, the list of citations can be printed so you can take it with you. Some database programs will also allow you to download, or transfer, the list of citations to a computer disk so you can easily use them in your research report.

When you use electronic databases, you will have to learn how to use and combine keywords to select citations on desired subjects. The normal problem with electronic databases is in defining the subject too broadly and coming up with far too many references that are not germane to the topic at hand.

• • • Online databases

Electronic databases are available in two formats, online and CD-ROM. Online databases are physically located (in a computer) in one location, and researchers in libraries and other locations around the world can access the database with computers and telephone-line connections. The single location makes it easy for the compiler of the database to add new material to the database on a frequent basis. The major disadvantage is cost; companies that compile databases charge users a per-minute or per-hour fee to search through the database, and the cost of a single search session can be quite high. (Many fees are more than $100 per hour, and some are considerably higher than that.) When you are paying that kind of money, you want to be sure to be knowledgeable about search processes to minimize the time needed to make the search.

. . . CD-ROM databases

CD-ROM stands for Compact Disc—Read Only Memory. To use such a database, you need a computer with a compact disc player attached. The database information is stored on compact discs just like the ones you can buy with prerecorded music. The compact disc holds incredible amounts of information, and the CD-player enables the computer to access any piece of data on the disc. The search process is the same as for an online database; you instruct a software program to search for articles on the basis of the appearance of certain keywords or phrases in the title and text.

Many libraries have computers and CD-players, and they purchase data discs from database suppliers. Beyond that, however, researchers do not usually pay to use databases. The major disadvantage is timeliness; updated discs may be available only on a quarterly basis. That is a small disadvantage when you consider the savings in cost over using an online database. However, even if you have to pay to search an online database, the savings in time and effort as opposed to looking through printed sources will usually be well worth it.

How do you know what kinds of CD-ROM discs are available? CD-ROM users can search a CD-ROM disc called the *CD-ROM Sourcedisk* from Diversified Data Resources. It contains descriptions of more than 300 commercially available CD-ROM services and includes simulations that show how to use many of them.

. . . Guides to Secondary Research

You should use the sources described in this chapter as starting points for your secondary research. They might suggest other sources, and so will reference librarians and a library card catalog (or its electronic equivalent). Addresses are provided in Appendix B for readers who wish to contact publishers and suppliers of such materials.

To begin your search and to give you some ideas about appropriate sources, you might want to look at sources that will help you to structure and outline your research. These can also help you to find information about more specific subjects.

. . . General Guides

A good source to start with is *Search Strategies in Mass Communication,* which is a textbook for courses about using mass communication databases. In addition to a discussion of the strategies for searching for information, the book describes several sources of advertising material.

Another useful guide is one used by reference librarians themselves, *Guide to Reference Books.* This book lists and describes hundreds of reference books. By using the index, you can locate reference sources for virtually any topic. Suppose, for example, that you did not know where to look for the names of advertising agency media directors. You could look in the index under the headings of "advertising, directories" or "advertising, guides," and it would tell you to look in a periodical called the *Stan-*

dard Directory of Advertising Agencies. Each entry in the *Guide to Reference Books* lists the author, title, and descriptions of the contents and uses of the reference source.

Business and Economics Databases Online is a guide to online databases in the business and economics fields. It includes instructions on how to access and use the databases.

• • • Guides to Business Sources

Some of the research guides deal specifically with sources of information about business, including advertising. One of them is *Handbook of Business Information: A Guide for Librarians, Students, and Researchers.* The first part of the book categorizes sources by their formats and includes basic reference sources, directories, periodicals (including newspapers), looseleaf services, government services, statistics, vertical file collections, and electronic databases. The second part of the book lists sources by business fields; a section on advertising media sources appears in the marketing section.

Another comprehensive guide used extensively by reference librarians is the *Encyclopedia of Business Information Sources,* which lists information sources for more than 1,000 business topics. The guide was designed for business executives, and sources are listed by subject or industry. For example, a listing for the airline industry includes two directories, two periodicals and newsletters, and two trade associations. Each citation includes addresses, telephone numbers, and costs of the sources.

• • • Indexes to Articles in Periodicals

You can find valuable secondary information in trade magazines, scholarly journals, and other publications. Fortunately, you do not need to search through every publication to find that useful information. Indexes in printed and electronic forms can tell you where to find articles about specific subjects. The key is knowing which indexes are appropriate and how to use them. Subjects are listed alphabetically, and you will need to take a few minutes to browse through a particular index to learn how it categorizes and lists subjects.

One of the best-known indexes is an old standby you are probably already familiar with—the *Readers' Guide to Periodical Literature.* It is published monthly, with quarterly and annual accumulative volumes. Authors and subjects are listed alphabetically, and article titles are listed under each subject heading. It indexes approximately 200 general interest magazines, so it is not likely to list many articles with specific information for advertising research. However, the articles might provide useful background information, such as stories about how families use computers.

Magazine Article Summaries: EBSCO's Weekly Index to Periodical Literature is published more often (58 times a year, with periodic accumulative volumes) than *Readers' Guide* and also has summaries of the articles cited. It indexes 220 periodicals that are popular in public schools and public libraries. Articles are selected for inclusion on the basis of their value as reference material and whether they will be useful to high school and college researchers. This index is also available on EBSCO CD-ROM.

Info-track is a CD-ROM database index of articles in more than 1,100 publications. It is available in many academic and public libraries and is updated monthly. The basic service includes the most recent four years, but a backfile of previous years is available.

UMI NEWSPAPER ABSTRACTS ONDISC is a CD-ROM database that indexes and abstracts articles in nine so-called "elite" newspapers, including the *New York Times* and *Wall Street Journal*.

An index that will probably be more useful to you in advertising research is *Business Periodicals Index* (BPI). The format and classification systems are identical to those of *Readers' Guide*; the difference is that BPI indexes business publications instead of consumer magazines. Like *Readers' Guide*, it is published monthly with quarterly and annual accumulative volumes. If you wanted to know something about marketing and advertising strategies for personal computers, you could look in BPI for articles from *Advertising Age* or other trade publications.

ABI/INFORM is a CD-ROM database index of business information in more than 800 different journals. It is an excellent source of information on companies, products, business conditions, trends, corporate strategies, and management techniques. Marketing and Advertising is one of its subject areas.

Another very useful database is *Dow Jones News/Retrieval*, which includes information from the *Wall Street Journal*, Dow Jones News, *Barron's*, the *Washington Post*, major business publications, and specialized journals. You can find current news, sports, and weather; a reference library of historical articles; company and industry statistics and forecasts; stock market quotations; airline schedules; online shopping; an encyclopedia; and book and movie reviews. While it is available in libraries, many business firms and individuals also access Dow Jones News/Retrieval with their personal computers and telephone modems.

A similar online database service is NEXIS, which indexes articles and other citations from hundreds of publications and reports, including newspapers, consumer magazines, business publications, the *Encyclopaedia Britannica*, and government documents.

VU/TEXT is an online service that allows users to access several databases, including many U.S. newspapers, stock market quotations, public relations news releases, and Securities and Exchange Commission data about publicly held companies.

U.S. government agencies publish hundreds of periodicals, books, and other publications, and many articles or items in them can be useful in advertising research. The U.S. Department of Commerce publishes *Commerce Publications Update*, a biweekly listing of its publications. An added feature of this index is the inclusion of the biweekly report of Key Business Indicators, which includes the latest data or estimates about the U.S. population, personal income, gross national product, unemployment, and the consumer price index.

The best single source for U.S. government publications is *GPO on SilverPlatter*, which is a CD-ROM listing of documents published by the U.S. government, including books, reports, serials, and maps. Compiled and distributed by a private firm and not the government, the disk is an electronic version of the printed *Monthly Catalog of U.S. Government Publications*.

In addition to consumer and business periodicals and U.S. government publications, you may also want to search scholarly or academic publications. Several indexes list articles in such publications. *Social Sciences Index*, published quarterly with an annual accumulative volume, includes author and subject entries from periodicals in anthropology, economics, geography, medicine, psychology, sociology, and other related fields. The CD-ROM version is called Social SciSearch.

Psychological Abstracts includes abstracts of research studies in psychology and related disciplines. It is available in printed, online, and CD-ROM formats. Advertising researchers are likely to find useful citations in the Marketing and Advertising section in the monthly and semiannual accumulative volumes. *PsycLit* is a CD-ROM database of literature in psychology from 1974 to the present that includes *Psychological Abstracts*.

A specialized but potentially useful source is *Dissertation Abstracts*, which contains summaries of doctoral dissertations available on microfilm or as Xerographic reproductions. Dissertations related to advertising are listed in the Humanities and Social Sciences volume of *Dissertation Abstracts*. This source is not as up to date as others and is therefore more likely to be a good source for historical purposes. It is also available on CD-ROM.

The *Public Affairs Information Service* (PAIS) indexes journal articles, books, government documents, and reports on politics and public affairs from 1976 to the present. It is especially useful because it covers trade and scholarly publications, newspapers, government documents, and books written in several languages from around the world. It is also available as *PAIS on CD-ROM*.

ERIC (Educational Resources Information Center) indexes documents and journal articles from more than 750 journals in the field of education. It is sponsored by the U.S. Department of Education and is a network of 16 separate clearinghouses that each cover a specific area.

• • • Useful Periodicals

A few periodicals are so useful that they should be considered separately, although they are indexed in one or more of the sources listed in the previous section. To find articles listed in those indexes, you would have to go to a library to find the periodicals. The periodicals listed in this section might be worth the price of a subscription to advertisers and advertising researchers.

Advertising Age has regular features and special sections on research. Special issues, like "The 100 Leading National Advertisers," can be particularly useful sources of information for secondary researchers. Listings like that can also be considered as sampling lists for surveys of agencies or other organizations.

A more specialized trade publication is *Marketing and Media Decisions*, which has regular columns and stories about research. The July issue each year is particu-

larly useful because it includes advertising expenditure data for the top brands in several product categories. Other useful trade publications include *Adweek* and *Madison Avenue*.

The *Journal of Advertising* and the *Journal of Advertising Research* are even more specialized. They emphasize reports of research findings more than theoretical discussions, but they also include articles about methodological problems in advertising research.

The *Journal of Marketing* has articles about marketing and advertising research as well as articles about trends, opinions, and forecasts. An even more specialized publication is the *Journal of Marketing Research*, whose articles tend to be more academic and theoretical than those in the *Journal of Marketing*.

American Demographics calls itself the "Magazine of Consumer Markets," and many of the articles in that monthly publication are relevant to advertising research. Here are a few titles and descriptions from some recent issues:

"Inside America's Households." America's 91 million households are changing in three important ways. Businesses need to track those trends to keep up with their customers.

"Death of the Frito Bandito." L'il Black Sambo, the Frito Bandito, and other negative stereotypes are out. Positive realism is in when it comes to advertising to minorities.

"Why They Buy." Food retailers now have the data to link people with products. But they need to know more about their customers' needs and buying habits to lure them to the store.

"Meet Jane Doe." The average American is fictitious, but her importance is not. The characteristics of the average American reveal important trends in how people live and what they buy.

• • • Information About Periodicals and Other Media

Advertisers and advertising researchers frequently need data about media: advertising rates and circulations of newspapers and magazines, coverage patterns of radio and television stations, and owners and managers of periodicals and stations. You can find such information in a variety of sources. Many can be found in public and university libraries, and many are useful enough to be included in a company library. You can also use many of these sources to build sampling lists for surveys of media organizations.

You might want a comprehensive list of periodicals in a particular field. If so, you can consult periodical directories, which list thousands of publications by subject area. Periodical directories can also be used to generate sampling or mailing lists.

Ulrich's International Periodicals Directory lists more than 110,000 periodicals under more than 550 subject headings. Each entry describes the editorial content, when the magazine was first published, how often it is published, its cost, the publisher's address, and the editor's name. An extremely useful feature is a notation for periodicals that are available online or on CD-ROM. (The 1989–90 edition listed more

than 2,100 available online and more than 170 on CD-ROM.) *Ulrich's* itself is available online.

The *Standard Periodical Directory* lists similar information for more than 65,000 periodicals in the United States and Canada and includes magazines, newsletters, directories, and journals. Two of its subject categories are Advertising and Marketing and Media and Communications.

The *Working Press of the Nation* is a five-volume source of information about media in the United States, including newspapers, magazines, radio and television stations, feature writers and photographers, and internal publications of more than 3,100 companies, government agencies, and other groups. Listings include addresses, telephone numbers, mechanical information, subscription prices, top editorial staffers, a content description, a description of readers, and deadlines.

The *Gale Directory of Publications* is a two-volume listing of nearly 25,000 newspapers, magazines, and similar publications in the United States and Canada. Each entry includes information about the audience and purpose of the publication, frequency of publication, editors, publishers, advertising directors, circulation, subscription rates, and advertising rates.

A well-known source is *Standard Rate and Data Service*, which includes separate volumes for different media categories: newspapers, consumer magazines, business magazines, spot radio, spot television, transit, and direct mail. Some volumes are published as often as monthly. Each gives advertisers virtually all they need to know about individual newspapers, magazines, stations, and other media vehicles. Similar information for outdoor advertising can be found in the *Buyer's Guide to Outdoor Advertising*.

Editor and Publisher International Yearbook lists newspapers published in the United States and other countries. Entries give circulation and advertising data, addresses, names of officers, and mechanical specifications for ad sizes and color printing. The *Yearbook* also lists news and syndicate services, equipment suppliers, schools and departments of journalism, and other industry organizations and services.

You can find information about radio and television markets and stations, including cable television, in *Broadcasting/Cablecasting Yearbook*. In addition to market statistics, it includes directories of stations, advertising agencies, station sales representatives, network affiliate stations, and commercial producers and distributors. Other sections describe the Federal Communications Commission and the history of broadcasting.

Similar information about broadcasting can be found in *Television and Cable Factbook*, an annual two-volume edition. The volume about stations has data about broadcast stations around the world, including coverage maps, personnel, and Arbitron audience estimates. The volume about services is a directory of agencies, manufacturers, and cable systems. The *Cable Advertising Directory* lists cable television systems, including number of subscribers, number of homes passed by cable, and advertising rates.

Two sources provide specialized information useful for media planners and buyers who have to estimate the costs of advertising schedules. Both sources are actually quarterly magazines. *Media Cost Guide* has cost estimates, demographic data, and other information about all media. *Media Market Guide* is more specialized because

of its inclusion of cost-per-rating point estimates for local radio and television markets in the United States.

• • • Data About Business Conditions

To help them make decisions about where to advertise, advertisers need research data about business conditions in specific markets. Data such as population, number of households, age distributions, disposable income, automobile registrations, and retail sales, to name a few, are very important. Several reference sources provide that kind of information, and most are readily available in printed or electronic formats at many libraries.

In addition to information about media, certain volumes of *Standard Rate and Data Service* include data about local market conditions. In SRDS volumes for newspapers, spot radio, and spot television, the beginning of each state section has data for county, city, and metropolitan areas. They include population estimates, number of households, consumer spendable income, retail sales, passenger car registrations, and farm population. Federal government agencies are the primary sources of those data. SRDS volumes also include rankings of national markets on such dimensions as population, income, and retail sales.

A very useful and widely quoted source of market information is the *Survey of Buying Power Data Service*, which is available in both a printed and a CD-ROM format. It provides demographic data for cities, counties, and states, including population, age distributions, buying income, and retail sales.

Editor and Publisher Market Guide is an annual compilation of data about U.S. and Canadian newspaper markets. Entries give location, transportation facilities, population, households, banking facilities, automobile registrations, industries, climate, retail sales data, names and circulations of newspapers, and newspaper sales representative firms. The *Market Guide* also ranks markets by population, income, retail sales, and food sales.

Rand McNally's *Commercial Atlas and Marketing Guide* has large maps detailing commercial and marketing information about the United States and other countries. One section has U.S. aggregate data about agriculture, communications, manufacturing, population, retail trade, and transportation. It includes detailed information on zip code zones, rail and highway distances, military installations, shopping centers, and manufacturing. A section on states has similar information.

D & B — Donnelley Demographics provides demographic information from the latest U.S. census — with updates based on its own estimates — for the current year and for five-year projections. Data are available for zip code zones, cities, television markets, and states. Reports include population, age, gender, household income, education, and mobility. This database is available online through the Dialog Information Retrieval Service.

The U.S. Department of Commerce publishes several sources of data about business conditions. The *U.S. Industrial Outlook* is an annual volume containing information about past and current conditions and forecasts for more than 350 industries. The monthly *Survey of Current Business* includes data on national business conditions, including gross national product, personal income, savings, and employment. The Commerce Department's Census Bureau offers several publications with data about population estimates, department store sales, retail businesses, and wholesale businesses. The *Census Catalog and Guide* describes those sources. Some data are also available on the Census Bureau's online data system, CENDATA.

Congressional Information Service (CSI), a private company, provides three services that might provide information relevant to advertising research. *American Statistics Index* (ASI) contains references to statistical information published by more than 500 sources within the federal government. *Statistical Reference Index* (SRI) contains references to statistical information published by U.S. associations and institutes, businesses, commercial publishers, independent research organizations, state governments, and university research centers. *CIS/Index* cites information from working papers of the U.S. Congress, including hearings, prints, documents, reports, and special publications issued from 1970 on. All three CIS services are published monthly with quarterly and annual accumulations.

Many universities have research bureaus that can provide valuable data about business conditions in their state and region. These research bureaus conduct original research and also compile it from other sources, and they are usually associated with schools or departments of business, economics, and commerce. Many also publish journals.

A local chamber of commerce can be another source of data about business conditions and potential. Some of this information is compiled from published sources, but some may come from local original sources such as tax offices or building permit offices. The annual *World Chamber of Commerce Directory* has information about chambers of commerce, tourist offices, convention bureaus, and economic development organizations in the United States and foreign countries. However, you should remember that the purpose behind such information is usually to attract business and industry to a community, so it may feature only positive data.

You can find data about the consumer electronics industry, including sales and history, in the *Consumer Electronics Annual Review*.

••• Directories

If you want to find names of advertisers, agencies, or market research organizations, you can look at one of several directories of such companies. Those directories can also help you to develop sampling lists.

The *Standard Directory of Advertisers* is an annual guide to advertising practices of U.S. companies. In addition to an alphabetical index of the companies and a list of approximately 20,000 trade (brand) names, it has entries for each of the companies, classified according to type of industry. Entries include addresses, corporate officers, advertising agencies, types of advertising media used, and advertising expenditures. The *Standard Directory of Advertising Agencies* lists agencies alphabetically and by region. Entries include addresses, agency billings, officers, and clients. It also lists agencies by specialty and has lists of service organizations and sales promotion agencies. *Adweek* magazine also publishes regional and national directories of advertisers, agencies, and media.

The *Encyclopedia of Associations* is a guide to more than 30,000 national and international organizations in several categories. Advertising associations are listed in the section on trade, business, and commercial organizations.

The *Madison Avenue Handbook* is a special source of a variety of information, including lists of companies that do animation, sound effects, production, and other services.

If you don't know what directory to look at, you can start by consulting the *Directory of Directories*, which indexes more than 5,000 directories by title and subject.

··· Miscellaneous Information

Several dictionaries or glossaries of advertising include definitions for research terms: *Dictionary of Advertising Terms; Dictionary of Advertising and Direct Mail Terms; Macmillan Dictionary of Marketing and Advertising; Dictionary of Marketing, Advertising, and Public Relations;* and the *Encyclopedia of Advertising*.

Suppose you or a fellow worker creates a new advertising slogan for a client. How can you check to see if such a slogan has ever been used before? You can look in one of several compilations of advertising slogans. They include *Advertising Slogans of America; The Effective Echo: A Dictionary of Advertising Slogans; Slogans and Slogans in Print;* and the *National Register of Advertising Headlines and Slogans*.

If you are looking for biographical information about advertising people or even an advertising professor, you might find it in *Who's Who in Advertising*.

Survey of World Advertising Expenditures is an annual compilation of estimates of advertising expenditures in many countries. Data include total expenditures, per capita expenditures, advertising expenditures as a percent of gross national product, and totals by medium.

Evaluating Advertising: A Bibliography of the Communication Process was edited by Benjamin Lipstein and William J. McGuire and published by the Advertising Research Foundation in 1978. Although it is now out of date, it can still be useful because of its compilation of more than 7,000 published and unpublished research studies about evaluating the communication (message) effects of advertising. Most studies are abstracted and classified by an elaborate classification and cross-reference system. For example, the book has approximately 240 entries on the topic of repetition and frequency.

A similar book, *Effective Advertising: The Relationship Between Frequency and Advertising Effectiveness*, was written by Michael J. Naples and published by the Association of National Advertisers in 1979. It reviews published research dealing with advertising frequency and effectiveness.

Information Sources in Advertising History lists several sources of information about advertising. It includes a bibliographic essay on sources of data for research and a list of more than eighty sources related to advertising and copy research.

You might also need to do research about a particular company's financial condition. For example, you might be asked to provide the president of your agency with data about the balance sheet or profit and loss statement of a publicly held agency. You can find such information in a CD-ROM database called *Compact Disclosure*. It contains financial and management information on more than 12,000 public companies. That information includes a company profile, current and past financial statements, annual reports, cash flow statements, and stock and earnings information.

● ● ● Summary

Secondary research—searching for information that has already been collected and published—is an early and important part of the research process. Once you have defined the research problem, secondary research into that or related problems can suggest appropriate approaches for primary research. Analyzing secondary research can save unnecessary duplicative research and can suggest research questions that are still unanswered. It is even conceivable that analyzing secondary research will eliminate the need for primary research.

Large public or university libraries are the best sources for secondary research materials, although some materials might be purchased for a company library. The electronic storage of information in online and CD-ROM databases has revolutionized secondary research by making it much easier and faster to search vast numbers of secondary research sources.

● ● ● Self-Test Questions

1. Where could you find the names and addresses of advertising directors at U.S. daily newspapers?
2. Where could you find the number of households in Richmond, Va., with annual incomes greater than $50,000?
3. Where would you look to find citations for magazine articles about household use of personal computers?
4. Where would you look to find the estimated cost of spot radio advertising in Fort Wayne, Ind.?
5. Where would you look to find information about forecasts for the farm machinery industry?
6. Where could you find information about the Association of National Advertisers?
7. Where could you find names and advertising rates for Canadian newspapers?

8. Distinguish between online and CD-ROM databases. In which type would you look if you were interested in finding the most recent citations? In which type would you look if you were concerned about cost of using the service?

9. Suppose you wanted to determine what kinds of reference books are available for a particular topic. Where could you find such a listing of reference books?

10. What is a CD-ROM database index of more than 800 business magazines?

11. If you wanted to look at articles published in the *Wall Street Journal* about advertising, where could you look?

12. What is the best single source of information on articles in U.S. government sources?

CHAPTER 5

Sampling

Many times in advertising research, you will be interested in the characteristics, knowledge, attitudes, or behavior of groups of people. (We'll call those groups of people *populations* for the sake of discussion in this chapter.) The size and nature of the populations you might study can vary greatly. For example, you might be interested in the career plans of the population of advertising seniors at just your school—or the career plans of the population of thousands of advertising seniors across the country. In another study, you might want to know about the level of computer skills among the population of students at your university. If you worked for an agency or a research company, you might study the population of the readers of a certain business magazine or the population of all business executives in a certain industry. If you worked for a national media audience measurement firm, you might study the population of all U.S. adults, or the population of women aged 18 to 34, or even the entire population of nearly 250 million Americans.

In any such study, you have to answer a fundamental question: How many people in the population do you need to study if you want to ascertain certain things about the population? If you want to make general statements about the career plans of advertising seniors across the nation, do you have to question every single one of them? Or can you question only a limited number and still be able to make general statements about the entire population of advertising seniors?

Some research studies rely on a *census* of the population being studied. Theoretically, that means the researcher attempts to question or study every single member of the population. Most studies, however, rely on smaller groups, or *samples*, of the population, and that is the major topic of this chapter.

... Using a Census

We will talk a little about censuses because there are a few times when they are more appropriate than samples. We will discuss sample sizes later, but at this point we can say that samples need to be a certain size before you can confidently make generalizations about the population at large. Therefore, if the population you were studying consisted of only a few hundred people, a census would probably be more appropriate than a sample. So, if you wanted to ascertain the career plans of advertising seniors at your school, a census would be appropriate. However, if you wanted to study the career plans of seniors from across the country, a sample would be more appropriate and more practical than a census.

If you settle on a census of the population you are studying, you theoretically should try to get data about every single member of the population. Otherwise, you have to doubt the representativeness of your data. You cannot be certain that the people in the population who did not respond to your study are similar to the group of people who did respond. Notice that we said "theoretically." In practice, of course, that is impossible. The best-known census of all is the one conducted by the U.S. Bureau of the Census every ten years. Theoretically, every single person is supposed to be queried for that census, but that is far from practical. Still, just like the Census Bureau, you should do all you can to get responses from as many members of the population as you can if you decide to use a census.

The Utility of Sampling

Most advertising research is based on a sample of the population being studied instead of a census. With large populations, it would simply not be practical to attempt a census. The tremendous expense of trying to poll all readers, viewers, or customers would be too high. More important, it would not be necessary to measure the population just to try to increase the accuracy of the study. The increased accuracy or precision that you might gain from a census would not be worth the added cost. It's another example of the cost-benefit principle.

A properly selected sample represents the larger population — the group of persons you are studying. If 18- to 34-year-old women comprise 10 percent of the population you are studying, then a carefully selected sample of that population will include approximately the same percentage of women aged 18 to 34. More important, if that sample is properly drawn and is large enough, you can generalize our findings about the sample to the population. In other words, if you find that 20 percent of the sample reads Magazine A, then you can generalize that approximately 20 percent of the population you sampled from reads it.

Although some people are skeptical about sampling and are uncomfortable with the concept, sampling has repeatedly been shown to be a valid procedure if planned and executed carefully. Skeptics might criticize the Nielsen national sample of television households because it includes one or two atypical viewers (or because the skeptics themselves are not in the sample). The flaw in that argument is that the atypical household is not supposed to be representative of viewers generally. Instead, the entire sample is supposed to be representative of the entire population of television households.

A person who is unconvinced about sampling should consider the problem of testing light bulbs (or other products) without using samples. Suppose General Electric wants to test the average life span of a 100-watt bulb manufactured in a new plant. It would not make sense to test the life span of all bulbs that come off the assembly line. A sample would work just fine. Consider another example: How does Campbell's test canned tomato soup? Certainly not by consuming an entire production run. Or how does a medical technician test your blood? Certainly not by removing all of your blood! A blood test requires only a tiny sample from the tip of your finger or a slightly larger sample from a blood vessel in your arm. It's a good thing medical technicians believe in sampling!

Probability Sampling

There are two types of samples: probability and nonprobability. Members of a *probability* sample are chosen with great care, and every member of the population has a known chance of being selected for the sample. Notice that we said a *known* chance; it is not always an equal chance. Members of *nonprobability* samples are not chosen with great care, and the researcher is more concerned with the convenience of selection than with representativeness.

The important thing about probability samples is the fact that you must establish and follow careful procedures for selecting sample members. A sample can never be completely representative or never be a perfect microcosm of the population from which it is selected. However, probability samples are likely to be much more representative than nonprobability samples. That's the primary reason that probability samples are more important than nonprobability samples in research and why we devote much more space to them in this chapter. Another reason is the simple fact that probability samples are much more widely respected and accepted in the research community. There are situations where nonprobability samples are appropriate, however, and we will discuss those in a later section of this chapter. Right now, we will explain the major types of probability samples: simple random and stratified random samples.

. . . Simple Random Samples

Every member of the population has an *equal* chance of being selected for a simple random sample. Nothing is done to alter that probability. Conceptually, a simple random sample is the purest approach to sampling, and it is the kind that most easily lends itself to statistical analysis and to confident generalizations about the population.

As in the case with any sampling procedure, you must begin by *defining the population* you are studying. This may not be as obvious as it seems, and it is a very important step. Suppose you were trying to ascertain the career plans of advertising seniors from across the country. If you defined your population as "advertising seniors at universities in the United States," it would raise some questions and have several implications for your sampling and research. For example, do you mean *universities* in the strictest sense, meaning that students at *colleges* would not be included? Do you mean students just in journalism and mass communication programs? What about students in schools or departments of business? You would also need lists of students, which you would probably get from the schools. That means you would have to have a list of schools. One source of such a list would be the membership of the Association of Schools and Departments of Journalism and Mass Communication (ASJMC). If that is the source of your list, then your sample would be more properly defined as "advertising seniors at ASJMC-member schools." As we will explain a bit later, this idea of a list of the population members is extremely important, so the definition of your population may be given by the source of a list of the population.

The next step is to determine the appropriate size of the sample. We'll cover that topic a bit later in this chapter. All we will say right now is that the appropriate size of a sample is not determined by the size of the population but rather by the desired degree of confidence and precision of generalizations about the population.

Next comes the actual selection process, and to do that, you have to have a list of people in the population. In our advertising senior example, you would actually have to use a two-step process because no single source would have a list of all the seniors in advertising programs at ASJMC schools. The first step would be to write to the heads of those schools or departments and ask them to send you a list of the advertising seniors at their schools.

Now you have to deal with another important question. There are approximately 180 schools in ASJMC, and it might be very expensive and time consuming to write to all of them. And if they all responded to your request, you would probably have several thousand names of advertising seniors. What can you do to keep this project manageable? Well, you could do a two-stage sampling procedure. The first step would be to sample from the list of schools and ask only those in the sample to send you lists of seniors. You would then select your sample from those lists. Let's do it that way. (Some of our more astute readers might raise the question of school size or location and might suggest that we should make sure that our sample of schools includes large and small schools as well as schools from all parts of the country. We'll save that problem for the selection on stratified random sampling.)

So, let's draw the sample of schools and then decide how to draw the sample of students. The sample of schools would be fairly easy. You first need a list of all the

ASJMC schools, and you can get that fairly easily from the *Journalism and Mass Communication Directory*.[1] The 1989 edition lists 182 ASJMC member schools in alphabetical order. (The same directory also lists the names and addresses of the deans, directors, and chairs of those schools and departments.)

The purest way to select a simple random sample is to write the names of all of the population members on separate pieces of paper, put those into a container, and to draw them out without looking. That procedure might be practical for office or family gift exchanges, but it won't work very well for large populations, even 182 schools. It is acceptable, therefore, to use systematic procedures for selecting names for a sample as long as those procedures do not detract from the representativeness of the sample. You can use these systematic procedures for simple random or stratified random samples.

Interval Sampling

Interval sampling is the simplest of the systematic approaches. You can use it whenever you have a list of the population. You randomly designate a starting point on the list and then count down the list, selecting names at predesignated intervals. The interval depends on the size of the population and the desired size of the sample.

Back to the problem at hand—selecting a sample of schools. Let's select 25 percent of the schools for our sample of schools, meaning you will want to select every fourth name on the list. But first you have to select a *starting point* for your counting, and technically, you should leave that starting point to chance. You could do that in a couple of ways. One, you could close your eyes and put your finger on the page containing the list. The school under your finger would be the starting point. You would start counting there and select the fourth school, eighth, and so on. Two, you could use a table of random numbers like the one in Appendix A. It doesn't matter which page of the appendix you use, so arbitrarily look at page 349. Those numbers all have five digits, and you don't need five digits because your list includes only 182 names. Therefore, you should decide in advance that you will use only a portion of the number—the first two digits on the left, for example. Suppose you closed your eyes and pointed to the page and your finger landed on the number in the eighth column of line 36: 99730. Because you have already decided to use the first two digits, you will start your selection process with the 99th name on the list. You then count—100, 101, 102, and 103. The 103rd school on the list becomes part of your sample, and you continue the process until you have 45 names, which is approximately 25 percent of the list. You have a simple random sample, and each school in the population had a known and equal probability (.25) of being selected.

That interval sampling procedure might not be appropriate with very long lists or with an unnumbered list, such as a telephone directory. In such a case, you might want to modify your interval sampling procedure. If your interval were 5, you could take a name from every 5th page. You might pick another random number, such as 14, and take the 14th name from every 5th page. You could refine it further and say that you would take the 14th name from the middle column of every 5th page. Instead of counting names in a column, you could decide in advance that you will use a ruler and take the name closest to the 18th centimeter mark on the ruler—in the middle column of every 9th page, or whatever. The important thing is that you establish your interval, starting point, and selection procedure before you begin and that you not deviate from it once you begin selecting names. It is also important that your interval size permit you to take names equally from all parts of the list.

Cluster Sampling

Using an interval selection procedure can sometimes be impractical, especially if you plan to interview subjects in their homes. Taking names at intervals would most likely mean that your sample members would be widely scattered, and the transportation costs to conduct those interviews might be prohibitive. If you were doing a national survey, you might spend days traveling from one subject to the next. Cluster sampling would probably be appropriate in such cases.

With cluster sampling, you draw a cluster of several names or units instead of one name or unit at a time. *Area sampling* is based on geographic location of the elements of the population. Here's an example of one way to do it, based on a map of numbered census tracts in Charlotte, N.C. (Figure 5.1). If you used an interval selection method to choose names from a telephone directory, you would undoubtedly end up with a sample of people from all over the city, which would be somewhat impractical for in-home interviews. Instead, you could use a table of random numbers to select a sample of census tracts by number. You could then go to each selected district and make a list of addresses of all the occupied houses or apartments and use an interval selection process to pick households from the district. Another variation is to use a combination of cluster and interval procedures to select a starting point household and then to interview people at any number of houses on either side of that starting point.

As with interval sampling, the important thing is to establish your procedure in advance and to stick to it. If a home in the cluster is unoccupied, you will have to decide whether to replace it with another dwelling. If no one is home at an occupied dwelling, you should return to that house for a predetermined number of times (at various times of the day) before you drop that household from the sample. Otherwise, your sample may be biased against households in which both adults work during the day.

The problems with area sampling may not be obvious. In low income areas, houses may be closer together than in upper income areas, so there would be more of them on each block. Area sampling might tend to oversample low income households in such a situation, and your sample would not be representative. A solution to this overrepresentation of low income households may be to employ stratification with the area approach. (We talk about stratified samples later in this chapter.) You could classify your sampling units, such as on income, and draw subsamples from each stratum. This approach is sometimes called *multistage area sampling*.

Another cluster sampling procedure is called *chunk sampling*. You might want to use that method if you have a very long list of the population and if you are drawing a large sample of names. It might take an inordinate amount of time to count through the list, taking one name at a time at a prescribed interval. Instead, you could randomly pick your starting point and intervals but take groups of names instead of individual names at each interval.

A few pages ago, we were working through an example of drawing a sample of advertising seniors. We had progressed as far as a simple random sample of schools

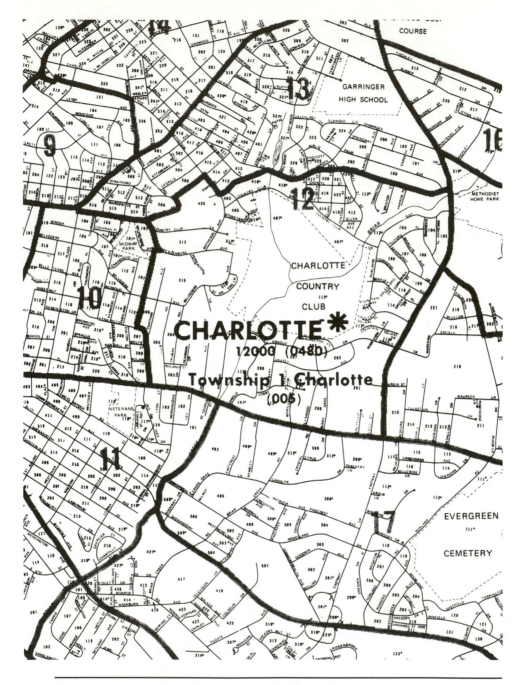

Figure 5.1 Map of Charlotte, North Carolina. U.S. Census Bureau.

but had not yet determined how to sample students. Your next step would be to write to the heads of the schools and ask them to send you names of their advertising seniors. These would come to you in the form of lists of names. After you have all of those lists, you should put them in some order. (The way you order the lists does not really matter.) At that point, you will have an ordered list of several hundred names, and you could use interval sampling to select names of students for your sample. Following that two-step strategy (random selection of schools and then random selection of students from the sampled schools) will give you a probability sample.

...Stratified Random Samples

In drawing a simple random sample, there is always a chance that through luck (bad luck), the sample will underrepresent certain segments of the population. This is more likely to be true of small samples than large ones, but it can be a problem with large samples too. For example, suppose you are asked to survey a sample of charge account customers of a large department store. You analyze the customer list and learn that customers come from three cities: approximately 15 percent from City A, 35 percent from City B, and 50 percent from City C.

Suppose also that you suspect city residence is an important variable to consider in this study—perhaps people from City A are more affluent and account for considerably more than 15 percent of the store's business. If you were to draw a simple random sample from the entire list, you might be unlucky and end up with only a handful of customers from City A—a number too small for meaningful statistical analysis. In your simple random sample, you would naturally end up with more people from City C than from the other two. However, you would have no assurance that the cities would be represented in your sample in the same proportions as in the population.

You could overcome the underrepresentation of City A by drawing a very large sample to increase the likelihood of having enough customers from City A. Remember, however, that increasing the sample size also increases the cost of the survey. And it does not guarantee that you will get enough people from City A.

This situation lends itself to another type of random sampling—*stratified random sampling*. As in simple random sampling, you begin by defining the population, determine the sample size, and secure your list of the population. At this stage, however, you would determine the population characteristics you believe are critical to the study. You would categorize (stratify) people on the list according to those characteristics and draw simple random samples from each of the categories. Stratification assures you that each key group in the population is represented in the sample in the desired proportion, either as it exists in the population or disproportionately as necessary.

In the example, you would begin by dividing your list into three smaller strata or lists, one for each city. You would determine the total sample size needed. If you decided you needed a sample of 300 names, you would take 15 percent (45 names) from the City A list, 35 percent (105 names) from the City B list, and 50 percent (150 names) from the City C list. That would be a stratified random sample, with each stratification represented in the sample in the same proportion as in the population.

You must, of course, use a random procedure for selecting the people for each stratum. That is necessary to maintain the representativeness of the entire stratified sample. That also gives you separate random samples from each city, so you can make generalizations about the customers from each city.

In some circumstances, you might want to oversample from certain segments. In our example, you might conclude that customers from City A are more important than those from the other two cities because they are more affluent. That might lead you to want to have customers from City A represented in your sample in a larger proportion than they are in the population.

The advantages of this approach are that sample size (and costs) can be smaller than with simple random sampling, and you can be assured of an appropriate number of responses from each key segment in the population. The strata need not be equal in size, and in many cases they won't be, because you usually want them to represent the distribution of the key characteristic as it occurs in the population.

When Can Stratified Random Samples Be Used?

Nearly any situation in which a simple random sample can be used lends itself to stratification. Samples are frequently stratified by gender, age, income, census region, place of residence, or level of product usage. Remember, however, that you should stratify on only the characteristics you think are important.

Consider the following example dealing with consumers who use powder or liquid laundry detergents. You might learn that 55 percent of consumers use powders and that 45 percent use liquids. If you were studying detergent users, you might want to draw a sample that would parallel usage-share data: 55 percent powder users and 45 percent liquid users. Or you might conclude that the proportions in the population are close enough that you would not need to worry about stratification in the sample.

In contrast, what would you do if 95 percent of consumers use powder and 5 percent use liquids? Strict stratification here would give you a very large stratum of powder users and a very small stratum of liquid users. In this situation, you would probably want to oversample the liquid users so that both sample strata would be large enough for generalizations.

• • • Sampling Distributions

We will try to keep our discussion of precision, sampling size, sampling distributions, and related topics as nontechnical as possible. For students who wish a more detailed and technical — yet very clear and readable — explanation, we highly recommend *The Practice of Social Research* by Earl Babbie.[2] However, we do need to say a few words about those concepts, beginning with the idea of sampling distributions because it is important to an understanding of appropriate sample size.

Imagine that you had a container filled with 1,000 marbles: 200 red ones and 800 white ones. If you thoroughly mixed the marbles and reached into the container without looking and drew out a sample of *one* marble, it is quite possible that you could select a red marble, which would not be at all representative of the population of 1,000 marbles. If you put that marble back in the container, mixed the marbles again, and drew another sample of one — and repeated that process several times — you would draw red marbles quite often. It is true that you would probably draw white marbles more often than red ones, but the point of the example is to illustrate that small sample sizes are prone to considerable imprecision.

Suppose you were to mix the marbles and draw several samples of *five* marbles each — replacing the marbles each time to maintain the population of 1,000. If you recorded the number of red marbles in each sample of five, you would find that it would range from zero to five. Many of the samples of five would have the same percentage of red marbles as the population (20 percent or one marble), but a considerable number would have more than 20 percent. In other words, if you did not know the actual number of red marbles in the jar and if you were trying to determine that number based on a sample of five marbles, you would not have much confidence in your estimate.

Imagine using a simple line graph with a horizontal axis and numbers from 0 percent (no red marbles) to 100 percent (five red marbles). If you drew out 100 or more samples of five each and plotted the number of red marbles in each sample by putting a dot above the appropriate number on the horizontal axis, a large number of the dots would be at the 2-mark on the line. However, there would be enough dots at other places on the line to raise doubts about the accuracy of any single sample. Think of it this way. Suppose you drew those 100 samples of five marbles each and plotted the number of red marbles on the graph. Based on the pattern of those dots, what are the chances of predicting the number of red marbles in the 101st sample?

If you increased your sample size to ten marbles, drew 100 such samples without looking, and plotted the number of red marbles on a graph, you would see a greater cluster of dots at the 2-line. If you kept increasing the size of your samples, you would find that the dots would cluster with greater precision. Even if you picked only one sample of 100 marbles, you would not expect to find a 20–80 split just because of luck. (Actually, we call it *sampling error*.) However, if you drew 100 samples of 100 marbles each, many of the red-white splits would be at or near 20–80.

Think of those dots on the line graph again. As you increase the size of the sample, the cluster or width of the dots becomes narrower. That is analogous to what statisticians call reducing the *margin of error*. You could never completely eliminate that margin of error — unless, of course, you drew out a sample of all 1,000 marbles. In fact, cutting the margin of error in half requires making the sample four times larger — and making the research four times more expensive. It is obvious, then, that researchers have to settle on a compromise when it comes to sample size. The sample must be large enough to reduce the margin of error to an acceptable level and yet not be prohibitively expensive.

You must remember that when we talk about appropriate sample size, we are talking about the number of cases for which you have usable data in your study. If you are doing a mail survey and believe that you will get responses from only 50 percent of your sample, you would need to send out twice as many questionnaires as you need in the sample. For example, if you were willing to tolerate a 5 percent error range at the 95 percent confidence level, you would need to have approximately 400 completed questionnaires. That would require you to select at least 800 for your sample. You should probably be conservative and select more than that.

Nonprobability Sampling

In nonprobability sampling, members of the population do not have a known or equal chance of being selected for the sample. One type is a *convenience sample*, in which people are selected because they are easily accessible or convenient for the researcher. To draw a convenience sample, you can select telephone numbers from the same page of the directory. Or you can go to a shopping mall and interview the first ten, fifteen, or one hundred shoppers who pass your location.

Another type of nonprobability sample is a *quota sample*. This appears similar to stratification, but there is no randomness to the selection of people for the various strata. For example, you might instruct an interviewer to interview one hundred people: twenty-five African-American males, twenty-five African-American females, twenty-five white males, and twenty-five white females. The interviewer would interview people in each category until fulfilling the quota for each group.

When Nonprobability Samples Are Appropriate

If you use a convenience or quota sample, you can be almost certain to have sample bias because interviewers are almost always likely to select subjects who are easy to reach and who appear to be easy to interview. For example, a white, female, middle-class interviewer instructed to complete fifty interviews in a shopping mall will tend to select white, female, middle-class people to interview. Interviewing the first one hundred people who walk into a store after it opens in the morning will prevent you from getting information from people who work during the day and who shop after work.

In other words, by their nature, nonprobability samples are not representative of the populations from which they are selected. This means you cannot make accurate generalizations from the sample to the population. You can talk about the results from your sample, but your results will have no external validity to the population.

That does not mean that nonprobability samples have no value at all, because they are satisfactory for certain kinds of research. A convenience sample can be useful when you are pretesting a questionnaire you plan to use with a probability sample. A quota sample can be useful if you are trying to determine product characteristics that are important to consumers. (Quotas will help you make sure that you have a variety of consumers.) You could then survey a probability sample about those same characteristics.

To take another example, a financial institution was considering a name change from Anytown Savings and Loan to Anytown Federal Savings and Loan. At the same time, it was considering a range of new services for customers. Management wanted to reduce risk by learning reactions to the changes in name and services, and the most logical people to ask were current customers. However, those customers were scattered in large and small towns throughout an entire county. Researchers used a convenience sample. Armed with maps and customer addresses, they interviewed customers until they had an appropriate number. Customers were nearly unanimous in their neutral opinions about the name change and in their positive opinions about new services. The researchers confidently limited their study to a convenience sample of 120 customers because they believed that a more expensive probability sample would not have improved the precision of the data or of the results.

You should be aware that samples are rarely perfect and rarely need to be. It is a matter of the cost-benefit ratio. Attempts to make a sample more representative almost always increase research costs more than they increase representativeness or benefits.

Keep in mind that precision is not necessarily synonymous with accuracy, because you can be accurate without necessarily being precise. We might say that the viewers of a television program are primarily adults over the age of 24. That statement may be accurate, but it is hardly precise. It would be more precise to say that the viewers are primarily adults between 24 and 34 years of age.

To minimize costs, researchers decide on an appropriate confidence level and the degree of error they are willing to tolerate as they generalize from the sample to the population. In the television rating example, we might accept an error range of plus or minus 2 percentage points at the 95 percent level of confidence. That means we would expect a rating of 25 percent for the sample to be within two percentage points of the rating for the population, and that if one hundred estimates were obtained through one hundred different samples of viewers, at least ninety-five of the ratings would fall between 23 and 27 percent. Traditionally the 95 percent level of confidence has proved to be popular among researchers. The lower the necessary confidence level and the higher the tolerable error, the smaller (and less expensive) the sample may be.

Table 5.1 shows the approximate sample sizes needed for 95 percent and 99 percent confidence levels for different error ranges. For example, if you were willing to accept an error range of plus or minus 3 percentage points at the 95 percent confidence level, you should have a sample of 1,100. You should note that sample size

Table 5.1 Approximate Sample Sizes Needed for Various Levels of Precision

Error Level	95% Confidence	99% Confidence
1%	9,600	16,600
2%	2,400	4,150
3%	1,100	1,850
4%	600	1,050
5%	400	650
6%	250	450
7%	200	350

Source: C. H. Backstrom and G. D. Hursh, *Survey Research* (Evanston, Ill.: Northwestern University Press, 1963), 33. Reprinted by permission of Northwestern University Press, Evanston, Illinois.

is not affected by the size of the population but rather by the degree of precision and confidence desired. Note, too, that a sample of 600 will mean a margin of error of 4 percentage points at the 95 percent confidence level. To cut that error in half—to only 2 percentage points—would require a sample 4 times larger—2,400. That would also be four times more expensive.

• • • Determining Sample Size

Precision, the degree of exactness of an estimate, is a key criterion in determining sample size. The greater the degree of precision desired, the larger the sample must be. Remember, however, the principle of the cost-benefit ratio. To double the precision (reducing the margin of error by one-half) requires quadrupling the sample size (and quadrupling the cost).

Some degree of imprecision is tolerable. We normally do not need to know that a television program's rating is exactly 25 percent. We are usually satisfied if we know that there is a very high probability that it is somewhere between 24 and 26 percent or between 23 and 27 percent.

In other words, appropriate sample size depends primarily on the purposes of the research study. Simmons Market Research Bureau uses a sample of approximately 19,000 people to gather data about magazine readership and product usage. By contrast, Nielsen uses a sample of approximately 4,000 households for its metered measurement of network television viewing in more than 94 million households.

And a researcher interested in learning if a proposed advertisement makes any sense to people could get useful information from a sample of twenty-five or fewer. It's yet another example of the application of the cost-benefit ratio. You must consider whether the added cost of a larger sample is worth the added benefits of greater precision.

The four photographs in Figure 5.2 show how the well-known research firm Nielsen Media Research demonstrates sampling's effectiveness. The four photographs illustrate how you can take different size samples and produce a generalizable conclusion. Photograph 1 is finely screened, printed in thousands of ink dots. Because of the fineness of detail or degree of precision, we can say that this photograph contains nearly all the detail, or information, that can be provided.

In the other photographs, not all the detail is provided. Photograph 2 is made up of approximately 2,000 dots. The face is still very clear, but not as clear as in Photograph 1. Some of the detail is missing, but not so much that the face is not recognizable. Photograph 3 is made up of only 1,000 dots, which constitute a sample that is half as large as that in Photograph 2. You can still recognize the face. In Photograph 4, the sample is down to 250 dots. Yet if you look at the photograph from a distance, you can still discern a face and identify it as the same one that is in the other photographs. The 250-dot sample is still useful, even though it contains only a fraction of the number of dots in the other photographs. *Precision* has suffered, but *accuracy* has not.

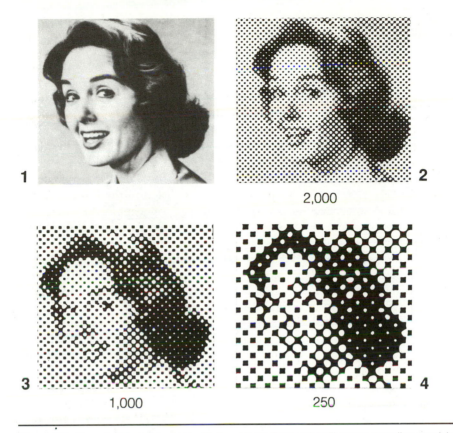

Figure 5.2 Four photographs used by Nielsen Media Research to illustrate sampling precision. Reprinted by permission of Nielsen Media Research.

Sample Bias

A critical problem associated with sampling is sample bias, which occurs when a sample is not representative of the population from which it was drawn. This is especially important for probability samples, which are supposed to be representative. When the sample is not representative of the population, we cannot have much confidence that are generalizations about the population are correct, and that raises questions about the value of the research.

Telephone Directories and Bias

A common source of sample bias can occur when samples are drawn from telephone directories. To draw a probability sample, remember, you need a list of all of the people in the population. Unfortunately, no such list exists for most populations. There are some exceptions, though, such as lists of store customers or magazine and newspaper subscribers.

If you wanted to draw a random sample of people in your city, the closest approximation to a complete list of everyone in the city would be the telephone directory. However, a sample drawn from that list is not likely to be representative of the population because it would exclude three groups who are not included in that directory: (1) people who have moved into the city since the directory was published, (2) people who choose (and pay extra for the privilege) to keep their names and telephone numbers out of the directory, and (3) people who do not have telephones.

You must be concerned with whether those three groups of people differ in significant ways from the people whose names are listed in the directory. If you are confident that they are like the listed people in every relevant aspect, then you would not have to worry about their exclusion. Or you might consider how relevant those groups are to the advertising problem you are investigating. For example, you might argue that most people without telephones cannot afford them, and people who cannot afford telephones cannot afford most discretionary products, either. Therefore, their exclusion from the sample would not be a critical loss. On the other hand, the other kinds of nonlisted people are critical to most research studies, and their exclusion would likely result in sample bias. For example, most people who elect to have unlisted numbers are upper income professionals such as physicians or attorneys. Despite this fault, the telephone directory remains the best (although imperfect) source of names of the population.

Researchers have devised ways to overcome this problem, usually with some type of *random-digit dialing* procedure. In one variation of this procedure, you begin by randomly selecting names and numbers from the telephone directory using an interval procedure. However, you replace the last four digits of the listed and selected numbers with numbers you get from a table of random numbers. There would be a very good likelihood that some of the numbers generated in that fashion would be the same as unlisted numbers in that city.

Here is an example of how that might be done. Suppose that you use an interval selection procedure and choose a listed number like 555-1212. Turn to the table of random numbers in Appendix A again, this time looking at the very first page of the table. These are five-digit numbers, but we need only four digits for the telephone number, so let's arbitrarily say that we will use the four digits beginning with the left digit. Suppose you closed your eyes and pointed to that page and your finger landed on the number in line 20 and column 4: 09998. The telephone number for your sample would therefore be 555-0999. You would repeat that procedure for all telephone numbers in your sample.

In another variation on the procedure, you could begin with a list of all possible numbers in each exchange, such as 555-0000 to 555-9999. You can get a list of all the known and listed numbers in that sequence from the telephone company and eliminate them from the list. That will leave you with numbers that are not listed. You could draw a regular sample from listed names in the telephone book and supplement it with a sample of numbers from the list of unlisted numbers.

You can use another procedure for surveys involving personal interviews at respondents' homes. (Even with personal interviews, you normally use a telephone directory to select the sample because it is the only list of the population.) Begin by randomly selecting names and addresses from the directory using an interval procedure. Send interviewers to those addresses. However, instead of interviewing people in those households, instruct the interviewers to go to the household next door (or to a group of households for an area cluster sample). Some of those adjacent households could have unlisted telephone numbers.

. . . Other Sample Bias Problems

Our explanation of sampling in this chapter has focused on samples of people because that is what researchers are most likely to be concerned about. In some research studies, however, you may also face other sampling problems. One of those problems has to do with selecting time frames for interviewing or analysis. Suppose, for example, that a local restaurant hired you to survey its customers to provide background information for an advertising campaign. It would not be practical for you to spend every hour of every day interviewing every patron of the restaurant, so you will have to devise a procedure for sampling. You have two sampling decisions: when to conduct interviews and what people to interview during those times.

Let's consider the time sampling first. Suppose the restaurant opens at 11:30 and does a brisk lunch business until 1:30 or 2:00 P.M. Monday through Friday. Business drops off for a while but picks up with a cocktail hour crowd at 5:00 and dinner customers beginning at 6:30 or 7:00. It also has a very popular Sunday brunch between 10:00 and 2:00 and is closed for the rest of Sunday. In addition to varying by time of day, the number and type of patrons vary by day of the week. Your problem is to make sure your interviews cover the various dayparts. You could draw up a grid like the one in Figure 5.3. You would want to make sure that you interviewed patrons at Sunday brunch, as well as weekday lunches, afternoons, cocktail hours, and evenings. The restaurant manager tells you that business is especially heavy on Friday and Saturday nights, so you want to make sure that some of your interviews take place on those nights. Your careful analysis might lead you to conduct interviews during the times marked with asterisks on the grid.

After you have selected the days and time periods, you will have to decide whether to interview all patrons in the restaurants during those times or just a sample. Trying to interview them all might be impractical or impossible, so let's think of a sampling procedure. You could decide in advance on an interval (say every third one) and interview every third customer as he or she leaves the restaurant. Because most people do not dine alone, you will also have to decide whether to interview all members of a selected party or just one. If you decide to interview one, how will you do that? The point we are trying to emphasize is that you must have these procedures worked out in advance and must follow them without deviation. Otherwise, your selection of persons to interview is likely to be biased, which will bias your sample and results.

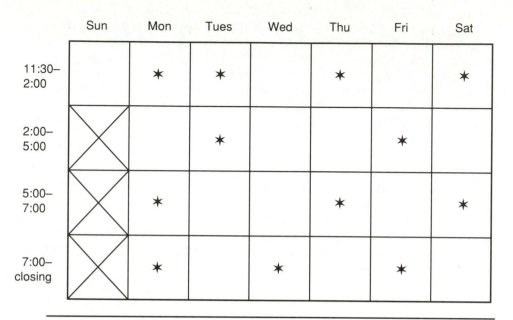

	Sun	Mon	Tues	Wed	Thu	Fri	Sat
11:30–2:00		✳	✳		✳		✳
2:00–5:00	✕		✳			✳	
5:00–7:00	✕	✳			✳		✳
7:00–closing	✕	✳		✳		✳	

Figure 5.3 This grid illustrates how a researcher might plan interview sessions in a research study of restaurant patrons.

Let's go back to that question of how to select one person from a designated group. That same problem can also arise when you conduct interviews in households or even over the telephone. Suppose you want to speak to one adult at each selected address or telephone number. If more than one adult lives in that house (or if more than one person is in the dining party), how do you decide which one to interview? If you make that decision on the spot, you cannot trust yourself (or your interviewers) to be unbiased in the selection of respondents. Instead, you must have a procedure worked out in advance. One commonly used technique is to select the person in the group or the household who has the next birthday. It's easy to do, and the arbitrariness of it reduces the likelihood of sample bias.

• • • Testing for Sample Bias

How can you tell if a sample is biased? It can be done fairly simply if you plan in advance. Suppose you do a telephone survey in your city to measure awareness of a new radio station. You carefully select a random sample using the telephone directory as your population list and using random-digit dialing to overcome the problem of unlisted numbers. Even though you were as careful as possible in selecting the sample, you have an obligation to yourself and your client to try to assess the representativeness of that sample.

Most surveys logically include questions about demographics about respondents, so you will want to include questions about age, gender, and possibly the area of the city in which respondents live. After the survey is completed, you can analyze the demographics of the sample and compare it to known characteristics of the population—in that case the city. For example, if you know (from U.S. Census data, for example) that the city's population is 55 percent female and if you find that females comprise 75 percent of your sample, you can conclude that you have a problem with overrepresentation of women and possible bias. If the problem is too severe, you may have to start over. You at least have an obligation to your client to report the sample-population comparisons and your interpretation of how the results might be affected.

• • • Summary

Some advertising research is conducted as a census of all members of a population, but only when the total size of the population is relatively small. Most research, therefore, studies samples of the population. When those samples are properly drawn, researchers can use information they learn about the sample to make generalizations about the population from which the sample was drawn.

A probability sample, in which all members of the population have a known chance of being selected, is the most useful and important kind of sample. By establishing and following careful procedures for sample selection, researchers can be very confident that the sample will be representative of the larger population.

In a simple random sample, every member of the population has an equal chance of being selected. In a stratified random sample, researchers categorize members of the population according to relevant criteria and select appropriate numbers for each stratum. Although each subsample is usually a simple random sample, the entire sample may not always be a simple random sample because some strata may be overrepresented. For both simple random samples and stratified random samples, interval and cluster selection procedures simplify the actual selection of units for the sample.

The size of the sample is important, and the appropriate size is a function of the degree of precision (margin of error) and confidence level desired and not of the size of the population. The margin of error cannot be completely eliminated with a sample, so researchers must strike a compromise between precision and practicality.

Nonprobability samples are typically chosen for the convenience of the researcher, and they do not permit the researcher to make generalizations about the population because the samples are not likely to be representative. They are appropriate for pretesting research procedures or for qualitative research such as a focus group interview.

The nonrepresentativeness of a nonprobability sample creates a problem of sample bias, which means the sample is not representative of the population. Sample bias can also be a problem with the selection of probability samples, especially if telephone directories are used as the population list. Researchers using such directories should use random-digit dialing procedures to increase the likelihood of including unlisted telephone numbers. Researchers should do all they can to reduce sources of sample bias and should report comparisons between the sample and population.

Probability sampling can be used for units other than names or telephone numbers, as in the case of selecting dates and times for interviews.

••• Notes

1. Association for Education in Journalism and Mass Communication, *Journalism and Mass Communication Directory*, Vol. 7, 1989.
2. Earl Babbie, *The Practice of Social Research*, 5th ed. (Belmont, Calif.: Wadsworth, 1989).

••• Self-Test Questions

1. Under what circumstances would you consider using a census of the population instead of a sample?
2. Under what circumstances would you consider using a nonprobability sample?
3. Suppose you are going to do a telephone survey of students at your college or university and decide to use a simple random sample. What source will you use as your list of the population? Are you likely to have a problem with a significant number of students who are not on that list? If so, what can you do about it?
4. Let's assume that you are going to use a student telephone directory and that you are convinced that 99 percent of all students are listed. Assume that there are 12,000 students in the population and that you want a sample of 1,200 completed interviews. If you assume that 75 percent of the students you call will cooperate and complete interviews, how many names do you have to select for your initial calls? If you are willing to accept the 95 percent confidence level, what will be the margin of error for the interpretation of your results?
5. Look at one page of your local telephone directory and assume for the sake of this question that it is a complete list of the population you are surveying. Use a table of random numbers to select a starting point on the list and use an interval of eight to select the first ten telephone numbers in a hypothetical sample.
6. Assume that you are going to do a telephone survey of a random sample of students at your college or university. Suppose that 25 percent of the students live off campus and that it is important for your sample to include a sufficient number of those students. What sampling method would you use to ensure that? Describe how you would do it.
7. You have been hired by your campus bookstore to conduct an advertising research study based on interviews with students leaving the store. Devise a plan for sampling time periods during the week and for randomly selecting students in those time periods.
8. Interval sampling is usually used to select names for a random sample, but it is really a substitute for a more pure method. What is that pure method? What do we mean by cluster sampling?

Suggestions for Additional Reading

Babbie, E. *The Practice of Social Research*. 5th ed. Belmont, Calif.: Wadsworth, 1989.

Backstrom, C. H. *Survey Research*. 2nd ed. New York: Macmillan, 1981.

Jones, W. H., and J. R. Lang. "Sample Composition Bias and Response Bias in a Mail Survey." *Journal of Marketing Research*, 17 (1980), 69–76.

Meyer, P. *Precision Journalism*. 2nd ed. Bloomington, Ind.: Indiana University Press, 1979.

Stempel, G. H., III, and B. H. Westley. *Research Methods in Mass Communication*. 2nd ed. Englewood Cliffs, N.J.: Prentice-Hall, 1989.

CHAPTER 6

Questionnaire Design

A properly designed questionnaire can simplify data collection and standardize responses for efficient analysis. Well-phrased questions make it as easy as possible for respondents to understand what the investigator is seeking and to answer as concisely and accurately as possible.

Questions are of several types. A screening question is designed to determine whether a respondent meets certain qualifications for answering the remaining questions. Before asking a respondent for an opinion of local newspaper advertising, you might first determine whether the respondent subscribes to the newspaper or buys it at a newsstand. If the respondent is a nonreader, the interview should come to an end.

If the respondent does read the newspaper, an additional screening question concerning degree of use might be asked, so the sample will include only those people who appear to be loyal readers of the newspaper.

A second type of question concerns substance of the research itself. These questions deal with whether the respondent has read all or part of certain advertisements, the respondent's attitudes toward the advertisements, or the respondent's intentions to buy certain items advertised in the newspaper.

A third kind of question produces information that makes the other information usable to the advertiser. It is demographic information, such as age, gender, occupation, or income of the respondent; or it is psychographic data, such as the person's impulsiveness or conservatism; or it is buyer behavior information, such as heavy versus light usage of the product. These questions are used to classify respondents' answers by important variables related to the research problem.

... Nature of the Questionnaire

Several conditions determine the nature of the questionnaire: purpose of the study, type of results needed, and method of collecting data.

... Purpose

In some studies you'll be looking for new ideas — ideas that may lead to development of general principles. These are especially numerous in academic journals. In such a study you may conclude, for example, that reader attitudes are more affected (or less affected) by positive claims than by negative claims. You may conclude that this finding is applicable broadly and is not product-specific. This is a generalizable finding, and uncovering it may require a lengthy questionnaire or series of questionnaires. Authors of academic journal articles go to some length to ensure that their questionnaires are scientifically correct.

In other studies, considerably more common than the first type, you will be studying specific problems that your product or company faces, measuring performance of your print advertisements, or measuring reactions to a new communications program. The kinds and number of questions necessary frequently differ from those required for more analytical studies.

... Results Needed

In some kinds of research, precision of answers is not important, and the questionnaire can be designed accordingly. Focus group research seeks a richness of responses in the respondents' own words, so open-end and probing questions are essential.

Survey research usually seeks more precise answers from larger groups of respondents, so closed-end questions are essential. Occasionally, survey research seeks

The Durham Morning Herald
The Durham Sun Shopping Survey

This excerpt from a marketing survey demonstrates a technique for consolidating three questions into one on a questionnaire that was administered by telephone. By looking at it carefully, you can see that a less clever format would have required as much as three times the space. You can also understand that the interviewers must be carefully trained to follow the instructions precisely.

To compensate for the possible biasing effect of starting each interview with *The Chapel Hill Herald*, the author of the questionnaire provided for highlighting each newspaper's name in turn and instructing interviewers to rotate the starting point with each interview.

In this study, several questions were consolidated as these three were. Such consolidation requires care, to avoid excessively complicated question formats that will confuse the interviewer.

1a. For the following newspapers, please tell me if you have read or looked into a weekday copy, that is, a Monday through Friday copy, of the newspaper during the past seven days. What about the . . . ? **(READ LIST, THEN ASK:)** Are there any others?

1b. **(FOR EACH NEWSPAPER READ PAST 7 DAYS, ASK:)** Not counting today, when was the last time you happened to read or look into a weekday, that is, a Monday through Friday, copy of **(name of paper)**? **(IF READ "TODAY," ASK):** When was the last time before today that you read or looked into a weekday copy of (name of newspaper)?

1c. **(FOR EACH NEWSPAPER READ PAST 7 DAYS, ASK:)** During the past seven days how many weekdays, Monday through Friday, did you read

both precise answers and comments in respondents' own words, so a combination of closed-end and open-end questions will be needed on the questionnaire.

In some studies, it may be inadequate simply to report that 63 percent of the respondents liked a food marketer's new advertising spokeswoman. The marketer may need to know something about the intensity of respondent beliefs about the new spokeswoman. How many, or what percentage, of the respondents liked the new personality? How well did they like her? Of those who did not like her, how strongly did they dislike her? Were there many respondents who had no opinion at all? Management may need more than a yes-no or an agree-disagree response.

Envisioning the way results will be presented in the final research report is an essential part of planning. Precisely what do you intend to do with the study? For what purposes are you conducting the study? One way to force yourself to think ahead and to frame the study for appropriateness, precision, and efficiency is to construct a number of dummy tables, charts, and graphs before you design the questionnaire itself. With the dummy tables, you can easily visualize the way the data will appear. Taking this step will help you decide exactly the kinds of questions you will need to ask.

• • • Data Collection Technique

A telephone interview must be kept short in comparison with other techniques. Therefore, the questionnaire must be tightly constructed and easy to administer. A conversational tone is preferable to a monotonous recitation of complicated questions; this is why a colloquial expression is sometimes inserted in the questionnaire to lend a casual air.

In comparison, some personal interviews are conducted with a lengthy questionnaire, one that may require a half hour, hour, or even two hours to administer. And some mail questionnaires may require more than just a few minutes to complete. Researchers who use a mail survey must take special care to ensure that respondents can follow directions and answer questions properly because the researcher will not have a chance to clear up misunderstandings.

Questionnaires are not restricted only to survey research. In conducting a focus group study, you must have your questions and probes in mind before facing the group. The same admonition applies to experimental research because questionnaires are often used to measure changes in variables.

Types of Questions

A well-designed question meets several requirements: It is clear and understandable; it is as concise as possible; it is neutral in that it elicits responses without adding any bias of its own; it generates responses that are easy to use; and it provides an acceptable level of precision.

Closed-End Questions

In a closed-end question, respondents are given two or more choices from which to select the answer that best represents their position. In most of these questions, respondents are prohibited from diverging from the list of acceptable responses. An exception is a question with a provision for answering "other." This enables, but may not encourage, respondents to insert their own answers and a brief explanation.

A dichotomous question is one that provides only a yes-no, agree-disagree, or similar two-way response option. Although such questions provide no degrees of variation, they are the easiest of all question types to tabulate. The important consideration is whether or not they provide adequate precision in the responses. For example, it may be enough to know that half the respondents in a survey were 21 years of age and older. But you may need a more precise description of the sample, with age breaks of ten years or so, which a dichotomous question would be unable to provide.

If you were asking respondents about their reaction to a print advertisement, you might ask:

"Did you happen to see this advertisement, which appeared in today's morning newspaper?"

—— yes

—— no

If you were looking for reactions to the advertisement, you might use a multiple-choice question:

"If you were to read this advertisement, would you . . ."

___ believe the claims made in it?

___ doubt the claims made in it?

___ have no opinion?

Some questions may resemble the multiple choice format but may allow for multiple responses:

Which of the following media did you use at all yesterday? Please check as many as apply.

___ radio

___ television

___ morning newspaper

___ afternoon newspaper

___ any magazine

___ none of the above

In the preceding question, the sixth option, "none of the above," might seem unnecessary, depending on the nature of the sample. If you were asking the question of business executives, you would probably make the assumption that all of them would have used at least one of the media. But you can't know for sure. What seems obvious to you may not be to some of your respondents. So including the sixth option is probably a good idea. And if you are using the question to screen for media users, you would definitely need to include the option.

A ranking question asks for an ordering of several alternatives. For example:

Here is a list of qualities of powdered detergents. Please number them in the order of their importance to you, with the most important quality ranked Number 1:

___ cleaning ability   ___ price

___ fragrance   ___ resistance to lumping in the box

___ grease-cutting power

___ gentleness to hands

In a variation of this ranking question, you may need to know only the top one or two characteristics of the product. Especially if your list of characteristics is long, you may not want to ask for a ranking of all of the items because respondents may have trouble deciding on some of the rankings.

With a rating scale, the researcher is trying to detect very fine differentials in the responses of numerous subjects. A rating scale may have three points, which give a yes-maybe-no or agree-neutral-disagree continuum. It offers an advantage over the straight yes-no question because it allows respondents to take the middle ground if they insist. With a dichotomous question, the respondents have no option, and the forced choice may not be appropriate in representing their opinions.

A further extension of the rating scale is to use four, five, or more points along the continuum. This may result in exact responses, as long as respondents are careful and thoughtful in completing the questionnaire. For example:

What is your opinion of Miller's return policy?

fair __ __ __ __ __ unfair
    1 2 3 4 5

In some situations it is a good idea to use rating scales that have an even number of possible responses. Scales with an odd number of responses have a middle category, which makes it easy for respondents to choose the middle or neutral category instead of answering with a more definite opinion. An even number of responses forces respondents to one side of the issue or the other.

Exhibit 6.1 is an example of the use of three rating scales simultaneously in a study of executives' opinions of three magazines.

The closed-end questions that you will need to ask will produce a variety of types of data. Some data are *nominal* data. That means that the data are in the form of categories of responses. You ask this type of question with no intention of applying quantitative statistical techniques. You are simply counting, assigning each respondent (or the respondent's answer to a question) to an established category. This is what you see when you look at Simmons Market Research Bureau data (see Chapters 15 and 16). In the left-hand column of SMRB tables, you see the characteristics by which users of products are categorized. Geographic area of the country, County Size A, B, C, and D (which relates to population densities of urban, suburban, and rural counties), and other objective characteristics are the bases on which product and media usage data are tabulated.

With nominal data, you simply count the number of people in a category. The numbers are independent of one another. That is, you can't figure averages with nominal data. It makes no sense to say that the average consumer lives in a county that is between an A county and a B county. The counties are mutually exclusive; a metropolitan dweller lives in an A county or a B county but not in an average of the two.

Ordinal data have relative values. If the data can be put into rank order, for example from heaviest user to lightest user, they are ordinal data. You are still putting

MAGAZINE RATING SURVEY

We would like to know how you rate several magazines on such points as EDITORIAL CONTENT, RELIABILITY, etc. Just circle the appropriate number under each of the magazines to indicate whether you feel it rates *very high, high, average, low,* or *very low,* for each of the points listed. PLEASE CIRCLE ? IF YOU FEEL YOU *DON'T KNOW* HOW THE MAGAZINE RATES ON ANY POINT.

PLEASE RATE ALL THREE MAGAZINES ON EACH POINT

1—Very High 2—High 3—Average
4—Low 5—Very Low ?—Don't Know

	MAGAZINE A					MAGAZINE B					MAGAZINE C				
	Rating Scale					Rating Scale					Rating Scale				
	High			Low		High			Low		High			Low	
LEADERSHIP . . . is it a leader in the industry . . . does it have stature in your field?	1	2	3	4	5	?	1	2	3	4	5	?	1	2	3	4	5	?
BUSINESS TRENDS . . . does it keep you up-to-date on legislation, market developments which may affect your business?	1	2	3	4	5	?	1	2	3	4	5	?	1	2	3	4	5	?
EDITORIAL CONTENT . . . is it well-written . . . does it hold your interest . . . is it easy to follow?	1	2	3	4	5	?	1	2	3	4	5	?	1	2	3	4	5	?
VALUE OF THE MAGAZINE . . . does it make a real contribution to your day-to-day efforts?	1	2	3	4	5	?	1	2	3	4	5	?	1	2	3	4	5	?
TECHNOLOGY . . . does the editorial content usually display expert knowledge of the subject and the industry?	1	2	3	4	5	?	1	2	3	4	5	?	1	2	3	4	5	?
RELIABILITY . . . are the articles or news stories believable, truthful . . . accurate, unbiased?	1	2	3	4	5	?	1	2	3	4	5	?	1	2	3	4	5	?
ILLUSTRATIONS . . . are they interesting . . . do they help clarify the articles . . . do they increase your interest in the articles?	1	2	3	4	5	?	1	2	3	4	5	?	1	2	3	4	5	?

Please check the magazine(s) you receive regularly   Thank you.

Exhibit 6.1   Example of a rating instrument used to evaluate magazines. Reprinted with permission of The Conference Board.

things into categories, but the categories are related to one another. In studying preferences for Test Advertisements A, B, and C, you could ask people to rank the three ads, with Rank One being the best. Clearly, Rank One is higher than Ranks Two and Three. But the respondent has no way of showing that the Rank One ad was a much stronger or only slightly stronger choice.

Interval or *ratio* data are based on objective measures, always numerical. A particular magazine advertisement may be read by 60 percent of the magazine's readers. Another may be read by only 30 percent of the magazine's readers. The readership of one of the advertisements is exactly twice that of the other. These are interval data because the differences are not ambiguous or arbitrary; they are mathematical. And because there is a zero point (0 percent) implied in the use of percentages, these are also ratio data.

∙ ∙ ∙ Open-End Questions

Especially in personal interviews, you might use a general question as an opener. Put respondents at ease by asking them to respond to a broad question any way they want. Such questions may be used to set the stage, and in a very few situations the responses to them may not be considered important. (Generally, however, you'll want to avoid asking any question that you don't intend to use later.) Some kinds of questions must be open-end because a researcher cannot anticipate and list in advance on the questionnaire all the possible answers to a question. For example, a researcher may ask, "What college or university did you attend?" A closed-end format would be awkward with that question because of the number of colleges and universities. Often at the end of a formal interview with closed-end questions, open-end questions are asked as a final means of appraising respondents' feelings on the topic. They are a sort of backstop, designed to cover those areas that for some reason were not included in the rest of the questionnaire.

In a large survey, a serious weakness of open-end questions is that the answers do not lend themselves to quantification. Equally serious, perhaps more so, is that the answers cannot usually be coded or tabulated easily; each response must be considered individually.

For some kinds of research, open-end questions are necessary. Researchers can get some degree of uniformity in responses to open-end questions by asking probe questions. A researcher might ask an open-end question about consumers' perceptions of potential product uses. For example:

"What are some of the ways that you think you might use this product?"

It is important that respondents be allowed to answer such a question without additional prompting. The order in which they list characteristics would approximate the order of importance for them. However, if the researcher is specifically interested in learning about reactions to the package, the research effort will be wasted if respondents don't comment on the package. Therefore, a probing question would be in order — when respondents don't mention the package on their own. The questionnaire should include instructions to the interviewer. For example:

Instructions to Interviewer: Allow respondents to talk about the product without prompting. If respondents don't mention the package, ask the following probe, "What about the package specifically? Do you think the package might have some particular uses?"

How Question Formats Affect Responses

If you are comparing two or more sets of data, you must be aware of the questions used in obtaining the data. There are many ways of asking a question, and each will give differing results — results that may be difficult to compare safely.

Here are several ways of asking respondents for their consumer magazine reading habits, as described by Bernard Guggenheim in *Media Decisions*:

1. "Which of the magazines listed below have you read or looked into in the past month?" In this closed-end question, respondents are given a prepared list of magazines to help them remember magazines they have seen.
2. "Which of these magazines do you read regularly, that is, at least three out of four issues?" This question is more generalized than the first one in that it asks for an estimate of repetitive behavior over a long period of time.
3. "What magazines do you read regularly, that is, at least three out of four issues? Please write in the names of the magazines." In this question, respondents are not assisted with a list of magazines from which to choose. They must be able to remember their magazine usage.
4. "Next, the monthly publications. Next to each magazine listed below, please check the box that describes how many different issues of the magazine, if any, you personally have read or looked into for the first time in the last four months." In the table that would accompany this question, respondents would indicate the number of issues they have read over the four-month period. An additional response option is "Read now and then but not in last four months."
5. "For each of the magazines listed below, will you please check:
   (a) Whether or not you personally read the most recent issue?
   (b) Whether or not you personally read the issue before that one?"
   This is a highly structured question, with boxes for checkmarks indicating readership of several magazines.[1]

It is not unreasonable to expect different answers for these questions. Although they all relate to magazine readership, their different formats and phrasing make them materially different from one another.

Guggenheim compared the effects of open-end with those of closed-end questions. The survey was designed to discover magazine reading habits of those buying Aspen automobiles. Matched samples of Aspen buyers received mail questionnaires.

Table 6.1 Magazines Read by Aspen Owners (Total Adult Respondents)

Magazine	A Open End (Read Regularly 3 or 4 of 4 Issues)	B Closed End (Read Regularly 3 or 4 of 4 Issues)	Percent (Plus or Minus)
Reader's Digest	29.9%	32.2%	α 2.3%
Time	20.3	13.1	α 7.2
Newsweek	13.4	14.0	α 0.6
National Geographic	13.0	22.5	α 9.5
U.S. News & World Report	7.7	7.6	α 0.1
Sports Illustrated	6.5	12.7	α 6.2
Playboy	5.7	8.1	α 2.4
Business Week	2.3	3.0	α 0.7
People	—	5.5	α 5.5
TV Guide	—	20.3	α 20.3
Base	261	236	

Question A: "What magazines do you read regularly, that is, at least three out of four issues? (Please write in the names of the magazines.)"

Question B: "Which of these magazines do you read regularly, that is, at least three out of four issues?"

Source: Bernard Guggenheim, "It Depends on How You Ask It!" *Media Decisions*, Vol. 12, No. 7 (July 1977), 82–90.

For one sample, the question was "What magazines do you read regularly, that is, at least three out of four issues?" No help was given in this open-end question. The other sample received a similar question plus a list of magazines.

Results of the study are shown in Table 6.1. For seven of the ten magazines, the two methods of asking questions produced differing results. In those instances, claimed readership differed by as much as 20 percentage points. Two of the magazines — *People* and *TV Guide* — didn't even show up in the open-end responses. In the closed-end question, *TV Guide*'s readership was an impressive 20.3 percent.

Obtaining Accurate, Honest Answers

Several problems can arise when designing a questionnaire. They all affect the accuracy of respondents' answers and should be avoided.

Questions Can Create Answers

Charles Ramond, past editor of the *Journal of Advertising Research*, demonstrates how questioning can bias respondents:

"Suppose I were to call you on the telephone as follows: 'Hello, this is Charles Ramond of the XYZ Poll. We are trying to find out what people think about certain issues. Do you watch television?'

"Whatever your answer, the next question is, 'Some people say that oil tankers are spilling oil and killing the fish and want to pass a law against this, do you agree or disagree?' Your answer is duly recorded and the next question is, 'Have you ever read or heard anything about this?'

"Again your answer is recorded and I ask, 'Is this important to you personally?'

"Again your answer is recorded and finally I ask 'Do you think anyone should do anything about this? Who? What?'

"And now the main question: 'I'd like you to rate some companies on a scale from minus five to plus five, minus five if you totally dislike the company, plus five if you totally like and zero if you are in between or indifferent.' First, 'U.S. Steel.' You give a number and I say 'The Gas Company.' You give another number and I say 'Exxon.'

"You see what is happening? Or do you? Suppose I now tell you that this form of questioning is given only to a random half of a large sample called the experimental group. To the control group, the interview is as follows: 'Hello, this is Charles Ramond from the XYZ Poll. We are trying to find out what people think about certain things. Do you ever watch TV?' You answer and then I ask, 'Now I'd like you to rate some companies on a scale from minus five to plus five . . .' Any difference in average rating between the experimental and control group can be attributed to them having thought about tankers spilling oil and killing the fish, for that is the only difference in the way the two groups were treated."

Source: Charles Ramond, "What's Wrong with Our (Misnamed) Attitude Research," *Advertising Age*, Vol. 48, No. 28 (July 11, 1977), 124–128.

. . . Leading Questions

Intentionally or not, an investigator can inject bias into responses through implication of values or use of emotionally charged words. For example, one blatant attempt at biasing responses asked for a simple answer: "Do you think our tax money should be used for a plush new luxury office building for fat politicians, or do you think it should be used for a new bridge across the river to help reduce the traffic problem south of the city?"

Here is an example of a value implication that may generate biased responses:

"If you were free to do either, would you prefer to have a job outside the home, or would you prefer just to stay home and take care of a house and family?"

Another Example of Bias in Questioning

Here is another example to show how question wording can affect results.

In June 1978, both the Harris Poll and the CBS/New York Times Poll conducted national surveys to measure opinions about relations with the Soviet Union.

The Harris Poll asked the question in the following manner:

"Do you favor or oppose detente—that is, the United States and Russia seeking out areas of cooperation and agreement?"

That question showed 69 percent favorable and 19 percent opposed. (The others were undecided.)

The CBS/New York Times Poll used this question:

"What do you think the U.S. should do—should the U.S. try harder to relax tensions with the Russians or instead should it get tougher in its dealings with the Russians?"

That question showed 30 percent in favor of relaxing tensions and 68 percent in favor of getting tougher.

In other words, both polls dealt with the same issue with comparable national samples at the same time. Yet the wording of the questions produced dramatically different results.

Source: "The Slippery Art of Polls," *Politics Today*, January/February 1980, 21–24.

In using the word "just" in the above example, the investigator is implying something about the value of one kind of activity—that of taking care of a house and family. In a study conducted by The Roper Organization, the question was phrased in a somewhat more objective fashion:

"If you were free to do either, would you prefer to have a job outside the home, or would you prefer to stay home and take care of a house and family?"

Even the revised question is potentially biased or troublesome. It implies that the respondent must choose only one of the alternatives presented, and many people feel they can do both. At the very least, a third alternative should be added.

The use of emotionally charged words is another potential cause of unwanted bias:

"It has been suggested that women who are housewives ought to be paid a decent weekly wage by their husbands for the work they do in the home. Do you approve or disapprove of this?"

In the same Roper survey, the word "regular" was substituted for "decent." But the revised question still implied values and could have been troublesome for some respondents, for "regular" can mean "usual or customary" or "proper." Perhaps the question should have been worded as follows:

> "It has been suggested that housewives ought to be paid for the work they do in their homes. Do you approve or disapprove of this?"

To avoid using leading questions, try to look at the questions from the respondent's viewpoint: "How would I interpret this question?" Does the question let the respondent know what you are really looking for?[2]

... Threatening Questions

A question may not be intended to lead to a given response, yet it may contain elements that may generate incorrect answers. If you're asking about media usage, one area of concern may be time spent in reading the local newspaper. Here is an example of a poorly worded set of alternative responses:

____ 3 or more hours per weekday

____ 2–2 hr. 59 minutes per weekday

____ 1–1 hr. 59 minutes per weekday

____ less than 1 hour per weekday

____ do not read

To soften the "do not read" response (in certain socioeconomic strata, who would want to admit not reading a newspaper?), you might substitute "I do not care to read the local paper" or a similar statement. Depending on your purpose, the "less than 1 hour per weekday" may even be adequate.

Similarly, a person may not want to admit to being in the lowest income group in an array of ranges. So you may add an extra category, below the lowest response you expect. Thus a low income respondent needn't admit to being at the bottom.

The story is told of a respondent in a door-to-door television survey who, after naming a number of situation comedies, country music, and other nonintellectual programs as among his favorites, then added class to his list by including "Meet the Press," "Face the Nation," and the "CBS Evening News."

In other words, some people may feel a degree of embarrassment over their preferences. You may reduce that tendency by asking them what they watched last time instead of what their favorites are. The implication would be that most recently viewed fare was more important than respondents' *usual* choices. That procedure allows them to suggest casually that they don't *usually* watch those programs. The assumption is that respondents' actual viewing selections are valid indicators of their favorites.

...Ambiguous Questions

"What do you think of our company's scholarship program?" may be an important question to you, but it may be difficult for respondents to answer. Do you refer to the number of scholarships, the amount of funding, the method by which winners are selected? Respondents who earnestly try to complete your questionnaire soon find it peculiarly difficult and begin to lose interest in filling it out. You can't blame them, of course, because after all, they are giving you their time and opinions, free of charge. Why should they wade through an unanswerable question?

For some purposes, especially in small group interviews, you'll want some ambiguous questions. They may help you draw out thoughts and opinions you had never considered. In a sense, any open-end question is ambiguous because it doesn't tightly channel respondents' thought processes, as does a true-false or multiple-choice question.

Except for those applications, ambiguity is generally regarded as something to avoid. Respondents must know what you're asking if they are to respond to it.

...Incomplete Questions

If a multiple-choice question is to generate representative answers, it must contain *all possible* answer options. That sounds reasonable, of course, but questions sometimes appear in incomplete form.

Ideally you'll include three, four, or five answer options that are all-inclusive and mutually exclusive. If the answers are likely to cluster in one, two, three, or four options, you may not need an "other" category. Otherwise, be sure to use the extra catchall category. Your pretesting will show whether the "other" category is generating excessive responses. Normally you will not want the "other" category to receive a large number of responses, because that would mean that you may have overlooked some very important answer that should have been given a space by itself.

...Unusually Difficult Questions

It's easy to assume that respondents are knowledgeable about a given topic. Yet, to answer a given question, they may have to look up financial records or other historical data. You can't expect respondents to go to that trouble for you.

Or if you're asking about their media usage, they may not remember which program they "usually" watch at 8 P.M. Sundays. That is one reason for asking, instead, which program they watched last Sunday at 8 P.M. Their memory won't be as taxed as if you had asked them to remember over a long period of time.

The Evolution of a Questionnaire

In a telephone survey of television viewers, investigators proceeded through several stages in arriving at a questionnaire that they considered refined adequately for the survey.

The purpose of the survey was to learn viewing patterns of television set owners who lived midway between two television markets, Columbia, South Carolina, and Charlotte, North Carolina, cities that are approximately 100 miles apart. Respondents were asked twenty questions, including the usual questions on demographic characteristics.

First the investigators made a list of the topic areas they wanted to cover. Next, they wrote a rough draft of the questionnaire. They then edited and rewrote questions for the final version.

One of the first questions was a screening question, designed to learn whether respondents had a television set in the home.

Initial version: "Do you have TV in your home?"
Final version: "Do you have a television set in your home?"

The purpose of another question was to track changes in viewing patterns. The NBC television network had moved from a VHF station to a UHF station in Charlotte, and the NBC affiliate in Columbia was interested in learning the effect of that change on viewing patterns.

Initial version: "Were you watching the same NBC station last spring?"
Revised version: "Thinking back to last spring, which station would you most frequently watch for NBC programs?"
Final version: "Thinking back to March or April, which station would you normally have watched for NBC programs?"

Careful editing and rewriting of individual questions, plus pretesting, can result in questionnaires that are streamlined and unambiguous.

Tips on Constructing a Questionnaire

1. Keep it as short as possible. Respondents are in a hurry too.

2. Include complete instructions, remembering that although you know what you mean, respondents may not. This goes not just for the beginning of the questionnaire. Within the questionnaire, hold respondents' hands by assisting

them on individual questions. You can save them time by directing them around some questions that do not apply to them: "If 'no' please skip to question 6."

You can help respondents, and yourself, by making clear that an answer box goes with a specific question item. For example, in an agree-disagree question, the following design would be confusing because the blanks could be associated with either the preceding or the following response:

Strongly agree ___ agree ___ neutral ___ disagree ___ strongly disagree ___

This one, however, is clear:

Strongly agree ___

agree ___

neutral ___

disagree ___

strongly disagree ___

3. Use simple language throughout. Your respondents may not be familiar with *rollouts, dayparts, share of market,* or other technical terms.

4. Be polite! Try to make respondents feel important; after all, in this survey they *are*. Show them that their responses are necessary to the study. You can say *please* and *thank you*, and you can write a short, courteous cover letter. And you can emphasize their importance (by remembering egos) through use of an important-sounding questionnaire title. "A Survey of Our Customers" or "A Confidential Survey of Consumer Opinions" would be better than "Survey" or some other nondescript label.

5. Position easy and interesting questions first, to allow respondents to become accustomed to the task of completing the questionnaire. Although ours is a questionnaire-intensive society, with thousands of business forms, federal and state income tax forms, and other questionnaires, not everyone is experienced in completing formal questionnaires. Don't assume too much.

6. Position potentially embarrassing or controversial questions toward the end if possible. Respondents may be reluctant to answer a question about age early in the questionnaire, whereas they may be willing to answer it if it is near the end and they have invested their time up to that point. For these questions, such as age, income, political affiliation, stock holdings, home ownership, and religious affiliation, you can refer to them as "a couple of final questions that will help us in tabulating your answers." That statement tells respondents that the time and effort they have expended will be worthwhile only if they answer the last questions.

7. Be careful to order all questions so that one question does not bias the next.

8. If the questionnaire is self-administered, include the return mailing address plus a return envelope. The address should be included on the form in case respondents misplace the envelope. Another alternative, useful in limited situ-

ations, is to use a self-mailer. The questionnaire can be on one side and the mailing address on the other, along with return postage.

9. Don't forget that after you've collected the information, you're going to have to analyze it. If you administer the questionnaire to 1,000 respondents and ask primarily open-end questions, you'll think it impossible to go through the responses. Especially if you're under a time constraint, analyzing open-end questions may prove impossible. Wherever possible, pose closed-end questions, and be sure to allow space to code them at the edge of the page for easier tabulation. (See Chapter 10 for a more detailed discussion of questionnaire coding procedures.)

. . . Pretesting

Although a questionnaire may be subjected to rigorous perusal by several investigators, one or more questions in it may cause a variety of problems. Respondents may not understand a question. In a multiple-choice question, respondents' answers may not fit well. A telephone survey may be bogged down because interviewers have to repeat a question or feel the need to explain a question. In a mail survey, an unusual number of respondents may fail to answer a probing question.

The solution? Pretesting. Try the questionnaire on a number of people ahead of time, starting with the people in your own office. Using a standard checklist, they can evaluate individual questions and make recommendations for questions suffering from any of a number of problems, including:

1. Question can be answered through secondary resources; no need to ask it of respondents.
2. Answer would be nice to know but is not important.
3. Ambiguous.
4. Awkwardly phrased.
5. Biased phrasing.
6. Response categories not all-inclusive.
7. Response categories not precise.
8. Question sequenced poorly in questionnaire.
9. Question embarrassing to respondents.
10. Question threatening to respondents.
11. Question has no answer.
12. Respondents are asked a knowledge question on a subject about which they probably know very little.
13. Question can be answered only if respondents refer to their records or other source.
14. This open-end question should be stated in multiple-choice or other form.
15. Instructions vague or nonexistent.
16. Jumbled format difficult to follow.
17. Format too open. Makes questionnaire look longer than it is.
18. Format too crowded. Makes questionnaire difficult to fill out.

Then, after the initial informal pretesting of the questionnaire, you can make revisions and pretest it formally among a small sample of respondents. That type of pretesting gives you an idea of how the actual sample will react, and you can make additional changes as necessary.

••• Keying the Questionnaire

Although in most surveys you don't need to know the name of the person who completed your questionnaire and mailed it to you, frequently you need to key the questionnaire in some way.

If one of your primary variables is geographic region, you would want to know where all the responses to your mail survey are coming from. A business reply envelope, with no cancellation mark on it, won't tell you. Including a question about region of the country adds unnecessarily to the length of the questionnaire. Therefore you might choose to identify each questionnaire. You might produce the questionnaire on various colors of paper, one for each region: white, buff, beige, or other pastels. The keying is built in.

Or you might use slightly different sizes of paper: $8\frac{1}{2}'' \times 11''$ as the basic size, with questionnaires for the East trimmed $\frac{1}{4}''$ at the bottom, and the questionnaires for other parts of the country trimmed in other ways.

You can use various techniques to key the questionnaire without engendering hesitation on the part of the respondent. Many researchers go to great lengths to avoid letting respondents know the questionnaire is keyed.

Some researchers have found that for some audiences, open and obvious keying can be successful. A study of magazine publishers contained such keying. Each questionnaire contained the name of the publisher and the magazine. Response to the question was better than 71 percent, very acceptable in most mail surveys.[3] A later survey produced somewhat lower response.[4]

Mail surveyors have also noted that a well-written explanation to respondents can also allay their skepticism over positive identification.[5] Simply telling respondents that the reason for the identification number in the upper right corner of the questionnaire is for tabulation purposes can be reassuring.

••• Summary

The ideal questionnaire is a neutral instrument. That is, it enables the investigator to obtain accurate information while it remains completely unobtrusive. It does not color the responses in any way. It is simply the carrier of messages — the questions the researcher is asking.

Such a questionnaire is surely rare; composing a truly neutral question is difficult. Yet that is the ideal toward which you should strive. Ingenuity is important.

Questions must be simple, clear, and nonthreatening, as well as unbiased. They must appear in a logical order, and the answer to one question must not suggest the answer to the next one.

During the question-writing process, it is helpful to remember that the use to which you will put the data will influence the form the questions will take.

... Self-Test Questions

Suppose that you were doing research for a retail client called The Energy Store, which specializes in energy-saving products for the home.

1. You have decided to conduct a survey of a simple random sample of the population. The store's management believes that homeowners may be better prospects than renters for certain products. Devise an appropriate screening question.
2. One of your purposes is to learn awareness of your client. What question would you ask to measure this? Explain your reasoning.
3. You want to find out how respondents learned about The Energy Store. What closed-end question could you ask? What screening question would be necessary?
4. Devise a closed-end question that you could ask to learn the relative importance of energy-saving products to your respondents. Write one question that you could use for a face-to-face interview and another version that would be more appropriate for a telephone survey.
5. Your client wants to learn consumer attitudes toward a proposed income tax credit for woodstove owners. Such a tax would presumably benefit your client because it would stimulate the sale of woodstoves. Write three questions to measure consumer attitudes toward this proposed tax. Slant the first version to produce mostly favorable reactions to the tax. Slant the second question to produce mostly unfavorable reactions. Write the third question to be as objective as possible.

... Notes

1. Bernard Guggenheim, "It Depends on How You Ask It!" *Media Decisions*, Vol. 12, No. 7 (July 1977), 82–90.
2. "The Virginia Slims American Women's Opinion Poll," Vol. III (New York: The Roper Organization, Inc., 1974).
3. Alan D. Fletcher, "City Magazines Find a Niche in the Media Marketplace," *Journalism Quarterly*, Vol. 54, No. 4 (Winter 1977), 738.
4. Alan D. Fletcher and Bruce G. Vanden Bergh, "Numbers Grow, Problems Remain for City Magazines," *Journalism Quarterly*, Vol. 59, No. 2 (Summer 1982), 313–317.
5. Paul L. Erdos and James Regier, "Visible vs. Disguised Keying on Questionnaires," *Journal of Advertising*, Vol. 17, No. 1 (February 1977), 13–18.

Suggestions for Additional Reading

Babbie, E. *The Practice of Social Research*. 5th ed. Belmont, Calif.: Wadsworth, 1989.

Boyd, H., Jr., R. Westfall, and S. F. Stasch. *Marketing Research*. 7th ed. Chap. 9. Homewood, Ill.: Irwin, 1989.

Chowins, C. W. "Constructing a Mail Questionnaire." In A. D. Fletcher and D. W. Jugenheimer (eds.). *Problems and Practices in Advertising Research*. Columbus, Ohio: Grid, 1982.

Jugenheimer, D. W. "Improving Telephone Questionnaires." In Fletcher and Jugenheimer, 1982.

Payne, S. L. *The Art of Asking Questions*. Princeton, N.J.: Princeton University Press, 1951.

CHAPTER 7

Surveys

A survey is a means of gathering information by asking questions. It is a common method of conducting advertising research. In its simplest form, a survey is conducted at one time, with little or no follow-up to obtain data that were missed the first time around. This type of survey is commonly referred to as a *simple survey* or a *one-shot survey*.

A survey can be used as part of an experiment. In such an application, the researcher can track changes. The investigator can manipulate some of the variables to identify relationships among them. In an experiment, the survey may be administered more than one time or to one or more groups of subjects.

The Technique

A survey consists of several steps. First, the researcher must set the objectives. What, precisely, is the researcher trying to find out? The objectives, which may be stated in the form of hypotheses, will direct the researcher toward a desired end.

In much applied research, the word "objective" is used more commonly than the word "hypothesis." An objective simply states what the researcher wants to learn:

What products do my audience members buy? To what extent did they read my magazine advertisement? To what extent did they respond to my direct mail piece?

Hypotheses, usually associated with experiments in academic research, can be very important in directing a study, especially a large-scale and complicated study. For example, in a study of reach and frequency, a researcher may attempt to predict the outcome of some manipulation of reach and frequency plans. In making the predictions of the outcome, the researcher states a hypothesis or several hypotheses. A hypothesis may be something like, "Doubling the gross rating point weight over a four-week period will double the awareness score as measured by the unaided recall method."

The purpose of stating the objective or the hypothesis is to direct the study. The intellectual rigor that is required for effective objective or hypothesis setting makes for an efficient study, one that addresses the research question and goes no further. It's a process of asking "What do I want to know, and what's the most efficient way of finding out?"

Sample selection is usually the next stage in a survey. You should choose these respondents from those people who are representative of the specified universe.

Next is selecting the data collection technique — mail, telephone interviews, personal interviews, or observation.

Constructing the data collection instrument, usually a questionnaire, is the fourth step. It is dependent on the data collection technique and sophistication of the members of the sample.

Executing the data collection phase follows. And finally, tabulation and interpretation complete the process. The last task is to write the report and present it to the appropriate user.

••• Gathering the Data

Four methods of gathering data for surveys are mail questionnaires, personal interviews, telephone interviews, and observation. For various applications, they all have merit.

••• Mail Questionnaire

The mail questionnaire is relatively easy to manage for several reasons. It involves no direct contact with the large number of sample members. There is no crucial period during which interviewers must be supervised, and there is no need for the minute-by-minute monitoring of telephone interview progress.

The mail questionnaire is also relatively inexpensive. It does not require a large staff of trained workers. Instead, it requires only the questionnaire, envelopes, and postage.

Another advantage of the mail survey is that you can be very selective in drawing the sample. The U.S. Postal Service goes just about everywhere, and one can, if necessary, address the questionnaire to specific respondents.

However, in a mail survey the questionnaire must stand on its own. It must be totally self-explanatory because respondents who have questions cannot ask them. And respondents who incorrectly think they understand a question may supply an invalid response. A mail questionnaire cannot generate as much data as a personal interview, because of the difficulty in obtaining the subtleties of an interview and the impossibility of following up on spontaneous statements by respondents. Because there are no interviewers to control the conditions under which questionnaires are completed, some answers may be incomplete or biased. Respondents may peruse the entire questionnaire before starting to respond to it; in so doing, they may confound the careful ordering of the questions.

Probably the most serious drawback associated with mail surveys is the low response rate, however. Although some surveys may achieve a return rate of 75 percent, 85 percent, or higher, that is rare. Some studies may generate a response rate of only 5 percent, which can hardly be considered adequate for most uses. The problem is that it is just too easy not to respond to a mail survey. Even a follow-up letter has little effect on the recipient who forgets to complete the questionnaire or just procrastinates. It's difficult to specify an adequate response rate. That is something that must be determined by the researcher.

A low response rate means much more than simply too few questionnaires to evaluate. If that were the only problem, you could mail twice as many questionnaires in order to double the number of completions. A low response rate is highly likely to be biased. That is, the resulting sample of respondents is not representative of the population whose opinions are being studied. More about that later.

. . . Personal Interview

If interviewers are properly trained, the personal interview is potentially the most productive technique for most surveys. (It may not be the most productive for all surveys, because productivity must be measured on a cost-benefit basis, and some surveys do not require all the advantages of the personal interview technique.) Effective interviewing is an art; expert interviewers can ask probing follow-up questions, rephrase questions that respondents don't understand, and occasionally ask additional questions that may lead to further research. With some open-end questions, interviewers can classify answers as the session progresses. None of these advantages accrue to the mail questionnaire.

Additionally, interviewers can develop rapport with respondents and may be able to ask questions that would go unanswered on a mail questionnaire. If interviewers can succeed in initiating interviews, the interviews will probably be completed.

The two major drawbacks associated with personal interviews are their cost and the chance for bias to develop. If you plan to conduct personal interviews with 1,000 recent college graduates and are using a simple random sample, your travel, food, and lodging costs will be extensive. By contrast, a mail survey would be inexpensive.

Clearly, personal interviewing is a costly undertaking. For many firms, the technique is not worth the cost. That is why many studies using personal interviews do not employ simple random samples; instead, they may be restricted to one or two cities to hold travel expenses and time requirements to a minimum. The question is whether a limited random sample with personal interviewing is desirable over a national or regional sample with a mail questionnaire. They both have their advantages and disadvantages.

. . . Telephone Interview

The telephone interview is a cross between the mail survey and the personal interview. It *is* a personal interview in the strictest sense because it involves a conversation between two human beings. However, it also is similar to a mail survey because it employs a fairly uncomplicated questionnaire.

Because of the growing consumer resistance to in-home interviews, many marketing researchers prefer telephone interviews. Increasingly, people are reluctant to allow a stranger into their homes, even if an introductory letter precedes the visit. With the telephone's approximately 90 percent coverage of U.S. households, a telephone sample can be fairly representative. In all likelihood, most nontelephone homes are low income homes. Generally, marketers have least to gain with the low income market; therefore, the omission may not be serious.

If your research problem is basically simple, one that can be handled with a few straightforward questions, a telephone interview may be for you. It is easy, fast, and inexpensive.

You must be cautious, however, because the drawbacks are numerous. You begin with the fact that much telephone "research" is not research at all, but rather selling by telephone. Cemetery lots, mountain property, and studio portraits are among the many items sold by telephone, often under the guise of research. This use of the telephone combines with other factors to produce telephone subscribers who refuse to cooperate from the start or are at least reluctant to answer some of your questions.

Sample bias can also reduce the value of telephone interviews. People not at home can be a problem if the telephoning is done during the day, yet conducting the survey during evening hours reaches people when they may not want to talk. Unlisted numbers and numbers that are incorrect because people have moved also create problems. One study recently reported that .8 percent of telephone listings were listed incorrectly, 13.3 percent were unlisted by request, and 3.7 percent were too new to be listed.[1]

According to another study, the percentage of unlisted numbers is highest in the West (26.1 percent), major metropolitan areas (29 percent), among nonwhites (31.7 percent), and persons 18–34 years old (26 percent).[2]

The problem of unlisted numbers would not be serious if people with unlisted numbers were like people with listed numbers in all other respects. That is definitely not true, however. People who have unlisted numbers by request are often doctors and other professionals with incomes and spending patterns that make them different from people with listed numbers. Those who do not have telephones are usually at the other end of the socioeconomic ladder. So a sample based on a telephone directory will differ from the population in important respects.

For this reason, some researchers endorse random-digit dialing as a means of including all possible telephone numbers in the sample frame. By such a method,

"Er . . . you wouldn't like to answer some questions, would you?"

Figure 7.1 How not to obtain respondent cooperation in a personal interview.

telephone numbers for the survey are generated by basically the same procedure used to generate tables of random numbers. Thus an unlisted number has the same probability of being selected as a listed number. Such a procedure also dispenses with the need to cut up telephone directories for chunk sampling purposes. Chapter 5 explains the random-digit dialing process in more detail.

. . . Observation

In interviewer-administered and respondent-administered surveys, the emphasis is on the respondents' oral or written responses to questions. Experience has shown that in certain circumstances some of these responses do not necessarily reflect reality. For example, a question concerning brand preference may elicit one response despite the fact that the person usually buys another brand. Through observation, you can go beyond simple *statements* of preference and can look at actual behavior. The technique is relatively limited in its applications; yet what it can do, it can do well.

Because a respondent may not remember which magazines are in the house, an interviewer may ask to see those that are there. The result may be greater accuracy of the estimate.

In television, electronic recording devices were the standard for measuring national audiences for many years. Although such a device did not involve actual observation, it was a measure of a type of behavior. It did not rely on a respondent's statement of viewing behavior. The meter, connected with the television sets in the home, kept a continuous record of the channels to which the sets were tuned.

The meter had an advantage over other usual techniques of estimating television audience size because it eliminated respondent error. The drawback was that it provided no identification of the viewers who were in the room during a program. It could not detect whether or not anyone was even in the room with the television set. Essentially, what the meter measured was *tuning* behavior rather than *viewing* behavior.

The newer form of the meter is the People Meter, which involves electronic connections and computer data handling plus a hand-held data input device with which a viewer can push buttons to identify the persons watching a program. Obviously, even this technique is not perfect because it cannot measure the degree of attention, if any, the viewers are giving to the program. And it makes no distinction between viewing of the commercials and viewing of the program.

Direct observation, sometimes through one-way mirrors, is also used on occasion, and it is, in a literal sense, observation. It may be used in a laboratory to observe reactions to any number of stimuli: new packages, television commercials, or print advertisements. Verbal behavior may also be of interest, as when two young mothers discuss the merits of competing detergents or the believability of several new print advertisements.

Direct observation may also be used in a grocery store to determine consumer reactions to a new promotional display. Do shoppers stop and look at the display? Do they pick up the product from the display? How do they seem to react to the display?

• • • The Problem of Bias

As with other approaches to studying an advertising problem, surveys must be executed cleanly and as nearly free of unwanted bias as possible. Bias is distortion, and it can result in unrepresentative findings. The only kind of bias that is desirable in a survey is that which is exhibited by the respondents themselves—their attitudes, apprehensions, likes, and dislikes of the topic of the survey—in other words, their honest answers to the questions.

Unwanted bias can crop up at every turn.

• • • Interviewer Bias

Like the unsuccessful door-to-door magazine vendor who begins a sales pitch with "You don't want to buy a magazine subscription, do you?" interviewers can

Minimizing Interviewer Bias: The National Association of Broadcasters' Recommendations

Interviewer instructions are important, especially if you are employing inexperienced interviewers. All interviewers in a project must follow a similar nonbiasing procedure in asking questions. The National Association of Broadcasters' (NAB) recommendations are valid in personal interviews as well as telephone interviews:

Your job as an interviewer is to communicate *our questions to the respondents* and to communicate *their answers to us* by means of the questionnaire. Think of yourself as a *communicator* only, not as a helper, prompter, explainer, or educator. Here are some basic rules:

a. Read the questions exactly as worded. Ask them in the exact order listed. Skip questions only when the instructions on the questionnaire tell you so. There are no *exceptions* to this.

b. Never suggest an answer, try to explain a question, or imply what kind of reply is wanted. Don't prompt in any way.

c. If a question is not understood say, "Let me read it again," and repeat it *slowly and clearly*. If it is still not understood, report a "no answer."

d. Report answers and comments exactly as given, writing fully. If an answer seems vague or incomplete, probe with neutral questions, such as "Will you explain that?" or "How do you mean that?" Sometimes just waiting a bit will tell the respondent you want more.

e. Act interested, alert, and appreciative of the respondent's cooperation. But never comment on his replies. Never express approval, disapproval, or surprise. Even an "Oh" can cause a respondent to clam up. Never talk up or down to a respondent.

f. Follow all instructions carefully, whether you agree with them or not.

g. Thank each respondent. Leave a good impression for the next interviewer.

Source: A Broadcast Research Primer (Washington, D.C.: National Association of Broadcasters, 1974), 37–38. Reprinted by permission.

inadvertently direct respondents toward certain responses. By showing disdain for an answer, however slight that disdain may appear, interviewers may have a chilling effect. An interview is supposed to be nonthreatening to the participant.

Showing agreement with an answer may act as a stimulant for similar answers to other questions. Failure to ask the questions carefully and patiently may also confound the interviewing procedure.

The solution to the problem of interviewer bias is a comprehensive training program. Although a simple interview can be administered by a novice, a long, complicated questionnaire is best administered by a trained interviewer who understands the subtleties of the interview situation.

. . . Source Bias

A razor blade manufacturer asked men to evaluate recent magazine advertisements for various brands of razor blades. The manufacturer was pleased to learn that the men overwhelmingly preferred the sponsoring firm's ads. A later study with controls for sponsor anonymity showed quite different results. There's no doubt that respondents like to please interviewers by giving the "correct" answers. Therefore, in many studies the sponsor's name is omitted, and a dummy name is used. If an outside research firm is conducting the study, that firm's name can be used as a means of masking the identity of the sponsoring firm.

. . . Sample Bias

Samples are the most commonly blamed source of bias in survey research and must be chosen carefully. In a study of the desirability of instituting a statewide holiday in honor of Dr. Martin Luther King, Jr., a university organization selected a sample consisting of "no more than 35 percent" African-American respondents. If African-Americans are highly likely to say "yes" to such a proposal and whites are less likely to agree, the results of the study will naturally be biased, since African-Americans do not constitute 35 percent of the population of the United States.

In a study of its local image, a savings and loan association surveyed only its own patrons. Perhaps a valid sample would consist of patrons of all such associations in the area; or, even better, perhaps it would be a random sample of all adults in the area, whether or not they were patrons of any savings and loan association. By surveying only the association's own patrons, the marketing director who conducted the study should have *expected* a highly positive rating.

. . . Nonresponse Bias

A novice researcher may not understand the need for a high response rate. "If our sample is too small, we'll just conduct more interviews or send out more questionnaires," the novice might say. But research has shown that nonrespondents differ from respondents. There is no randomness in the respondent-nonrespondent problem.

Overcoming nonresponse bias is difficult. Incentives, such as a one dollar bill, can help, but the additional expense is often out of the question. Follow-up letters are almost imperative in mail surveys, for they are a relatively inexpensive way of reminding nonrespondents of the importance of their answers. Using a stamp on the return envelope is preferred over a business reply envelope. Keeping the questionnaire as short as possible is an obvious way of ensuring good return. In telephone interviews or personal interviews, callbacks are usually advisable; "not-at-homes" are different from "at-homes."

In a survey in which the return rate is considerably less than 100 percent after one or two or more follow-ups and incentives have been used, the researcher can only try to analyze the probable significance of the nonresponse bias and then carefully account for it in the written report. That is why a complete survey report contains the response rate.

Obtaining Adequate Response Levels in Mail Surveys

In addition to using an incentive such as a monetary reward, researchers commonly send a follow-up letter to people who have failed to respond to a questionnaire.

In some surveys, it may be desirable to send not only one follow-up letter, but two or even three. Exhibits 7.1 and 7.2 are two letters, an initial request plus a follow-up request, that might serve as models for other surveys.

XYZ Research, Inc.
123 Cumberland Avenue, N.W.
Dayton, Ohio

February 1, 1991

Dear Homeowner:

May we ask a favor?

We would appreciate your help in a research project
that is designed to provide an understanding of
buying habits of American families. Studies of this
kind enable manufacturers to produce products that
people want.

Will you please help us by answering the enclosed
questionnaire? Most of the questions can be answered
quickly. Please understand that your answers will be
kept in confidence and will be used only in
combination with those of others.

A stamped, self-addressed envelope is enclosed for
your convenience. Perhaps you know a child who would
like to have the quarter we have also included as a
token of our appreciation.

In advance, thank you for your cooperation.

Sincerely,

President

Exhibit 7.1 Initial request sample letter.

```
                    XYZ Research, Inc.
                123 Cumberland Avenue, N.W.
                       Dayton, Ohio


     March 1, 1991

     Dear Homeowner:

     Recently you received from us a questionnaire
     relating to buying habits of American families.  If
     you have already returned the questionnaire to us,
     please accept our thanks for your help.  But if you
     have misplaced the original copy, we would sincerely
     appreciate your filling out the new one we have
     enclosed and returning it to us in the enclosed
     stamped envelope.

     Because the survey is going only to a very select
     sample of people, your answers are very important to
     us.  That is why we hope you will complete the
     questionnaire as soon as possible.  Please understand
     that your individual responses will be kept in
     confidence.

     Thank you for your help in this study.

     Sincerely,


     President
```

Exhibit 7.2 Follow-up request sample letter.

...Questionnaire Bias

Designing an effective questionnaire is an art. The type of question, order of appearance of the questions, and phrasing of questions can produce bias. The questionnaire should be interesting, if possible, to elicit a high response rate. Questions should be clearly phrased, easily understood, and should be ordered so that one question does not suggest an answer to the questions that follow it. Keep in mind the fatigue factor. Some questions can be rotated to balance hasty responses that may occur toward the end of a lengthy questionnaire.

When a questionnaire is long, a practical way of boosting respondent cooperation is to use a split-half questionnaire. This involves dividing the questions into two questionnaires, each of which contains common questions of demographic characteristics. But other questions are split between the two questionnaires. For example, if there are eight important open-end questions, each respondent receives a questionnaire with only four of them. If one or two of the eight open-end questions are so important that you need responses from every participant, you might include those questions on both forms and split the remaining questions between the two forms. That way you would obtain extensive responses on a large number of questions without demanding too much effort from any one respondent.

. . . Environmental Factors

Timing can be critical. Conducting a television audience survey during a week-long snow and ice storm will probably produce relatively high television ratings. Often such environmental factors cannot be predicted; changes in the weather, dramatic political events, social upheavals, competitive activity, or other events can alter the environment in which the survey is to be conducted. These can bias the results of a survey.

• • • Interviewer Recruitment and Training

Research directors use one of two approaches to gather interview data. One is to hire a research company that has a staff of experienced interviewers. That will minimize many of the problems associated with interviewers, but the researcher should still brief the experienced interviewers on the purposes of the survey and the questionnaire.

The other approach is to hire and train interviewers for the particular survey. This is usually the more feasible option for small companies because of the added expense of hiring experienced interviewers. Note, however, that if you consider the time spent to train interviewers as well as the risks of using inexperienced interviewers, hiring experienced ones may be more economical in the long run.

If you do hire your own interviewers, you will want to be careful in your selection to make sure they are well trained before they go into the field to conduct interviews. All the time and money put into a representative sample and an excellent questionnaire can be wasted by untrained or incompetent interviewers.

When you select interviewers, you must make sure they are articulate and that their physical appearance and characteristics are appropriate to the kinds of people they will be interviewing. If your sample includes large numbers of African-Americans or Hispanics, you should consider using African-American or Hispanic interviewers for these interviews. A high school education is essential for interviewers, and you may want to hire only persons with some college training. You will need people who feel at ease with strangers and who are capable of making judgments on their own.

All interviewers must receive thorough training. You must tell them precisely how to locate respondents (if they are doing in-home interviews) and what to do if respondents are not home or if they refuse to cooperate. You should require that all interviewers conduct several mock interviews with you as the respondent.

Interviewers should know that you will systematically check their work. If you are doing telephone interviews, you might want to be able to monitor interviews as they are conducted. You need do only a sample of these, but interviewers should not be aware of when you do it. If you do in-home interviews, you should select a sample of completed questionnaires and contact the respondents to verify that the interviews were conducted. This requires respondents' telephone numbers on the questionnaire, of course.

Regardless of who does the bulk of the interviewing, the researcher should do a few of the actual interviews to get a feel for what is happening. This is especially important in the pretest of the questionnaire.

• • • Summary

Simple survey research is the most common of all methods of learning about consumer product usage, media habits, and attitudes toward companies, advertising, and issues. Much of the data you will collect or analyze will probably be survey data.

Conducting a survey seems easy, yet such research should not be designed hastily. Sample selection requires care if the data are to be representative. Questionnaire design also demands attention.

Whether the data are collected by mail questionnaire, personal interview, telephone interview, or observation, the investigator must take precautions to guard against several sources of bias: source, sample, interviewer, questionnaire, timing.

• • • Self-Test Questions

1. Continue the earlier example of The Energy Store. Evaluate the appropriateness of each data gathering method: mail, personal interviews, telephone interviews, and observation. Which one would you recommend?
2. Anticipate possible bias problems you may experience in your survey and explain how you would minimize bias.
3. Assume that your survey will be extensive enough to require the assistance of three other interviewers. Describe how you would recruit, train, and evaluate potential interviewers.

Notes

1. A. B. Blankenship, "Listed Versus Unlisted Numbers in Telephone Survey Samples," *Journal of Advertising Research*, Vol. 17, No. 1 (February 1, 1977), 39–42.
2. Gerald Glasser and Gale D. Metzger, "National Estimates of Nonlisted Telephone Households and Their Characteristics," *Journal of Marketing Research*, Vol. 12 (August 1975), 359–361.

Suggestions for Additional Reading

Backstrom, C. H., and G. Hursh-Cesar. *Survey Research*. 2nd ed. New York: Wiley, 1981.
Erdos, P. L. *Professional Mail Surveys*. rev. ed. Malabar, Fla.: Krieger, 1983.

CHAPTER 8

Qualitative Techniques

t is common to speak of *quantitative* and *qualitative* techniques in advertising research. Understanding what is meant by quantitative research is simple enough. Quantitative research employs statistical techniques in analysis of data. It also involves the measurement of specifically identified variables, such as readership scores for a magazine advertisement, number of persons viewing a television program, or dollar amount of advertising done by a competing firm.

In qualitative research we describe or analyze a situation or condition without the formal measurement of variables. Often this means we conduct exploratory research, which can include historical research, focus groups, field observation, depth interviewing, and case studies.[1] This is not to say that numbers have no place in qualitative research.[2] In a qualitative research project, the investigator may note commonalities that can be counted.

Let us clear up a minor misunderstanding that sometimes exists concerning the nature of the differences between the two types of research. The implication is that if one type of research is "qualitative," the other type is not "of quality." Of course, that conclusion is absurd, but it is a quick one which some persons draw. Both types of research are important in advertising, public relations, and marketing research programs, and they both can be of high (or low) quality.

Among some agencies and advertisers, qualitative techniques have become more prevalent in recent years. One reason is cost; individual or group interviews with a small number of carefully selected consumers can be much less expensive than a large survey. In addition, the advent of supermarket scanners has given many advertisers and researchers large amounts of quantitative data about brand sales. Consequently, some researchers argue, there is a greater need for qualitative data to complement the quantitative data. In particular, some researchers are using qualitative techniques to try to learn more about the "bonding" between consumers and products. As one agency executive puts it, "Brands have become so similar to one another that the real leverage in the advertising is no longer the content of the product but the placement of the product in the consumer's life."[3]

The best-known qualitative technique used in advertising research is the focus group interview. Others include the Thematic Apperception Test (TAT), cartoon technique, sentence completion, and other methods.

The applications of qualitative techniques are varied. As part of an initial situation analysis, you can use them to provide general background information about consumer beliefs and attitudes. They can help make clear some of the specific questions that should be included in a questionnaire. As part of the creative process itself, the qualitative techniques can help generate ideas you can incorporate into the creative strategy of the advertising campaign.

••• Focus Groups

A focus group usually consists of five to ten persons selected on the basis of some important similarity. The group may consist of young mothers, and the subject may be baby foods — what babies like, preferred jar sizes, preferred packaging combinations, label recognition, and advertising memorability. The focus group interview could be designed to elicit ideas for a survey questionnaire to be distributed to a large sample of young mothers.

The popularity of the focus group technique is shown in a *Journal of Advertising Research* article based on interviews with eighteen advertising agency research executives in New York City. The executives reported using the results of focus group interviews to generate hypotheses, to form preliminary evaluations of product concepts, to create copy and rough advertisements, and to develop product concepts and advertising copy.

Although the focus group technique has its merits, it also has its drawbacks. The executives noted the speed and low cost of focus groups as their primary advantages but noted too that agency and client personnel have a tendency to accept focus group interview results as final. They noted that recruiting participants is sometimes difficult and that the projectability of focus groups is limited.[4] Other researchers have been more critical of focus groups, emphasizing the problem with projectability.

. . . Conducting a Focus Group Interview

You should have a minimum of five participants to facilitate good discussion and interaction. However, if you have more than ten people, you will probably have one or two who feel intimidated and who will not take part in the discussions. You must have people who are familiar with the product or service or who are likely to use it. You should probably offer some kind of financial incentive, such as cash or a gift certificate. You might also consider recruiting participants from a church or civic organization and making a donation to that group. You will find that most people feel honored to participate.

Physical arrangements for focus group interviews are very important. The setting should be as casual as possible. You will want to make an audiotape of the session, so your arrangements must make such recording possible. For that reason, a conference table or a circle of comfortable chairs works best. A good audio recording is essential because you cannot possibly write fast enough to record everyone's comments. Be sure you have enough microphones to record every participant. If necessary, you should seek professional assistance in setting up the recording equipment.

Once the participants are in place, you will need to take great care in conducting the session. You will probably want to address people by their first names, so it would be a good idea to have a seating chart in front of you. Although you should not reveal the name of the client at the start of the session, you will need to explain the purpose of the interviews—to get opinions about the product. Stress the fact that you want everyone's opinion and that you are recording the session so you can analyze the comments later. Stress the fact that no one will be identified by name in the report of the session. Your role is to encourage discussion by all participants and to prevent one or two people from dominating the session and intimidating others. Have a series of questions written out so you can keep the discussion going in your intended direction. (See Case 8.1 for an example of a focus group interview.)

When the session is over, you will need to prepare the report for the client. The first step is to write a transcript from the audiotape. (See Case 8.1.) Participants should not be identified by name, but you may want to identify them by characteristic, such as "mother of three children, works outside the home." The verbatim transcript will be valuable to the client, for it may suggest ideas for creative strategies. You also need to identify and discuss patterns and common threads in the responses. That will lead you to make recommendations about the implications for advertising strategy.

Focus groups are often preliminary to more extensive survey research, so you may need to make recommendations for further research. For example, the comments in Case 8.1 might lead a researcher to conduct a larger survey of a representative sample, and the survey might seek reactions to this question: "How important are specialty items in your decision to use products from a given company?"

On the other hand, the researcher may conclude that more extensive research is unnecessary because it probably would produce the same results as the focus group interviews. You might decide that the comments in Case 8.1 are so one-sided about the value of specialty items that further research would not be worth the cost. It's another example of the cost-benefit ratio: The added expense would not be compensated by any added precision in results.

Focus Group Study of Opinions of Specialty Advertising

These notes and questions were used by a researcher who conducted several focus group sessions to learn recipients' reactions to various types of specialty advertising items they had received during the previous year. Examples of specialty advertising items are writing instruments, calendars, and numerous other items of value that companies and other organizations give to customers and potential customers to build goodwill and cultivate customers.

The session ran for nearly two hours, with the interviewer, eight to ten participants, and two tape recorders (both running, one at each end of the table) in each session. The sessions started with introduction of the interviewer and each participant. The interviewer pointed out that the tape recorders were for accuracy only, and that no names would be attached to any of the comments made during the sessions.[1]

1. What kinds of specialty items have you received over the past year or so?
2. Were there any specialty items you were especially happy to receive? What was there about them that made them special to you? (probe)
3. Were there any specialty items you have received that you would like to receive again? (probe)
4. Not all specialty items are useful to all persons. Can you think of any that you have received that were not useful to you?
5. Are there any specialty items that you find yourself using constantly, such as daily? (probe)
6. Have you received any specialty items that you thought were really special? How did you react to receiving those items? (probe)
7. What kinds of companies gave out those items that you use constantly or think of as special?
8. To what extent, if any, would you say that the specialty items you use most often contribute to your perceptions of the firms that gave them to you?
9. Do you think more highly of any firm that routinely gives you some sort of specialty item when you do business with the company?
10. On the other hand, if a firm does *not* give you some sort of specialty item, do you think any less highly of it?
11. Are there any specialty items you have received in the past year or so that were not useful to you? (probe) If there were, what did you do with them?
12. What kinds of companies gave out those items?
13. (Ask only if a respondent reported discarding a specialty item) To what extent, if any, would you say that the specialty items you discarded contributed to your perception of the firm that gave them to you?

For Consumer Groups Only:
14. Do you think that distribution of specialty items influences the prices of items the company sells? (probe)

(*continued*)

CASE 8.1 (*continued*)

15. Do you receive more specialty items now than in the past? Fewer than in the past?

For Business-to-Business Groups Only:
16. Do you now have on your desk any specialty items that you use? (probe)
17. How important would you say specialties are in helping you form your perceptions of a given supplier or other firm with which you routinely do business? Do you think any less of a company that does not give specialty items?
18. To what extent, if any, do you regard specialties as important to your decision to use products from a given company?
19. At Christmas, do any companies with which you do business give you a gift? (probe) Do you ever wish the company would give you enough of the item to let everyone in the office have one? (probe)

An essential part of the report of a focus group study is a verbatim transcript of participants' responses. In the main body of the report, the researcher summarizes the responses and draws conclusions. But the responses themselves should also be given to the client.

Here are several responses to some of the questions raised in the study.[2]

- Considering specialty items you get at your place of business, how important would you say things like that are in helping you form your perceptions of the companies that gave them to you? What role, if any, do those items play in your views of what the company stands for, what it is, what it is like?

"From that standpoint, any gift that you would receive from a place of business, it seems to me that it would make an impression on the mind that if someone would ask you about a product that you know they can purchase at this place, it would probably be this place that would come into your mind, and you would normally refer them to this particular place. And if there are others you know about you might send them there too, so they can make their own choice. I think with a lot of this today, people receive it and just take it for granted. It's commonplace. Now if it's a special type gift, it becomes a conversation piece, which is many times what you want."

"That's the whole idea of the thing."

"That's a well thought out point, but I think that the majority of people who receive things like that of most any consequence, they appreciate the fact that somebody is thinking enough of them that they mail them whatever they are sending. They lean toward a party that does that. Most everybody in business has three factors before they buy anything. One is price, one is quality, and the other is service. And as we have heard, there is no product that is better than the service you can get on it. When a business firm sends most anything like that to a prospective customer, that customer appreciates it. I really believe they do."

- What if you are dealing with a company and the rep *doesn't* give you something? Do you think any less of a company for not giving you something?

"If a company has a good product and has a good representative, then I don't expect anything, just a personal touch, with a phone call, a 'can I help you?' That means more than any pen. Anything they send me is just extra."

"You feel important. The personal touch is important."

"I think it depends on where it's coming from. If you are buying something from a man and you're getting good service and a good product, he doesn't have to send you anything, but when he does you feel kind of nice about it, whether it be a ballpoint pen or whatever, that he took the time to send it to you, not as an inducement, because you're already doing business with him. It's just a little thank you, and the bigger the thank you the better you feel about it."

- How important would you say specialties are in your decision to do business with a given company?

"I would say the only importance attached there would be the importance of knowing what type of product that party had, and if you had the need, and you had that specialty item he had given you, and you know his product was good quality and so forth you are automatically going to remember him. But I don't believe that the specialty item he gives you is going to make any man feel obligated to give his business to him. It's just something to keep his name forward in your mind."

"It's a reference point, to keep that name right there."

"It's got to be a keeper. If it's not a keeper it's a waste."

"If you know the man for what he is and would do business with him regardless, then it doesn't make any difference if you get something or not. But to have it right in front of you, by the phone, or whatever, it does make a difference because you see it all the time and you know where to go to find something."

- Do you think any more highly of a firm that just routinely gives you some sort of specialty item when you do business with them?

"That's really hard."

"Depends upon the item or items, I think. If they are giving you something small, useful, and not so large that you feel some kind of obligation like this is a really nice expensive gift and next time I have to reorder maybe I ought to reorder from him but if it's something like a ruler or pen that's handy or useful but not of value to feel like you're under an obligation."

"I much prefer the idea that it's something simple enough that you don't feel obligated. That's a turn off to me to feel obligated to purchase something because they gave me an extravagant item."

Source 1: Summarized questions from several focus group interviews. Reproduced with permission of Specialty Advertising Association International.
Source 2: Example of a focus group transcript. Reproduced with permission of Specialty Advertising Association International.

• • •

Projective Techniques

Projective techniques, which allow respondents to answer questions more freely than with direct questioning, are used in two ways. They are sometimes used alone, without a follow-up survey, and advertising decisions may be based on the findings. The other application of projective techniques is to use them as the foundation for a survey questionnaire. As with focus group interviews, these approaches can overcome respondents' inabilities to express true feelings about a topic.

For example, asking respondents why they like a particular television program may not produce a meaningful answer. Their preferences for a show may be based on something they're unaware of. Likewise, homemakers may be unable to explain why they do or do not like to use a cake mix.

Instead of asking "What do you think about this cake mix?" you might be considerably less straightforward and use a Thematic Apperception Test. With the TAT, you can ask respondents to analyze several photographs showing the stages in the process from purchasing the mix, taking it home, baking the cake, and serving it to the family. Respondents may be asked to tell a story about the homemaker who made the purchase. Somewhere within that story may lie some important but subtle attitude toward the kind of person who would buy the cake mix. And those attitudes and perceptions might be helpful to the investigator in preparing a questionnaire for a larger sample of respondents.

A well-known example of one of the first applications of a projective technique concerned consumer attitudes toward women who used instant coffee rather than ground coffee. It was conducted by Mason Haire and set the pattern for thousands of such studies to follow. In the literature of marketing, it remains a classic study.

Direct questioning of women had not appeared to have produced complete and valid results. Most women who did not use instant coffee claimed they simply did not like its flavor. It was believed that other reasons were more important than flavor. So the investigator made two shopping lists containing commonly used grocery items and showed each list to a different sample of women. The lists were identical except for one item, the type of coffee purchased:

Table 8.1

List 1	List 2
pound and a half hamburger	pound and a half hamburger
two loaves Wonder Bread	two loaves Wonder Bread
bunch of carrots	bunch of carrots
1 can Rumford's baking powder	1 can Rumford's baking powder
Nescafé instant coffee	1 lb. Maxwell House coffee (drip grind)
5 lbs. potatoes	5 lbs. potatoes
2 cans Del Monte peaches	2 cans Del Monte peaches

Source: Mason Haire, "Projective Techniques in Marketing Research," *Journal of Marketing*, Vol. 14, No. 5 (April 1950), 649–656.

Then the two samples of respondents were asked to evaluate the kind of woman who would have such a shopping list.

What were the responses? Respondents characterized the woman who purchased the instant coffee as lazy, a spendthrift, not a good wife, a failure at planning household purchases. She just didn't measure up as a "good" wife. In contrast, the woman using list 2, which contained "drip grind" coffee, was characterized favorably.

Where did the responses originate? The assumption was that the respondents, many of whom would claim they didn't use instant coffee because it didn't taste good, in reality were concerned that using the brand would say bad things about them. They were apprehensive about using the product and risking the disdain of their friends and acquaintances. This technique enabled the investigator to get at the deeply held attitudes that people had toward the product.

It should be noted that although the Haire study has been heralded by many authors over the years, there have been questions about the validity of using brand names in the shopping lists. Whether using brand names invalidates the study or not, the study is an excellent example of how a projective approach can be used.

Another indirect questioning technique is sentence completion. For example, you might present consumers with this statement: "The kind of person who uses a liquid detergent rather than a powder . . ." This too allows respondents to give a thoughtful answer without the pressure that a direct question may imply.

In the cartoon technique, respondents are shown a cartoon and are asked to complete it by adding the dialogue. In such a procedure, two homemakers may be pictured talking over coffee. Empty dialogue balloons float over their heads, and respondents are asked to fill them in with a conversation relating to a given product category or brand (see Figure 8.1).

Figure 8.1 The cartoon technique calls for asking a respondent to provide a part of a conversation.

The obvious intent of using these techniques is to enable respondents to relax, play a role, and experience an enhanced ability to express themselves. The other purpose, not so obvious, is to probe more deeply than is usually possible with more direct questioning.

A simple technique that puts the respondent in the position of answering questions posed by a third party rather than by you is to ask a question in the following manner:

"Suppose a friend asked your opinion about carpet dealers in this community. What would you tell your friend?"

This is a very open-end question. The respondent might mention dealers whose prices are low. If you were also interested in the respondent's views of quality of service and product selection, you might follow with other questions, such as this:

"If your friend were interested in other factors, such as the quality of service, what would you say?"

You might follow with this question:

"What if your friend asked about the varieties of carpeting carried?"

Questions such as these, which ask only indirectly for answers, may draw more meaningful responses than those in which you ask the respondent to state an opinion directly.

Although projective techniques are potentially helpful in discovering attitudes, they are not usually a substitute for larger-scale survey or experimental research. On a per-respondent basis, they are expensive to use, and they provide only very specialized information. They require large quantities of time as well as the expertise of trained interviewers and psychologists. For these reasons, the projective techniques are usually used with only twenty to thirty respondents.

New Applications of Observational Research

Observation is a common survey technique that can also be used in qualitative studies. A relatively new approach, one that has not caught on widely, it sometimes involves placing a researcher in a home or in a store to discover "the often-hidden impulses that prompt people to buy an expensive car, eat gourmet ice cream, and wash their clothes with a particular detergent."[5] Some companies hire cultural anthropologists to conduct such observational research because of their special training in observation techniques. Although questions have been raised about the validity of such close observation and the legal implications of potential invasion of privacy, it is estimated that companies nationally are spending millions on such studies.

It's easy to see why. According to the director of product strategy for Nissan, "People are often not aware of what they are actually doing and why. . . . The way consumers use products symbolizes how they view themselves."[6] A Toyota study showed that some car buyers think of their cars as art objects; a subsequent Toyota campaign portrayed the Lexus as an art object. A gourmet ice cream producer found that eating ice cream is a ritualized procedure, with ice cream lovers having their own special bowl, spoon, and chair; a subsequent campaign focused on the personal joy of eating something that did not belong on a weight-control diet. A U.S. Postal Service study showed that many people consider their letter carriers as friends; a subsequent campaign placed emphasis on the people carrying the mail.

Like most qualitative research, these applications of observational techniques do not usually stand alone. They are typically used in conjunction with other methods of research.

••• The Need for Care in Using Qualitative Research

For several reasons, you should be very careful in using qualitative techniques. Although practitioners generally agree that the techniques can be helpful, they also agree that the techniques are subject to considerable abuse.

For example, the moderator of a focus group has enormous potential to bias the group in some way. If members of the group don't mesh well, their responses may be stilted. If group members are too much alike, obtaining a broad range of responses may be difficult.

Sometimes clients are willing to accept results of qualitative studies as definitive. That may not be wise, of course, because in a group of eight to ten people, a single unusual, unrepresentative opinion can be blown out of proportion. It can alter the remainder of the discussion. And as with all types of research, it is sometimes tempting to believe only those findings that happen to correspond to preconceived notions about the product or how it should be promoted.

••• Summary

Controversial as they are, the qualitative research techniques have important applications in advertising. Used improperly, they can provide invalid data that will result in poor decision making. But the same can be said for simple surveys and experiments.

The danger inherent in much qualitative research is that it is very easy to jump to quick conclusions. But seldom, if ever, can you attach the same statistical significance to results of qualitative research that you can to results of large-scale survey research. Because of the nature of qualitative research, it is best to use the techniques to explore attitudes in a preliminary sense, laying the groundwork for later research (which may involve a questionnaire that will be administered to a relatively large sample) or generating ideas for the development of creative strategy.

••• Self-Test Questions

1. Describe the types of bias that can creep into a focus group interview. What can you do to minimize the various types of bias?
2. A critic might comment, "You can say what you want, but a person taking part in a TAT session isn't fooled that you aren't really asking about his or her opinions about the product or the advertising. So how can you say that you are creating an imaginary situation in which he or she is supposed to answer your questions?" How would you respond to the critic?
3. Describe how you might use focus group research to gather data about consumer perceptions of The Energy Store. Under what conditions might you recommend a focus group instead of a survey? How would you use a focus group in conjunction with a survey?

••• Notes

1. Roger D. Wimmer and Joseph R. Dominick. *Mass Media Research*, 2nd ed. Belmont, CA: Wadsworth, 1987, p. 49.
2. Clifford G. Christians and James W. Carey, "The Logic and Aims of Qualitative Research," in Guido H. Stempel III, and Bruce H. Westley. *Research Methods in Mass Communication*, 2 ed. Englewood Cliffs, NJ: Prentice-Hall, 1989, p. 357.
3. Randall Rothenberg, "Ad Research Shifts from Products to People," *New York Times*, April 6, 1989, p. 27(Y).
4. George J. Szybillo and Robert Berger, "What Advertising Agencies Think of Focus Groups," *Journal of Advertising Research*, Vol. 19, No. 3 (June 1979), 29–33.
5. Kim Foltz, "New Species for Study: Consumers in Action," *New York Times*, December 18, 1989, p. 1(Y).
6. Foltz, "New Species for Study," p. 1(Y).

••• Suggestions for Additional Reading

Green, P. E., and D. S. Tull. *Research for Marketing Decisions*, 4th ed. Englewood Cliffs, N.J.: Prentice-Hall, 1978.

Hammond, Meryl. "Creative Focus Groups: Uses and Misuses." *Marketing and Media Decisions*, July 1986, pp. 154–156.

Rago, Rosalinde. "Finding the Magic: Cognitive Aspects of Mood and Emotion in Advertising." *Review of Business*, 11 (Summer 1989), 9–10.

CHAPTER 9

Experiments

· · · · · · · ·

At times, conducting a survey is not enough. A survey can provide useful descriptions of a situation. Most of the syndicated data sources that we use in advertising are the result of surveys; some surveys involve large samples of respondents and very long questionnaires. But surveys cannot provide all the information we need.

In advertising, we often make assumptions about how advertising works, how different kinds of people react to different stimuli, and why some advertising strategies work better with some markets than with others. For example, we might assume that a high readership score for a print advertisement will produce a high level of goodwill or sales or intention to buy. We usually assume that a high readership score helps improve a person's perception of a product, service, or company. We almost always assume that the greater the frequency with which a person sees our advertisement, the greater the likelihood the person will buy the product.

It is very easy to see how quickly advertisers draw conclusions about the effects of advertising. When a product sells well, you can bet that advertising people compliment themselves on having devised such clever strategy. And if the product does not sell well, you can bet that the advertising people are decrying the poor quality of the product or claiming that the product is not in tune with the times.

Correlation and Causation

One type of conclusion we sometimes reach is *causation*. We try to go beyond the *what* of a problem or situation to arrive at the *why*. We also want to know the direction of a relationship: whether X caused Y or Y caused X.

Many types of advertising research cannot tell us why certain things happened; they merely verify that they did happen. What appears to be a causal relationship may merely be an associative or correlational relationship. Correlation is not necesarily causation. It may seem very apparent that A caused B. But perhaps A did not cause B, and perhaps B did not cause A. Perhaps A and B just happened to occur together for no reason other than pure chance. The following statements may be true, but they show correlation and not causation.

"The number of alcoholics in the United States has increased at the same rate as the number of teachers."
"As the number of cats in this country increases, so does the number of rats."
"Most people who eat supper also watch television."

We need three kinds of evidence to support an assumption that Variable A *causes* Variable B. The first is correlation: Variable B has to appear when Variable B appears, or Variable B has to change in value when Variable A changes. The second is sequence: Variable B has to appear *after* Variable A appears or has to change in value *after* Variable A changes. The third is the absence of other causal factors: No other variable could cause B to change.

For example, suppose we run a magazine ad with a coupon inviting readers to write in asking for a product information booklet. The ad with the coupon is Variable A; the response to the coupon (the volume of letters we get) is Variable B. The letters start to arrive after the ad appears, and no other ad has made a similar offer. We can safely conclude that the ad caused the response.

The Nature of Experimental Research

We must be careful about drawing conclusions in advertising research. We must be wary of jumping to conclusions and assuming relationships among advertising and other variables. It is because of the limitations of simple survey research and the need to draw conclusions that experimentation is an important technique in advertising research.

Experimentation is a research design whose essential elements are *control*, *independent variables*, and *dependent variables*. The purpose of experimentation is to detect the direction of relationships; that is, whether A causes B or vice versa.

Control in experimental research means the ability to manipulate. For example, you might expose some people to an advertisement once and others twice, to learn how well a second exposure implants a brand name in the audience. Or you might use a highly overstated advertising claim in an experimental advertisement that you show to some people, and the company's tried-and-true advertising claim in one of the company's current advertisements that you show to other people. You have control over the stimulus or stimuli; you can manipulate as you see fit.

The group to whom you administer the experimental stimulus or treatment is called the *experimental group*. The experimental stimulus or treatment is the independent variable, the thing or phenomenon you are studying, such as a magazine advertisement with a coupon. You administer the independent variable and observe, measure, or assess the dependent variable, which is the reaction of the experimental group. That reaction might be measured by the number of coupons redeemed or some questionnaire-based response.

The other group — the *control group* — is important to the process of inferring the relationship between the experimental variable and the measured response. It receives either a modified version of the experimental variable, no version at all (which would be impractical in this example), or the old advertisement. Then, by comparing the redemption rates for the two advertisements, you can draw conclusions about the relative merits of the two advertisements.

In another example, you might show a new television spot to one group of viewers (the experimental group) and a current spot to a second group (the control group). After the exposure, you could ask members of each group about the brand they intend to buy next time they need that kind of product. If the purchase intentions of the two groups differ, you can assume that the new television spot had something to do with the differences.

The whole point in having control groups is to allow the researcher to draw the conclusions that are so important to draw. If you added television to your media plan in a city in which you had been using only newspapers, and you compared sales during a base period (a month, say) with sales one month after you added the television, and you found a five percent sales increase, you would have no way to know whether television was a useful addition to the media plan. For all you know, maybe people really liked the product. But if you also used a control city, one in which you had been using a comparable level of newspaper advertising space and made no changes whatsoever in your media plan, and you found a sales increase of two percent, you would see immediately that the addition of television to the test city was not solely responsible for the increase in sales. If the control city sales increase was two percent, you would assume a similar sales increase in the test city, which would mean that television contributed approximately three percentage points of the sales increase in that city.

It should be clear that proper experimentation requires careful design and execution. In using two groups of consumers, for example, the two groups should be matched — that is, they should be similar in important demographic characteristics. Otherwise, the differences in results might be due to differences in gender, income, or age of the subjects. One way to do this is, where possible, to use some kind of random procedure for assigning subjects to the experimental and control groups. Random assignment assures us that the groups are similar to each other and that we are controlling for differences among subjects.

If you are testing individual advertisements, you should make sure that the subjects view the ads under similar conditions. That is, you try to make the environments in which your variables are being tested as nearly alike as possible.

... Ideal Conditions for Experimentation

Although meeting all of the ideal conditions for experimentation is difficult, the researcher should strive to create an unbiasing, neutral environment for such studies. If the project involves advertising messages, the ideal procedure is to distribute the messages in as realistic a way as possible. If the ads are designed to be run in consumer magazines, they should appear in consumer magazines in the testing stage. The objective is to test the advertisements in as natural an environment as possible. That will give generalizability to the results. With good camouflaging, recipients of the messages will not be aware that they are seeing an experimental advertisement and are more likely to react naturally.

The measures of effect should be totally unobtrusive, if possible. This is not always feasible; it is easy to see that keeping the measures unobtrusive is legally and ethically impossible for example if you are studying television viewing habits of any demographic group—since you cannot study them surreptitiously. But if you are testing two different coupon offers, the procedure can be unobtrusive because sales measures will give you the information you need.

Experimental Designs

Four experimental procedures or designs are commonly used in advertising research studies. One of the designs is not really experimental because it omits a control group and a second observation or measurement. Another is a weak design because it has no control group.

It is convenient to use a set of symbols to describe and denote the elements of experimental designs. Researchers commonly use the system developed by Campbell and Stanley.[1] In this notation system, X indicates that a group of subjects has been exposed to an independent or experimental variable. The letter O indicates some method of observation or measurement of a dependent variable. The letter R denotes random assignment of subjects to the groups. The sequence of letters from left to right indicates the order of treatments and measurements, and vertical alignment of letters indicates simultaneous treatment or measurement.

... After-Only, No Control Group

Experimental group: **X   O**

Control group: **(No control group)**

Campbell and Stanley call this design a "one-shot case study," and it has very little value in research. In this design, you administer a treatment or stimulus to one group (X) and later take an observation or measurement (O), without using a control group. The group may be a small number of consumers, a national mail sample (as in mail-order advertising offers), or consumers in a test market city. You should avoid this design whenever possible because it cannot show the actual effects of the treatment itself. Because you do not measure the group before the treatment, you cannot tell if there was any change.

If you were using this design to test a mail-order advertisement for a laptop computer, you might conclude that your advertisement was a good one because it resulted in many orders. But without a measure of sales before the ad, you really cannot tell what effect the ad had. And during the time that the ad appeared, the product may have been enjoying unusual success throughout the country. Without a control group, how would you know whether your ad was responsible for the satisfying order rate or whether you simply happened to be in the right place at the right time with the right offer?

··· Before-After, No Control Group

Experimental group: O_1 X O_2

Control group: (No control group)

In this design, you use only one group, obtain an initial (baseline) measure (O_1), administer a treatment or stimulus (X), and measure the same group a second time (O_2). You presume that the difference in the measurement ($O_1 - O_2$) is due to X. Campbell and Stanley also call this a bad design because it lacks a control group.

Suppose your company has been publishing a mail-order catalog for several years and that laptop computers have been featured in each year's edition. Then you decide to promote the computers with extra funding to take advantage of the boom. So you send a new mailing piece to everyone on your mailing list. Then you count the returns — the inquiries and orders.

Because the people who received your new mailing piece have also been receiving your annual catalog, you have a "before" measurement that you can use as a base — the old rate of sales. You can then compare the "after" measurement (the number of returns that arrived after you sent the new mailing) with the "before" and conclude that the difference is due to the mailing. Or can you?

Not necessarily, because you still do not know for sure whether the mailing was responsible for the increased sales or whether the new sales were a result of the growing interest in laptop computers. You know that sales increased, but that is all you know. In other words, this design is weak because it does not have a control group — a way to test what would have happened if you had not sent the new mailing piece.

. . . After-Only, With Control Group

Experimental group: **R   X O_1**

Control group: **R O_2**

In this design, you expose the experimental group to the stimulus (X) and measure the effect after the treatment (O_1). You do not measure the experimental group before the exposure, but you do measure a control group (O_2) at the same time you measure the experimental group — after its exposure. Because subjects are randomly assigned to the groups, you can assume that differences in the measurement of the dependent variable ($O_1 - O_2$) are the result of the independent variable. In other words, random assignment means you have "controlled" for, or neutralized, external variables that might have caused differences in O_1 and O_2.

With this approach, you can test the effect of a new mailing piece. If we assume that conditions are the same as in the previous example — that you have been using annual catalogs and have a good mailing list — you could send the new mailing and detect its sales-generating ability. You would send the new mailing piece to an experimental group, a randomly selected sample of names from the mailing list. To the remainder of people on the mailing list (the control group), you would send only your usual catalog. You would compare sales for the experimental group with the sales for the control group. If 5 percent of the control group ordered the laptop computer and 15 percent of the experimental group ordered it, you could assume that the mailing piece (the independent variable) did have a positive effect. You can assume that the 5 percent sales level for the control group represents what would have happened without the mailing, so the difference of 10 percentage points was due to the mailing.

. . . Before-After, With Control Group

Experimental group: **R O_1 X O_2**

Control group: **R O_3 O_4**

This design is generally regarded as the most rigorous and most careful of the simple experimental designs because it allows a comparison of the effect of one treatment with the effect of other treatments and with changes in control groups. It also permits comparison of conditions both before and after the experimental variable has been manipulated.

The simplest version of this design employs before and after measurements of a single experimental group (O_1 and O_2) that is exposed to the treatment (X). It also employs before and after measurements of a control group (O_3 and O_4), even though the control group is not exposed to the treatment. The difference between $O_1 - O_2$ and $O_3 - O_4$ is presumed to be due to the effect of X.

In our example, the experimental group would be exposed to the new mailing piece, and the control group would see the regular catalog. You could compare sales before the mailing piece with sales after the mailing piece. You might expect sales to increase for both the experimental group (because of the mailing) and for the control group (because of increased general interest in laptop computers), but you would expect a greater increase for the experimental group. The difference between the sales increase for the experimental group and the control group could be attributed largely to the mailing piece.

Of course, you would not necessarily have to limit yourself to testing one mailing piece. You could use one control group but test two or more mailing pieces, each with a different experimental group. You could compare the results from each experimental group to results from other experimental groups and from the control group.

••• Extraneous Variables

In experimental studies, researchers are interested in the effect of an independent variable on a dependent variable. However, other variables—extraneous variables—can also influence the dependent variable and complicate your analysis. One of those extraneous variables could be consumer income. Let's assume that the laptop computer we have been talking about costs approximately $2,500. That means some low income consumers might not be inclined to buy it. Suppose our experimental group, the one receiving the new mailing piece about the computer, has a lot of low income members and that the control group has few or no low income people. That would probably mean that few of the people in the experimental group would buy the computer, and we would probably conclude that the mailing piece was not very effective, especially if we did not know about the problem of the low income people. External publicity about laptop computers could be another extraneous variable.

••• The Hawthorne Effect

One of the best-known extraneous variables arises from the unnaturalness of the experimental situation itself. It was first noted in studies of worker productivity at the Hawthorne Western Electric Plant in Cicero, Illinois. Researchers were interested in the effect of certain working conditions, such as the level of illumination, on worker productivity. The researchers measured productivity of experimental and control groups and then changed lighting conditions for experimental groups. They found, however, that productivity increased for both experimental and control groups. Further investigation revealed that workers in the control groups (where the lighting had not been changed) were very conscious of the attention being paid to them by the researchers and increased their productivity as a response to that attention.[2]

Hawthorne effect now often refers to any experimental situation, including advertising research, in which the conditions of the experiment or the attention being paid to the subjects has a possible effect on the dependent variable. If you measure a control group and measure it again a few weeks later without an intervening exposure to an independent variable, you are likely to see change simply because of the attention you are paying to the control group.

Furthermore, if you bring a group into a laboratory setting and measure a change in a dependent variable after exposing the group to an independent variable, you can assume that at least part of the change resulted from subjects' reactions to the unnatural laboratory setting. Or if you bring subjects into a room and tell them you are going to ask them some questions after you show them some television commercials, they are going to anticipate the questions and view the commercials accordingly, which is not a natural way to view television commercials.

... Controlling for Extraneous Variables

Extraneous variables can seriously weaken your experiment unless you control for them. Controlling for extraneous variables means to eliminate or neutralize them. In laboratory experiments, you control for extraneous variables by randomly assigning subjects to groups. Suppose you were working with two groups of thirty students each. If they all came to see you at once, you could line them up and assign every other student to the control group and the others to the experimental group. If they were coming individually, you could place sixty pieces of paper in a box; thirty would say "experimental" and thirty would say "control." As the subjects came in, they would draw a slip of paper and that would designate their assigned group.

In a field experiment, like the example we have been discussing, you could start with a list that is in some order—alphabetical or zip code sequence. You could take every other name on the list for the experimental group and the remainder for the control group. Or if you did not intend to use all of the mailing list for the experiment, you should use a random method for selecting and assigning people to the two groups.

Random assignment of subjects will let you assume that the resulting groups are very similar on a number of characteristics. You could assume, for example, that you have the same proportion of low income people in each group; that would allow you to say that the possible effect of income would be the same for each group. That in turn would allow you to say that you had controlled for the possible effect of income, or any other possible extraneous variables.

A stratified sampling procedure, you will recall from Chapter 5, is another way of controlling for possible extraneous variables. If you knew the income levels of all the people on your list, you could stratify your two samples (experimental and control groups) to make them similar on the income dimension.

... Using College Classes

A lot of experimental research has been conducted with college psychology or advertising classes serving as experimental or control groups. It is more convenient for researchers to use such classes intact than to bring individual students into a laboratory and randomly assign them to groups. Researchers justify this practice with a casual statement about an assumption that the classes were similar and extraneous variables were therefore controlled. However, the fact that such a practice is more convenient to the researcher cannot hide the fact that classes of college students cannot be assumed to be equal. Classes that meet at different times of the day or that have different instructors could easily attract very different kinds of students. And because students' ages center around the early twenties, they can hardly be considered representative of the overall adult market.

Laboratory Experiments

Advertising research experiments are often conducted in laboratories or in other specialized testing facilities. The term *laboratory* can refer to a number of environments besides a so-called clinical laboratory. A specially outfitted motor home or van can be used as a laboratory in shopping mall parking lots. You can conduct laboratory research in a plain room in a shopping mall or in classrooms. *Laboratory* means a location in which a researcher can maintain relatively tight controls over conditions and treatments. It may also mean that conditions are relatively unreal or artificial.

The ability to control conditions is a real advantage of a laboratory experiment. Experimental studies are done usually on a smaller scale than surveys or other kinds of research, so the savings in time and money can be important too. Researchers sometimes use laboratory research to pretest procedures they plan to use on a larger scale in field experiments.

The artificial conditions of a laboratory experiment can be a serious disadvantage. Tests of television commercials or print ads take place under conditions that are not even remotely similar to real-life situations. The type of person willing to participate in an experiment may not be representative of the target audience for the product. For example, experiments conducted during daytime hours usually cannot include men or women who work outside the home during those hours.

Theater Tests

Theater tests are a type of laboratory experiment often used to pretest television commercials. The name stems from the fact that such tests are sometimes conducted in movie theaters, although many researchers now use television sets and videotape recorders in rooms in shopping malls or mobile vans in mall parking lots. You can use the same setting and procedures to test print ads too.

To use this technique to test alternative ads, you could prepare one or more versions of a commercial to be tested. To avoid expensive production costs for test commercials, the ads are sometimes rough commercials instead of finished versions. For example, you can show still photographs or slides of the commercial storyboard with an accompanying sound track.

You can recruit subjects as they come through the mall, or you can arrange for groups of subjects to come to the theater for the test. You will probably use convenience samples, which is generally acceptable as long as the people you recruit are similar to the kinds of people likely to purchase the product. Even though you are using a convenience sample, you should randomly assign subjects to your experimental or control groups.

You will probably want to reward those who participate in your test. This can be a relatively small gift certificate. Some research companies recruit test subjects from church or civic groups and make donations to the organization or to a charity.

You should begin by taking a measure of the dependent variable. You could do this by showing your subjects a list of products and services and asking them to indicate their brand preferences. This list should include more products and brands than the one you are testing. Otherwise, your research intentions will be quite obvious and could contaminate the results of your test. Collect those questionnaires before you show the commercials.

Let's suppose you are testing two commercials (C and D) for a frozen food product. You should imbed the test commercials in some kind of entertainment program and include commercials for one or two other products. Ideally, these commercials should be in the same form (rough or finished) as your test commercials. Otherwise, the commercials' production quality could be an extraneous variable. To control for another possible extraneous variable, the program should be the same for both groups. Before you show the commercials, you should tell the subjects that you are interested in their reactions to the program and that you have added the commercials for a touch of realism.

Your subjects should be randomly assigned to group C or group D. After they view the program and commercials, ask them to complete a questionnaire about their reactions to the television program they just saw. On that questionnaire, you would include the same question you asked earlier about preferences for certain brands and services.

After all subjects view the test program and commercials, you would analyze data from the questionnaires to see how much change there was in brand preference from before the commercial to after. The commercial that brought about the greatest positive change would be deemed more effective.

After you show the commercials, you should probably tell the subjects the purpose of your research. Most researchers consider this an ethical obligation. It is acceptable to disguise the purposes of your research during the experiment to avoid possible contamination. It is unacceptable to lie to subjects after the test is completed. Of course, it goes without saying that you should never do anything threatening or stressful to subjects.

• • • Mechanical Measurements in Laboratories

A common way to measure a dependent variable in a laboratory or field experiment is with a paper and pencil test, usually a questionnaire with rating scales or questions. This technique requires subjects to verbalize their attitudes and reactions. Such verbalizations may not always be an accurate reflection of subjects' true reactions or attitudes. Some reactions, such as emotions, are simply impossible to verbalize. In other cases, subjects may not want to tell you the truth about their reactions.

For those reasons, researchers sometimes use mechanical devices to measure involuntary responses to stimuli. Because subjects cannot control such responses, researchers assume these responses are accurate indications of true responses. The assumption underlying mechanical devices is that the greater the physiological change, the greater the effectiveness of the advertisement, at least in attracting the subject's attention.

A *pupillometer* measures eye pupil dilation in response to visual stimuli. If you were testing the effect of an attractive model (male or female) in an automobile advertisement, you could ask subjects to view a test ad with the model as well as a control ad without the model. Some subjects might not want to tell you they were attracted to the model, so they would tell you they had the same reaction to the two ads. However, measuring the dilation of their pupils might tell you that they had a more pronounced reaction to the ad with the model. The dilation was involuntary and did not lie.

An *eye-movement camera* can identify the point where a person's eyes first focus on a page and can trace the movement of the eyes throughout the ad. Used in the previous example, it could tell you if it was the car or the attractive model that first attracted the subject's attention. It could also tell you whether a headline or an illustration is more likely to attract the reader's initial attention.

A *psychogalvanometer* records physiological changes (such as perspiration or pulse rate) when the subject is exposed to a stimulus such as advertising. A *brainwave scanner* can measure variations in electrical impulses in a subject's brain (in response to an ad) and can pinpoint the location of the activity in the brain.

• • • Field Experiments

Experimental methods can also be used in the field, such as in split-run tests, test markets, and panels. These are good research methods because they are natural to consumers. Consumers do not usually realize that they are taking part in a field experiment; therefore, the Hawthorne effect or respondent conditioning is minimized.

• • • Split-Run Tests

A *split-run test* (sometimes called an *inquiry test*) is a special kind of field experiment that offers important advantages to advertising researchers. It takes advantage of the ability of a newspaper or magazine publisher to place alternate versions of an advertisement in alternate copies of the publication as the copies come off the press. Every other copy of a magazine could have Version A of an ad, and alternate copies could have Version B. Half the readers (Group A) see Version A, and half (Group B) see Version B. Because Versions A and B are distributed randomly to the magazine's subscribers, Groups A and B are assumed to be matched samples in all characteristics — gender, age, place of residence, and income, for example.

So you can prepare two versions of an ad. Ideally, they should be identical except for one variable: the one being tested. For example, an ad could have identical copy and illustrations but different headlines. The ads also must have a way for readers to respond: a coupon, reply card, or telephone number. The address or the telephone numbers would be different for the two versions of the ad so you can tell which response came from which ad.

You would have to make arrangements with the publisher (not all publications have split-run capability), the ads would appear, and you would count the responses as they come in. An attractive feature of this kind of research design is that subjects are normal readers. Unaware of a testing situation, they are reading the publication and responding (or not responding) to the ad. Because the groups are matched samples, differences in response to the ad (the coupons or inquiries) can be attributed to the manipulated variable (the test headline). That is another attractive feature of a split-run test. You can assume that extraneous variables (such as income level) have been controlled because both groups are matched on income levels.

⋅ ⋅ ⋅ Market Tests

Advertising strategies and individual advertisements can be evaluated in market tests under natural conditions. Such field experimentation will involve at least two markets, one a test market and the other a control market.

Identifying test and control markets should take into account several factors. The first step is to select the cities themselves, then divide them into subgroups of test and control markets. The markets should meet the following criteria:

1. They should all be approximately the same size.
2. They should be of moderate size, so that they are manageable for the study and so that their media rates will not be higher than the media budget will cover. For example, it probably is better to use Peoria, Illinois, than New York City. The media charges in New York will destroy a modest media budget.
3. They should be demographically representative. A city with a heavy retired population will be inappropriate for some studies.
4. They should have a broad economic base. Some heavy industry, light industry, brisk retail trade, and low unemployment all contribute to a good economic base.
5. They should have all the major television networks, a newspaper, a variety of radio stations, and perhaps a metropolitan magazine. You want access to the media you are considering using in the actual advertising campaign.
6. There should be as little intrusion of media from other markets as possible. This is called *spill-in*, and it can be a major newspaper from a nearby city or a television station from an adjacent market. This criterion is difficult to meet, because cable penetration is so great and because many local media are distributed over a wide area.
7. The test and control markets should be far enough apart to prevent mixing of media between them. In other words, you wouldn't want people in a control city to be able to see your test commercial on a television station in a test city.

8. Climate should be taken into account where appropriate. Advertising for a product associated with cold climates should be tested in northern locales.
9. Product distribution in the test markets should be on a par with that in the rest of the company's marketing area.
10. The competitive situation in the test markets should approximate that in other markets. Unusually weak or strong competition will distort the results of the experiment.

Then, through a random selection process, you assign cities to the experimental group and to the control group. The number of cities you include in your study will depend on the needs of the study and the research budget.

With market tests, you could test two different advertisements or two different advertising strategies. For example, you might want to conduct a test to compare the effectiveness of outdoor advertising with spot television as a way of complementing network television. Your network television commercials would appear in both cities. In the test city, you would use outdoor advertising to support the network schedule. In the control city, on the other hand, you would use spot television as the supporting medium. The media strategy would be the independent variable, and product sales would be the dependent variable. If the test markets are matched, and if your competitors do not confound your research by cutting their prices during the test, you can attribute differences in sales to the advertising strategy. The strategy that yields higher sales would be deemed the more effective one.

This kind of market test has the great advantage of being conducted under normal conditions. Most residents of the two cities would have no idea that they were subjects in a field experiment. On the other hand, setting up and conducting that kind of study would require weeks or months to give you reliable results. You or your client may not have that kind of time or money.

... Panels

A panel study can be simply a series of surveys, with no experimentation. But panels can become a type of field experiment in which the same group of people is studied over a relatively long time—several months or a few years. In most panel studies, researchers exercise some control over exposure to advertising and use experimental and control groups.

A panel study can be established in a city with a special kind of cable television system that permits researchers to divide cable homes into two groups that are nearly equally matched in important demographic characteristics. The cable system also permits researchers to show different commercials or to employ different media strategies with the two groups of subscribers.

The researchers can also measure product and brand purchases by households in the two samples. Panel families are asked to shop in grocery stores that have optical scanners to read the Universal Product Code on every package. When the subjects pay for groceries, they give the checkout clerk a special card that enables the store's computer to record their purchases electronically and indicate their group affiliation.

In a variation on this, some research companies place electronic meters in the panel households to record the programs (and therefore the commercials) that the family watched. The meters also have an electronic wand that can read the Universal Product Code and store information about the family's purchases. When families bring groceries and other products home, they record the purchases with the wand. Thus the researchers have a record of the family's television exposure and its purchases.

Researchers can show one version of a commercial to one group and another commercial to another group, or show television commercials to one group and no commercials to the other group. They can measure purchases by families in each group and gauge the effectiveness of the commercial or the strategy. Because the families are carefully assigned to the groups and because they are watching commercials under normal viewing conditions, researchers can conclude that differences in purchases are due to differences in advertising exposure. The random assignment and the normal viewing conditions mean that external variables have been controlled.

Limitations of Panels

Panels are an excellent method of gathering data under carefully controlled conditions. Yet they do have some limitations.

If you ask panel families to maintain diaries or detailed records of product purchases over long periods, they may resist or drop out because of the time and effort involved. They might not fill out the diaries until several days or weeks after the purchases and might forget important items. Of course, this problem can be alleviated by the use of the electronic devices described in the previous section, but those methods are very expensive. You may have to pay people a considerable amount to participate, and that could mean that your panel members come disproportionately from certain income levels — low income families who want the money and are willing to tolerate the inconvenience of keeping the records.

If families are aware of their participation in a panel, they may become overly conscious of that role. They might avoid certain products (or purchase other kinds) because of how such products might make them look in the eyes of the researcher, even though the data would be anonymous. Researchers usually feel that such conditioning is more of a problem among new members of a panel than among the older ones. Consequently, data from new panelists are sometimes not tabulated with data from more experienced panelists until several weeks have passed and newer members have grown accustomed to the panel.

• • • Summary

Experiments are characterized by a considerable degree of control over test conditions and especially over extraneous variables. Because of this control, researchers often use experimental research in attempts to prove or demonstrate causal relationships among variables.

Advertising research experiments can be conducted in laboratories or in the field. Laboratory research usually offers more control but much less realism and external validity than field experiments. Field experiments—including panel studies, split-run tests, and market tests—involve considerably more time and expense.

Different types of research designs offer varying degrees of control over experimental variables. At a minimum, an experiment should compare a test group to a control group. Ideally, both the test group and the control group should be measured before and after the manipulation of the experimental variable. Subjects should be randomly assigned to groups.

··· Self-Test Questions

1. Suppose you decide to do a field experiment in your research work for The Energy Store. You will use direct mail to test the relative effectiveness of two advertising themes. Describe how you would conduct the field experiment and identify your control and experimental groups and your independent and dependent variables.
2. What extraneous variables can you anticipate in your field experiment?
3. What advantage do mechanical measurements have over traditional paper and pencil measures in advertising research? What disadvantages do they have?
4. Devise advertising research studies that could employ mechanical measurement devices such as a pupillometer, eye-movement camera, or psychogalvanometer. Identify your experimental and control groups and your independent variables.
5. Repeat the process in Question 4 for a test of television commercials using videotape facilities in a shopping mall.

··· Notes

1. D. T. Campbell and J. C. Stanley, *Experimental and Quasiexperimental Designs for Research* (Chicago: Rand McNally, 1963).
2. R. K. Merton, *Social Theory and Social Structure* (New York: Free Press, 1968), 120–121.

··· Suggestions for Additional Reading

Freund, J. E., and F. J. Williams. *Elementary Business Statistics*. 3rd ed. Englewood Cliffs, N.J.: Prentice-Hall, 1977.

CHAPTER 10

Data Processing and Analysis

The time to think about the data processing and analysis stage of the research process is before you even conduct the research itself. It would be a serious mistake to wait until after you have completed your survey or experiment to begin thinking about what you will do with your data. You must consider the statistical techniques, if any, that you will apply. And you must consider the appropriateness of your question formats and whether or not they will provide you with data that are precise enough for your purpose.

Advance Preparation

When your data are in, you probably will have accumulated many questionnaires or other data collection instruments. These will often be papers with marked responses. Because you almost certainly will want to use a computer to analyze your data, you will have to convert those marked responses on paper to a form that a computer can read and analyze. And even if you are using a computer to collect the data and therefore store it in computer-readable form, you need to think ahead of time how you want the data stored.

While planning the study, you should consider the kind of data tables and analysis you will need. An excellent way of forcing yourself to plan ahead is to devise dummy tables, charts, and graphs for every piece of data that you will collect. Dummy tables will give you a graphic portrayal of what form the data will take and may suggest modifications that you might want to make before gathering the data. If you skip constructing dummy tables, you might collect your data and then realize that you won't be able to do a particular kind of analysis because you did not collect the right kind of data or did not plan for the right kind of analysis.

We'll consider a simple example of a dummy table. Suppose you are interested in the ages of readers of your magazine advertisement that appeared in a recent edition of a popular magazine. In the back of your mind you have assumed that you will use broad age breaks, such as 18–24, 25–49, 50–64, and 65+. When you make up a dummy table showing the hypothetical age distribution of your advertisement's readers, you see that your table may not provide the precise description of the audience that you want it to provide. Your dummy table looks like this:

Age of Reader	Percentage Distribution of Readers
18–24	0%
25–49	79%
50–64	21%
65+	0%

If you believe your data will look like these, you may want to redefine the age breaks you are using. That large accumulation of readers in the 25–49 age group may be clustered in the top half of the category, meaning that your readers are older than you might expect. If it is important to you to have some precision in the description of the readership of the advertisement, reducing one age category and adding another will provide improved precision. Here is what your new table would look like:

Age of Reader	Percentage Distribution of Readers
18–24	0%
25–34	5%
35–49	74%
50–64	21%
65+	0%

This table shows that the heaviest readership is in the 35–49 age group, with second highest in the 50–64 age group. You now have some precision that the original dummy table would not provide.

In addition to devising dummy tables, it is also a good idea to conduct a pretest of the study. This is a useful way of finding and eliminating problems in the questionnaire and procedures. A good pretest will suggest changes in your research design that will let you conduct more meaningful analyses. To conduct a pretest, you will simply administer the questionnaire to a number of persons who are in the sample you will be using. If they don't understand Question 3, you will just rewrite Question 3. If they refuse to answer Question 14, you will rewrite or eliminate that question.

Coding

An essential part of the data processing phase of research is coding questionnaires or other data gathering instruments. Coding is the task of changing verbal answers to numerical answers or to codes that computers can read and process.

In cases where the answers you are collecting are numbers, you can code them directly. Interval data can be coded directly. For example, if a question asks how many children a respondent has and she answers "3," you could give that answer a value or code of 3. If you were asking respondents to rate an advertisement on a scale of 1 to 7, you could code a rating of "2" as 2, and so on.

Some questions may require respondents to answer with something other than a raw number, and that will require a different coding procedure. You will rarely ask people to tell you their exact income, for example. Although many people are unwilling to reveal their income, they are often willing to identify the range in which their income falls, as in this example:

—— under $10,000

—— $10,000 to $19,999

—— $20,000 to $29,999

—— $30,000 to $39,999

—— $40,000 to $49,999

—— $50,000 or more

In this case, you will need to assign a numerical value to each alternative. You can print or type those numerical values on the questionnaire before the interviews. Interviewers can mark the response, or they can write the code number on a line in the margin of the questionnaire. An example follows.

(1) ___ under $10,000

(2) ___ $10,000 to $19,999

(3) _X_ $20,000 to $29,999   ___3___

(4) ___ $30,000 to $39,999   Income

(5) ___ $40,000 to $49,999

(6) ___ $50,000 or more

It should be apparent that although it is appropriate to apply statistical measures to interval data, it is not always appropriate to apply certain measures to nominal data. If one of your questions concerns occupation, you could assign a numerical code to each of five or six occupational categories, starting with managerial-professional, 1, and ending with laborers and farm workers, 7. But the code *1* has no mathematical relationship to the code *7*. You could not take two persons, one coded as a 1 and the other as a 7, and average the two codes to arrive at 4. That would be like saying that the average of a Mercedes and a Subaru is an Oldsmobile.

. . . Coding Closed-End Questions

Preparing to code closed-end questions is usually not difficult; responses will fall into one of the predetermined categories. There will be little question about where a response belongs or how to code it.

It is important to make certain that the categories are precise enough but not too precise, because listing too many response alternatives may produce thin data — alternatives with too few responses to be useful. If that happens, you may have to *collapse* the categories, say from ten to five or even to four. To do so, you would combine adjacent categories into fewer categories that are still precise enough for your purposes yet large enough to be usable. You can do this after collecting all the data, but it is easier to anticipate this problem and to collapse the categories before administering the questionnaire.

Tables 10.1 and 10.2 show the benefits of collapsing data. In Table 10.1, the data for one hundred respondents are distributed unevenly over eleven categories, zero through ten. In several categories, the data represent only very few respondents. Collapsing the data, as in Table 10.2, enlarges the numbers for each purchase level and makes them more useful for the researcher. Unfortunately, it may make the results less precise, but such a loss is probably not serious.

. . . Coding Open-End Questions

Open-end questions are more difficult to code than closed-end questions. When you ask an open-end question, naturally you are likely to receive a wide variety of

Table 10.1 Frequency of Purchasing by 100 Respondents

Number of Purchases	Persons
10	1
9	1
8	3
7	7
6	3
5	12
4	20
3	3
2	8
1	10
0	32

Table 10.2 Frequency of Purchasing by 100 Respondents

Number of Purchases	Persons
7–10	12
4–6	35
1–3	21
0	32

responses. Many of those responses may be essentially alike, but you may be uncertain about others.

For those responses that are similar — such as "I bought it because my next-door neighbor bought one" and "I bought it because a friend bought one" — you would probably code them alike. The common thread of those responses is that the person bought the product because "someone he knew bought one," and that is how you would categorize or code those responses. But if the response is "I bought one because a neighbor's friend told me they are durable," it would require a different code, depending on the purpose of your research.

If you are going to have open-end questions, you can probably anticipate the general categories of responses you will receive. Even so, you will need to develop a *coding scheme* after you have collected your data and before you begin to code. That means you will have to write instructions and definitions to tell you (and other coders) how to categorize various responses. The instructions must be written so that you and other coders can refer to specific definitions and use the same rules for coding every response.

You will have to look through several returned questionnaires to get a flavor for the kinds of responses you have. You may even want to look at a randomly selected sample of questionnaires. The best procedure is to write a coding scheme, pretest it with a sample of questionnaires, revise the scheme as needed, and then use it on the complete set of questionnaires (including the sample).

... Intercoder Reliability

After you have written a coding scheme, you must test it for reliability. You must demonstrate that several coders, working independently, can read an open-end answer, follow your written coding instructions, and agree on the proper coded response.

It is easy to see how coders will not always agree. There may be inadequate definition of categories, lack of a common frame of reference among the coders,[1] and simple errors. Yet there may also be the appearance of agreement where agreement does not exist, for any of the same reasons. Just as you'd like to avoid accidental disagreement, you would like to avoid accidental agreement.

Of the various methods of testing for coder reliability, one is especially easy to apply and to understand. It is simply the percentage of cases in which the judges were in agreement. Here is how to do it. Assemble the coders and review the coding instructions with them. Have coders work separately to code the same set of questionnaires (20 or 25 or so). You will have to make photocopies of the questionnaires for this purpose or have the coders record their responses on separate sheets of paper. This work must be done without any discussion among the coders.

When the coders finish, look at their coding decisions to see the number and percent of times all agreed (chose the same coded alternative). For example, if you have 20 questionnaires with 10 questions, you have 200 coding decisions to make. If coders agree on 90 percent of the coding decisions, you have a 90 percent coder reliability score, and you'll probably be happy with your coding instructions. You would prefer 100 percent reliability, but that may not be practical in some studies, especially those involving extensive open-end questions.

If your intercoder reliability score is not satisfactory to you, you will need to improve your coding instructions and your training of coders. You can read through the questionnaires you used for the reliability test and talk with coders about their answers. After you have improved the coding instructions, you will need to do another measure of intercoder reliability with a different set of questionnaires.

Even if you have only one coder (such as yourself), you need to do a reliability test. Select a sample of questionnaires and code them. Several days later, go through the same set and code them again. Measure the agreement between your first and second coding.

• • • Coding Multiple Answers

With many questions, you will be coding a respondent's single answer, such as income level or brand awareness. Even a lengthy and detailed answer to an open-end question can be coded as a single response. In other cases, respondents may give you two or more answers, either voluntarily or because your question calls for more than one answer.

For example, you might ask, "What brands come to mind when you think of toothpaste?" That kind of question presents a special problem for coding because computer software for analyzing data will not usually allow you to count more than one answer per variable. A common solution to this problem is to accept only the respondent's first answer, the assumption being that respondents begin with the answer that is most relevant and significant to them. In other words, your variable would be the first brand mentioned. In the toothpaste brand example, respondents' first answers would give you an indication of top-of-mind brand awareness. If you are going to code the first answer given, you must tell interviewers to record answers as accurately as possible and in the order given by respondents.

You could code multiple answers in other ways. In the toothpaste example, you might be interested in knowing how many times each brand was mentioned at all, not just as the first one mentioned. In that case, you would treat each brand as a separate variable and count every time each brand was mentioned. Thus you could report the total number of times Brand A was mentioned (frequency) or the percentage of respondents who mentioned Brand A. You could even do this in a way that would give more weight to a first mention than to a second or third mention. Instead of just recording each incidence a product is mentioned, you could assign a weight of 3 for a first mention, 2 for a second mention, and 1 for a third or later mention.

• • • Tabulating Data

The result of data collection is an enormous quantity of raw data, even for a small study. In their natural state — answers from all respondents for all questions — data don't tell much. Therefore you must put the mass of data into a form that lends itself to analysis, a step called *tabulating the data*. You will want to do this with a statistical analysis program for personal or mainframe computers. It's possible to do it by hand with a small study, but you will be severely limited in the kind of subsequent analysis you can do.

Tabulation is a process of combining raw data into aggregate and manageable form and involves counting all the answers that have already been coded. You will almost certainly find it necessary to construct several tables that reduce your data to manageable form.

Tables consist of several parts: *title*, *identifying number*, *stubs* (labels for the rows) of data), *captions* (labels for the columns of data), *footnotes* (sometimes needed to explain complicated data), and *source reference*. The source reference is not needed when you are reporting your own data. Table 10.3 illustrates typical table organization.

Table 10.3 Consumer Magazines Circulation Price Index

	Average Single Copy Price		Average Yearly Subscription		Consumer Price Index
	Price	Index	Price	Index	
1970	.63	100	7.16	100	100
1977	1.11	176	13.39	187	156
1978	1.21	192	14.86	208	168
1979	1.33	211	16.30	228	187
1980	1.48	235	16.75	234	212
1981	1.62	257	18.06	252	234
1982	1.80	286	20.28	283	249
1983	1.97	313	21.53	301	258
1984	2.07	329	22.61	316	269
1985	2.10	333	23.15	323	279
1986	2.16	343	23.84	333	287
(est.)					

Caption

Row

Column

Stub

Source: J. B. Kobak, in R. Fannin, "Can Publishers Jump the Hurdles?," *Marketing and Media Decisions,* Vol. 21, No. 9 (August 1986), 89. Reprinted by permission.

Source reference

The units of measure — dollars, thousands of dollars, units purchased, percentages, and so on — must be made clear. If you have large numbers (in the thousands or millions), you can drop three zeros from the large numbers and report that data are for thousands. You can also indicate this by placing (000) or '000 in the caption. This reminds the reader to add three zeros to the reported numbers.

When you plan your dummy tables, it is a good idea to think about the titles, captions, rows, and columns for each table you think you might prepare. That precaution can help ensure that you will collect appropriate data.

...Cross-Tabulating the Data

Straight tabulation of data is the starting point of analysis. Relationships become apparent, and you can begin to draw conclusions. Yet simple tabulation may obscure many relationships. Gross numbers or percentages, not broken down into parts and not cross-tabulated, may produce the appearance in the data of tendencies that do not exist. The mirages thus created can lead to inaccurate conclusions.

Take, for example, a situation in which adult males and adult females indicate whether they watch a particular television program. Table 10.4 shows the proportions of respondents watching Program A.

You might initially conclude that in a given advertising campaign, Program A would be a wise media buy. After all, it is very popular among both men and women and would be a good vehicle for advertisements for products that appeal to both men and women.

Further analysis, however, reveals that the audience for Program A is not evenly distributed among members of each gender. Table 10.5 shows that the program is especially popular with younger men in the sample but not so popular with older men. It shows that the program is equally popular with both female age groups. That difference may be important to an advertiser whose product sales are a function of age as well as gender.

When you analyze data, it is important to consider the logic of cross-tabulations. In a study of the patrons of a fast food outlet, researchers found that men made the most purchases, a finding that led to a conclusion that men were more important customers than women. But additional tabulations, in which gender was cross-tabulated with size of purchase, showed that women were more important because they made larger purchases. Further, the cross-tabulation revealed that women who

Table 10.4 Percentage of Male and Female Adults Watching Program A

	Male ($N = 100$)	Female ($N = 100$)
Program A	30%	30%

Table 10.5 Gender and Age Characteristics of Adults Watching Program A

	Male		Female	
	18–34 (N = 50)	35–49 (N = 50)	18–34 (N = 50)	35–49 (N = 50)
Program A	50%	10%	30%	30%

brought their children with them made the largest and most frequent purchases. That finding led to a decision to promote the restaurant with a family and child theme.

Basic Descriptive Statistics

When you analyze your data, you will probably need to employ one or more statistical measures. At a minimum, you will want to use descriptive statistical measures. They help you answer several questions:

1. What is the most common response?
2. What is the range of responses?
3. How widely are the responses scattered?
4. How strongly do the respondents agree?

You should understand how to compute and how to interpret six common descriptive statistical measures:

1. mean
2. standard deviation
3. median
4. mode
5. percentage
6. index

... Mean

The term *average* is commonly and loosely used to refer to a common or typical value in an array of data. It is sometimes termed a *measure of central tendency*. People often equate, sometimes erroneously, the term *average* with an *arithmetic mean*. Strictly speaking, a mean is one type of an average. Others are *median* and *mode*, which are explained in later sections.

Table 10.6 Exposures to Advertisement A

Person	Number of Exposures	
A	3	
B	7	
C	3	
D	5	
E	3	
F	1	
G	2	
H	6	
I	4	
J	4	
Total 10	Sum = 38	Mean = 3.8 exposures (38 ÷ 10)

Table 10.7 Exposures to Advertisement B

Number of Exposures Per Person	Number of Persons	Total Exposures	
1	10	10	
2	8	16	
3	5	15	
4	2	8	
	25	49	Mean = 1.96 exposures (49 ÷ 25)

We find the mean of an array of values by summing the values and dividing the sum by the number of values. Table 10.6 illustrates how a mean is calculated for an array of ten numbers.

Table 10.7 shows how grouped data can be averaged through a weighting process. If you divide the total exposures (49) by the number of persons (25), you will find that the mean is 1.96.

A mean is a simple and very convenient statistic you can use in describing data. Means can be deceptive, however. That is why you should generally try to determine the width of the *range* over which the raw data fall. For example, you might have data indicating that the average frequency of exposure to your advertisement is 8, as shown in Table 10.8.

Table 10.8 Exposures to Advertisement C

Person	Number of Exposures	
A	3	
B	7	
C	9	
D	3	
E	3	
F	11	
G	20	
H	14	
I	2	
J	8	
Total 10	80	Mean = 8 exposures

Table 10.9 Exposures to Advertisement C

Person	Number of Exposures	
A	6	
B	10	
C	6	
D	8	
E	10	
F	7	
G	9	
H	8	
I	7	
J	9	
Total 10	80	Mean = 8 exposures

That mean of 8 may be satisfactory to you; that is, it may *appear* satisfactory. The range, however, runs from 3 to 20. This means that some people are not seeing the ad often enough, and others may be seeing it more often than you think is necessary. The mean of 8 obscures this fact. On the other hand, compare the distribution in Table 10.8 with that in Table 10.9.

In this distribution, the mean is the same—8—yet the range is from only 6 to 10. Exposures are clustered relatively tightly around the mean. If your plan calls for a mean exposure of 8, on the assumption that 8 exposures is an optimum level, this distribution would be more to your liking than the previous one.

. . . Standard Deviation

The desirability of looking at the range of an array of data is obvious. Yet a range can have a major weakness. A single value can throw it off. In the preceding example, if Person J had been exposed to the ad 20 times instead of 9, the range would have increased from 6–10 to 6–20. The range would be wide, but it would not be truly representative of the state of affairs. Therefore, statisticians use more refined statistics, such as the *standard deviation*, to represent the amount of dispersion in a set of data.

We can use the previous example to show how the standard deviation is calculated. If you are doing your own research, you will probably use a computer to tabulate and analyze your data, and computer statistical analysis programs routinely calculate standard deviations. If someone else does your research, you won't need to calculate it either. However, in both situations, you may need to interpret the standard deviation.

In essence, the standard deviation is a measure of the variance or differences of individual values or scores from the mean of a group of values. For example, let's find the standard deviation for the values in Table 10.8, using the calculations in Table 10.10.

Person A had 3 exposures, or 5 below the mean of 8, so A's deviation from the mean is minus 5. We will have both negative and positive numbers, so we will square

Table 10.10 Calculations to Find the Standard Deviation in Table 10.8

Person	Exposures	Mean	Deviations	Squared Deviations	
A	3	8	−5	25	
B	7	8	−1	1	
C	9	8	+1	1	
D	3	8	−5	25	$\frac{302}{10} = 30.2$
E	3	8	−5	25	
F	11	8	+3	9	
G	20	8	+12	144	
H	14	8	+6	36	
I	2	8	−6	36	$\sqrt{30.2} = 5.5$
J	8	8	0	0	
				302	

Table 10.11 Calculations to Find the Standard Deviation for the Values in Table 10.9

Person	Exposures	Mean	Deviations	Squared Deviations	
A	6	8	−2	4	
B	10	8	+2	4	
C	6	8	−2	4	
D	8	8	0	0	$\frac{20}{10} = 2$
E	10	8	+2	4	
F	7	8	−1	1	
G	9	8	+1	1	
H	8	8	0	0	
I	7	8	−1	1	$\sqrt{2} = 1.4$
J	9	8	+1	1	
				20	

the deviations to make them all positive numbers. We continue with the other people in our example, and the sum of the squared deviations is 302. We divide that sum by the number of people to get an average of 30.2. However, that is derived from squared deviations, so we find the square root of 30.2. An electronic calculator with a square-root key gives us the answer: 5.5. That is the standard deviation for our set of values.

For some purposes, especially when you are calculating a standard deviation for a sample and wish to make inferences about the population, you would divide the sum of squared deviations by $N - 1$, where N equals the number of scores in the sample. In our example, we would divide 302 by 9 and get 33.6. The standard deviation (square root of 33.6) would be 5.8.

Table 10.11 shows calculations to derive the standard deviation for the data in Table 10.9. The standard deviation of 1.4 confirms what we already suspected — that the variability of the data in Table 10.9 is much less than that of the data in Table 10.8. So the higher the standard deviation, the greater the spread, or range, of scores.

. . . Median

By definition, the *median* is the midpoint in an array of values arranged from highest to lowest or lowest to highest. Another definition is that the median is the value that divides the array so that half the values are above the median and half are below it. If 23 values are listed in order, then the 12th value is the median. If we have 22 items in the array, the median is the *mean* of Value 11 and Value 12.

The median is somewhat more stable than the mean because extreme values do not affect it. For example, if you added another person with an exposure level of 15 to

Table 10.12 Exposures to Advertisement A

Person	Number of Exposures	
A	3	
B	7	
C	3	
D	5	
E	3	
F	1	
G	2	
H	6	
I	4	
J	4	
K	15	
Total 11	53	Mean = 4.82

the data in Table 10.6 and calculated a mean, that new mean would jump from 3.8 to 4.8, as shown in Table 10.12. That new mean would be somewhat misleading because only one viewer was responsible for the increase.

In contrast, we can calculate the median for the same data and show a more stable average or central tendency. Without Person K, the median would be 3.5, or the mean of the values of 3 and 4. With Person K in the array, the median shifts to only 4. (See Table 10.13.) It makes no difference whether Person K's exposure level is anything above 3. It could be 4, 5, 20, or more, and it would have the same effect on the median.

... Mode

The mode is the value that appears most often in the array of values. In the advertisement exposure example (Table 10.13), 3 exposures is the most commonly occurring level. With interval data, the mode is not always as useful as the mean or median, because it is not necessarily a measure of central tendency. With nominal data, however, the mode can be very useful. In a question about the type of housing the respondent lives in, the response options might be single-family dwelling, duplex, fourplex, apartment. If the preponderance of answers was "apartment," you would have a pretty good idea of at least one dimension of the nature of your sample.

Table 10.13 Exposures to Advertisement A

Person	Number of Exposures	
F	1	
G	2	
A	3	
C	3	
E	3	
J	4	
I	4	
D	5	
H	6	
B	7	
K	15	
Total 11	53	Median = 4

. . . Percentage

A percentage is a convenient statistic that is easy to use and simple to calculate. You divide a number by another number and multiply the result by 100. If 17 persons out of 34 remembered your slogan, you could calculate the recall percentage by dividing the 17 by the 34 and multiplying by 100. The result is 50 percent.

What if 4,300 regular customers responded to your coupon offer and the remaining 72,000 did not. What percentage responded?

$$\begin{array}{r} 4,300 \text{ responded} \\ \underline{72,000 \text{ did not respond}} \\ 76,300 \text{ customers} \end{array}$$

4,300 divided by 76,300 equals .056
Multiply .056 by 100 to get 5.6 percent

The beauty of a percentage is that it provides an easy way to compare two or more sets of data that have unequal numbers of values. The percentage puts sets of data on the same footing. Because we are accustomed to using percentages, we can more quickly and more safely judge the meaning of a 5.6 percent response rate than we can a response rate of 4,300 persons out of a total of 76,300. If you don't agree, answer this: Which is a higher response rate — 283 out of 736, or 748 out of 2,200?

Percentages are also used to describe changes in variables over time or differences between two variables. Consider first how to use percentages to describe changes over time. Suppose a full-page, four-color (P4C) ad in Magazine A cost $80,000 in 1990 and $88,000 in 1991 and that a P4C ad in Magazine B cost $50,000 in 1990 and $58,000 in 1991. Both magazines increased their rates by $8,000, but because their 1986 rates were different, the *percentage increases* were different.

Magazine A
1991 rate	$88,000
1990 rate	80,000
difference	$ 8,000

Divide the difference by the base rate, or the rate that you are *comparing to*.
$8,000 divided by $80,000 equals .10
Multiply by 100: 10 percent increase

Magazine B
1991 rate	$58,000
1990 rate	$50,000
difference	$ 8,000

Divide the difference by the base rate.
$8,000 divided by $50,000 equals .16
Multiply by 100: 16 percent increase

Now let's calculate the difference between the 1991 rates for the two magazines. Consider first how we will state the difference. We could say that Magazine A's rate is _____ percent higher than Magazine B's. Here is what we would do to find that difference.

Magazine A	$88,000
Magazine B	58,000
difference	$30,000

Because Magazine B follows the *than* in the comparison statement, its rate is the base value.

Divide $30,000 by $58,000: .52
Multiply by 100: 52 percent
Magazine A's rate is 52 percent higher than Magazine B's.

Consider another way of stating the difference: Magazine B's rate is _____ percent lower than Magazine A's.
Because Magazine A follows the *than* in the comparison statement, its rate is the base value.

Divide $30,000 by $88,000: .34
Multiply by 100: 34 percent
Magazine B's rate is 34 percent lower than Magazine A's.

It is easy to make mistakes with percentages. In the two previous examples, you could divide by the wrong base number and get an incorrect answer. Consider another situation: An oven cleaner contains 3 percent active ingredient. The manufacturer increases the active ingredient to 4 percent. Is that a 1 percent increase? No, it is a 1-*percentage point* increase. The manufacturer's advertising claimed a 33.3 percent increase, which is correct.

"Don't Know" and "No Answer" Responses

"Don't know" and "no answer" responses are troublesome when you are calculating percentages of responses that fall in various categories. It may appear reasonable to stick to the facts and to include those kinds of responses when you calculate percentages. Or it may seem logical to eliminate such responses from your calculations and base the percentages on only the "real" answers to the question.

Consider the following example, which shows how "no answer" and "don't know" responses can affect tabulated data. In a survey, 400 people were asked whether or not they approved of a public service advertising campaign.

Approve	189
Disapprove	76
Don't Know	103
No Answer	32

The percentage distributions shown in Table 10.14 will vary, depending on whether we include "don't know" and "no answer" questions.

These differences can be very important because by using various approaches, you might conclude that (1) less than half the respondents approved of the public service campaign, (2) approximately half approved, or (3) nearly three-quarters ap-

Table 10.14 Audience Attitudes Toward a Public Service Advertising Campaign

	Percentages Based On		
	Total Sample	All but "No Answer"	Respondents Stating Opinions
Approve	47%	51%	71%
Disapprove	19	21	29
Don't know	26	28	
No answer	8		
	(*n* = 400)	(*n* = 368)	(*n* = 265)

Table 10.15 Percent of Respondents Preferring Brands of Compact Disc Players

Brands Named	Percent of Respondents
"A"	35%
"B"	25
"C"	13
"D"	5
Don't know	22

proved. Selecting different base numbers, as in this example, can result in widely divergent conclusions from a single set of data.

Nonresponses may result for several reasons. These reasons, some of which we list below, are important determinants of whether or not the nonresponses should be included in the calculations.

First, respondents may have no knowledge of the topic. For example, in a survey of brand preference, respondents may not know the names of available brands of compact disc players. In such a study, "don't know" is a very relevant response and should be included. In Table 10.15, the fact that 22 percent of the respondents are unable to specify a brand may indicate that compact disc players are still in the growth stage and are not familiar to many people.

Second, respondents may not have an opinion on the subject being studied. This too may be germane to the study because you will want to know what percentage of respondents have no opinion.

Third, respondents may not want to reveal their positions on the subject. For example, they may not want to admit that a certain television program is their favorite. In this case, "don't know" is an evasive answer. If you suspect that this is the case, you would probably eliminate those responses from the calculations.

Fourth, respondents may not understand the question, such as this one: "Have you, in the past twelve months, taken advantage of a self-liquidating premium offer?" That kind of question is likely to elicit numerous "don't know" answers in a consumer survey. In such a case, the questionnaire is at fault.

. . . Indexes

An index is similar to a percentage because it reduces data to a base with 100 as an average (or expected value). Indexes enable us to compare the sizes of two or more markets, compare one market area to the entire country, compare response rates to different advertising strategies, and compare media delivery. Other applications will become apparent as you work in advertising.

Table 10.16 Adult Purchasing Levels for a Hypothetical Product

Market	Percentage of Adults Buying Product		Index
U.S. total (base figure)	6.0%	6.0 ÷ 6.0(× 100)	100
Adult readers of *Time*	5.8	5.8 ÷ 6.0(× 100)	97
Adult readers of *Playboy*	15.2	15.2 ÷ 6.0(× 100)	253
Adult readers of *Rolling Stone*	14.1	14.1 ÷ 6.0(× 100)	235
Adult readers of *Motor Trend*	4.1	4.1 ÷ 6.0(× 100)	68

An index number relates the value of one number to a base value. The two values may be raw numbers or percentages. To calculate, divide the number by the base value and multiply by 100. (Multiplying by 100 moves the decimal to the right and eliminates it, thus making your tables much simpler to prepare and to read.) Index numbers are whole numbers with a value of at least 1 and a maximum value that is unlimited.

Table 10.16 shows how to calculate index numbers to compare product users among readers of some consumer magazines. It is estimated that 6 percent of all adults use the product; that is the base figure, or the average, so it has an index number of 100. According to the table, 5.8 percent of the adult readers of *Time* magazine purchased the product, somewhat below the national "average" of 6.0.

It is easy to see that readers of *Playboy* and *Rolling Stone* are more likely to have purchased the product than the U.S. average and more than the readers of other magazines. But how much more, in relative terms? If you divide the purchase rate for readers of *Playboy* (15.2 percent) by the national rate (6 percent), the resulting index number is a high one — 253. That means *Playboy* readers are 2½ times more likely to purchase the product than the average U.S. adult. But readers of *Motor Trend* are not nearly as likely, because its index number is only 68.

Because index numbers and percentages appear so similar, they can be confusing. Keep in mind that an index number of 67 is low, whereas a percentage of 67 may be considered high. An index number of 67 for a given market segment means the segment's purchase level is below average. But if 67 percent of the people in the market segment buy the product, a marketer would probably be delighted.

Selecting the Base for an Index Number

To make indexes work, you must be able to determine the base on which to compute the numbers. Table 10.17 shows data for three business magazines. The percentages represent the coverage of each magazine for each of the age categories of professional or managerial persons. For example, *Business Week* reaches 7.2 percent of the professional-managerial persons in the United States, *Forbes* reaches 4.8 per-

Table 10.17 Coverage Estimates of Three Business Magazines

	Business Week	Forbes	Fortune	Average
All prof./managerial	7.2%	4.8%	5.1%	5.7%
18–24	4.0	4.2	4.0	4.1
25–34	7.9	3.8	4.8	5.5
35–44	9.1	5.8	5.7	6.9
45–54	5.0	5.0	4.0	4.7
55–64	6.7	5.3	7.4	6.5
65+	7.3	4.1	4.3	5.2

Averages were calculated by the authors. *Source:* Simmons Market Research Bureau, *1983 Study of Media and Markets.* Used by permission.

cent, and *Fortune* reaches 5.1 percent. The average for the three magazines is 5.7 percent.

The data are not difficult to analyze as they stand, but index numbers will make it easier to compare the coverage of each magazine in the age categories. For example, you could calculate an average coverage for each age category. In the 45–54 category, the magazines have an average coverage of 4.7 percent.

$$5.0 + 5.0 + 4.0 = 14.0$$

$$14.0 \text{ divided by } 3 = 4.7$$

You could then calculate an index number to relate each magazine's coverage of the 45–54 segment to the average of all magazines for that segment. For *Forbes*:

$$5.0 \text{ divided by } 4.7 = 1.06$$

$$\text{Multiply by } 100 = \text{index of } 106$$

Table 10.18 shows index numbers calculated in this manner for all magazines and all age categories. The index numbers compare each magazine's age category coverage to the three-magazine average for each age category.

At first glance, *Forbes'* coverage of the overall professional-managerial market is 84, or somewhat below the average for the three magazines. *Fortune's* coverage index is somewhat higher at 89. In contrast, *Business Week's* coverage is indexed at 26 percent higher than the average.

If you thought *Business Week* was probably the best magazine to use in reaching the professional-managerial market, you might want to construct a different index, one that compares the other magazines' coverage to *Business Week's* coverage instead of to the average. In Table 10.19, the data are rearranged on that basis. The indexes for *Business Week* are set at 100, and the coverage percentages for the other magazines

Table 10.18 Market Coverage Estimates of Three Magazines, Indexed to the Average for Each Age Category

	Business Week	Forbes	Fortune
All prof./managerial	126	84	89
18–24	98	102	98
25–34	144	69	87
35–44	132	84	83
45–54	106	106	85
55–64	103	82	114
65+	140	79	83

Indexes were calculated by the authors. *Source:* Simmons Market Research Bureau, *1983 Study of Media and Markets*. Used by permission.

Table 10.19 Market Coverage Estimates of Three Magazines, Indexed to *Business Week* Coverage

	Business Week	Forbes	Fortune
All prof./managerial	100	67	71
18–24	100	105	100
25–34	100	48	61
35–44	100	64	63
45–54	100	100	80
55–64	100	79	110
65+	100	56	59

Indexes were calculated by the authors. *Source:* Simmons Market Research Bureau, *1983 Study of Media and Markets*. Used by permission.

are compared to *Business Week*'s percentages. You could have used any of the magazines as the base for comparison.

Testing for Significance

In addition to using descriptive statistics to analyze research results, researchers use other kinds of statistical analysis to compare results from two or more groups or to compare results to chance expectations. When researchers compare two or more groups, they want to know if differences in the dependent variable are due to the effect of the experimental variable or to chance occurrences. Researchers might also analyze one group's "scores" on a dependent variable to see if the scores or results are what could be expected to occur merely on the basis of chance—or if they are actually unique. Researchers call these procedures *testing for significance*; they want to see if their results are statistically significant.

Many statistical procedures are available to test for significance, and your choice of an appropriate test depends on the nature of the data and your purposes. This section describes a few basic statistical measures you are likely to use or encounter, and it provides only limited descriptions of the tests. The descriptions assume that you will use computer software programs to analyze your data, so we do not talk about formulas, calculations, or assumptions about the data. Such topics, as well as statistical analysis itself, are the subjects of countless books and courses. Some of the books are cited at the end of this chapter.

. . . Correlation Analysis

A published advertising research report illustrates how correlation analysis can be useful. Reid and Haan hypothesized that television commercials could be pretested by showing viewers just one scene from a storyboard.[2] They believed that the results they would get from showing such "key visuals" would be the same as results they would get from showing the entire commercial or the entire storyboard. If true, this would have practical applications because of the time and money it would save.

The researchers used four groups of subjects to test commercials for eight products. One group saw complete storyboards for all products; one group saw one frame from each storyboard; one group saw complete, finished commercials for all products; and another group saw single frames from the finished commercials. Subjects rated each stimulus on an interest scale of 1 to 100, with 100 being "absolutely interested" in the message and 1 being "absolutely not interested." The researchers calculated means of the interest ratings for each stimulus for each group. The results are summarized in Table 10.20.

Reid and Haan ranked the messages, according to their means, for each group. They noted the correlation—the degree of agreement—of the rankings for each group. They intuitively guessed that their hypothesis was correct: They obtained essentially the same results (same rankings) using key visuals as with using entire storyboards or commercials. (Note how the first four commercials were ranked in the top four among all the groups.)

Intuitive guessing was not enough, however; they also wanted to know the extent to which the correlation they observed might have been due to chance. In other words, they knew that pure luck might have given them the high correlation. Their computer program calculated *correlation coefficients* for them. One coefficient, the *Pearson correlation coefficient* (r), was used because each subject rated each stimulus on a numerical (interval) scale. Another coefficient, the *Spearman rank-order correlation coefficient* (r_s or *rho*), was also used to measure the correlation of the rankings. Such coefficients can vary from 0 to 1.00 and can be either negative or positive.

Table 10.20 Interest Ratings for Commercials: Key Visuals Versus Whole Commercials

Product Advertising	Storyboard				Finished Commercial			
	Key Visual N = 30		Whole Message N = 30		Key Visual N = 30		Whole Message N = 30	
	Mean	Rank	Mean	Rank	Mean	Rank	Mean	Rank
Tuna fish	58	(1)	56	(1)	62	(1)	65	(1)
Instant coffee	53	(2)	52	(2)	50	(2.5)	51	(2)
Breakfast cereal	46	(3)	48	(3)	50	(2.5)	49	(3)
Cookies	37	(4)	35	(4)	33	(4)	35	(4)
Gasoline	32	(5)	33	(5)	28	(6)	28	(7)
Frozen peas	30	(6)	32	(6)	27	(7)	28	(7)
Homeowner's insurance	29	(7)	27	(7)	31	(5)	32	(5)
Laundry detergent	24	(8)	22	(8)	36	(8)	28	(7)

Source: L. Reid, and D. Haan, "'Key Visuals' as Correlates of Interest in TV Ads," *Journalism Quarterly*, Vol. 56, No. 4 (Winter 1979), 865–868.

The agreement of the rankings for storyboard key visuals and storyboard whole messages was perfect (exactly the same order in both rankings), so the Spearman rank-order correlation coefficient was 1.00. The mean scores were also very similar, meaning the subjects' ratings were consistent, and that is reflected in the Pearson correlation coefficient of .99. To what extent could those coefficients have been that high merely by chance? The computer analysis told Reid and Haan that the probability of that happening was less than .001, meaning that it would happen by chance less than one time in a thousand.

It is customary to present correlation coefficients in tabular form, as shown in Table 10.21.

The Spearman rank-order correlation between whole finished spot and storyboard key visual was .88, and the probability of that being due to chance was less than .01, or less than one time in a hundred. Note that we cannot say for certain that the results were not due to chance; we can talk only of the probabilities of that happening. How high can the probabilities be before we are too uncertain to accept the results as being statistically significant (in other words, as being almost certainly not due to chance)? Researchers customarily say that if the probability is greater than .05 (more than five times in a hundred), they will not accept the results as being statistically significant.

So Reid and Haan could say with confidence that their results were statistically significant. More important, they could say with confidence that you probably don't need to show an entire finished commercial in pretests of viewer interest.

Table 10.21 Correlations Between Interest Scores for Various Treatment Stimuli

	Storyboard Whole Message		Finished Spot Whole Message	
	Pearson r	Spearman r	Pearson r	Spearman r
Storyboard key visual	.99[a]	1.00	.95[a]	.88[b]
Finished spot key visual			.99[a]	.97[a]

[a]$p < .001$

[b]$p < .01$

Source: L. Reid and D. Haan, "'Key Visuals' as Correlates of Interest in TV Ads," *Journalism Quarterly*, Vol. 56, No. 4 (Winter 1979), 865–868.

. . . Chi-Square

Another useful statistical test of significance for the association between two variables is chi-square, symbolized X^2. You can easily obtain chi-square measures with many computer programs for statistical analysis. An example of a published advertising research study shows how you can use chi-square.

Sheinkopf, Atkin, and Bowen were interested in the effect of televised political advertising on political party members, so they conducted a mail survey of a group of party leaders and a group of party subordinates.[3] The questionnaire included questions about the perceived usefulness of the televised advertising. For example, one question asked, "How much have you learned about your party's candidate for governor from his TV ads?" Table 10.22 shows the findings.

Table 10.22 is an example of a *contingency table*, which enables researchers to analyze a relationship between two variables, in this case party leadership position and amount learned. The researchers could look at the table and surmise that there was such a relationship: Party subordinates seemed to learn more than party leaders. However, the researchers wanted to do more than just surmise a relationship; they wanted to know the probability of those results being due to chance. The computer calculated the value of chi-square and estimated that the chances were less than one in a thousand that the results were due to chance. The researchers therefore concluded that the relationship between party leadership position and amount learned was statistically significant at the .001 level.

Chi-square analysis is particularly useful when you do not have numerical or interval scale data for your respondents. In this example, respondents answered on an ordinal scale (a lot, a little, or nothing) instead of on an interval scale. If they had responded on an interval scale (such as the number of facts known about the candidate), another kind of statistical test of significance might have been more appropriate.

Table 10.22 Perceived Usefulness of a Candidate's TV Commercials by Party Leaders and Subordinates

Amount Learned	Party Leaders	Subordinates
A lot	13%	32%
A little	45	39
Nothing	36	21
No answer	6	8

Source: K. G. Sheinkopf, C. K. Atkin, and L. Bowen, "How Political Party Workers Respond to Political Advertising," *Journalism Quarterly*, Vol. 50, No. 2 (Summer 1973), 334–339.

Table 10.23 Ratings of Ads and Ad Shapes by Housewives and Students

By Shape		By Group	
Triangle	80.67	Housewives	71.97
Square	74.85	Students	78.27
Circle	69.83		

A mean of 20 would have been most favorable; 140 most unfavorable. *Source:* S. H. Surlin and H. H. Kosak, "The Effect of Graphic Design in Advertising on Reader Ratings," *Journalism Quarterly*, Vol. 52, No. 4 (Winter 1975), 685–691.

. . . Analysis of Variance and *t*-Test

When you have interval scale data and wish to test the significance of differences between mean scores for groups, you should use statistical tests of significance like *analysis of variance* or *t-test*. For example, Surlin and Kosak investigated the effect of illustration design in print ads on recall scores and on evaluation of the ad and the product.[4] The independent variable was the shape of the illustration (circle, square, or triangle), and the dependent variables were recall scores and evaluations of the product and the ad. The product was a hypothetical brand of hand soap, and the test ads were inserted in copies of a real consumer magazine. Interviewers showed the magazine to two kinds of subjects (college students and housewives) and asked them to evaluate the ad and the product on seven-point rating scales. Table 10.23 shows the means.

An examination of the mean scores suggested differences between the shapes and between the two groups. But were the differences statistically significant or due to chance? An analysis of variance (done by the computer) revealed that the differences between design ratings were significant at the .001 level; in other words, chance occurrences would have caused the results less than one time in a thousand. Differences between students' ratings and housewives' ratings were significant at the .008 level, still considered acceptable.

Another statistical test, the *t*-test, was used to test the significance of differences between various pairs of ad designs. The difference between the circular shape (most favorable) and the triangular shape (least favorable) was significant at the .001 level. The difference between the square shape and the triangular shape was significant at the .05 level. However, the difference between the circular shape and the square shape was not statistically significant. The computer calculations said the differences could have been due to chance in more than five out of a hundred times.

Surlin and Kosak could have concluded that the subjects' evaluations of the three shapes were truly different and that the housewives rated all ads more favorably than the students did. However, they could not have concluded with certainty that the circular shape was more favorably rated than the square shape.

● ● ● Summary

A research project does not end with the collection of data, for the data must be processed, analyzed, and presented to decision makers. Advance preparation is essential, particularly the developing of a coding scheme for converting verbal responses to the numerical values needed for statistical analysis.

You should present data in tabular format to maximize comprehension. Descriptive statistical measures — mean, standard deviation, median, and mode — are useful ways to describe research results. Percentages and indexes are useful for making comparisons. You can use tests of statistical significance — such as correlation coefficients, chi-square, analysis of variance, and *t*-tests — to determine if observed differences are true differences or due to chance.

● ● ● Self-Test Questions

1. Assume that you ask respondents the following open-end question in a survey for The Energy Store: "What energy-saving purchases are you thinking about for the next six months?" Try to anticipate the variety of answers you might get. Develop a preliminary coding scheme for the anticipated responses, including numerical values for each possible response.
2. You probably will not be able to anticipate all possible answers to the open-end question, so how will you code the answers you do not plan for?
3. The open-end question is likely to produce more than one answer from some respondents. What will you do in those cases?
4. Develop a dummy table for the responses you anticipate for the question about planned purchases. Include a title, stubs, captions, rows, and columns.

5. If your survey includes both homeowners and renters, how would you cross-tabulate the data? Create a dummy table to show possible cross-tabulations.
6. Distinguish between a mean and a median and tell when each may be more appropriate.
7. Distinguish between a percentage and an index.
8. Distinguish between a Pearson correlation coefficient and a Spearman correlation coefficient. When is each more appropriate?
9. Assume that the following table resulted from your question about energy-saving purchases. In your own words, summarize what the data show. What test(s) of significance would be appropriate here?

| | Plan Energy-Saving Purchase? | | |
Own or Rent Home?	Yes	No	Totals
Own	120	60	180
Rent	20	80	100
Totals	140	140	280

Notes

1. G. H. Stempel, III, "Content Analysis," in G. H. Stempel, III, and B. H. Westley, *Research Methods in Mass Communication*, 2nd ed. (Englewood Cliffs, N.J.: Prentice-Hall, 1989), 132.
2. L. Reid and D. Haan, "'Key Visuals' as Correlates of Interest in TV Ads," *Journalism Quarterly*, Vol. 56, No. 4 (Winter 1979), 865–868.
3. K. G. Sheinkopf, C. K. Atkin, and L. Bowen, "How Political Party Workers Respond to Political Advertising," *Journalism Quarterly*, Vol. 50, No. 2 (Summer 1973), 334–339.
4. S. H. Surlin and H. H. Kosak, "The Effect of Graphic Design in Advertising on Reader Ratings," *Journalism Quarterly*, Vol. 52, No. 4 (Winter 1975), 685–691.

Suggestions for Additional Reading

Campbell, S. K. *Flaws and Fallacies in Statistical Thinking*. Englewood Cliffs, N.J.: Prentice-Hall, 1974.
Ernst, S. B. "Data Tabulation: The Fine Art of Pigeon Holing." In A. D. Fletcher and D. W. Jugenheimer (eds.). *Problems and Practices in Advertising Research*. Columbus, Ohio: Grid, 1982.
Freund, J. E., and F. J. Williams. *Elementary Business Statistics*. Englewood Cliffs, N.J.: Prentice-Hall, 1972.

Glover, D. R. "Getting the Most out of the Data." In Fletcher and Jugenheimer, 1982.

Hall, R. W. *Media Math: Basic Techniques of Media Evaluation*. Lincolnwood, Ill.: NTC Business Books, 1987.

Huff, D. *How to Lie with Statistics*. New York: Norton, 1954.

Keller, G., and others. *Statistics for Management and Economics*. Belmont, Calif.: Wadsworth, 1988.

Key, V. O., Jr. *A Primer of Statistics for Political Scientists*. New York: Macmillan, 1966.

Meyer, P. *The Newspaper Survival Book: An Editor's Guide to Marketing Research*. Bloomington, Ind.: Indiana University Press, 1985.

Siegel, S. *Nonparametric Statistics for the Behavioral Sciences*. New York: McGraw-Hill, 1956.

Stempel, G. H., III, and B. H. Westley. *Research Methods in Mass Communication*. 2nd ed. Englewood Cliffs, N.J.: Prentice-Hall, 1989.

Williams, F. *Reasoning with Statistics: Simplified Examples in Communication Research*. New York: Holt, Rinehart & Winston, 1968.

CHAPTER 11

Writing the Research Report

● ● ● ● ● ● ● ● ●

It is not uncommon for university students to complain that some of the articles they are assigned to read in academic journals are so poorly written that they are difficult to understand. Although good academic writing is precise and meticulous, on occasion it lapses into a style that is pedantic and not very readable.

But in the business of advertising research there is no room for such lack of consideration for the reader. The research report must clearly express the intent of the writer. Clumsy writing, ostentatious phrasing, and poor organization have no place in a research report. Although the typical report may not represent literary excellence, it should serve the specialized needs of its readers. It should contain a description and analysis of a problem, couched in accurate, unembellished, concise language. Unfortunately, not all business writing meets these standards.

Central to effective writing is knowledge of the purpose of such a report. It contrasts with the research itself, for while the research may be relatively complicated, the reporting of it must be as simple as possible. Communication of conclusions is a report's ultimate purpose, a purpose that cannot be fulfilled if its readers cannot easily understand it.

Is the report's purpose to sell an idea? Maybe not, because someone other than the researcher will normally make the advertising decisions based on the study. An author may draw some conclusions about the needed decisions but should only recommend useful alternatives. The researcher's purpose is to find and interpret facts and to relate those findings to the advertising problem.

• • • A Frame of Mind for Writing

Effective writing requires a specific frame of reference. As in any kind of communication, you must recognize your audience and its abilities. For some readers, you would assume very little; your writing would be designed to be read by people who know very little about research.

If your audience consists of moderately or highly sophisticated readers, you can exercise judgment and assume that your readers understand basic research techniques. Thus you can include somewhat more technical detail, at least in an appendix, no matter what the level of the audience. The point is that even the best research will not be used if your reader can't understand it quickly.

• • • Terminology: How to Handle It

Terminology can be a problem. You may be tempted to throw in technical terms without thinking of the audience. Resist this temptation, however, because excessive use of technical terminology does not result in readable writing.

You can express much research terminology in simple language. If a given term must be used several times in a report, the best practice is to explain it the first time, possibly in a parenthetical statement, just as a journalist defines an unusual term or abbreviation the first time it appears in a newspaper story: "Today the Federal Communications Commission (FCC) issued the first in a series . . ." The complete name of the commission having been established, the writer can then use "FCC" for the sake of brevity.

• • • Sentence Structure and Length

If you look at business reports of various types — research reports, advertising plans, public relations plans — you'll find at least one characteristic in common. The better ones are usually written simply. Sentences are short and uncomplicated.

A business report is not like an academic term paper that you might write in a sociology or psychology course. It's not written for a professor who may be as oriented toward learned-looking form and learned phraseology as toward high-quality content. The research writer is interested in form and phraseology only as they contribute to effective communication.

The Art of Writing Readable Reports

One Writer's Recommendations

1. Present tense works best. Results and observations expressed in *now* terms sound better and are easier to read.

   Don't say: "The test panel liked the taste of the juice."

   Say: "People like the taste of the juice."

2. Use active voice. Passive voice doesn't swing. Passive voice is stilted.

   There is nothing wrong with saying: "We believe . . ." rather than: "It is believed that . . ."

3. Findings, findings. Don't use the word *findings*. This word makes your report sound as if some archeologist just came across some old bones from the paleolithic stage. Or a pigeon just walked across your report.

   Jonas Salk uses Findings. And Findings was okay for Louis Pasteur. But marketers should use Results, Conclusions, or Observations.

4. Use informative headlines, not label headlines. "Convenience is the packaging's major benefit" is better than "Analysis of packaging."

   Follow newspaper headline editors and magazine editors. They know how to get readers with informative headlines.

5. Let your tables and charts work. Help them with words when necessary.

   Don't take a paragraph or a page to describe what a table already says.

   Purpose of a table or chart is to simplify.

   Use words to point out significant items in the table — something that is not readily clear.

6. Make liberal use of verbatims. Great nuggets of wisdom come from people's comments. Use verbatims if you have them.

   Bulova Accutron was born from verbatims.

   So was man-size Kleenex, the Lady Parker pen, Libby's bite-size fruit, United's Friendly Skies. They did not come from tables.

7. People who think research reports are readable, interesting, rewarding, and useful usually ask for more research.

Adapted from Howard Gordon, "Some Things I Have Learned About Producing Research Reports," in Alan D. Fletcher and Donald W. Jugenheimer, *Problems and Practices in Advertising Research* (Columbus, Ohio: Grid, 1982), 189–191.

● ● ●

To analyze your writing, you might try using Robert Gunning's "Fog Index," a readability formula. The formula, which has found its way into numerous textbooks and other places, was developed as a way to estimate the probable readability of written communication. With it, you can detect the level of difficulty readers will encounter with a given piece of writing.

Specifically, a Fog Index tells you the equivalent grade levels on which various types of material are written. Whereas a *Ladies Home Journal* article may be written on the sixth through eighth grade level, an article in *Time* is written on the eighth or ninth grade level, and a *New Yorker* article is written on the twelfth grade level.

To use Gunning's Fog Index, you follow this procedure:

1. Select a sample of at least 100 words. To analyze a research report, select several samples from throughout the report to test the degree of consistency of your writing.
2. Compute the average number of words per sentence. In compound sentences, treat independent clauses as separate sentences. "In school we studied; we learned; we improved" would count as three sentences.
3. Determine the percentage of hard words in the sample. Words of three or more syllables are considered hard words, with these exceptions: words that are capitalized; words made up of shorter words, such as *lawnmower* or *typewriter*; or verbs made into three syllables by the addition of *es* or *ed*, such as *transposes* or *repeated*.
4. Add the average number of words per sentence and the number of difficult words per hundred and multiply by .4. The figure that results is the Fog Index and indicates the minimum grade at which the material should be easily read.[1]

What is the significance of a high score? Although you may be impressed if your writing is measured as being at the twelfth grade level or above, such writing may not be appropriate for your purpose. You may need to reduce the writing level to make it more acceptable to the audience.

If your writing is measured as being at the eighth, ninth, or tenth grade level, you are probably on target for most audiences. By writing at that level, you need not talk down to your audience; instead, your writing will probably enable you to communicate more effectively than if you wrote at a higher level. As one observer noted, "One simplifies one's writing not because one's audience has a fourth grade education but because clear thinking is expressed by clear writing and the clearest writing is often the simplest."[2]

Another useful formula is the Flesch Readability Score. It is calculated on the basis of sentence length and the number of syllables per word. Using the Flesch formula is similar to using the Fog Index. With it, you select a passage of at least 100 words. You then calculate average number of words per sentence and average number of syllables per word. Multiply the sentence length by 1.015 and the average number of syllables per word by 84.6. Then add the two figures and subtract from 206.835. Finally, find the score in the Flesch readability table, shown in Table 11.1.

• • • Using an Outline

By now you have your own writing style. You have your own procedure for putting on paper your thoughts about a topic and your analysis of a situation. In writing

Table 11.1 Flesch Readability Table

Score	Readability	Grade Level
90–100	very easy	5
80–90	easy	6
70–80	fairly easy	7
60–70	plain English	8–9
50–60	fairly difficult	10–12
30–50	difficult	college
0–30	very difficult	college graduate

Source: Rudolph Flesch, *How to Write Plain English* (New York: Harper & Row, 1979), 25–26.

term papers, you may begin with rough notes on a legal pad. Or you may write your paper straight into the typewriter or word processor, making up the logical flow as you write. Another alternative is to use a formal outline.

There are good reasons for using a formal outline in writing a research report for your client. Advance thinking will help you write a well-ordered report. With a formal outline, you will have a logical arrangement of the parts of the report, an order that flows smoothly from beginning to end. You have followed meticulous procedures in designing the research project and in carrying it out, and your report should reflect that meticulousness. Your report should have the high degree of order that characterizes the project itself. Another important benefit is that your report is likely to be more concise.

Elements of a Research Report

As you might expect, not all research reports have identical elements or follow the same order. You must tailor your writing style and plan of organization to the project you are working on.

I. Introductory Material

    A. Letter of transmittal. If your study was done for a client, you'll need a short formal letter identifying the study and making clear that you or your firm performed the work.

    B. Title page.

C. Table of contents. The amount of detail will vary. In a long report the table of contents normally will display only the major sections or chapters. In a short report you'll probably include somewhat smaller divisions of the study. The table of contents is not an index, however; avoid trying to include every minor heading and subhead.

D. Executive summary. Especially in long reports, a preliminary summary can be useful in communicating the study's basic findings. Along with each individual finding you cite in this summary, you should include some sort of reference, such as "For additional information, see page 17" or "Details, page 8."

II. The Main Body of the Report

A. Purpose. Here you'll succinctly describe the reason the study was conducted. There's usually no need for detail; write only enough to position the study and explain its existence.

B. Methodology. In this section you should describe the approach — survey, experiment, observation — and the sampling procedure. If you used a questionnaire, it may fit here. If the questionnaire is long, it may be more appropriate in an appendix.

C. Findings. To many readers, this is the most important section. Obviously it is the section upon which decisions will eventually be made. In it, you should detail the findings one by one.

D. Summary. A summary should be more than merely a means of ending a report. It is your way of emphasizing the findings you believe are most significant. Depending upon the nature of your task, it is also the appropriate section in which to include your recommendations for action.

III. Other Material

A. Bibliography. If your advertising research project relates to or is partially based on previous research, you should include a complete listing of those materials. Don't forget that your study may be recurring, and you may need to refer again to earlier studies. And similar studies that you might later conduct may also be made easier (and remember *cheaper*) if you have ready access to valuable secondary sources.

B. Appendix. As noted above, a long questionnaire may be appropriate in an appendix. You should include technical details of sampling procedures, statistical techniques, and other materials supplementary to your main report. Be careful, however, not to include material that you specifically want to be read, because readers don't always give appendixes much attention.

It's clear, and experience has shown, that communicating effectively is an art. There's repetition in a research report; for example, you have the executive summary, then the detailed findings, then the summary. Remember the story of the old rural preacher? "First you tell 'em what you're going to tell 'em; then you tell 'em; then you tell 'em what you told 'em."

Using Visuals Effectively

Visuals—slides, posters, charts, graphs, maps—can make a boring oral presentation into a stimulating, even exciting, experience. They do so because they help communicate material that is inherently uninteresting even to the person who should be interested.

> Just like a clear piece of writing, a good data graph strives for transparency. Instead of calling attention to itself, it focuses the viewer's attention on the meaning of the data. A well-designed graph can help you understand a complex situation, then present your conclusions with precision and impact.[3]

If a table or graph will help you communicate important parts of your findings, use it. In some reports you may need numerous tables and charts. And additional graphic material may find its way into your report. The purpose of the written report is to communicate. Visuals are important.

You must keep several factors in mind. The graphic normally should be as simple and easy to understand as possible. Your layout should make good use of white space; it should have breathing room. A graphic that requires nearly an entire page should be placed on a page by itself. You should place each graphic immediately adjacent to the first paragraph in which reference is made to it. Try to cite specifically each graphic by writing ". . . as shown in Figure 1" or some similar phrase.

You should clearly identify visual material with a descriptive title. Because styles differ, you may prefer to put titles of tables at the top or at the bottom. With illustrations, the title should go at the bottom. Don't overlook listing the source of the data if they are derived from secondary materials.

. . . Tables

The most commonly used visual aids, which aren't necessarily very "visual," tables can help simplify complex findings. Typically tables in a final report are based on the tabulations of raw data, discussed in Chapter 10. Sometimes they represent statistical procedures that were performed on the raw data.

In the final report, you must display the data as simply and clearly as possible. Unlike the initial tabulations, these tables are meant to be seen and read by persons who may be unfamiliar with any of the data.

. . . Graphs

Several graphing techniques are used for various purposes. You can use a *line graph* to demonstrate changes over time, although it is also used for other purposes.

The time period is shown on the horizontal axis, and the value being tracked is shown on the vertical axis. The reason is that the eye naturally follows the left to right patterns.

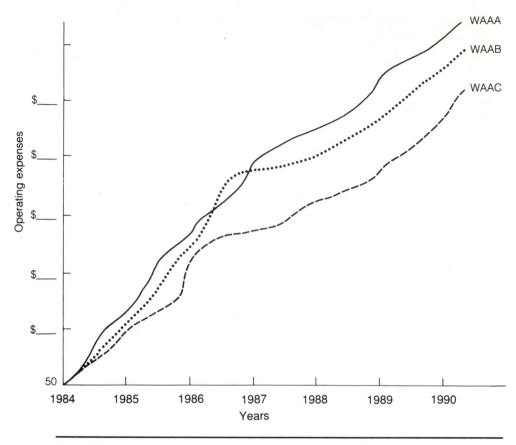

Figure 11.1 Increases in operating expenses of three hypothetical television stations.

You must clearly identify the two axes and give the scale. The time may be shown in days, weeks, months, or years. The other axis may show the rate of purchasing, awareness scores, or any other variable being measured. An example is shown in Figure 11.1.

It may be desirable to show more than one trend in a line graph, as demonstrated in Figure 11.2.

You can use a *bar chart* to compare values with one another, and, like the line graph, it can show changes over time. You can arrange it vertically or horizontally.

Bar charts come in several varieties. A bar chart may be simple, as shown in Figure 11.3. For many purposes, the bar graph is a dramatic way of displaying data because the reader can see some of the differences at a glance. The data are generally included within the bar graph for the sake of precision.

Or a bar chart may illustrate more than one variable, as shown in Figure 11.4. This is a *stacked bar chart*.

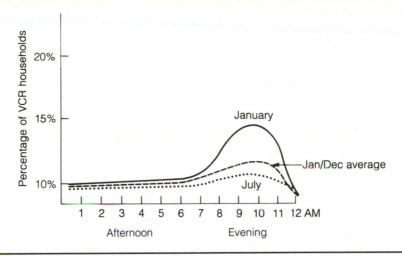

Figure 11.2 Hypothetical percentage of households using a VCR to tape programs throughout the viewing schedule. This example shows more than one trend.

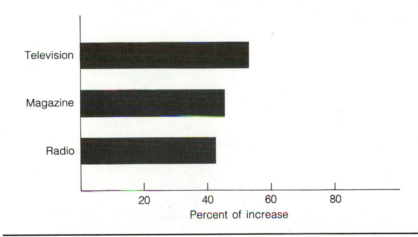

Figure 11.3 Hypothetical advertising cost increases of various media (1990–1995).

With a *pie chart* you can instantly illustrate percentage differences within a set of data. As a rule of thumb, you should use a pie chart only when you have three or more breaks in the data. If you have only two breaks, you needn't use the space for the chart; in that situation you could just as quickly show the data in text form. The visual characteristics of a pie chart give it eye appeal.

Pie charts are visually pleasing, and they lend themselves well to presentations. But because converting percentages to degrees (the 360 degrees found in every circle) is troublesome to some persons, you are smart to use a computer program to convert your data into a pie chart.

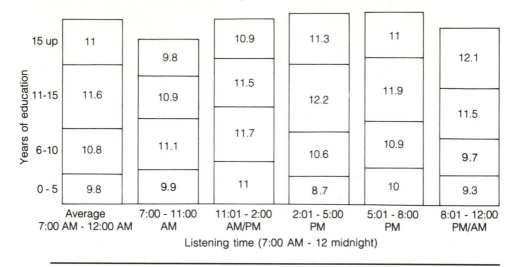

Figure 11.4 Early morning to late evening listening time for hypothetical radio station WAAA. This bar chart illustrates the measurement of two variables — listening time and years of education.

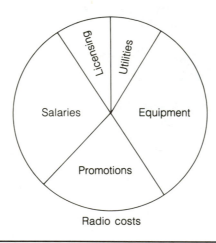

Figure 11.5 A simple pie chart illustrating the distribution of costs for hypothetical radio station WAAA.

To make a pie chart work best for you, consider exploding a key slice — that is, moving the key slice out from the circle by a fraction of an inch, to place emphasis on it. You can use different colors for the slices or different crosshatchings, as provided by your computer program. See Figure 11.5.

Although *pictograms* are popular in some consumer magazines and other publications, you should use them carefully in research reports. With a pictogram you can very easily mislead your reader. Even if you are careful to state the scale, the graphic component can be so overwhelming that the pictogram may suggest incorrect infor-

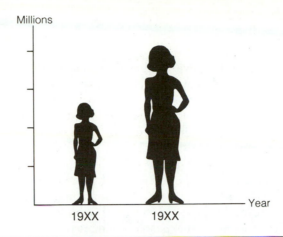

Figure 11.6 Women in the workforce.

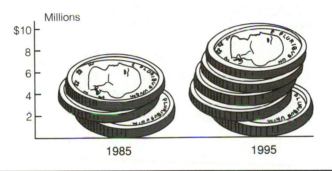

Figure 11.7 Revenue of hypothetical television station WAAA, 1985, 1995 (est.).

mation. Such is true if the width of a symbol increases along with its height. The height of the symbol is its measure, yet the increased width adds confusion, as shown in Figure 11.6.

A better application of the pictogram is shown in Figure 11.7, in which the width of the character does not vary with its height.

...Other Techniques

You can also use sketches, diagrams, maps, flowcharts, and photographs to illustrate relationships and explain data. If you can make your reporting task easier by using these graphic aids, you should use them. Just be careful that each one has a valid application in your report and that each says what you think it says. Ask yourself whether you would understand the graphic if you were unfamiliar with the basic problem. The people to whom you submit the report will not likely have exactly the same perspective as you; after all, they haven't spent the last few weeks working on the problem.

Summary

A common complaint that advertising managers make is that their new trainees and other young employees do not know how to express themselves on paper. The observation is a serious condemnation of the basic qualifications of young employees.

The inability to write may not be real in itself; instead, it may be a symptom of some other problem: carelessness. In some college programs where strict spelling and grammar policies constitute part of the grading system, students suddenly begin using proper spelling and grammar. Perhaps the apparent inability to write is similar to the supposed inability to spell. Being careful is one of the most important ingredients in writing effectively. Becoming an *author*, with all the ramifications of that word, is not important; the advertising business doesn't need "authors" in the research department. It does, however, need capable people willing to put forth the effort to communicate effectively.

Self-Test Questions

1. How might you use Gunning's Fog Index or a similar technique to analyze your writing? What kind of score would please you?
2. Write a letter of transmittal that might accompany your report to The Energy Store.

Notes

1. Drawn from Robert Gunning, *The Technique of Clear Writing*, rev. ed. (New York: McGraw-Hill, 1968), used with written permission of the author and copyright owner. Fog Index is a service mark of Gunning-Mueller Clear Writing Institute, Santa Barbara, California.
2. Memorandum from Richard Tino, Department of Journalism/Communication, University of Bridgeport, Bridgeport, Conn., August 3, 1981.
3. Richard Scoville, "Ten Graphs (and How to Use Them)," *PC World*, September 1988, p. 216.

Suggestions for Additional Reading

Flesch, R. *How to Write Plain English*. New York: Harper & Row, 1979.
Lesikar, R. *Report Writing for Business*. 7th ed. Homewood, Ill.: Irwin, 1986.
Lewis, P. V., and W. H. Baker. *Business Report Writing*. 2nd ed. Columbus, Ohio: Grid, 1983.

PART THREE

Syndicated Research Sources

Our purpose so far has been to describe the process of advertising research, to help you understand research procedures, and to show you how to conduct limited research studies.

In addition to conducting and interpreting their own research, advertising practitioners commonly use research conducted by other companies. Customized research is done for one company, and the results are usually not available to other companies. Syndicated research, in comparison, is done by research organizations that sell the results to many advertisers and agencies.

Just as advertising practitioners should understand how to conduct their own research, they should understand the procedures that research syndicators use. This is particularly important because of the limitations of syndicated research, limitations brought about because of the desire to cut the time and cost of research.

In this part of the book, we describe the major sources of syndicated advertising research, based on material supplied by the research organizations themselves. Chapter 12 explains the important limitations of the research and shows how to evaluate the results. Chapters 13 and 14 describe major sources of syndicated message research, and Chapters 15 and 16 describe audience research companies. Chapter 17 describes companies that supply data about competitors' media expenditures. ■

Syndicated Research

In his proposal that advertising agency research departments be eliminated, Edward Tauber emphasized that he was making a recommendation rather than a prediction: "I believe agencies would be wise to eliminate their research department."[1] He wrote that agency research departments are expensive and not needed by clients. He claimed that current advertising agency research departments are not providing much new thinking. But he added that some agencies would probably continue operating as they have in the past.

Tauber pointed out that during the 1980s, research suppliers and consultants were providing the real leadership in research. He noted a brain drain in which the most notable researchers were leaving agencies to open their own research firms.

The shift did not have to lead to total abdication of the research function, wrote Tauber. He suggested that agencies have four key research personnel, each a specialist. They would provide counsel to their agency rather than conduct the research themselves. In Tauber's scheme, there would be a Director of Advertising Development, who would provide general data on trends and markets. Next would be the Director of Advertising Effectiveness, who would help develop copy and media strategies, using the best data sources available. The Director of Research Methods would be the resident expert on the technology of research. Finally, the Director of Promotion Research would become an expert on research in direct marketing.

The need for outside suppliers of research continues to grow, whether that need is being met by advertising agencies or by research companies. "Client research staffs are disappearing in some cases or becoming smaller in others, often consisting of a single person having other responsibilities and who may consequently function largely as a purchasing agent."[2]

As emphasis on all types of research increases, research firms have the opportunity to provide a service that increasingly requires well-trained specialists. They are organized to handle questions that are too large and costly for a client company or its advertising agency to cope with using personnel who are limited in number and who lack specialized training.

These research firms conduct a variety of types of research, many of which have been discussed in earlier chapters. These firms' research products can be categorized by the degree to which they are designed to meet the unique needs of advertisers paying for the service.

Some of the research firms conduct what is called *customized* research. Customized research is designed for a specific client and is conducted at the direction of that client. Because the results of those studies are given only to that client and not to the public or to competitors, they are known also as *proprietary* research.

Other research firms conduct *syndicated* research for clients. They conduct the research on a regular and recurring basis and sell the results to as many clients as need the information and are willing to pay for it. The Nielsen television ratings are a well-known example of syndicated research.

Although there are important weaknesses inherent in some syndicated research and the way it is used, syndicated research is very important in the advertising decision-making process.

Most syndicated research falls into three categories: message research, media audience research, and competitive media activity research. The following five chapters, which discuss these three categories, are not intended to provide comprehensive coverage of companies supplying syndicated research services and data. Many other companies exist, and the turnover is great. We have tried, however, to include widely used companies that provide data useful to most companies and their agencies. Inclusion in this book does not represent the authors' approval, and exclusion does not represent the authors' disapproval.

General Problems with Syndicated Research

General criticisms of applied research on message effects, audience media usage, and competitive activity center on validity and reliability. Because syndicated studies are conducted for use by hundreds of clients, they cannot be tailored specifically for individual clients. What results is the search for the "best" measure that can satisfy as many clients as possible.

A wide range of empirical questions remains unanswered. These questions involve the influence of the method of exposure, of the media environment, and of differences related to single versus multiple exposures to an ad. There is also a need to understand the degree to which the obtrusiveness of a measure influences its resulting score. The problem of measuring campaign effects, as opposed to the effects of a single execution, has received rather little attention. Finally, the relationships between measures obtained at the individual level versus the aggregate level have not been specified.[3]

Problems with Syndicated Message Research

Much message research is concerned with what consumers remember about the advertising messages they have seen. Consumers are asked about their recall of advertising slogans, of specific advertisements, or of specific selling points in advertisements. The research is based on the assumption that advertising cannot influence purchase decisions unless it is remembered. It further assumes that an advertisement's memorability is an indication of its effect on sales. According to the assumption, if Advertisement A is remembered by more people than Advertisement B, then Advertisement A will generate more sales than Advertisement B. Similarly, advertisements that are pretested and fail to achieve a certain level of memorability will probably not be used.

These assumptions are not entirely valid, however, and users of message research should avoid applying such a scorecard analysis to the results of message research. You should consider at least two factors when using message research: problems of memory and the lack of evidence of a relationship between memory and purchase decisions.

Problems of Memory

When we talk about message effects, we are talking about phenomena that occur inside consumers' heads. We cannot see the phenomena and usually do not observe their immediate and direct consequences. We must rely on consumers to tell us, and that means we must rely on consumers' memories. Unfortunately, those memories are less than completely reliable. As Lucas and Britt warn:

> . . .numerous experiments over the years by psychologists have demonstrated that most of us rapidly forget (do not remember); that the speed of forgetting (not remembering) rapidly accelerates; and that different measurement scores are obtained, depending upon whether we measure by the recognition method or by the recall method.[4]

Recognition and recall methods are used to measure memory of advertising. In the *recognition method*, respondents are shown an advertisement and are asked whether they remember seeing (recognize) the advertisement when they read the publication in which the advertisement appeared. Most recognition studies are limited to people who say they read the issue of the publication in which the advertisement appeared. In the *recall method*, respondents are asked what they remember about an advertisement, but they are not shown the advertisement. Researchers frequently use aided recall — they prod respondents' memories by suggesting a product category. In true, or unaided, recall, respondents are not given any hints and are merely asked to name the advertising they can remember from a particular publication or program.

Lucas and Britt say that memory tests are based on *noting* the advertisement when it was first seen and *remembering* it when the interviewer asks. Unfortunately for the researcher or user of such data, it is impossible to distinguish between the noting and the remembering at the time of the test. Furthermore, according to Lucas and Britt, recognition and recall scores are affected by both message factors (size, placement, color, and illustration) and nonmessage factors (exposure to other advertising, need for the product, interest in the product, and similarity of advertising for like products).[5]

To check the validity of recognition and recall measures, researchers can insert dummy advertisements into magazines or suggest product categories not advertised on the program in question. Some respondents will invariably claim that they recognize or recall the advertisement even though it was impossible for them to have done so. Lucas and Britt cite several reasons for such errors:

1. Genuine confusion with other advertising
2. Guessing when uncertain
3. Deliberate exaggeration
4. Deduction that the advertisement was seen, based on recognition of surrounding material
5. Deduction of likely noting, based on memory or knowledge of one's own reading or viewing habits
6. Eagerness to please the interviewer
7. Hesitation to appear ignorant
8. Misunderstanding of instructions given by the interviewer
9. Guessing based on general familiarity with, or interest in, the advertised product or service
10. Tendency to rate or not rate advertisements on the basis that they look like advertisements that the respondents think they would have noticed.[6]

... Memory, Liking, and Purchasing

Tests that measure the memorability of advertisements, or the degree to which audience members actually like the ads, rely on surrogate measures rather than on the measures of desired outcomes, such as attitude change or purchasing. These tests are used with the assumption that advertising cannot affect purchase decisions if consumers cannot remember the advertising or do not like it.

The assumption is not entirely without support. A study of television commercials by the Ogilvy Center for Research & Development showed that people ". . . who like commercials are more likely to be persuaded by them."[7] And by using humor, attractive illustrations, and other pleasing devices, advertisers daily demonstrate their belief that there is some relationship between a pleasant ad and the desired result.

That explanation may have some merit for ads that are designed to be attractive and pleasing, but it appears not to apply to the shouting, intrusive advertisements that may reflect an advertiser's desire for memorability at any cost.

Unfortunately for proponents of memory-based tests, many studies that have tried to examine the relationship between memory of advertising and subsequent purchase decisions have failed to provide support for that basic assumption. Haskins reviewed twenty-eight studies of the relationship between memory and purchase and between memory and attitude change, and he reached this conclusion: "Learning and recall of factual information from mass communications does occur. However, recall and retention measures seem, at best, irrelevant to the ultimate effects desired, the changing of attitudes and behavior."[8]

• • • The Copy-Testing Controversy

One of the advertising industry's enduring issues is the role of research in the creative process. It pits agency creative personnel against agency researchers and clients, and the debate has threatened to undermine the credibility of message research and advertising research in general. Advertising researchers have devised numerous ways of testing messages — broadcast and print — and all have come under attack.

In an American Marketing Association–sponsored panel discussion of research, John Doig characterized the intensity of the differences between the creative people and the research department. "I have yet to hear a creative team come in and say, 'We've got a terrific idea here; let's take it to the researchers and see how they can improve it.' The battle will be over the day that happens."[9]

The debate has become more strident in recent years because of the increasing costs of advertising, and most of the controversy has been about testing television commercials. More and more, advertisers who spend millions of dollars on advertising are reluctant to risk their money without assurance that the advertising will be effective. These advertisers insist that their agencies test commercials before they are produced and aired. For economy reasons, most commercials that are pretested are tested in rough, unfinished form. This is so because testable unfinished commercials can be made at considerably lower cost than finished commercials.[10]

Clients often specify the research methodology and the syndicated researcher they want used to test their advertising. Most clients also insist on quantification — scores or numbers that indicate the performance of the advertising message. Agency creative people take offense at the idea that their messages can be reduced to numbers. In addition to the scorecard mentality, they also object to the practice of using the numbers in a "go or no-go" fashion. That refers to the practice of accepting or rejecting a proposed commercial instead of trying to find out why it got the response it got.

Some creative people believe that traditional copy-testing methods penalize emotional or soft-sell commercials more than hard-sell commercials that attempt to drive home the brand name by repetition.[11] Such critics often cite the case of Quaker Oats' famous "Mikey" commercial, which was produced and aired without being tested. After the commercial received wide acclaim, it was tested for recall. The result:

a lower-than-average score. If the commercial had been pretested, it might not have aired.[12] Critics of copy testing also cite examples of how some commercials that had low recall scores in pretests have proved to be winners as far as brand sales were concerned. On the other hand, some commercials that pretested well have been real losers at the cash register.[13]

It is also alleged that the perceived threat of copy testing leads some copywriters to make commercials deliberately loud and grating so the commercials will receive high test scores.[14]

Pretesting of television commercials is criticized on two other grounds. One, pretesting a commercial with one exposure is not realistic, because it does not account for the role of repetition in a commercial's eventual effectiveness.[15] Two, the recall score of a commercial probably depends on the program environment in which it is placed and the level of audience involvement in the program. Some evidence has shown that commercials placed in blockbuster movies usually have higher recall scores than the same commercials placed in other shows.[16]

Fortunately there seems to be a lessening of the traditional antagonism between researchers and creative people. Many work more closely together from the beginning of campaign planning, and both sides develop a better appreciation of what the other is doing. In addition, both sides are more willing to accept the idea that research is only a part of the process of evaluating advertising. Greater attention is being paid to how research data are interpreted and applied.[17] Or as one creative director sums it up:

> Research is one of advertising's finest tools, but like any tool, you have to know how to use it. . . . Research does not come up with ideas. You come up with the ideas. Research can help you to assess and strengthen them. Research is a dirty word only when misused and abused. Properly used, research is good clean words like "share of market," "brand leader," "competitive edge," and "sales."[18]

... Other Problems

Other characteristics of message research should be considered. One is the problem of nonrepresentative samples. Because of cost and interviewer convenience, personal interview studies are sometimes limited to urban and suburban areas. Some studies are conducted only among people who meet rigorous proofs of readership of the original issue of the magazine, meaning that casual readers are likely to be excluded. The nonrepresentative samples that can result from these practices weaken the predictive power of the research.

Atypical or abnormal readership or viewing can sometimes result from certain message-research techniques, and the results from such studies must be considered carefully. In some magazine studies, readers are sent a second copy of the issue being studied or are otherwise notified in advance that an interviewer will call them with questions about advertising readership. Some television message studies notify viewers in advance and ask them to watch a particular program because an interviewer will call them with questions about the program and advertising.

Long interviews can present a problem too. Respondents may tire of the questions and make more mistakes toward the end of the interview. Others may try to speed up the interview by claiming that they did not see the advertisement when they first read the magazine. To control for such problems, careful studies do not begin at the front of the magazine for each respondent but start on a different page in each interview. Such procedures do not eliminate the problem of fatigue; they merely attempt to distribute the problems evenly across all ads in the publication.

Another potential problem arises because some message-research studies rely on self-administered data gathering techniques. For example, one company sends readers second copies of a magazine issue being measured and asks them to mark the ads they read. Although such methods cost less than personal interviews, researchers can never be sure that respondents fully understood the instructions or that the right person filled out the questionnaire. A few companies send out questionnaires and limit their samples to the first fifty or so that are returned. That practice adds the problem of sample unrepresentativeness to that of self-administered questionnaires.

Despite the inherent problems, message research can provide valuable information to advertisers. After all, researchers will never be able to devise a perfect and economical method that overcomes problems of memory. Suppliers of syndicated message-research data use methods that are necessary compromises between an unobtainable perfect method and one that is affordable and practical.

• • • Problems with Syndicated Media Audience Research

The problem of consumer memory haunts audience research too. Most audience research studies ask consumers to remember programs they watched or listened to or newspapers or magazines they read, and we know that some consumers forget what they read, watched, or listened to. This is especially true when consumers must provide a self-report of their media behavior (with diaries and self-administered questionnaires). Even if interviewers ask about media exposure, researchers cannot be sure that respondents always provide accurate answers.

• • • Minority Group Representation

Audience research studies use samples based on telephone directories and are subject to problems of sample bias explained in Chapter 5. Most audience researchers use random-digit dialing or similar techniques to reduce those sample bias problems.

The problems can be particularly acute for those in minority groups, who are less likely to have telephones and are therefore less likely than nonminority people to be included in samples based on telephone directories. In addition, members of minority groups are less likely than those in nonminority groups to complete and return diaries or questionnaires. For example, the normal response rate for Hispanics is about 15 percent to 20 percent, compared to 55 percent for the general population.[19]

Because of sample bias and lower cooperation, minorities can be underrepresented in audience data. The problem has been particularly acute in radio and television, where audience estimates for stations that appeal to African-Americans and Hispanics are frequently lower than they apparently should be. Two examples show

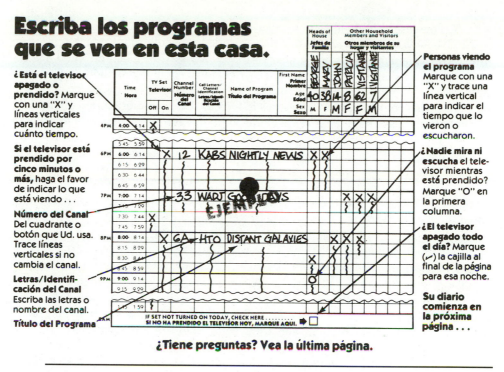

Figure 12.1 Example of Spanish-language Arbitron television diary. Reprinted by permission.

how serious the problem can be. Arbitron used a special telephone survey in San Antonio, Texas (to increase Hispanic representation), at the same time it did its regular diary measurement. The results of the special telephone survey showed that a Hispanic station's audience estimate was ten times greater than the estimate from the diary measurement. Arbitron did a similar study in New York, and audience estimates for two Spanish-language stations were two and one-half times greater in a special telephone survey than in a diary survey.[20] The problem has obvious consequences for stations that appeal to minority groups; it can also be a serious problem for advertisers trying to decide what stations to use to reach such audiences. (See Figure 12.1.)

Audience researchers have taken steps to reduce such problems. One technique gives additional weight to responses received from groups underrepresented in a sample. A simple example illustrates how weighting can be done in such cases. Suppose you are doing an audience survey and you know that a particular minority group comprises 20 percent of the population. When you examine the completed diaries or questionnaires, however, you discover that the minority group comprises only 10 percent of your sample. You could attempt to correct this underrepresentation by counting your minority group responses twice. Audience-research companies use more complicated weighting methods, but the principle is the same. Weighting techniques and similar statistical manipulations are used in other kinds of research, but they introduce an artificial and unknown element into the interpretation of the results. In other words, they do not eliminate the problem.

To increase the likelihood of minorities being included in samples, audience-research companies try to ensure that they include households not listed in telephone directories. Their methods are similar to those discussed in Chapter 5 and are explained in more detail in the descriptions of individual company methods in Chapters 15 and 16.

Research companies also take steps to increase the cooperation rate of minority group households. These steps can include additional letters or personal contacts in advance of the measurement period, greater financial incentives for returning a completed diary, additional telephone calls or personal visits during the measurement period, bilingual diaries and interviewers, and personal visits to retrieve the diaries.

The results of such efforts are mixed, however. Arbitron has learned that special retrieval efforts can produce lower audience estimates among African-Americans than when the firm uses the mail diary method. But it concluded that the differences were due to the different methodologies involved instead of the response rates or samples.[21] Arbitron conducted a special telephone survey of two groups: people who had completed radio diaries and people who had not. Additional efforts to contact people by telephone (which increased the costs of the survey) did not produce a higher response rate than a traditional mail survey. Arbitron also learned some important differences between those who kept diaries and those who did not. Diary-keepers tended to be more affluent, better educated, and from larger families than non-diary-keepers. Diary-keepers were more likely to prefer middle-of the-road, beautiful music, and news/talk formats, while non-diary-keepers preferred contemporary and African-American radio formats.[22]

. . . Small Samples

Audience research is sometimes criticized because samples are too small to permit meaningful examination of demographic groups within audiences. If a local television or radio audience measurement study is based on 400 completed diaries, 200 of those might be from women, which is no problem as long as you are analyzing data for the entire group of women. However, if you want to know something about women aged 18 to 34 in the audiences, there might be only 100 diaries from women in that segment. If only 20 were watching or listening during a particular daypart, you could not place much reliance on the ratings, because they would be based on such small numbers of respondents.

The problem does not lie entirely with the research companies, because their reports advise users of the shortcomings of the estimates. The problem also lies with users who do not heed or understand the warnings. Media representatives who use the data to promote their media may also not mention the weaknesses.

Even if the data did not have these weaknesses, some advertisers and agencies would probably still misuse them. Even if we had almost complete confidence in the numbers, advertisers and agencies might still place too much emphasis on quantity and not enough on quality of the audience. And quality means more than just characteristics of the audience—age, income, and gender. It also includes the audience's attitudes toward media and toward programs. It includes the nature of their media exposure—whether they are relaxing, reading, driving, or talking to someone. It includes the degree of attention they pay to the media vehicle as well.

... Timeliness

Another problem of audience research is that by the time users receive audience information from research suppliers, much of the information is out of date. It takes companies several months to complete their interviews and process and publish their reports, and by the time agencies and advertisers are ready to use the audience estimates, they are using six-month-old data (or older) to make decisions about advertising in the next six months or later. In addition, by the time some broadcast rating reports are available, some television programs listed in them may have been canceled. Only the major television markets have overnight television ratings.

To be fair, this problem is somewhat beyond the control of audience researchers. It simply takes a long time to collect and publish data about media audiences. Electronic data processing innovations are making it possible to provide data more promptly than in the past.

... Media Manipulation

Media manipulation occurs when broadcast stations (especially television) try to increase their audience size during audience measurement periods. The audiences of most stations are not measured continuously throughout the year because of the tremendous cost of such measurement. Instead, research companies like Arbitron or Nielsen measure the audiences three or four times a year. These measurement periods, which are usually for one to four weeks, are called sweeps.

The sweeps are very important to the stations because the resulting ratings are used to determine advertising rates. The ratings are also important because advertisers tend to buy advertising time on stations or programs with the highest ratings. Consequently, stations desire large audiences (high ratings) during the sweeps. That leads stations and even networks to run special programming and use other techniques during the sweeps to temporarily inflate the size of their audience.

Broadcasters can use several techniques to inflate their audiences artificially.

- By scheduling programs before and during the sweep that are likely to draw unusually large audiences for the time period. If competing stations do not also schedule special programs, a station can add several percentage points to its reported audience size. And even if other stations do schedule strong programming, the overall ratings for a particular station may increase slightly.
- By scheduling "Dialing for Dollars" or other contests temporarily during morning or afternoon time slots. Special contests may have the same effect as special programming.
- By conducting a major promotional campaign for the station during the broadcast day and on other local media. Large stations can more readily afford the increased promotion costs, although small stations may have the most to gain by a promotional campaign.

- By giving viewers participating in the ratings sweep visual and spoken instructions for filling out the viewing record. This is a simple trick, especially for a station with unsold air time. Instead of running a public service announcement, a station can run instructions for filling out a ratings diary.

These practices mean that reported ratings for these stations will be artificially inflated over the ratings that would have resulted from an unencumbered audience survey. In one television market, competition was so severe that one broadcaster leased a helicopter to transport its news team when it learned that a rival station had purchased for its news team a van for improved remote news coverage. When the ratings sweep ended, the helicopter lease was terminated, and the first station went back to reporting local news with its station wagon for transportation.

Networks often schedule blockbuster movies or other programs that will temporarily boost their audience figures. *Gone With The Wind, Elvis in Concert,* and *One Flew Over the Cuckoo's Nest* once faced one another on the networks' prime-time schedule at sweeps time.

The Advertising Research Foundation has reported that network television audience estimates for some time periods were nearly 10 percent higher in survey periods than in nonsurvey periods.[23]

Several solutions have been proposed, but none seem to offer much chance of success. If the rating periods were longer than four weeks, it would be more expensive and difficult for stations to sustain their audience inflation practices, but increased costs of lengthening the ratings periods make that solution unfeasible. In addition, federal antitrust regulations prohibit Arbitron and Nielsen from agreeing to measure audiences at different times — which could expand the rating survey period.

The Federal Communications Commission (FCC) has found it difficult to stop the practices without interfering with stations' programming rights. The FCC has taken action to halt fraudulent practices, however. A radio station in Wichita, Kansas, took diaries that had been sent to some of its employees and filled out the diaries to indicate that the employees listened to that station exclusively. The FCC disciplined that station by granting only a short-term license renewal and warned other stations that it would take away their licenses if the situation got worse.[24] About the only practical solution to the problem of audience inflation is for advertisers and agencies to be aware of the problem and to use data accordingly. Arbitron and Nielsen customers who use the ratings books with care can be alert to ratings that are intentionally distorted. The ratings companies note dates and times during which individual stations have employed techniques that will distort the data. (They also note dates and times during which stations have experienced technical difficulties such as power outages.)

. . . Researchers' Responses to Criticisms

Researchers generally agree that there are problems with audience research. Improvements can be made, they agree, but only at considerable cost. Researchers contend that the users of audience data are not willing to pay the extra costs required to improve sampling procedures, to offer people enough incentive to cooperate with interviewers, to pay for competent and reliable interviewers, and to lengthen the period of audience surveys.

The cost of research is a major problem. Stations and publications have to pay audience-research companies to include them in the measurements. The costs are usually related to advertising revenue or audience size: Larger stations or publications pay higher rates than smaller ones. In addition, advertisers and other users must pay for audience data. The conclusion is clear: High costs of audience research and higher costs for improved research make it unlikely that significant improvements will occur.

Even if users would pay for the improvements they wanted, some researchers believe that users would still complain about audience research. The problem, according to researchers, is that users expect too much, demand too much, and use audience data in the wrong way, even if the data are accurate. In other words, researchers believe that users often do not understand the limitations of research. Or as the president of one leading syndicated research company told *Marketing and Media Decisions*: "People look to research for the absolute truth, when the truth about research is that there is no such thing as absolute truth."[25]

In an editorial accompanying the article about the credibility crisis in audience research, *Marketing and Media Decisions* concluded that audience research was oversold, overused, and overrated:

> . . . audience numbers have suffered their greatest beatings, not because of any inherent dishonesty in the services themselves, but because buyers and sellers alike have yielded to the temptation to oversell their importance.
>
> Information which at the collection end is soft and subjective — a matter of 'by-guess and by-golly' for many a respondent — later becomes the unquestioned gospel for the media buyer.
>
> It takes on an aura of inviolable truth, when in point of fact it is only one barometer of public opinion.
>
> Sense will emerge from the ratings war only when media planners and buyers refuse to buy the inflated and exaggerated importance of one analytical tool — however critical. The numbers have indeed been oversold, overused, and overrated.[26]

••• Limitations of Syndicated Competitive Activity Research

Users of competitive media activity research should consider four questions about the data they use:

1. Are all media vehicles measured, or only a sample?
2. Are all time periods measured, or only a sample?
3. Are the data collected by observation or by self-report?
4. What are the expenditure estimates based on?

. . . What Vehicles Are Measured?

For certain types of media, all vehicles are measured. This is true, for example, of network television: All three commercial networks are monitored for measurement of advertising activity. That would not be practical for spot television, however. So only a sample of stations are monitored, and data from that sample are projected to yield estimates for a larger number of stations. Whenever estimates are used in advertising research, they introduce an element of uncertainty and are generally less accurate.

. . . What Time Periods Are Measured?

Not all media are measured continuously for advertising activity. Again, that would be impractical for a medium like spot television; so activity is measured for one week and projected to yield estimates for four weeks. On the other hand, network radio and television are measured continuously, and it is not necessary to project estimates. Measuring all time periods will generally produce more accurate data than will result from projecting estimates from samples of time periods.

. . . How Are Data Collected?

Most competitive activity data are collected by observation by the research company. In other words, company personnel monitor advertising activity and make a record of what they hear or see. For some types of media, however, advertising activity data are reported by the media themselves. For example, outdoor advertising plant operators report advertising by national advertisers to Leading National Advertisers, Inc. Users of competitive activity data should generally have more confidence in data collected by the research company than from reports by the media.

. . . On What Are Expenditure Estimates Based?

No one knows exactly how much competitors actually spend on advertising. The cost figures that are reported are estimates of what companies spent, based on what media rate cards say they probably spent. For example, Broadcast Advertisers Reports can say that a competitor placed a thirty-second commercial on a program and can estimate that the competitor paid $125,000 for that commercial. Even though that estimate may be based on information supplied by the network, only the advertiser and the network know exactly how much the commercial cost.

In other words, competitive activity data are based on estimates. Expenditure data are always estimates, and the volume of advertising may be based on samples of media vehicles and samples of time periods. Within a particular medium, however, the errors that are likely to arise are likely to be spread evenly across all advertisers. That means the data are still useful for others advertisers.

Evaluating Externally Supplied Research

Users of externally supplied research must know how data are collected and what limitations arise because of that collection method. They should also be familiar with the concepts of sampling, questionnaire design, surveys, and other research techniques. The following checklist can also be useful in evaluating research data.

... The Sample

1. The supplier should define the universe or the population that the sample is supposed to represent.
2. The supplier should name the source of the list of those in the universe. If the source is a telephone directory, the supplier should indicate what it did to overcome the biases of such a source. If the source is likely to change (telephone directory, for example), the supplier should indicate what steps it took to update the list.
3. The sampling procedure should be clearly described.
4. The supplier should explain the reasons for using a particular sampling method.
5. Regardless of the sampling method, the supplier should describe potential biases that might result.
6. If a stratified sample is used, the supplier should describe the methods used to establish the strata.
7. The supplier should specify the number and percentage of completed interviews and the methods used to increase the completion rate.
8. The supplier should indicate if substitutes are used for people in the original sample and how those substitutes are selected.
9. If a panel sample is used, the supplier should explain how the representativeness of the panel is maintained.

... The Questionnaire

1. The complete questionnaire should be available to the client.
2. If telephone interviews are used, the questions should be concise and easy to understand, and the questionnaire should not be too long.
3. Closed-end questions should include all possible answers.
4. Rating questions should include appropriate gradations.
5. Early questions should not discourage accurate answers and good cooperation in the remainder of the questionnaire.
6. Probing questions should be used with open-end questions.
7. Questions should be objective and should not be structured to elicit a particular kind of answer.

8. The questionnaire should not include any embarrassing or threatening questions.
9. Self-administered questions should have clear instructions to minimize misunderstanding by respondents.

... Interviews and Fieldwork

1. The supplier should explain the training and level of experience of interviewers.
2. The supplier should tell how interviewers' work is supervised and verified.
3. The supplier should provide the dates and times of field interviews.
4. The supplier should specify how much freedom interviewers are given to make judgments about persons to interview.
5. In interviewing in ethnic areas, it is especially important to use African-American or Hispanic interviewers.
6. The supplier should specify the procedures used for households that cannot be contacted initially.

... Monitoring Externally Supplied Research

Two organizations help to assure advertisers that research suppliers follow approved procedures. The Advertising Research Foundation (ARF) and the Electronic Media Rating Council (EMRC) perform a monitoring role over many suppliers of syndicated data. Both organizations provide services that most advertisers and their agencies are unable to provide.

... Advertising Research Foundation

Formed as a joint venture of the Association of National Advertisers and the American Association of Advertising Agencies, the Advertising Research Foundation became known as "the bureau of standards for advertising research."[27] Its founders' objective was to promote better advertising through impartial and objective research.

ARF maintains thirteen research councils, each addressing a specialized research area or issue. Several of them work toward improvement of syndicated research standards and practices.

Business Advertising Research Council

A committee of this council, the Business Audience Measurement Committee, published guidelines for preparing or evaluating business magazine audience studies.[28]

Copy Research Council

This council has worked on validity of copy research, to develop improved understanding of how various testing methods can be used to predict performance in the marketplace.

Magazine Research Council

This council was formed because of industry concern about the validity of magazine audience measurements. Its Auditing Committee has developed auditing techniques for magazine audience research. The Validity Committee has developed a method for studying audiences that can be validated against observed reading behavior. The Research Development Committee has developed new research approaches that will help detect the actual impact of advertising.

Newspaper Audience Research Council

This council's *ARF Guidelines for Newspaper Audience Studies*, first published in 1986 and recently revised, is the result of extensive research on syndicated audience studies. The guidelines are designed for individual market newspaper audience studies as well as for syndicated studies.

Radio Research Council

The Ethnic Committee has investigated the different response rates obtained in telephone surveys and in-person interview studies. It has been particularly concerned with data retrieval techniques on the Hispanic audience. The Response Rates Committee has worked on clarifying to users of the data the importance of high response rates in audience research.

Other ARF research councils are concerned with measurement of the children's audience, conducting test market research, carrying out original research in effective frequency of exposure, qualitative research methods, and other issues of importance to the advertising research community.

• • • Electronic Media Rating Council

Concern over the validity of broadcast ratings, capped by Congressional hearings on broadcast audience measurement, led to the formation of an organization that would help ensure the integrity of the ratings. Originally known as the Broadcast Rating Council, the organization in 1982 became the Electronic Media Rating Council.

The council's primary purpose is to secure audience measurement services that are valid, reliable, effective, and viable. To that end, the EMRC provides several services:

1. Develop minimum standards of ethics and operational practices for rating services. The EMRC has also worked with several industry groups to develop further technical standards that amplify and interpret the basic minimum standards.

2. Audit broadcast measurement services to ensure that they conform to established criteria and procedures. These audits are conducted continually by certified public accountant (CPA) firms under contract to the EMRC. Auditors examine several areas of a company's operations. They analyze and verify sample design and sample selection. They talk to interviewers and supervisors to determine their training and thoroughness. They confirm with respondent households that interviews took place or that mailed diaries were received and returned to the research organization. The auditors also check household and people meters to make sure they are properly calibrated, and that the information is properly transmitted and recorded at the central office.

   Auditors also review data processing procedures. They analyze personnel and the steps they follow in editing, coding, and keypunching data from returned questionnaires and diaries. Auditors even recalculate some ratings to verify their accuracy.

3. Provide accreditation for rating services. This is the EMRC's most visible service because accredited rating services may use the council's "double check" symbol on all accredited reports.

All broadcast rating services are invited to apply for accreditation. To apply, a rating service must request accreditation and must provide the EMRC with all requested information. In addition, rating services must agree to comply with criteria established by the EMRC and must submit to continuous and unannounced audits of their procedures and records. Rating services pay for audits, but these costs are passed along to their subscribers in the form of surcharges.

••• Summary

Much advertising research is conducted by companies that syndicate or sell results of the research to advertisers, agencies, and media. Most of these users could not afford to conduct that kind of research, so the cost is spread among them. It is important for users of syndicated research to know how that research is conducted and to know the limitations of the results.

Some syndicated research studies the effect of advertising messages and attempts to measure the influence of advertising on purchase decisions. Problems and limitations of message research include faulty consumer memory and lack of proof of relationship between memory and purchase.

The most common type of syndicated research measures audiences of media vehicles. Problems and limitations of audience research include sample bias, small samples, controversy over methodology, and media inflation of audiences.

Competitive activity research tells advertisers about their competitors' media strategies. Limitations of such data include incomplete measurement of all vehicles and all time periods, collection of some data by media self-report, and inability to report actual media expenditures.

Self-Test Questions

1. Discuss how you would do customized and syndicated research on your college campus or in your community. What kinds of research in your community or on campus would probably be appropriate for customized research? For syndicated research?
2. Think of a television program you saw or a magazine you read in the last twenty-four hours. What product ads can you remember? What does that tell you about some problems of advertising message research?
3. Discuss how you would conduct a recognition test for advertisements in your college newspaper.
4. How would you measure the validity or dependability of your recognition and recall tests? What are you likely to learn from that measure of validity? What factors might account for those results?
5. How would you design a research study to learn the relationship between recall of advertising for a product advertised in your college newspaper and purchase of that product by students? What would you expect to learn?
6. What conditions have led to the controversy about advertising copywriting and research?
7. When you look at ratings books for local television stations, what can you assume about the stations' programming during the measurement period? How will this knowledge affect your use of the ratings?
8. What are some consequences of the following problems or limitations associated with advertising research?
   a. nonrepresentative samples
   b. respondent fatigue
   c. use of self-administered reports or questionnaires
   d. small samples
   e. timeliness
   f. use of samples in competitive activity research

Notes

1. Edward M. Tauber, "Agency Research Department: 1990," *Journal of Advertising Research*, Vol. 27 (April/May 1987), 6.
2. Gerald Zaltman and Christine Moorman, "The Management and Use of Advertising Research," *Journal of Advertising Research*, Vol. 29 (December 1988/January 1989), 18.
3. David Stewart and others, "Methodological and Theoretical Foundations of Advertising

Copy Testing: A Review," in James H. Leigh and Claude R. Martin, Jr., *Current Issues and Research in Advertising* (Ann Arbor: University of Michigan Press, 1985), 63.

4. Darrell B. Lucas and Steuart Henderson Britt, *Measuring Advertising Effectiveness* (New York: McGraw-Hill, 1963), 47–48.

5. Lucas and Britt, *Measuring Advertising Effectiveness*, 47–48.

6. Lucas and Britt, *Measuring Advertising Effectiveness*, 47–48.

7. Richard Edel, "New Technologies Add Dimensions to Copy Testing," *Advertising Age* (November 24, 1986), s-20.

8. Jack B. Haskins, "Factual Recall as a Measure of Advertising Effectiveness," *Journal of Advertising Research*, Vol. 4 (March 1964), 7.

9. John Doig, "Why Agencies See Research as Enemy," *Advertising Age* (November 27, 1989), 38.

10. Jack Honomichl, "A Rough Look at Tests of TV Commercials," *Advertising Age* (April 14, 1980), 32.

11. Jack Honomichl, "TV Copy Testing Flap: What To Do About It," *Advertising Age* (January 19, 1981), 56–62.

12. Max Gunther, "To Burke or Not To Burke?" *TV Guide* (February 7, 1981), 3–8.

13. Harry McMahon and Mack Kile, "Testing Copy Research: An Old, Nasty Sore," *Advertising Age* (August 3, 1981), 40.

14. Jack Honomichl, "TV Copy Testing Flap."

15. McMahon and Kile, "Testing Copy Research."

16. Sonia Yuspeh and David Leach, "A Recall Debate," *Advertising Age* (July 13, 1981), 47–48.

17. Theodore J. Gage, "With Data, Ideas Come in Numbers," *Advertising Age* (August 10, 1981), s-6 to s-7.

18. Herman Davis, "Is It Blasphemy? Creative Director Praises Research," *Advertising Age* (June 11, 1979), 41–42.

19. Rene Anselmo, "Minority Undercount Remains Severe Research Problem," *Advertising Age* (April 16, 1979), s-1.

20. Anselmo, "Minority Undercount," s-1.

21. David Lapovsky, "Arbitron Seeks to Improve Minority Measuring Methods," *Advertising Age* (April 16, 1979), s-35.

22. "Arbitron Testing Diary Boosters," *Advertising Age* (February 26, 1979), 81.

23. James P. Forkan, "ARF Index Discounts 'Hyped' Sweep Ratings Diaries," *Advertising Age* (July 11, 1977), 156.

24. "FCC Warns It May Lift Licenses if Stations Try to Distort Ratings Diaries," *Advertising Age* (July 11, 1977), 164.

25. "Can You Count on the Numbers?" *Marketing and Media Decisions* (April 1978), 116.

26. "Can You Count on the Numbers?", 116.

27. "ARF: Sleeping Giant On Our Doorstep," *Advertising Age* (March 17, 1986), 49.

28. "ARF Guidelines for Audience Research on Business Publications," (New York: Advertising Research Foundation, 1988).

• • • Suggestions for Additional Reading

Baldinger, A. L. "Trends and Issues in Simulated Test Markets: Results of an ARF Pilot Project." *Journal of Advertising Research*, 28 (October/November 1988), RC3–RC7.

Dimling, J. "Measuring Future Electronic Media Audiences." *Journal of Advertising Research*, 25 (February/March 1985), RC3–RC7.

Goldberg, M. A. "Broadcast Ratings and Ethics." *Review of Business* (Summer 1989), 19–20.

Laczniak, R. N., D. D. Muehling, and S. Grossbart. "Manipulating Message Involvement in Advertising Research." *Journal of Advertising*, 18 (1989), 28–38.

Radding, A. "Researchers Making a New Impression: Outdated System to Determine Consumer Exposure Gets Revamp." *Advertising Age* (October 9, 1989), S2.

Schillmoeller, E. A. "Tackling Declining Response Rates." *Journal of Advertising Research*, 27 (December 1987/January 1988), RC10–RC11.

Sing, S. N., M. L. Rothschild, and G. A. Churchill. "Recognition Versus Recall as Measure of Television Commercial Forgetting." *Journal of Marketing Research*, 25 (February 1988), 72–80.

Stewart, D. W. "Measures, Methods, and Models in Advertising Research." *Journal of Advertising Research*, 29 (June/July 1989), 54–60.

Sudman, S., and N. Schwarz. "Contributions of Cognitive Psychology to Advertising Research." *Journal of Advertising Research*, 29 (June/July 1989), 43–53.

CHAPTER 13

Message Research: Broadcast

Operating on the premise that an advertisement cannot have an effect on consumer purchase behavior if the person cannot remember the ad, most message research continues to focus on recall. Although the ideal measure of message effect may be found in field experiments with controls for differences in subjects' media usage and other sources of influence, such studies are expensive and often impractical. Current efforts to develop useful single-source studies, and especially to provide purchasing data along with other data, have had to contend with the problem of research costs.

Because of the large number of variables that are associated with the consumer's purchasing decisions, it is difficult to isolate the effect of creative strategy of an advertising campaign. Even more difficult is isolating the effect of one creative execution among several that an advertiser may be using at a particular time. Who's to say that an advertiser's subtly humorous television spot that airs tonight at 8:00 P.M. will produce sales at a given level, and that the advertiser's slightly more humorous spot that airs at 9:00 P.M. will produce sales at a higher or lower level?

The result of the difficulty and expense of making the desired direct connection between an advertiser's creative strategy (and executions) and actual sales is that most message research addresses memorability. Some research, however, does address purchasing behavior or changes in brand preferences.

• • • ASI Market Research

ASI provides two television commercial testing services, Recall Plus and Persuasion Plus, both of which can be used for pretesting finished or rough commercials. Approximately one-third of the tests are of roughs. A client can purchase the services together, in what ASI calls the Apex system.

• • • Recall Plus

For Recall Plus, the standard sample size is 200 males, 200 females, or 100 males and 100 females. Recruiting is controlled so that 45 percent of the sample is 18–34 years of age, 30 percent is 35–49, and 25 percent is 50–65. Respondents are drawn from cable television households in at least two cities.

Respondents are invited to preview a proposed new television program that will be screened on an unused local cable channel. The test program is an unaired, thirty-minute situation comedy that includes four noncompeting test commercials and one nontest "filler" commercial. Scheduling of the commercials is similar to typical television commercial scheduling; the commercials are in pods throughout the program. The first pod appears about five minutes into the program, the second about fifteen minutes into the program. The filler commercial, whose purpose is to help establish a realistic viewing environment, appears by itself immediately following the opening credits.

The day following exposure, respondents are recontacted by telephone and viewership is established. The first several questions concern the program itself. Then the questions turn to the commercials that appeared. Four unaided product category cues are given to each respondent; if the respondent cannot correctly identify the advertised brand, for each commercial a brand prompt is given. For each commercial the respondent claims to remember, detailed recall prompts are administered to obtain levels of recall and communication.

Exhibit 13.1 is a sample page of an ASI Recall Plus Report for a well-known grocery product.

ASI provides extensive additional information for clients. Exhibit 13.2 contains data that enable the client to compare a test commercial's performance with the performance of a large number of other commercials.

ASI MARKET RESEARCH, INC.
FEBRUARY, 1990

SURVEY NO. 2107882
TABLE 1

Test Commercial

838 A) Now please tell me ANYTHING AT ALL you remember about the commercial that you saw last night. (IF "DON'T KNOW OR "DON'T REMEMBER", REPEAT QUESTION. IF INITIAL ANSWER GIVEN, ASK:) What else can you remember about last night's commercial? B)What (else) did the commercial LOOK LIKE, what did you see in the commercial last night? (PROBE) What else) did they show about the product (last night? What else? (PROBE) C) What (else) did they say about the product in the commercial? What else? (PROBE) D) What ideas about the product were brought out in the commercial last night? (IF RESPONSE GIVEN, ASK:) What other ideas about the product were brought out in the commercial last night?

	STANDRD FEMALE SAMPLE	HOUSTON	PITTS- BURGH	18-34	35-49	50-65	25-49
BASE - TOTAL RESPONDENTS	①166	90	76	73	64	29	115
RECALL OF THE COMMERCIAL							
Related recall score	②24%	20%	29%	27%	25%	14%	27%
Product cue	13%	10%	17%	14%	17%	3%	16%
Brand cue	11%	10%	12%	14%	8%	10%	11%
Measured Attention	47%	47%	47%	52%	③39%	52%	45%
Brand Linkage	.51④	-	-	-	-	-	-

Exhibit 13.1 ASI Recall Plus data for a test commercial for a well-known grocery product. Reprinted with permission of ASI Market Research.

1. One hundred sixty-six women participated in this test, which is for a commercial for an item purchased most commonly by women.
2. The Related Recall score of 24 percent means that 24 percent of the respondents who were at their television sets while the commercial was on were able to recall correctly some of the key elements of the test commercial.
3. Of the young respondents (18–34 years of age), 52 percent claimed to have seen the commercial after hearing a verbal description of the test execution.
4. Brand Linkage Ratio of .51 is calculated by dividing the Related Recall score by the Measured Attention score. The higher the Brand Linkage ratio, the better the test commercial is getting its brand identification across to those persons who recall it at all.

	Test Commercial	ON-AIR COMMERCIAL NORMATIVE DATA			
		30-SECOND ALL COMMERCIALS*		30-SECOND FOOD PRODUCTS**	
		AVERAGE	RANGE	AVERAGE	RANGE ②
RELATED RECALL SCORE	24%	24%	3% - 62%	27% ①	8% - 56%

* THIS NORM WAS UPDATED IN JANUARY, 1989 AND INCLUDES 5336 CASES.
** THIS NORM WAS UPDATED IN JANUARY, 1989 AND INCLUDES 1924 CASES.

Exhibit 13.2 Additional ASI Recall Plus data for the test commercial described in Exhibit 13.2. Reprinted with permission of ASI Market Research.
1. The Related Recall score of 24 for this grocery product commercial is slightly below the average for the 1,924 food product commercials tested by ASI by January 1989.
2. The range of Related Recall scores for food product commercials is 8–56 percent.

. . . Persuasion Plus

This service parallels Recall Plus but provides additional information useful to the advertiser. It employs the same broadcast, number of commercial breaks, sample definition, interviewers, and pool of cities. It provides information about the persuasiveness of the test commercial and the effects of brand loyalty on sample members' responses to the commercial.

The procedure is similar to that followed in the Recall Plus studies. It starts with recruitment of respondents, screening of the program over an unused cable television channel, and a follow-up interview via telephone.

In Persuasion Plus studies, the recruitment interview includes questions on brand usage and brand preference. Arrangements are made for a second interview, to be conducted within a two-hour period following exposure to the test program.

This interview is the key to the Persuasion Plus test. After exposure to the test program, respondents are recontacted by telephone, and viewership for the program and the commercials is established. Within the context of a prize drawing for an assortment of products in a given category, respondents are asked to select the brands they would most like to receive. This provides a measure that goes beyond simple recall. Because ASI uses controls to compensate for existing brand loyalties, this procedure shows the relationship between respondents' expected brand selections and their actual brand selections as demonstrated when they are given the opportunity to select a brand assortment in the prize drawing.

In the Recall Plus and Persuasion Plus tests, ASI provides diagnostics for clients wanting them. *Diagnostics*, which are gathered after the main portion of the test, are detailed respondent comments on the test commercials — what they liked about the commercials, visual or aural features that stood out, and components that they did not understand. This information is gathered by asking respondents to turn their television sets to the appropriate channel to view a commercial (or the commercial is exposed to a different sample of viewers, as the test design dictates). The diagnostic questionnaire is then administered. Most of these interviews are no longer than seven minutes.

••• Gallup & Robinson, Inc.

Through its In-View service, Gallup & Robinson provides on-air pretesting of rough or finished new commercials and posttesting of existing commercials. In-View provides an evaluation of the visibility of a commercial within a television program, the degree to which the commercial communicates, and the degree to which the commercial persuades. The service provides these basic measures of the impact of commercials:

1. *Proved Commercial Registration (PCR)*. PCR is a measure of a commercial's ability to cut through competitive clutter and make an impression on the viewer. It is the percentage of viewers who, aided by company or brand name cue, can prove recall by describing the commercial accurately the day after telecast.

2. *Idea Communication Profile*. A measure of the ideas and feelings the commercial communicates to the respondent, idea communication is the percent of viewers recalling specific sales points.

3. *Favorable Buying Attitude or Favorable Attitude*. The first of these measures is an indicator of the commercial's ability to persuade; the second, which applies to corporate or institutional advertising, is a measure of the commercial's ability to make a strong case for a position taken by the advertiser.

4. *Net Effectiveness*. Net effectiveness is the product of proved commercial registration and favorable buying attitude or favorable attitude. It provides a net measure of the commercial's ability to permeate the clutter and deliver a persuasive message successfully.

For advertisers seeking additional evaluation, Gallup & Robinson provides several options:

1. *Attitude Change Option*. This option uses an exposed/unexposed (independent samples) design or a preexposure/postexposure (same-person) design.

2. *Extra Question Option.* Extra open-end or closed-end questions can be included.
3. *Multiple Exposure Option.* If desired, the commercial can be aired more than once during a test.
4. *Target Sampling Option.* The option provides a specialized sample of respondents.

Commercials to be tested via In-View are inserted into prime-time programs aired on independent stations in any of three metropolitan areas in the East, Midwest, and West. Cities currently being used are Pittsburgh, Louisville, and San Diego.

For most studies, the sample consists of 150 men and 150 women between the ages 18 and 65. Some studies require different sizes or more specialized samples.

Test commercials can be in finished form, or they can be in Animatics or Photomatic form, to allow for economical modification if the test reveals weaknesses.

To test commercial impact, Gallup & Robinson telephones randomly selected households the day of the test and invites the youngest targeted-age-range person then at home to watch the program in which the commercial will be broadcast. The next day, interviewers call the respondents. After determining that the respondents did watch the program, the interviewers read a list of advertisers or brand names and ask the respondents which commercials they can recall. For each one recalled, the interviewers ask probing questions to elicit details.

To test attitude change, the firm invites eligible respondents to view the test program. During the invitation call, respondents are questioned about their awareness of and attitudes toward six product categories, three of which will be advertised on the test program. The day after the telecast, they are called back and asked the same questions about attitudes and awareness. For those who saw the program, changes in attitude or awareness are presumed to have resulted from exposure to the commercial.

Exhibits 13.3 to 13.7 show the application of a Gallup & Robinson In-View test to a thirty-second commercial for Lilt brand home permanent.

Exhibit 13.3 is the storyboard for a thirty-second television spot for Lilt Home Permanent.

Exhibit 13.4 is the performance summary for the Lilt commercial. Because this product is purchased and used by women, the sample consists only of women.

Exhibit 13.5 provides detailed information on the Intrusiveness/Proved Name registration measure.

Exhibit 13.6 shows detailed information on the idea communication performance of the Lilt commercial.

Exhibit 13.7 shows the Persuasion/Favorable Effects of the Lilt commercial.

Starch INRA Hooper

The name *Starch* is one of the oldest in the study of magazine advertisement readership. Starch INRA Hooper now offers its Impression Study for television commercials as well as for print advertisements.

COMMERCIAL: LILT HOME PERMANENT

LENGTH: 30 seconds   **DATE: 4/8/87**

1. (Musical Background) F/SINGER: Let Lilt's Home Wave

2. put your hair in the pink.

3. F/ANNCR: Lilt's little pink holding sponges keep roll-ups tight, . . .

4. so the style you want comes out . . .

5. CHORUS: Just right.

6. F/SINGER: Luxurious, furious, . . .

7. tame or carefree.

8. The look is whatever you want it to be . . .

9. when you put it in the pink.

10. CHORUS: Put it in the pink, pink, . . .

11. F/SINGER: Let Lilt's Home Wave . . .

12. put your hair in the pink.

Exhibit 13.3 Storyboard for thirty-second Lilt Home Permanent television spot. Reprinted with permission of Gallup & Robinson, Inc.

In its broadcast version, Impression Studies are designed to tell advertiser the meanings people find in commercials and how much importance they attach to these meanings. The Impression technique, which can be used for pretesting and posttesting, places emphasis on the commercial itself rather than on comparisons with other commercials in the same product category.

As in the magazine Impression Studies, the broadcast application is designed to answer several questions:

1. What image of our company and our product does the commercial communicate?

```
                    30" LILT HOME PERMANENT
                   Wednesday, April 8, 1987


PERFORMANCE SUMMARY

Sample Composition:  171 Women


                                                    Women

        INTRUSIVENESS/PCR

            Proved Commercial Registration (PCR)     36 ①
            Norm:  Women's Hair Products           ②   33


        IDEA COMMUNICATION

            Lead Idea: Refer to sponges             57%
            Norm:  Women's Hair Products            75


        AVERAGE NUMBER OF IDEAS COMMUNICATED

            Average Number of Ideas per Respondent  2.8 ③
            Norm:  Women's Hair Products            2.8


        PERSUASION/FBA

            Favorable Buying Attitude (FBA)         42%
            Norm:  Women's Hair Products            47


        NET EFFECTIVENESS

            PCR X FBA                               15 ④
            Norm:  Women's Hair Products            16
```

Exhibit 13.4 Performance summary for thirty-second Lilt Home Permanent commercial. Reprinted with permission of Gallup & Robinson, Inc.
1. Of the 171 women interviewed, 36 percent were able to prove that they had seen the commercial.
2. The average PCR for women's hair products is 33 percent. In statistical terms, this average score is not significantly different from the score for the Lilt commercial.
3. The average number of ideas communicated in the Lilt commercial was 2.8, which was same as the norm for the category.
4. The net effectiveness score is 15. In statistical terms, this is not significantly different from the norm for women's hair products.

2. Do the verbal and visual messages work together?
3. Do the product features we are highlighting give us a competitive advantage?
4. Do viewers find the same meanings in our commercials — the meanings we want them to find?

30" LILT HOME PERMANENT

Wednesday, April 8, 1987

INTRUSIVENESS/PCR*	PCR Measure	Standard Error	Sample Base
Total Sample, Women	36 ①	3.7	171 ②
By Age			
Ages 18-34	33	5.3	78
Ages 35-49	37	5.1	89
DK/NA/Refused	**	**	4
By Income			
Income Under $20,000	30	7.0	43
Income Over $20,000	35	5.2	84
DK/NA/Refused	43	7.4	44

30" Norms	Women
All Products	33
Women's Hair Products	33 ③
18 - 34	35 ④
35 - 49	32

* Proved Commercial Registration (PCR) is defined as the percent of qualified viewers of the program who, given the brand name/product, can recall and accurately describe the commercial on the day following the telecast.

**Base too small to compute a PCR Measure.

Exhibit 13.5 Intrusiveness/proved commercial registration scores for thirty-second Lilt Home Permanent commercial, by demographic category. Reprinted with permission of Gallup & Robinson, Inc.

1. This score is the one reported in the previous exhibit and reflects the percent of the total sample proving their recall of the Lilt commercial.
2. The number of women in the total sample was 171.
3. The norm for women's PCR for all products and for women's hair products is 33 percent.
4. Younger women, those 18–34, have somewhat higher PCR scores for women's hair products than women 35–49.

IDEA COMMUNICATION	Total Recailers	
	#	%
Refer to sponges	35	57 (1)
Pink	16	26
Beautifies/improves appearance	24	39
Leaves hair soft	8	13
Quality/better/best	23	38
Simple/easy to use	20	33
Good/better roll up	19	31
Keeps roll ups tight	14	23
Refer to styles	13	21
Variety	7	11
Makes hair look natural	9	15
Natural looking curls	6	10
Economical/inexpensive	6	10
Favor to commercial	1	2
Disfavor to commercial	0	0
Average Number of Ideas per Respondent	2.8	
Respondents with one or more Ideas Communicated	58	95 (2)
Base (# of women respondents)	61	

Norms: Women's Hair Products	Women
Lead Idea Communicated	75%
Average Number of Ideas Communicated	2.8
Respondents with one or more Ideas Communicated	>90% (3)
Favor to commercial	<10%
Disfavor to commercial	<10%

IRISTAB

Exhibit 13.6 Idea communication scores for thirty-second Lilt Home Permanent commercial. Reprinted with permission of Gallup & Robinson, Inc.
1. In this study, respondents mentioned the use of sponges with Lilt more often than any other copy point. Fifty-seven percent referred in some way to the sponges.
2. Ninety-five percent of the respondents were able to demonstrate that they had understood at least one idea in the thirty-second Lilt commercial.
3. For women's hair products, more than 90 percent of the respondents can cite at least one copy point. That is slightly below the performance of this Lilt commercial.

Wednesday, April 8, 1988

PERSUASION/FBA	Recallers – Not Users of Brand	
	#	%
Increased Buying Interest	23	42 ①
Increased considerably	4	7
Increased somewhat	19	35
Not Affected	21	38
Decreased Buying Interest	8	15
Decreased somewhat	3	5
Decreased considerably	5	9
DK/NA/Refused	3	5
Base (# of women respondents)	55	100

Norms: Women's Hair Products	Women
Favorable Buying Attitude	47% ②
Increased considerably	11
Increased somewhat	36

Exhibit 13.7 Persuasion/favorable buying attitude for thirty-second Lilt Home Permanent commercial. Reprinted with permission of Gallup & Robinson, Inc.
1. Of the nonuser women interviewed, 42 percent showed an increased interest in buying the brand.
2. For women's hair products generally, 47 percent showed some increased interest in buying the brand. This is better than the score for the Lilt commercial.

In Impression Studies, the sample is determined by the client's specifications. Members of the sample are shown a videotape of the commercial twice. Then a Starch probing procedure is used to determine the viewer's reactions toward the commercial as a whole; the product, service, or company; and verbal and visual messages. The viewer tells in his or her own words what he or she extracted from the commercial.

After respondents' spontaneous reactions have been obtained, respondents are questioned directly about the importance of ideas in the commercial, new information they have received, changes in their perception, purchase intent, and areas of confusion and believability.

Exhibit 13.8 is a storyboard for a K mart commercial that was analyzed in a Starch Impression Study.

Exhibit 13.9 is part of the summary section of the Starch Impression Study for the K mart commercial.

1. (BACKGROUND VOICES THROUGHOUT)
MAN 1: What do you think?

2. (BACKGROUND VOICES)

3. (GIRLS LAUGH)

4. (GIRLS LAUGH)

5. MAN 2: She'll love it.
MAN 1: Price is right...

6. WOMAN 1: I'll break 90 with these...

7. WOMAN 2: Where will you find a better price than that?

8. P.A. ANNCR: ...more incredible savings on top quality, name-brand appliances...

9. GIRL: Definitely...

10. MAN 3: Valerie, Valerie...

11. MAN 2: You know, you look pretty good in pink?

12. ANNCR: (VO) K Mart, the saving place and more.

Exhibit 13.8 Storyboard for K mart commercial, "Day in the Life/Burly Guys." Reprinted by permission of K mart.

K MART COMMERCIAL

"Day in the Life/Burly Guys"
(30")

EXPERIMENTAL STUDY

MAY 1988

SUMMARY HIGHLIGHTS

1. This commercial performed well on an overall basis. Seven of ten viewers expressed positive attitudes and resistant attitudes were not widespread.

2. Viewers appreciated the humor of the commercial. They welcomed its "positive," "light-hearted" approach and found it "entertaining" and "fun" to watch.

3. The visual messages were generally favorable. The commercial showed "a clean, well managed store;" an environment that was "comfortable," "relaxed" and uncrowded; products that were "attractive" and nicely displayed and shoppers that were "satisfied" and obviously "enjoying themselves."

4. The vast majority of viewers (78%) offered spontaneous comments about prices. Most respondents (60%) agreed that K mart had "the goods you want at the right prices." K mart was "a good place to get a good buy."

-1-

Exhibit 13.9 Portion of summary highlights from a Starch Impression Report for the K mart commercial. Reprinted with permission of Starch INRA Hooper, Inc.

5. K mart was also given much positive weight by viewers for having "something for everyone." This store had "a wide selection" of merchandise including "clothing," "sporting goods," "personal" and "household" items. Respondents were impressed both with its variety of merchandise and its widespread appeal to a broad spectrum of consumers.

6. K mart was well regarded by the vast majority of commercial viewers as "a good place to shop." K mart offered "low prices" on "quality merchandise" and a "friendly" atmosphere.

7. Nearly two in five viewers reacted to the commercial in terms of positive and personal involvement. These respondents spontaneously indicated that they definitely would or "might want to shop" at K mart because "they have something for everyone."

8. When questioned directly regarding the importance of the ideas communicated by the commercial, seven of ten viewers mentioned one or more messages. The possibility of "saving money" and the "variety" of merchandise were considered to be the key elements of the commercial.

-2-

Exhibit 13.9 continued

9. Over one in four viewers (28%) learned new
    information from this commercial. The primary message
    learned was the variety of merchandise available at
    K mart.

10. The commercial improved perceptions of K mart for nearly
    half the sample. The major reasons for this shift in
    attitude were the many "different items" offered and the
    "casual," "relaxed" shopping environment.

11. Based on direct questioning, nearly two of three viewers
    expressed positive interest in shopping at K mart in the
    future.

12. Respondents generally did not find anything in the
    commercial confusing or hard to understand (78%). Among
    those who did, the most common complaint was that the
    commercial "tried to make too many points."

13. Only twelve percent questioned the credibility of any
    aspect of this commercial. These responses were diffuse
    with no clear pattern evident.

-3-

Exhibit 13.9 continued

EXHIBIT I.
COMMERCIAL PROFILE

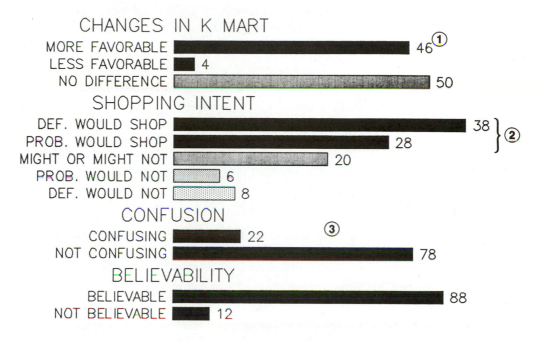

Exhibit 13.10 Commercial Profile for K mart commercial.
1. Of the respondents in the study, 46 percent claimed a more favorable attitude toward K mart as a result of seeing the commercial.
2. If the two positive categories under Shopping Intent are combined, 66 percent of the respondents said they definitely or probably would shop at K mart.
3. Somewhat more than one-fifth of the viewers of the K mart commercial were confused in some way by it.

Using a bar graph format, Starch provides clients with a graphic portrayal of respondents' reactions to specific commercials. This commercial profile shows general attitudes toward the company or brand, intent to shop, confusion that may have resulted from the commercial, and believability of the commercial. Exhibit 13.10 is the commercial profile for the K mart commercial.

••• Summary

Advertisers want to know how effective their advertising messages are, and syndicated message research services attempt to measure such effectiveness. In one form or another, most measures of message effectiveness are related to recall or recognition—how well people can remember advertisements they have seen. This reliance on recall and recognition is based on the assumption that advertising cannot have any effect on sales (the measure that most advertisers would really like to have) unless consumers can remember it. There is a body of research that suggests that recall of advertisements may have only a weak relationship to subsequent purchase of the product.

A common way to measure broadcast message recall is to telephone people and ask them what they remember about commercials they saw the day before. This is the method used by Gallup & Robinson and ASI. Starch shows respondents a videotape of the commercial and follows up with questions.

... Self-Test Questions

1. Look at Exhibit 13.2. Numerous factors can account for a given commercial's score. Suggest at least two possible explanations for the performance of the test commercial.
2. Look at Exhibit 13.4. What percentage of the female readers recalled a reference to sponges in the commercial?
3. Look at Exhibit 13.10. Would you say that this commercial was understandable to the respondents? What information tells you this?
4. Look at Exhibit 13.10. To what extent did the respondents consider this to be a believable advertisement?

... Suggestions for Additional Reading

Appel, V., S. Weinstein, and C. Weinstein. "Brain Activity and Recall of TV Advertising." *Journal of Advertising Research*, Vol. 19, No. 4 (August 1979), 7–15.

Greene, W. F. "Does the Medium Affect TV Commercial Performance?" Thirtieth Annual Conference of the Advertising Research Foundation, New York, 1984.

Greene, W. F. "Quantifying the Effect of Zapping and Zipping on Commercial Intrusiveness." Sixth Annual Advertising Research Foundation Copy Research Workshop, New York, 1989.

Greene, W. F., and J. E. McCullough. "Animatic, Photomatic to Live-Action Rough Pre-testing Predictability vs. Production Cost Tradeoffs." Second Annual Advertising Research Foundation Copy Research Workshop, New York, 1985.

Gunther, M. "To Burke or Not To Burke." *TV Guide* (February 7, 1981), 3–8.

Lissance, D. M., and L. E. Ott. "What Every Young Account Representative Should Know About Creative Research." New York: American Association of Advertising Agencies, 1978.

Lukeman, G. "No Attention, No Recall: Getting It and Losing It." Sixth Annual Advertising Research Foundation Copy Research Workshop, New York, 1989.

Murphy, J. P. "What Makes Ad Winner, Loser?" *Advertising Age* (October 20, 1980), s-32 to s-34.

Rapp, S., and T. L. Collins. "In Search of Research." *Advertising Age* (November 24, 1986), 43.

Walker, D., and M. F. von Gonten. "Explaining Related Recall Outcomes: New Answers from a Better Model." *Journal of Advertising Research*, Vol. 29 (1989), 11–21.

CHAPTER 14

Message Research: Print

The timeliness of a television commercial is especially beneficial during the testing process. Because the viewer can see the advertisement only when it is broadcast, day-after recall studies are convenient. The commercial airs, and the next day selected viewers answer questions posed by researchers.

In contrast, magazine readers' typical use of magazines takes place over some period of time. Some readers purchase the magazine on the first day the edition appears on the newsstand. Some subscribe to it and receive it early. Others buy it the day before the next edition appears on the newsstand. And any of them may read the magazine immediately or much later.

The disparity in times during which readers may actually see a given advertisement makes recall research difficult for print messages because of the desirability of interviewing all respondents within an equal time after their exposure.

If interviewing all respondents in a magazine study is crucial, the researcher can arrange for recipients to read the magazine on a prearranged day. More commonly, to overcome the problem of scattered exposure to print advertisements, researchers use recognition testing. They show respondents the original ad and ask whether they remember seeing it and reading it when they read the publication.

••• ASI Market Research

ASI Market Research, which is known for its television commercial testing service, also provides its Print Plus system for pretesting magazine advertisements.

Print Plus studies are based on tip-in advertisements placed in current editions of *People, Time, Newsweek, Sports Illustrated, McCalls, Better Homes and Gardens, Cosmopolitan, Redbook,* or ASI's control magazine, *Reflections. Reflections* is a 96-page magazine that provides a constant editorial and advertising environment that is appropriate for both male- and female-directed products and services. This publication eliminates the need to conform to publishing schedules of the major national magazines.

The tip-in procedure involves carefully gluing test advertisements into copies of the magazines, in order that testing of the ads be done in the natural environment. An ad that has been tipped in is as much a part of the magazine as any other advertisement in the edition.

ASI places the magazines in qualified respondents' homes in at least five geographically dispersed markets. Usually, the sample includes 175 males and 175 females, or 100 males and 100 females. Sample characteristics are generally reflective of the magazine's readership.

Respondents are asked to participate in a survey on the public's opinion of magazines and are screened for demographic information prior to placement of the magazine. They are asked to read the magazine that evening and to participate in a telephone interview the next day. They are also told that there will be a prize drawing after the test is over.

Print Plus provides three key measures:

1. *Day-After Recall.* Day-after recall is the percent of respondents who can accurately describe the ad the day following their exposure, with the magazine closed, when given the brand name.
2. *Persuasion.* Attitude change is measured through comparison of preexposure brand preference with postexposure preference.
3. *Product Interest.* This is the degree of change in indicated interest in the product or service as a result of having seen the advertisement.

••• Gallup & Robinson, Inc.

Gallup & Robinson's print research services are Magazine Impact Research Service (MIRS) and Rapid Ad Measurement (RAM). Each employs a sample of 150 adults of either gender, depending on the magazine tested. Respondents are selected from ten metropolitan areas and qualify by having read at least two of the last four editions of the test magazine or others in the category.

. . . MIRS

The Magazine Impact Research Service is a subscription posttesting service designed to track client advertising appearing in selected issues of major consumer magazines, including *Better Homes and Gardens, Bon Appetite, Cosmopolitan, People, Sports Illustrated, Time,* and others. The service also provides tracking information on competitors' ads placed in the same magazines.

MIRS can also be used to pretest ads that are in the development stage through use of a tip-in. The ad is prepared for insertion into copies of the magazine and is added to the copies distributed to respondents. Then it is tested along with the other ads that actually were published in the magazine.

MIRS has three applications: to assess performance of individual ads in a natural environment, to analyze overall print campaign effectiveness compared with past performance and with the performance of competitors' ads, and to analyze general patterns in creative strategies within specific industries.

MIRS produces three measurement scores that correspond to the three scores Gallup & Robinson provides for its television commercial tests.

1. *Intrusiveness (Proved Name Registration).* This is the percent of respondents who can accurately describe the ad the day following exposure. This measure is an indicator of the ad's ability to command attention. For comparative purposes, percentages are adjusted for space/color unit cost and issue level.
2. *Idea Communication.* This profile reflects the extent to which various copy points have gotten through to those persons able to prove ad recall.
3. *Persuasion (Favorable Buying Attitude).* This is the distribution of respondent statements of how the ad affected purchase interest. This measure is a relative indicator of the ad's ability to persuade. For corporate advertising, the persuasion measure indicates the extent to which the ad made a strong case for the advertiser.

In the June 27, 1988 edition of *Sports Illustrated* appeared a four color, full page advertisement for Kodak 35mm film. It featured a child sitting in a barber's chair, holding a teddy bear. The headline was, "True Courage," and the copy consisted of three lines: "Introducing new Kodacolor Gold 100 film. The truest color, the most realistic color, the most accurate color of any film, anywhere." It ended with "Show Your True Colors."[1] Exhibit 14.1 is the Gallup & Robinson summary report for the advertisement. Exhibits 14.2 to 14.4 provide additional information for each of the three measures of MIRS.

. . . RAM

Rapid Ad Measurement (RAM) is Gallup & Robinson's service designed for pretesting magazine ads. In it, test ads are placed in copies of *Time* or *People*. To

KODAK FILM

Sports Illustrated - June 27, 1988

PERFORMANCE SUMMARY

Sample Composition: 156 Men

Page Location: 28
Size/Color Unit: One page, Four color

	Men
INTRUSIVENESS/PNR	
Proved Name Registration (PNR)	21 ①
Norm: All Photographic Products	② 13
IDEA COMMUNICATION	
Lead Idea: Preserve/keep memories	34%
Norm: All Photographic Products	64
AVERAGE NUMBER OF IDEAS COMMUNICATED	
Average Number of Ideas per Respondent	1.4 ③
Norm: All Photographic Products	2.4
PERSUASION/FBA	
Favorable Buying Attitude (FBA)	61% ④
Norm: All Photographic Products	53
NET EFFECTIVENESS	
PNR X FBA	13 ⑤
Norm: All Photographic Products	7

Exhibit 14.1 MIRS Performance Summary for the Kodak advertisement. Reprinted with permission of Gallup & Robinson, Inc.
1. Proved Name Registration was 21 among the respondents.
2. The PNR for this ad was considerably stronger than the norm for all photographic products.
3. Respondents played back fewer ideas than the norm for the product category.
4. As a result of having seen this ad, respondents' Favorable Buying Attitudes were considerably stronger than the norm.
5. The Net Effectiveness score was nearly double the norm for the product category.

reduce the number of competing ads and hold the ad exposure universe to a constant twenty-five to thirty ads, four-page forms that are all advertising and do not interrupt article content are removed. Test ads are placed in the first half of the magazine and are rotated through at least two positions so as to offset any influence of adjacent material.

```
                        KODAK FILM

              Sports Illustrated - June 27, 1988


                                    PNR          Standard      Sample
INTRUSIVENESS/PNR                  Measure         Error        Base

Kodak Film
  Pg.  28  1P4C           Men    21①             3.1           156


-----------------------------------------------------------------------


Norms                          Men

All Products                    11
All Photographic Products       13
Film & Film Development         11②
```

Exhibit 14.2 MIRS data on intrusiveness/proved name registration. Reprinted with permission of Gallup & Robinson, Inc.
1. Of the 156 male respondents, 21 percent demonstrated recall of this one-page, four-color Kodak advertisement.
2. PNR for this Kodak ad was nearly double that of the film and film development category.

The sampling method is similar to that used for MIRS, as are the measurements: proved name registration, idea communication, and favorable buying attitude. The report formats are similar.

RAM differs from MIRS in several ways. Where two or more versions of an ad are to be compared, full-size samples are obtained by including each version in two successive tests of the same magazine or by splitting the test sample into two cells. In each test, half the total sample is exposed to Version A and half to Version B. Special arrangements can be made to add a special target audience to the standard sample. Finally, since advertisers testing new advertising strategies don't like to let competitors know what they are doing, RAM reports are confidential to the client.

Exhibit 14.5 is a Performance Summary page from a report on a Smirnoff Vodka advertisement that was tested in *Time*, October 5, 1987.

... Starch INRA Hooper

Starch INRA Hooper provides three widely used services for measuring advertisement readership. The Starch Readership Service measures readership of advertisements and editorial items in consumer and business magazines and newspapers

```
                             KODAK FILM

                    Sports Illustrated - June 27, 1988


                                                    Recallers
IDEA COMMUNICATION                              #              %
Preserve/keep memories                          10             34①

Quality/better/best                             8              28

Good/better color                               7              24
   Accurate/realistic colors                       3              10

Takes good/beautiful pictures                   5              17
   Clear/crisp pictures                            4              14

New                                             4              14

Refer to kind/type                              3              10


Favor to ad                                     4              14
Disfavor to ad                                  2              7

Mentions:
Child                                           28             97②
"Show your true colors"                         5              17

Average Number of Ideas
      per Respondent                               1.4

Respondents with One or More
      Ideas Communicated                        26             90③

Base (men)                                      29             100

-----------------------------------------------------------------

Norms: All Photographic Products                             Men

Lead Idea Communicated                                       64%
Average Number of Ideas/Respondent                           2.4
Respondents With One or More Ideas
   Communicated                                              >90%③

Favor to ad                                                  <10%
Disfavor to ad                                               <10%




IRISTAB
```

Exhibit 14.3 MIRS data on idea communication. Reprinted with permission of Gallup & Robinson, Inc.
1. Thirty-four percent of the respondents recalled the copy point, "preserve/keep memories."
2. Almost all respondents (97 percent) mentioned the child in the ad.
3. Most respondents (90 percent) were able to identify at least one idea contained in the ad. This was same as the norm for the product category.

Sports Illustrated - June 27, 1988

PERSUASION/FBA	Recallers - Did Not Buy Brand Last Time	
	#	%
Increased Buying Interest	17	①61
Increased considerably	4	14
Increased somewhat	13	46
Not Affected	11	39
Decreased Buying Interest	0	0
Decreased somewhat	0	0
Decreased considerably	0	② 0
DK/NA/Refused	0	0
Base (men)	28	100

Norms: All Photographic Products	Men
Increased Buying Interest	①53%
Increased considerably	15
Increased somewhat	38

IRISTAB

Exhibit 14.4 MIRS data on Persuasion/Favorable Buying Attitude. Reprinted with permission of Gallup & Robinson, Inc.
1. Of the men asked, 61 percent reported increased buying interest, compared with the norm of 53 percent.
2. The ad produced no adverse effects on the respondents who saw it.

through personal interviews with a sample of issue readers. The Starch Impression Study measures the meaning that readers attach to given advertisements. The Starch Ballot Readership Study measures readership of advertising and editorial items in business, professional, and agricultural publications through mail questionnaires with a sample of subscriber issue readers.

... Starch Readership Report

Each year, Starch studies the readership of more than 75,000 advertisements in 1,000 individual issues of consumer and business publications. It employs samples of at least 100 adult readers of each gender and uses specialized samples where appropriate, such as in studying readership by teenage girls. The company estimates that in a given year, it interviews more than 100,000 readers.

```
                          SMIRNOFF VODKA

                      Time - October 5, 1987


PERFORMANCE SUMMARY


Sample Composition:   153 Men
                      153 Women

Page Location: 91
Size/Color Unit: One page, Four color


                                              Men      Women
    INTRUSIVENESS/PNR

      Proved Name Registration (PNR)          14    ①    27
      Norm:  Vodka                            19          16


    IDEA COMMUNICATION

      Lead Idea: Enjoyable/pleasurable        59%        59%
      Norm:  Vodka                            40          44


    AVERAGE NUMBER OF IDEAS COMMUNICATED

      Average Number of Ideas per Respondent  2.3        2.5
      Norm:  Vodka                            1.3        1.6


    PERSUASION/FBA

      Favorable Buying Attitude (FBA)         24%   ②    31%
      Norm:  Vodka                            43          43


    NET EFFECTIVENESS

      PNR X FBA                                3    ③    8
      Norm:  Vodka                            8           7
```

Exhibit 14.5 RAM Performance Summary for a Smirnoff Vodka advertisement. Reprinted with permission of Gallup & Robinson, Inc.
1. The Proved Name Registration score for women was 27, compared with only 14 for men. The women's score was higher than the women's norm.
2. Neither the men's nor the women's Favorable Buying Attitude scores were at or above the norms.
3. The Net Effectiveness score was better for women than for men. The women's score was slightly higher than the women's norm for vodka advertisements.

Samples are selected from twenty to thirty urban areas and reflect the geographic circulation pattern of each magazine. Interviews are conducted with people of varying ages, income levels, and occupations to make samples broadly representative of the magazine's circulation. Samples for certain business publications are selected to be representative of the publication's readers, taking into account the type of industry and job responsibility. For publications having small circulations, Starch uses subscriber lists to help locate eligible respondents. Starch cautions that because the data are based on interviews with readers of specific editions of the magazines, the data are not necessarily projectable to the entire regular readership.

Face-to-face interviews are conducted by a permanent staff of Starch interviewers during the early life of a publication. Following a suitable waiting period after the appearance of a publication to give readers an opportunity to read or look through their issue, interviewing continues for two days for a daily publication, one week for a weekly publication, two weeks for a biweekly publication, and three weeks for a monthly publication. Interviewers first verify that a person is an eligible reader of the issue—one who meets the age, occupation, and gender requirements and who has glanced through or read some part of the issue being studied before the interviewer's visit. To minimize the effect of respondent fatigue, each interviewer begins at a different page in the issue and continues through to more than ninety ads in the issue.

Using the recognition method, the interviewer goes through the publication page by page, pointing to and asking about each advertisement designated for study. Respondents are first asked, "Did you see or read any part of this advertisement?" When the answer is "yes," respondents are then asked a prescribed series of questions to determine observation and reading of the component parts of the ad—illustrations, headline, signature, copy blocks. Based on the responses to these detailed questions, each respondent is classified by the interviewer as follows:

1. *"Noted" reader:* one who remembered having previously seen the advertisement in the issue being studied.
2. *"Associated" reader:* one who not only noted the ad but also saw or read some part of it that clearly indicated the brand or advertiser.
3. *"Read Most" reader:* one who read half or more of the written material in the ad.

Starch Readership Reports contain a labeled issue of the magazine, with "ad as a whole" and component part readership scores on each tested ad, a Summary Report listing all studied ads in the issue, and Adnorm data, wherever applicable, showing readership norms for ads of the same size, color, and product category for that publication.

Exhibit 14.6 shows a page from a labeled issue of *Reader's Digest*. Readership scores for an Oatmeal Goodness® advertisement are printed on stickers attached to the ad.

How did the Oatmeal Goodness® advertisement perform compared with other ads in this issue of the magazine? A page taken from the Starch Readership Report for the November 1989 edition of the magazine is reproduced as Exhibit 14.7.

Because the Oatmeal Goodness® ad was most likely targeted at women, readership data on women are more important to the advertiser than data on men or on all adults. Therefore, it is not surprising that the Oatmeal Goodness® ad scored considerably less well with male readers. Exhibit 14.8 shows these differences.

Exhibit 14.6 An Oatmeal Goodness® advertisement from *Reader's Digest*. Reprinted with permission of Starch INRA Hooper, Inc., and Continental Bakery Company. Oatmeal Goodness® is a registered trademark.

1. The Ad-As-A-Whole sticker shows the performance of the entire ad. Among male readers, 41 percent noted the ad, 40 read enough to learn the brand, and 5 percent read most of the copy.
2. Among women readers, 37 percent read the headline.
3. Twenty percent of the women readers read some of the body copy.
4. Just over half (51 percent) of the women readers read the signature.

Reader's Digest
Total of 65 1/2 Page or Larger Ads

November 1989
Women Readers

[1A]

PAGE	SIZE& COLOR	ADVERTISER	RANK BY ASSOC.	PERCENTAGES			READERSHIP INDEXES		
				NOTED	ASSOC-IATED	READ MOST	NOTED	ASSOC-IATED	READ MOST
		AUTOMOTIVE ACCESS./EQUIP./MISC.							
72	1P4B	GENERAL MOTORS PARTS & SERVICE	57	27	24	6	64	62	55
		BAKERY GDS. (FRESH/FROZEN/REFRIGERATED)							
24	1P4B	OATMEAL GOODNESS BREAD	10 ①	53	53	17	126	136	155 ②
		BUILDING EQUIP./FIXTURES/SYS.							
20	H1/2S4B	GENIE GARAGE DOOR OPERATOR	43	40	31	9	95	79	82
		BUILDING MATERIALS/PRE-FABRICATED HOMES							
18	1P4	MARVIN WINDOWS	51	38	29	3	90	74	27
		COMMUNICATIONS/PUBLIC UTILITIES							
38	1P4B	AT&T TELEPHONES	9	56	54	16	133	138	145
		CONFECTIONERY/SNACKS							
233	H1/2PB	PAYDAY CANDY BAR	**	25	**	7–	60	**	64–
235	H1/2P4B	PAYDAY CANDY BAR	40	35	34	9–	83	87	82–
243	V1/2P4B	MARS CANDY BAR	23	46	44	17–	110	113	155–
247	H1/2P4B	PLANTERS NUTS OFFER	29	43	40	13–	102	103	118–
		COOKING PRODS./SEASONINGS							
55	1P4B	SHAKE 'N BAKE CHICKEN COATING MIX	18	49	46	17–	117	118	155–
215	1P4B	LOG CABIN LITE SYRUP	12	53	51	14–	126	131	127–
		DAIRY PRODS./SUBSTITUTES							
208	1S4B	NATIONAL DAIRY BOARD	21	55	45	15	131	115	136
237	1P4B	KRAFT VELVEETA CHEESE	23	47	44	12	112	113	109
		ELEC. ENTERTAINMENT EQUIP.							
69	1P	MAGNAVOX SMART WINDOW COLOR TELEVISIONS	**	38	**	10–	90	**	91–
70	1S4B	MAGNAVOX SMART WINDOW COLOR TELEVISIONS	27	47	43	14	112	110	127
		FLOOR COVERINGS/FIBERS							
49	1P4B	DUPONT MASTERSERIES CARPET CARE SYSTEM	43	36	31	11	86	79	100
		FOOD BEVERAGES							
31	1P4B	FOLGERS DECAFFEINATED COFFEE CRYSTALS	3	62	61	12–	148	156	109–
44	1P4B	MINUTE MAID READY-TO-SERVE & FROZEN PINK GRAPEFRUIT JUICE COCKTAIL	5	58	56	12–	138	144	109–

[*] Less than 0.5%   [–] Fewer than 50 Words
[**] Not Applicable   [=] Fewer than 4 Words
[#] Page/Copy varies

Exhibit 14.7 Part of a Starch Readership Report for women readers of the Oatmeal Goodness advertisement. Reprinted with permission of Starch INRA Hooper, Inc.

1. The Oatmeal Goodness advertisement was ranked tenth in readership by women among the 65 half-page or larger ads carried in the issue. The "rank by association" column shows ranking by the second readership score.

2. The read-most index for the Oatmeal Goodness ad was 155, which means the ad was considerably better read than the average in this edition of *Reader's Digest*. To be specific, women read this ad at a rate that was 55 percent higher than the average of all tested ads in the magazine. Of ads containing at least 50 words of copy, no ad had a higher index than the ad for Oatmeal Goodness.

Reader's Digest   November 1989   [1A]
Total of 65 1/2 Page or Larger Ads   Men Readers

PAGE	SIZE& COLOR	ADVERTISER	RANK BY ASSOC.	PERCENTAGES NOTED	ASSOC-IATED	READ MOST	READERSHIP INDEXES NOTED	ASSOC-IATED	READ MOST
		AUTOMOTIVE ACCESS./EQUIP./MISC.							
72	1P4B	GENERAL MOTORS PARTS & SERVICE	15	49	43	10	129	126	143
		BAKERY GDS. (FRESH/FROZEN/REFRIGERATED)							
24	1P4B	OATMEAL GOODNESS BREAD	18 ①	41	40	5	108	118	71 ②
		BUILDING EQUIP./FIXTURES/SYS.							
20	H1/2S4B	GENIE GARAGE DOOR OPERATOR	27	44	36	7	116	106	100
		BUILDING MATERIALS/PRE-FABRICATED HOMES							
18	1P4	MARVIN WINDOWS	52	36	26	4	95	76	57
		COMMUNICATIONS/PUBLIC UTILITIES							
38	1P4B	AT&T TELEPHONES	24	42	37	8	111	109	114
		CONFECTIONERY/SNACKS							
233	H1/2PB	PAYDAY CANDY BAR	**	27	**	3-	71	**	43-
235	H1/2P4B	PAYDAY CANDY BAR	53	30	25	3-	79	74	43-
243	V1/2P4B	MARS CANDY BAR	34	35	33	11-	92	97	157-
247	H1/2P4B	PLANTERS NUTS OFFER	29	36	34	5-	95	100	71-
		COOKING PRODS./SEASONINGS							
55	1P4B	SHAKE 'N BAKE CHICKEN COATING MIX	39	35	30	10-	92	88	143-
215	1P4B	LOG CABIN LITE SYRUP	24	38	37	7-	100	109	100-
		DAIRY PRODS./SUBSTITUTES							
208	1S4B	NATIONAL DAIRY BOARD	61	30	19	1	79	56	14
237	1P4B	KRAFT VELVEETA CHEESE	60	22	20	8	58	59	114
		ELEC. ENTERTAINMENT EQUIP.							
69	1P	MAGNAVOX SMART WINDOW COLOR TELEVISIONS	**	41	**	10-	108	**	143-
70	1S4B	MAGNAVOX SMART WINDOW COLOR TELEVISIONS	5	61	57	14	161	168	200
		FLOOR COVERINGS/FIBERS							
49	1P4B	DUPONT MASTERSERIES CARPET CARE SYSTEM	59	23	22	5	61	65	71
		FOOD BEVERAGES							
31	1P4B	FOLGERS DECAFFEINATED COFFEE CRYSTALS	12	48	44	3-	126	129	43-
44	1P4B	MINUTE MAID READY-TO-SERVE & FROZEN PINK GRAPEFRUIT JUICE COCKTAIL	20	42	39	9-	111	115	129-

[*] Less than 0.5%   [-] Fewer than 50 Words
[**] Not Applicable   [=] Fewer than 4 Words
                 [#] Page/Copy varies

Exhibit 14.8 Part of a Starch Readership Report for men readers of the Oatmeal Goodness advertisement. Reprinted with permission of Starch INRA Hooper, Inc.
1. The rank by association was 18 out of the 65 advertisements under scrutiny.
2. The read-most index was 71, which means that the advertisement's read-most score among men was only 71 percent of the median for the issue.

How did the Oatmeal Goodness ad perform compared with other ads analyzed by Starch in *Reader's Digest* over a two-year period? The Adnorms Report that accompanied the analysis of the *Reader's Digest* readership showed average scores that can be used in making comparisons. This report is reproduced in Exhibit 14.9.

. . . Starch Impression Study

By asking readers to relate the meaning of the ad to them, this qualitative study measures how well an ad communicates. It is used for both pretesting and posttesting. A Starch Impression Study is designed to answer the following questions:

- What image of our company and our product does the advertisement communicate?
- Do illustration and copy work together?
- Do the product features that we are highlighting give us a competitive advantage? Are these features important to readers?
- Do most readers find the same meanings in our advertisements—the meanings we want them to find?

The sample is determined by client specifications. This usually means that respondents are drawn from readers of the magazine or magazines in which the advertisement was published or scheduled to be published. For the analysis of the Hellmann's Mayonnaise advertisement shown in Exhibit 14.10, the sample consisted of fifty women who were primary household shoppers and who regularly read at least one of the following magazines: *Better Homes and Gardens, Family Circle, Good Housekeeping, Ladies' Home Journal, McCalls, Redbook,* or *Woman's Day.*

The first step in the interviews is to verify that respondents meet target audience requirements. Interviewers then record respondents' verbatim responses to a series of questions about the ad:

1. When you first looked at this ad, what was outstanding to you? Tell me more about it. What does that mean to you?
2. In your own words, what did the ad tell you about the product, service, or company? Tell me more about it. What does that mean to you?
3. What did the pictures tell you? Tell me more about them. What do they mean to you?
4. In your own words, what did the written material tell you? Tell me more about it. What does that mean to you?

Starch analysts categorize responses and prepare reports for clients. Exhibit 14.11 is an example of a summary section of the Starch Impression Report for the Hellmann's Mayonnaise advertisement.

For greater detail, Starch provides an analysis of reader responses that reflects the degree to which the ad met the specific objectives set by the client. Exhibit 14.12 breaks down the findings by the set objectives.

STARCH READERSHIP ADNORMS

The following are average readership scores for all studied advertisements in issues of this magazine Starched in 1985-1986. Percentage
figures are shown for Noted, Associated and Read Most and are grouped
by product classification, size and color. Where fewer than five ads
were studied, average figures are not shown.

READER'S DIGEST   MF

	SEX	H1/2S4 NO.	N	A	R	1P4 NO.	N	A	R	1P3 NO.	N	A	R
MEDICAL EQUIPMENT/SUPPLIES	M					15	36	29	11				
	F					15	37	31	11				
MEDICAL APPLIANCES & EQUIPMENT	M					10	38	30	9				
	F					10	40	32	9				
MISCELLANEOUS MEDICAL SUPPLIES	M					5	31	27	14				
	F					5	32	28	14				
FOOD & FOOD PRODUCTS	M					① 157	38	31	6				
	F					157	56	51	14				
COOKING PRODUCTS & SEASONINGS	M					② 40	38	30	6				
	F					40	62	57	20				
SHORTENING & OILS	M					7	31	26	3				
	F					7	51	49	10				
DESSERTS & DESSERT INGREDIENTS	M					15	41	30	6				
	F					15	69	63	25				
CONDIMENTS, PICKLES & RELISHES	M					7	40	33	8				
	F					7	53	47	15				
SALAD DRESSING, & MAYONNAISE	M					8	36	32	5				
	F					8	63	59	23				
PREPARED FOODS	M					66	38	32	6				
	F					66	55	50	13				
CEREALS	M					32	39	34	5				
	F					32	50	45	9				
MAC., SPAGHETTI, NOODLE PRODS.& DIN.	M					7	41	35	7				
	F					7	60	56	15				
OTHER DINNERS & PREPARED DISHES	M					24	35	30	7				
	F					24	60	54	19				
DAIRY PRODUCTS	M					20	37	30	4				
	F					20	56	51	12				
CHEESE	M					17	38	31	4				
	F					17	57	52	12				
FRUITS & VEGETABLES	M					9	30	21	4				
	F					9	44	34	10				
OTHER FRUITS (INCLUDING FRESH NUTS)	M					9	30	21	4				
	F					9	44	34	10				
FOOD BEVERAGES	M					15	41	38	6				
	F					15	49	47	8				
COFFEE, TEA, COCOA & DERIVATIVES	M					15	41	38	6				
	F					15	49	47	8				
CONFECTIONERY, SNACKS & SOFT DRINKS	M					48	44	40	11				
	F					48	57	53	16				
CONFECTIONERY & SNACKS	M					43	44	40	12				
	F					43	57	53	17				
CANDY & GUM	M					42	44	40	12				
	F					42	57	53	17				
SOFT DRINKS	M					5	43	35	6				
	F					5	57	53	12				
NON-CARBONATED	M					5	43	35	6				
	F					5	57	53	12				
BEER, WINE & LIQUOR	M					12	53	49	18				
	F					12	37	30	11				
LIQUOR & WHISKEY - TOTAL	M					12	53	49	18				
	F					12	37	30	11				

(CONTINUED)

178

Exhibit 14.9   Page from a Starch Adnorms Report. Reprinted with permission of Starch INRA
Hooper, Inc.
1.   In the period shown for this Adnorms Report, Starch studied 157 advertisements for foods.
2.   The Oatmeal Goodness advertisement outperformed the average food advertisement covered in this Adnorms Report. For women, the associated and read-most scores for Oatmeal
Goodness were superior to the average scores for all food ads. Oatmeal Goodness's noted
score was slightly lower than the average. Among men, the Oatmeal Goodness scores for
noted and associated were higher than the average, and the read-most score was one
percentage point below the average.

Exhibit 14.10 Hellmann's Mayonnaise advertisement for which readership data are given in subsequent exhibits. Reprinted by permission of Best Foods, a Division of CPC International, Inc.

COMPARISON OF RESPONSE TO HELLMANN'S ADVERTISEMENTS

OCTOBER 1989

Ad A - "Give something tasteful for Father's Day. With Hellmann's."

Ad B - "Add a splash of creaminess to a tuna sandwich"

Overall response

Ad A generated well above average positive response. Readers liked an appealing picture and recipe and saw an "all occasions" attribute to Hellmann's mayonnaise.

Ad B drew well below average positive response and widespread resistance. The illustration was not well received. With only limited copy which related to the picture, readers unfavorable attitudes to the visual often colored their response to the ad as a whole.

Illustrations

The Ad A picture was widely seen as "delicious" looking and "appealing." It drew attention, underscored the theme of the ad and the "good result" of the recipe.

With Ad B, the clear majority response to the illustration was mixed or negative. The picture was seen as "off-putting," "not clear," overly "artistic," too abstract a representation of the food featured and not "appetizing."

Exhibit 14.11 Portion of summary highlights from a Starch Impression Report for Hellmann's Mayonnaise advertisement. Reprinted with permission of Starch INRA Hooper, Inc.

Food featured

The Ad A sample more often indicated positive interest in Irresistible Chicken than Ad B readers did in a tuna and mayonnaise sandwich.

Hellmann's mayonnaise

Favorable response to the product, a "good" mayonnaise, was equivalent for the two groups as was the number of readers reporting that they used Hellmann's. Ad B readers emphasized the mayonnaise's "creaminess." Two of ten Ad B women saw versatility: Hellmann's could be used in "any sandwich" or, less often, with "any" food. The versatility attribute was a widespread association, whether stated or implied, for Ad A women. These readers saw Hellmann's usefulness in a cooked dish, in a "variety" of dishes and as an ingredient in a dish which was "nice" for family and special meals.

Personal reaction

Resistance to Ad A was at category level and was as much based on attitudes toward food as on ad specifics. Positively involved response registered at an impressive 56% with most of these women saying they would like to try the recipe or would try it.

For Ad B, 18% indicated positive personal response, and a significant 48% registered resistance. One in ten women wanted a creamier mayonnaise or might buy Hellmann's. As seen, resistant attitudes here were heavily related to response to the visuals. While the strong content of responses suggested that many of the sample group shared the attitude, 14% (some of them Hellmann's fans) explicitly said that the ad would not induce them to buy Hellmann's mayonnaise.

Exhibit 14.11 continued

ADVERTISING OBJECTIVES

OBJECTIVE I:

To generate interest in using Hellmann's mayonnaise by establishing it
as an essential ingredient in an appealing dish.

FINDING: This objective was attained. A strong, attractive
illustration, together with a "good recipe," established the
"goodness" of the dish. Hellmann's was seen as a "fine" product.
More than one-half the readership indicated the desire or clear
intention to "make this dish," generally specifying the use of
Hellmann's mayonnaise.

OBJECTIVE II:

To determine what readers saw as the primary plus and minus areas of
the advertisement.

FINDING: A "yummy" illustration and an easy-to-prepare, "different"
and "good" recipe were productively positive elements of the ad.
Resistant response, which was not pronounced or entirely negative,
was generally related to a dislike of mayonnaise or occasional doubt
as to how healthy a food it was. Areas of the ad that readers argued
with were a "fried" look to the chicken, some confusion as to the
"connection" of the dish with the headline or gift articles pictured
and some doubt as to the suitability or satisfaction of cooking a
chicken dish for Father's Day.

- 3 -

Exhibit 14.12 Portion of a summary by objectives section of a Starch Impression Report for the Hellmann's Mayonnaise advertisement. Reprinted with permission of Starch INRA Hooper, Inc.

> - Roughly one-half the women in this sample explicitly singled
> Hellmann's mayonnaise out as "the best." While all readers
> understood that mayonnaise was an essential in Irresistible
> Chicken, these respondents saw Hellmann's as the specific
> product that "made" the dish, was a versatile, "high-quality"
> brand with a deserved good reputation and deserved place as
> a household standby.
>
> - 2 -

Exhibit 14.12 continued

The remainder of the Starch Impression Report contains verbatim responses and further analysis of general reactions.

・・・ Starch Ballot Readership Study

The Starch Ballot Readership Study measures readership of advertisements in business magazines. A random *n*th name sample of approximately three hundred people is drawn from the subscriber list. They receive postcards advising them that they will receive survey materials. After the group has had time to read their copies of the magazine, they are sent a fresh copy of the magazine, with ballots (short questionnaires) attached to selected pages of the magazines. Respondents mark the ballots to indicate the extent of their readership of the ads and mail the ballots back to Starch in preaddressed, postage-paid envelopes.

The readership studies produce several measures:

- *"Looked At" score:* glanced at the ad
- *"Read Partially" score:* saw the ad and read some parts, but less than half of the copy
- *"Read Thoroughly" score:* read half or more of the copy
- *"Advertising Recognition" score:* total of the "looked at," "read partially," and "read thoroughly" scores
- *"Partial and Thorough" score:* total of the "read partially" and "read thoroughly" scores

- *"Partial and Thorough Readership" index:* "partial and thorough" score divided by the median partial and thorough readership score for this issue
- *"Recognition" index:* recognition score divided by the median recognition score for this issue

Exhibit 14.13 is an excerpt from a Starch Ballot Readership Study for the April 1985 issue of *Office Products Dealer*.

••• Harvey Research Organization, Inc.

The Harvey Research Organization has two syndicated services that measure readership of advertising in business publications. The Communication Measurement Service uses personal interviews to assess readership and communication of advertisements. The other service, AD-Q, uses mailed questionnaires to measure readership of ads and editorial items.

••• Harvey Communication Measurement Service

The Communication Measurement Service measures readership and impact of advertisements in business publications. The publications sponsor the research and make the reports available to advertisers.

A sample of 100 respondents is drawn from the magazine's subscriber list. Three weeks after the publication date, interviewers telephone selected subscribers to determine whether they have read the issue being measured and to arrange for a personal interview.

In the face-to-face interviews, proof of readership is again established. Interviewers show respondents the magazine's table of contents and ask respondents about their interest in the articles listed.

After establishing readership of the specific issue, the interviewers ask a series of questions about each advertisement in the issue. Starting at different places to minimize the effects of ad placement and respondent fatigue, interviewers ask respondents if they can recall seeing or noticing the ad. Those who remember are asked if they can recall reading enough of the ad to understand the idea being discussed.

Respondents are then asked questions about the ads they read. These are a series of probing, open-ended questions designed to elicit readers' understanding of the ads. Interviewers record the verbatim responses.

Harvey's report for each advertiser includes two basic measures:

1. *Recall Seeing.* This measure gives the percent of respondents who recall seeing a specific ad when they originally read the issue. This measurement is an indicator of the power of a particular ad to attract notice. Harvey advises its clients that this score is affected by the type of headline, illustration, and layout.
2. *Recall Reading.* This measure gives the percent of respondents who read a sufficient amount of the advertisement to comprehend the principal subject

OFFICE PRODUCTS DEALER

ADVERTISING SCORES

BALLOT RESEARCH COMPANY

APRIL 1985

SUPPLIES/ACCESSORIES	PER CENT OF TOTAL READERS			ADVERTISING RECOGNITION SCORE		PARTIAL AND THOROUGH READERSHIP	
	LOOKED AT	READ PARTIALLY	READ THOROUGHLY	PCT	INDEX	PCT	INDEX
SOUTHWORTH CO. 1P4B Page 2C ,	63 ①	11	5	② 79	130 ③	16	④ 67
CAMPBELL STATIONERY/JAMES RIVER CORP. Page 1 , 1P4	41	20	2	63	103	22	92
TOPS BUSINESS FORMS Page 2 , 1P4B	41	14	3	58	95	17	71
DENNISON MANUFACTURING CO. Page 6 , 1P4	38	14	5	57	93	19	79
NEKOOSA PAPERS INC. Page 7 , 1P	53	17	8	78	128	25	104
DYSAN CORP. 1P4B Page 9 ,	36	9	16	61	100	25	104
TENEX CORP. S4B Page 10 ,	28	25	20	73	120	45	188
SWINGLINE 1P4B Page 13 ,	55	14	14	83	136	28	117
SCHWAN-STABILO USA, INC. Page 37 , 1P2	38	17	3	58	95	20	83
BEROL USA 1P4B Page 40 ,	41	11	8	60	98	19	79
HARPER HOUSE SYSTEMS Page 53 , 1P2B	20	11	11	42	69	22	92

Exhibit 14.13 Advertising scores summary from a Starch Ballot Readership Study. Reprinted with permission of Starch INRA Hooper, Inc.
1. Sixty-three percent of the respondents reported that they looked at the Southworth Company advertisement on Page 2c, which was a one-page, four-color bleed ad.
2. The advertising recognition score was 79. Seventy-nine percent of the respondents looked at, read partially, or read thoroughly the Southworth ad.
3. The 79 recognition score was 30 percent stronger than the median for the issue of the magazine.
4. The partial and thorough index was 67, which was below the median for the issue. Median index is 100.

**HARVEY
COMMUNICATION
MEASUREMENT**

Issue: October 23, 1989

SUMMARY OF SCORES

for_____Panasonic Video Communications_____**page**___Cover 2___

Size–Color of Ad_____1p4cb_____

	% Recall Seeing	% Recall Reading
Advertiser's Scores	64 ①	29 ④
Issue Average	53 ②	26
Size–Color Average Scores	57 ③	28

Exhibit 14.14 Portion of a Harvey Communication Measurement Service Report for a Panasonic Video Communications advertisement. Reprinted with permission of Harvey Research Organization, Inc.
1. Of the respondents interviewed, 64 percent reported seeing the advertisement. This was better than the average for similar advertisements in the issue.
2. The average recall seeing score for the October 23, 1989, issue of *Cablevision* was 53.
3. The average score for advertisements of similar specification was 57.
4. The recall reading score, 29, was slightly above the average recall reading score for ads with similar specifications.

discussed, and to identify the advertiser. These scores are affected by the quality and usefulness of the ad copy to the reader. Ads with long copy frequently get better recall reading scores than ads with short copy if the content is informative.

Exhibt 14.14 is a portion of a Communication Measurement Service Report for a one-page, four-color bleed ad that appeared on the inside front cover of the October 23, 1989, issue of *Cablevision*. The advertisement was for Panasonic Video Communications.

. . . Harvey AD-Q

Harvey AD-Q ("ADvertising Quotient") studies are conducted among at least 100 readers of the publications studied. Procedures are similar to those used in other Harvey studies.

The key feature of the Harvey AD-Q service is data on advertisement effectiveness among readers with buying influence. The advertising quotient score is the total of four other scores: the recall seeing and recall reading scores for all readers and for readers who buy or specify the advertised product. The maximum advertising quotient score is 400. Exhibit 14.15 shows the summary of scores for ads appearing in the September 1988 edition of *Heavy Construction News*.

Readex Readership Research

Readex, Inc., provides measures of readership and reader interest in advertisements and editorial items in business, professional, and farm publications. Publishers sponsor the research and make the results available to advertising agencies and advertisers.

Readex uses mailed questionnaires for its Reader Interest Plus Reports, Red Sticker Reports, and Message Impact Reports. A random, *n*th-name sample is drawn from the magazine's circulation list. Readex sends fresh copies of the magazine to respondents about midway between issue dates and bases reports on at least 100 responses.

. . . Reader Interest Plus Report

These reports measure reader interest for editorial items and for advertisements of at least half-page size. Respondents are asked to page through the magazine and mark those items that they found to be of interest. Then the respondents are asked to check the questionnaire for each ad they remembered seeing when they first saw the issue. The marked magazines and questionnaires are returned to Readex by return mail.

Reports contain data for two responses: "Remember seeing" denotes that a reader has remembered seeing a particular ad. "Found information of interest" means that the reader saw the item, read some or all of it, and then formulated a considered opinion of what was seen and read.

Exhibit 14.16 shows a portion of a Reader Interest Plus Report covering advertisements appearing in *The Office*.

SUMMARY OF SCORES

Page		ALL READERS		Readers Who Buy/Specify Advertised Product		ADvertising Quotient (Maximum: 400)
		% Recall Seeing	% Recall Reading	% Recall Seeing	% Recall Reading	
EARTHMOVING EQUIPMENT						
Cvr. 2	Komatsu Canada Ltd. (1p4cb) ②	60	27	67	47	201
12-13	JI Case Canada/A Division of Tenneco Canada Inc. (2p4cb)	55	32	67	53	207
22	JCB Inc. (1/2pbw)	28	12	37	20	97
23	JCB Inc. (1p4cb)	24	12	30	17	83
24B-C	Caterpillar Inc. (2p4cb Insert)	51	33	53	37	174
37	Truck & Tractor Equipment Ltd. (1pbw)	40	28	47	40	155
ROADBUILDING EQUIPMENT						
21	Caterpillar Inc. (1p4cb) ①	74	49	91	59	273
38	Dynapac (1/2p2c)	36	22	55	36	149
CRANES and SHOVELS						
33	TRAK International, Inc. (1p4cb)	23	18	21	12	74
34	Koehring Company (1p4cb)	42	23	47	33	145
TRUCKS including OFF-HIGHWAY						
Cvr. 4	Mack Trucks, Inc. (1p4cb)	36	29	38	31	134

Base: 100 issue readers.

Exhibit 14.15 Ad-Q Summary for *Heavy Construction News*. Reprinted by permission of Harvey Research Organization, Inc.

1. The Caterpillar Inc. advertisement that appeared on p. 21 of this edition of *Heavy Construction News* performed better than all other advertisements included in this exhibit. Seventy-four percent of all readers recalled seeing the advertisement. Other scores for the Caterpillar advertisement exceeded the comparable scores for other advertisements in this exhibit.
2. Sixty percent of all readers recalled seeing the first advertisement listed in this exhibit, which was a one-page, four-color bleed ad for Komatsu Canada Ltd.

the office

advertisements by product classification

RS	FI	SIZE	PAGE	ADVERTISEMENT
SOFTWARE				
36%	11%	1c4	145	**Wright Line FROLIC Software**
COMPUTER ACCESSORIES & SUPPLIES				
65%	20%	2c4	24-5	**3M Diskettes**
53	17	1	13	**Polaroid CP-50 Circular Polarizing Filter**
47	17	1c4	18	**Intel Modems**
40	17	1c4	147	**Ring King Computer Accessories**
TELECOMMUNICATIONS/TELEPHONE SYSTEMS				
49%	23%	1c4	26	**Plantronics Mirage Headset**
48	28	1c4	1	**Comlite Director Series**
35	11	1c4	41	**Executone Information Systems**
10	5	2/3	94	**Canamex Quiktel**
COMPUTER & W.P. FURNITURE/WORK STATIONS				
58%	25%	1c4	7	**Hamilton Sorter Furniture**
POWER CONTROLS & SUPPLIES				
59%	26%	1c4	C2	**Curtis Accessories**
49	19	1c4	141	**SL Waber Surge and Noise Suppressors**
46	31	1	113	**Panamax Surge Protectors**
34	14	1/2	152	**Certron Power-Pro Surge Suppressors**
17	6	1/2c4	128	**Winders & Geist Flexiduct Faxcessory Surge Suppressor**
WORD PROCESSING SUPPLIES & ACCESSORIES				
56%	18%	1c4	135	**Dysan Disks**
56	10	1c4	81	**Maxell Disks/Free Football Game**
39	7	1c4	79	**Verbatim Back Up Products**
20	13	1/2r	19	**M/H Group Software**
DESKTOP PUBLISHING				
55%	19%	1c4	93	**Hammermill Bond**
COLLATORS/FOLDERS/SORTERS/LAM./BINDERS/STAPLERS				
*46%	16%			**GBC Ad**
25	4	card	67-8	**Presentation Guide**
40	14	1/2c4	69	**Binding Systems/StyleWriter Lettering System**

*Percent of unduplicated readers who marked one or more items within the unit

advertisements by product classification

RS	FI	SIZE	PAGE	ADVERTISEMENT
COPYING MACHINES/DUPLICATORS				
73%	16%	1	5	**Lanier Copiers**
50	13	1	136	**Toshiba BD-9230 Copier**
46	19	1c4	123	**Panasonic FP-C1 Copier**
42	8	1c4	59	**Standard SP-9000 Copier**
36	5	1	45	**Xerox Midsized Copiers**
32	6	1	39	**Eastman Kodak Copiers**
31	7	1c4	86	**Canon Copiers**
28	3	1c4	10	**Gestetner Copiers**
24	5	1r	63	**AEG Olympia C1000 and C2011 Copiers**

① ②

RS	FI	SIZE	PAGE	ADVERTISEMENT
COPYING/DUPLICATING SUPPLIES & ACCESSORIES				
55%	12%	1c4	31	**Hammermill Copier Paper**
10	4	1/2r	46	**Hecon Copy Control Products**
BUSINESS PAPERS/FORMS/ENVELOPES				
47%	15%	1c4	C4	**Curtis 1000 Tyvek Envelopes**
26	9	1/2	156	**Sealed Air Jiffy Rigi Bag Mailers**
MICROGRAPHIC EQUIPMENT & SUPPLIES				
71%	20%	2c4	8-9	**Minolta Imaging Systems**
61	23	1c4	17	**Canon NP 780 FSII Reader/Printer**
41	13	1c4	36	**Canon Assisted Retrieval System**
22	7	1c4	143	**Micro Design Micro Copy 1000/Micro Copy 10**
ADDRESSING/MAILING/LABELING EQUIPMENT & SUPPLIES				
28%	4%	1g	64	**Pitney Bowes Mailroom Equipment**
17	6	1/2b	52	**Bowe Inserting & Mailing Systems**
FACSIMILE EQUIP./ELEC. MAIL SYSTEMS				
*56%	22%			**Lanier Ad**
34	8	1	53	**5400 Fax Machine**
33	8	1	55	**5400 Fax Machine**
46	21	1	57	**5400 Fax Machine**
55	14	2c4	100-1	**Murata Fax Machines**
55	19	1c4	110	**Sharp Fax Machines**
48	16	1c4	109	**NEC NEFAX 300**
46	21	1c4	2	**Telautograph Omnifax G55 Digital Fax**
46	13	1	96-7	**Toshiba Facsimile Systems**
43	19	1c4	107	**Canon Fax Machines**
41	14	1	98	**AT&T Fax Machines/24 Hour Hot Line Service**

(CONTINUED)

*Percent of unduplicated readers who marked one or more items within the unit

Exhibit 14.16 Portion of a Reader Interest Plus Report. Reprinted with permission of Readex Readership Research.

1. The advertisement earning the highest remember seeing score was in the copying machines/duplicators category. The Lanier copiers advertisement, on page 5 of *The Office*, achieved a score of 73 percent.
2. The found information of interest score for the Lanier copier ad was 16 percent. That score was lower than the scores for several other ads appearing in this edition of *The Office*.

・・・Readex Red Sticker Report

In this survey, duplicate copies of the magazine sent to subscribers have red stickers attached to selected (between twenty and sixty) editorial items and advertisements. Respondents check the appropriate space to give their answers to questions on the sticker. The three resulting scores are remember seeing, read half or more, and found information of interest.

Exhibit 14.17 shows a Red Sticker Report for the July 1989 edition of *Unix Review*.

・・・Message Impact Report

The Message Impact Report is a new service of Readex. It provides several measures of the performance of an advertisement. These measures include attention-getting ability, believability, an evaluation of information value, types of actions motivated by the advertisement, and the message or feeling perceived by the reader. Complete reports contain information about the performance of the individual and, for comparison purposes, the performance of other ads in the issue. Readex points out that the data should be used for making comparisons among ads and should not be projected to the entire universe.

Exhibit 14.18 is part of a Readex Message Impact Study for the August 1989 edition of *Video Systems*. Exhibit 14.19 shows one page of the issue summary, for comparing the performance of various individual advertisements.

・・・ Summary

Most print message research uses recognition as a measure of an advertisement's readership and communication. Respondents are shown copies of publications that they said they read before the interview. Interviewers show respondents the ads and determine whether or not the respondents did, indeed, read the ads. Examples of this kind of research are the Starch Readership Summary Report, Starch Impression Study, and Harvey Communication Measurement Service.

Some companies use another kind of recognition testing. They ask readers to mail back questionnaires that measure advertisement readership. Examples of this kind of research are the Starch Ballot Readership Study, the Readex Reader Interest Report, and Harvey AD-Q.

In some interviews, including those conducted by telephone, respondents are not shown the advertisements but are given product and brand cues and are asked to recall ads in issues of magazines they have read. This is the method used by ASI's Print Plus Test and by Gallup & Robinson's Magazine Impact Readership Service and Rapid Ad Measurement.

advertisements by product classification

RS	RM	FI	SIZE	PAGE	ADVERTISEMENT
CONTINUED					
64%	44%	31%	1b	17	**MKS Make & MKS RCS**
59	45	28	1c4	69	**Aesoft AEWINDOS**
59	40	26	1/3p	105	**MKS LEX/YACC**
56	44	38	1b	86	**Oregon Software C++ Compiler/Debugger**
55	31	21	1c4	27	**MetaWare High C/Professional Pascal**
43	33	21	1g	88	**Faircom D-Tree/C-Tree/R-Tree**
37	26	18	1c4	76	**Sherrill-Lubinski SL-GMS (3.0e)**
35	26	16	1/2g	16	**Oasys RISC Software Tools**
34	30	24	1/2g	100	**Language Processors NEW C**
DATABASE MANAGEMENT SYSTEMS					
92%	48%	36%	2c4Spr	2C-1	**Informix Software INFORMIX-4GL**
78	55	40	1c4	4	**Oracle Version 6**
73	47	31	1c4	18	**Relational Technology INGRES**
62	37	26	2c4Spr	54-5	**Interbase Software InterBase**
54	37	26	1c4 + card	65	**Unify ACCELL/SQL**
52	35	19	1c4	63	**Progress Software 4GL/RDBMS**
44	33	22	1c4	23	**Empress M-Builder 4-GL**
PRODUCTIVITY TOOLS & BUSINESS APPLICATIONS					
71%	60%	49%	1c4	4C	**Santa Cruz SCO Portfolio**
58	39	28	1/3g	103	**MKS Make**
50	35	26	2Spr	28-9	**UniPress Emacs 2.2**
47	39	31	1	110	**James River ICE.10**
PERIPHERALS					
84%	58%	22%	1c4	35	**Esprit Opus 3nl**
82	43	28	2c4Spr	36-7	**Imagen X320 Laser Printer**
59	47	36	1c4	107	**Microtek Scan Vu-300**
29	17	11	1/2Island	9	**Helios Memory Boards**
NETWORK & COMMUNICATIONS					
⌐67%①	⌐50%②	⌐40%③	1c4	78	**Advance Micro Research UnTerminal**
EDUCATION & TRAINING					
58%	52%	43%	1/2	32	**Prentice Hall X Window System Programming**
RECRUITMENT					
62%	59%	48%	1r	99	**Open Software Employment Opportunities**
29	22	16	1/2Island	8	**Stratus Employment Opportunities**

Exhibit 14.17 Portion of a Readex Red Sticker Report. Reprinted with permission of Readex Readership Research.

1. Fifty-eight percent of the readers of *Unix Review* remembered seeing the half-page advertisement for Prentice Hall X Window System Programming.
2. Just over half (52 percent) of the readers read half or more of the advertisement.
3. Forty-three percent of the respondents found the information to be of interest.

MESSAGE IMPACT STUDY
VIDEO SYSTEMS -- August 1989 Issue

Advertiser: Laird Telemedia
Product/Service Category: Video Effects, Graphics, Titles

Page: 59
Size/Color: 1/2 page, 2 color

	R E A D E R R A T I N G S*		
	attention-getting ability	believability	information value
this ad	2.4 ①	3.8	3.9
average - this product/service category	3.5	3.5 ②	3.5
average - this size category	2.8	3.3	3.2
average - all ads	3.5	3.5	3.3

* Ratings are based on a scale of 1 to 5, where 1 = low and 5 = high.

Exhibit 14.18 Portion of a Readex Message Impact Study Report. Reprinted with permission of Readex Readership Research.
1. This advertisement, which is for Laird Telemedia, had lower-than-average attention-getting ability among all ads in the category and all ads in the August 1989 edition of *Video Systems*.
2. The Laird Telemedia ad outperformed the averages for other ads in believability and information value.

MESSAGE IMPACT STUDY
VIDEO SYSTEMS -- August 1989 Issue

Issue Summary

page	READER RATINGS* attention-getting ability	believability	information value	size category	product/service category
	(1) 3.5	3.5	3.3		
Average for 44 Ads this Issue					
3M Magnetic Tape	47	3.6	3.3	2.4	1 page	Video, Audio Tape
Abekas Video Systems, Inc	7	3.0	3.4	3.4	1 page	Switchers, Editors, Time Codes
Alta Group, Inc.	30	2.5	2.8	2.9	1/2 page	Time Base Corrector, Synchronizer
Alta Group, Inc.	58	2.8	3.4	3.4	1/2 page	Switchers, Editors, Time Codes
Ampex AVSD	11	(2) 4.1	3.2	2.5	1 page	Video Effects, Graphics, Titles
Autodesk	24-	3.9	3.7	3.8	2 page	Video Effects, Graphics, Titles
Center Video Industrial Co., Inc.	48	3.0	3.1	3.3	1 page	Dealer, Distributor, Rental
Chyron Group	39	2.8	3.4	3.3	1 page	Video Effects, Graphics, Titles
Cipher Digital, Inc.	76	2.6	2.9	2.9	1/2 page	Time Base Corrector, Synchronizer
Columbia Audio/Video	57	3.0	3.1	3.2	1 page	Dealer, Distributor, Rental
Competitive Edge/Polar Video	61	3.3	3.3	3.5	1 page	Switchers, Editors, Time Codes
Cubicomp Corp.	51	3.2	3.0	2.7	1 page	Video Effects, Graphics, Titles
Discount Video Warehouse	31	3.4	3.5	3.4	1 page	Dealer, Distributor, Rental
Extron Electronics	81	2.7	3.1	3.1	1/2 page	Video Processing, Distribution
Fujinon, Inc.	43	3.7	3.9	3.5	1 page	Cameras, Lenses, Monitors
General Electric Company	44-	3.3	3.6	3.2	1 page	Cameras, Lenses, Monitors
Grass Valley Group, Inc.	79	4.2	3.8	3.1	1 page	Video Processing, Distribution
Hitachi Denshi America, Ltd.	27	3.1	3.2	3.0	1 page	Cameras, Lenses, Monitors
ITS, Inc.	69	3.7	3.2	2.3	1 page	Catalogs, Education
JVC Professional Products, Co.	13-	4.0	3.5	3.4	2 page	Cameras, Lenses, Monitors
JVC Professional Products, Co.	8C	4.1	3.8	3.5	1 page	Recorders, Players
Knowledge Industry Publications	65	2.3	3.1	3.2	1 page	Catalogs, Education
LTM Corporation of America	71	3.8	3.6	3.6	1 page	Miscellaneous
Laird Telemedia	59	2.4	3.8	3.9	1/2 page	Video Effects, Graphics, Titles
Leader Instruments Corp.	49	4.0	4.0	3.9	1 page	Test, Measurement Equipment

continued ...

* Ratings are based on a scale of 1 to 5, where 1 = low and 5 = high.

Exhibit 14.19 Portion of a Readex Message Impact Study Report. Reprinted with permission of Readex Readership Research.
1. At the top of the table is a row of average ratings for attention-getting ability, believability, and information value for all ads tested in the magazine.
2. The Ampex AVSD ad had a relatively high attention-getting ability rating, 4.1.

Some of the services described in this chapter report quantitative and qualitative measures of advertising readership. Quantitative measures tell how many people read or recalled reading the ad; qualitative measures tell what readers remember about the ad.

Self-Test Questions

1. Review the material in Chapter 12 about problems associated with message research and about ways of evaluating syndicated research. Critically review the companies and services discussed in this chapter. How would you evaluate their sample selection procedures: What about their reliance on interviews or self-reporting to ascertain readership? What about the accuracy of recognition and recall testing?
2. Look at Exhibit 14.2. What percentage of readers could recall the lead idea, which was "preserve/keep memories"?
3. Look at Exhibit 14.4. In terms of the average number of ideas per respondent, how did this ad perform compared with those for other photographic products? Look at the ad itself and suggest at least one reason that would account for the relative score.
4. Look at Exhibit 14.9. What percentage of readers truly read the advertisement for Genie Garage Door Operators? What is the Starch definition of the read-most score?

Notes

1. Kodak corporate policy prohibits reproduction of Kodak advertisements in textbooks.

Suggestion for Additional Reading

"New Lease on Life for Readership Studies." *Marketing and Media Decisions* (November 1980), 68.

Audience Research: Broadcast

Advertising researchers expend a considerable amount of money and effort to measure audiences of advertising vehicles because advertisers want to know the size and characteristics of the audiences they reach with their advertising messages. Although advertising agencies and other users of audience information must pay for the data, most of the cost of measuring audiences is borne by the media vehicles being measured. The cost can be extremely high; individual stations may have to pay thousands or even hundreds of thousands of dollars each to have their audiences measured.

There is no absolute requirement that media have their audiences measured. In fact, many publications and broadcast stations elect not to be measured because of the prohibitive expense. Audience measurement is a virtual requirement, however, for stations and publications that hope to garner significant amounts of national advertising. Many buyers of advertising, including agencies and advertisers, have policies against buying advertising from newspapers or magazines that do not have audited circulations.

While most vehicles in a market are usually measured by audience measurement companies, only the ones that pay for the service are allowed to use the resulting audience data for their own promotion purposes. For example, some radio stations may decide not to pay for the measurement services of either Arbitron or Birch. The stations of those audiences will still be measured and reported, but those stations will not be able to promote their audience figures.

The research companies discussed in Chapters 15 and 16 are the most widely used sources of syndicated audience data. Broadcast audience services discussed in this chapter include network radio (RADAR®), spot radio (Birch, Arbitron), spot television (Arbitron, Nielsen Station Index), and network television (Nielsen Television Index, TvQ). Print audience sources are discussed in Chapter 16.

Data Gathering Procedures

Companies that gather and report broadcast audience data use three basic methods. With *diaries* or other self-report techniques, respondents keep their own records of media exposure. *Interviews* rely on another person to question the respondent—in person or on the telephone—about media exposure. *Meters* are electronic devices that record television viewing automatically. Each technique has advantages and problems.

Diaries

A diary is a printed booklet in which individuals record their television viewing, radio listening, or other media exposure. Diaries are used primarily because they are inexpensive compared to other methods. About the only expense unique to diaries is postage, which is lower than the cost of interviews or meters. (All the methods have expenses related to sample selection, data analysis, and printing.) Diaries are the principal method used for local radio and television audience measurements, which require several hundred completed diaries in each market. Thus lower cost is a critical factor.

Problems with Diaries

Diaries are subject to the faulty memories of people who fill them out. Ideally, researchers hope that respondents keep diaries close to their television sets and radios and update them as they watch or listen. It is likely, however, that most diary entries are made only periodically or at the end of the survey period—usually one week. Respondents are likely to forget some details of their listening or viewing. It is also probable that only one family member (usually an adult female) reports viewing and listening for all others in the household. If she does that near the end of the diary week—as many probably do—the errors can be even greater.

Some respondents might also make honest mistakes in completing diaries because they get confused about station call letters and channel numbers. That can be a particular problem for people who watch cable television. For example, a person might

be watching WXXX-TV, which is broadcast over the air on channel 5. On the cable system, WXXX-TV might be carried on channel 9. Viewers have difficulty keeping all that sorted out in their minds. (Some viewers cannot even make the association between a station's call letters and its channel number.)

Diary information could also be incorrect because of deliberate untruthfulness by respondents. For example, some people who regularly watch daytime soap operas might not want to admit such behavior, even in an anonymous diary. It is easy for them to write the name of a more socially acceptable program — or nothing at all — in the diary. Another potential problem with diaries is the fact that people must be able to read and write to complete a diary. The U.S. Council on Literacy estimates that 20 percent of Americans are functionally illiterate, meaning they presumably do not have the verbal skills required to complete television or radio diaries.

Diaries require a considerable amount of time to process after the data have been gathered. Respondents must mail the diaries back to the company, and many forget to do that immediately. Diaries must be checked for completeness and accuracy and must be prepared for computer analysis before the rating books can be printed and mailed to users. That process can take several weeks.

... Interviews

Interviews can be conducted in person or by telephone. Either way, researchers have more control over data gathering than is true with self-report techniques such as diaries. Interviewers can probe for more complete answers or can explain questions that respondents might not understand. Such probing or explanation would not be possible with a diary or other form of printed self-report. Interviewers can also make sure that all needed information is collected. Diaries, on the other hand, are often returned to the company with important information left out. In some studies, interviewers call respondents and ask them to verbalize a diary by recalling their listening or viewing for the previous day.

Interviewers can also control the source of the information instead of leaving it to chance. In some audience surveys, for example, it might be important to have an equal number of male and female respondents, and interviewers could control that. Researchers have very little control over who fills out a diary.

Researchers can monitor and supervise telephone interviewers more easily than face-to-face interviews. Research firms that conduct telephone surveys usually do them from specially equipped facilities with many interviewers in one room. Supervisors are able to monitor telephone interviewers as they make their calls.

Problems with Interviews

Memory problems are not necessarily eliminated by interviews, for respondents may still be asked to remember their viewing or listening behavior for the previous few hours or days. They might legitimately forget what they watched or might lie to interviewers for fear of embarrassment.

A greater problem — and also true to a lesser extent with diaries — is a reluctance to cooperate with interviewers. Many people are reluctant to participate in surveys because they don't want to talk to strangers, they are too busy to be bothered, or they fear their name will be put on a mailing list. That reluctance to participate has become an acute problem for companies that use personal interviews; interviewers sometimes have doors slammed in their faces. In some urban areas, they may face dangers from physical assaults.

Finally, interviews are more costly and time consuming than some other methods. A single personal interview may require more than an hour to complete, and the transportation time required to get from interview to interview might make it difficult to complete more than three or four interviews per day. Telephone interviews can be done more quickly and more economically, of course, but they must be brief. In addition, a respondent can easily hang up before finishing a telephone interview. It also takes a long time to process and distribute the information gathered by personal or telephone interviews.

. . . Meters

Meters are electronic devices that automatically record the duration of time that a television set is turned on and the station to which it is tuned. No action or effort is required by viewers. That eliminates memory and accuracy problems associated with diaries or interviews. The meters are connected to the research company's central computer, which regularly and automatically collects data stored in the meters. That reduces the time needed to process and distribute audience data to users. Many large advertising agencies have online computer connections with audience measurement companies and can receive television audience data a day or two after a telecast.

The People Meter

Television audience measurement underwent significant changes in the late 1980s with the introduction of the people meter to measure network television audiences. Prior to that time, meters measured only television set usage — the station that a television set was tuned to. To ascertain the composition or characteristics (demographics) of network program audiences, research companies used a separate sample of households that maintained diaries to report the kinds of people who were watching the programs. The diaries allowed them to report on what individual family members watched. In addition to using a different sample of households than the metered households, that methodology suffered from the problems of diaries in general.

Nielsen Media Research's introduction of the people meter changed much of that. It is a small device that looks like a calculator or a remote control unit. (See Exhibit 15.1.) Each family member has a different assigned button, and there are extra buttons for guests. The meter automatically records the station being viewed, and individual viewers are supposed to press their buttons when they start to watch and press them again when they leave the room. The people meter is like a miniature computer, and each family member's age, gender, and other demographic information is stored in it. (Guests enter that information when they use the meter.) Both television viewing and demographic characteristics are now measured by people meters in one sample, and Nielsen no longer uses diaries for its network audience composition studies.

Exhibit 15.1 The Nielsen people meter that is used to record television viewing by different family members.

Problems with Meters

A major problem with meters is that they do not measure whether anyone is watching the television set while it is turned on. Some studies have shown that up to 25 percent of the time that sets are turned on, no one is in the room watching. That may be true during long program segments as well as commercial breaks. People meters have not solved that problem, for viewers must press a button to indicate they are in the room, and some may forget or ignore the button.

What is needed, and what the research industry is working toward, is a truly *passive* measuring device, one that can record viewing by individual viewers without requiring any action on their part. The technology for such passive meters is available, but costs and concerns about privacy are hindering their implementation. It would be technically feasible, for example, to give viewers a device to wear (or even to implant it under their skin) that would emit an electronic signal that could be read by a meter on the television set. It is also feasible for heat-sensing devices to identify and record the presence of individual viewers in the room while the set is turned on. (Such heat-sensing devices are sensitive enough to detect the presence of family pets.) To many people, however, devices like those pose threats of government surveillance. In addition, passive meters will detect only the presence of an individual in the room; they will not ascertain whether the person is watching or paying attention to the program or commercial.

Media researchers and television network executives are concerned about people meter problems with young children and with guests. Young children may not understand how to operate the people meter, and they are probably less likely than adults to remember to press the buttons. The requirement for guests in the household to provide demographic information when they watch is also seen as a hindrance.[1]

Another major problem with meters is the expense of installing and maintaining them. Consequently, meters are limited to the measurement of network television audiences and the audiences of television stations in the fifteen or so largest markets in the country. Stations in smaller markets simply could not afford to pay for audience measurement by meters.

A couple of other problems are associated with television audience measurement, although not necessarily only with meters. One is the problem of out-of-home viewers, people who watch television at work or in hotels, dormitories, or bars and who are effectively beyond the reach of audience measurement companies. One study estimated that 5 million people watch "Monday Night Football" in bars, hotels, and dormitories, that 3.1 million college students watch daytime television in dormitories, and that 2.6 million women watch daytime television at work.[2] It remains to be seen whether the costs of alleviating such problems can be justified in light of the improved precision of measurement.

The second problem concerns the difficulty of measuring the use of videocassette recorders to play prerecorded cassettes (rentals) and to play back programs recorded off the air. Nielsen Media Research does measure the viewing of prerecorded cassettes by families in its people meter sample, but there is not yet universal agreement about how to measure and to count viewers of programs recorded off the air. For example, should such viewing be counted if it takes place more than one or two days after the program was originally telecast?[3]

••• RADAR®

Network radio audiences are measured by Radio's All Dimension Audience Research (RADAR®). It was established in 1967 and has been operated by Statistical Research, Inc. (SRI) since 1972. Data are gathered by day-after telephone recall interviews of respondents for a seven-day period. Interviews with approximately 12,000 people are conducted throughout the year.

RADAR® reports audiences of stations that carry specific network programs and network commercials. To do that, it relies on network clearance reports — lists of stations that carried specific network programs and commercials.

••• RADAR® Samples

SRI first generates a sample of possible telephone numbers that are allocated among the 111 U.S. telephone area codes. In that procedure, a computer generates four-digit numbers that are paired with central office (exchange) prefixes. That random-digit dialing procedure gives each telephone household (even those with unlisted numbers) an equal chance of being selected, so SRI does not make any other effort to contact households that might otherwise be underrepresented, such as minority households.

Interviewers call the numbers to construct a list of the persons age 12 or older in each household. They make repeated calls at different times on different days to households that do not answer. Interviewers call in Spanish when necessary.

SRI then randomly selects one person from each selected household to be in the sample. Nearly 70 percent of those selected complete the interviews.

... RADAR® Data Collection

Interviewers call members of the sample every day for seven days to ask about their radio listening for the previous twenty-four hours. To make that task easier for respondents, interviewers ask them to think about three-hour blocks of time and to recall if they listened to a radio during those periods. If they did listen, they are asked when they started and stopped listening and the stations to which they listened. This procedure is repeated until the entire twenty-four-hour period is accounted for.

Respondents cannot always be reached every day. When that happens, interviewers ask respondents to reconstruct their listening for the time period back to the last interview. In a few cases when some daily interviews cannot be completed, listening for the missing days is presumed to be the same as the period reported listening for other specified days. In other words, if a respondent says he or she listened to the 8:00 A.M. newscast on a particular network on Monday, Tuesday, and Wednesday, and if the respondent cannot be contacted about Thursday's listening, it is assumed that the respondent also listened to the same newscast on Thursday. Such "simulated" days are typically less than 0.5 percent of all listening days processed.

Exhibit 15.2 shows a portion of a page from a RADAR® report of network radio audiences.

... Birch Radio

Birch Radio, a division of Birch/Scarborough Research Corporation, uses telephone interviews to measure audiences of local radio stations in approximately 250 U.S. markets. It represents one of the most extensive uses of telephone interviewing in research today.

... Birch Samples

Birch selects both listed and nonlisted telephone households in a random procedure that ensures representativeness. Special efforts are made to increase participation of Hispanic listeners by including additional sample households and by using Spanish-speaking interviewers. After households have been selected for the sample, Birch interviewers call and ask to speak to the person over age 12 in the household who had the last birthday. That procedure is used by many research companies to

RADAR 38 - FALL 1988

AUDIENCE ESTIMATES FOR XXX RADIO NETWORK
AUDIENCES TO ALL COMMERCIALS
NUMBER OF PERSONS IN THOUSANDS

MONDAY-FRIDAY PROGRAMS

PROGRAM TITLE (DAYS & DURATION)	AVG NUM STS	TOTAL PERS 12+	TOTAL ADULTS 18+	MEN TOTAL	18-49	25-54	25+	35+	WOMEN TOTAL	18-49	25-54	25+	35+	TEENS 12-17
900A HOURLY NEWS (M-F 5:00)	382													
AVG PER BROADCAST		1792	1784	721	239	311	696	618	1063	385	446	1046	912	*
5 DAY WEEKLY CUME		5159	5138	2216	859	1054	2091	1815	2922	1199	1279	2847	2428	*
FREQUENCY PER WEEK		1.74	1.74	1.63	1.39	1.48	1.66	1.70	1.82	1.61	1.74	1.84	1.88	*
1000A HOURLY NEWS (M-F 5:00)	375													
AVG PER BROADCAST		1797	1788	701	281	341	671	568	1087	413	482	1072	918	*
5 DAY WEEKLY CUME		4934	4908	2162	912	1066	2045	1699	2746	1174	1255	2675	2260	*
FREQUENCY PER WEEK		1.82	1.82	1.62	1.54	1.60	1.64	1.67	1.98	1.76	1.92	2.00	2.03	*
1100A HOURLY NEWS (M-F 5:00)	377													
AVG PER BROADCAST		1609	1585	606	276	318	573	465	979	357	412	968	858	*
5 DAY WEEKLY CUME		4756	4666	2040	946	1038	1898	1532	2626	1106	1183	2577	2179	90
FREQUENCY PER WEEK		1.69	1.70	1.49	1.46	1.53	1.51	1.52	1.86	1.61	1.74	1.88	1.97	*
1200N HOURLY NEWS (M-F 5:00)	(1) 378													
AVG PER BROADCAST		1318	1296	474	198	219	441	364	822	(2) 323	369	815	692	*
5 DAY WEEKLY CUME		3938	3859	1557	683	745	1453	1178	2302	989	1087	2273	1911	79
FREQUENCY PER WEEK		1.67	1.68	1.52	1.45	1.47	1.52	1.54	1.79	1.63	1.70	1.79	1.81	*
100P HOURLY NEWS (M-F 5:00)	368													
AVG PER BROADCAST		1320	1305	476	225	236	447	350	829	316	368	819	708	*
5 DAY WEEKLY CUME		4126	4068	1634	779	787	1501	1206	2434	1016	1173	2385	2054	58
FREQUENCY PER WEEK		1.60	1.60	1.46	1.44	1.50	1.49	1.45	1.70	1.56	1.57	1.72	1.72	*

Exhibit 15.2 A portion of a page from a RADAR® report of network radio audiences. Reprinted by permission.

1. For this network's 12:00 newscast, 378 stations carried the broadcast; the average audience was 1,318,000; and in five days, a cumulative total of 3,938,000 different people listened to that newscast. The average person listened 1.67 times.
2. For that same 12:00 newscast, the average audience of women age 18—49 was 323,000, the cume was 989,000, and the average frequency was 1.63.

minimize possible bias associated with persons who normally answer the telephone. It also helps to ensure that male interviewers do not always speak to male respondents or that female interviewers do not always speak to female respondents. If the person with the last birthday is not available or will not cooperate, the household is dropped from the list; another person in the household cannot be substituted. The individuals who are selected are called every day for seven days. Birch reported that in 1988, response rates for various markets averaged more than 60 percent.

• • • Birch Data Collection

Interviewing for all markets takes place in seven interviewing centers that utilize Wide Area Telephoning Service (WATS). Interviewers are carefully trained and are monitored during the interview process.

Interviewers ask respondents to recall the radio stations they listened to the day before the call — a procedure that is called *yesterday radio listening.*

"Now think about what you were doing yesterday, that is (name of day) and any radio listening you may have done yesterday at home, in a car, or some other place . . . whether you yourself turned it on or whether you heard a radio playing somewhere. I am going to ask you specifically about your radio listening yesterday, that is (name of day), during different times of the day. Did you do any listening between _____ and _____?"

Interviewers proceed with each daypart, asking respondents to report the exact times they started and stopped listening as well as the location (car, home, or other locations away from home). If respondents say they did not listen to any radio, interviewers use probes to stimulate recall, such as, "clock radio, driving to work, running an errand, during lunch, driving home from work or school, or after dinner."

Special efforts are made to ensure correct identification of the stations that respondents report.

"What station did you hear? Was that AM or FM? Where is it on the dial? What slogan or slogans does the station go by? Do you recall the name of a program or announcer? What city does it broadcast from? If sports broadcasts were heard, what type of sport? What teams were playing? Who was the sportscaster?"

• • • Birch Radio Reports

Birch measures more than 150 markets on a continuous basis — every month. Other markets are measured for a month at a time in the spring and fall. Reports are available in printed books or in electronic format (diskettes for personal computers, tapes or online) for agencies and other companies that want to do their own analyses of Birch data.

Exhibit 15.3 shows a portion of a page from a Birch Radio Report on radio station audiences in the Charlotte–Gastonia–Rock Hill market.

Target Demographics
WOMEN 25-49

AVERAGE QUARTER HOUR AND CUME ESTIMATES

CHARLOTTE/GAST/RK HILL NC-SC MSA
SEPTEMBER 1989 – NOVEMBER 1989

	MON – FRI 6:00AM-7:00PM				MON – FRI 6:00AM-10:00AM + 3:00PM-7:00PM				MON – FRI 6:00AM-3:00PM				MON – FRI 3:00PM-12:00 MID				SAT – SUN 6:00AM-12:00 MID			
	AQH PRS (00)	AQH PRS RTG	AQH PRS SHR	CUME PRS (00)	AQH PRS (00)	AQH PRS RTG	AQH PRS SHR	CUME PRS (00)	AQH PRS (00)	AQH PRS RTG	AQH PRS SHR	CUME PRS (00)	AQH PRS (00)	AQH PRS RTG	AQH PRS SHR	CUME PRS (00)	AQH PRS (00)	AQH PRS RTG	AQH PRS SHR	CUME PRS (00)
WAES	3	.1	.5	21	4	.2	.7	21	1		.2	21	1		.3	21	6	.3	1.6	114
WAME	22	.9 ①	4.0	220	23	1.0	4.0	187	3	.1	.5	21								
WBCY-FM																				
WBIG																				
WBT	19	.8	3.5	161	27	1.2	4.7	161	20	.9	3.6	181	11	.5	3.0	187	10	.4	2.7	161
WCKZ-FM	29	1.3	5.3	343	38	1.6	6.6	343	24	1.0	4.4	258 ②	31	1.3	8.4	186	17	.7	4.6	165
WDAV-FM	15	.6	2.7	38	17	.7	3.0	38	13	.6	2.4	38	27	1.2	7.3	300				18
WEZC-FM	18	.8	3.3	61	14	.6	2.4	61	19	.8	3.4	61	8	.3	2.2	38	13	.6	3.5	137
WFAE-FM	15	.6	2.7	186	23	1.0	4.0	186	11	.5	2.0	151	6	.3	1.6	49	29	1.3	7.8	144
WFGW	2	.1	.4	23	2	.1	.3	23	2	.1	.4	23	12	.5	3.3	176				
WGIV	8	.3	1.5	71	6	.3	1.0	52	6	.3	1.1	58	1		.3	23				
WHVN	1		.2	11	1		.2	11	1		.2	11	14	.6	3.8	89	7	.3	1.9	80

Exhibit 15.3 A portion of a page from a Birch Radio Report for the Charlotte–Gastonia–Rock Hill market. The material is copyrighted and may not be reproduced without written permission of Birch/Scarborough Research. Reprinted by permission of Birch/Scarborough Research.

1. During the average quarter-hour (AQH) between 6:00 A.M. and 7:00 P.M., 1,900 women age 25–49 listened to WBT. That was equivalent to .8 of one percent of women 25–49 in the market—the AQH person rating.

2. During the AQH between 6:00 A.M. and 3:00 P.M. WCKZ's AQH share was 4.4, meaning it attracted 4.4 percent of women 25–49 who were listening to the radio. In the period of a week, 25,800 different women 25–49 listened to WCKZ for at least five minutes sometime between 6:00 A.M. and 3:00 P.M.

Arbitron Radio

Arbitron Radio (The Arbitron Company) measures radio station audiences in more than 250 radio markets in the United States. Surveys are conducted during twelve-week periods in winter, spring, summer, and fall. The 100 largest markets are measured four times a year; practically speaking, that means they are measured continuously. The smallest markets are measured once a year; other markets are measured twice, and some are measured three times. The length of the measurement periods and the fact that some stations are measured continuously make it impractical for stations to engage in contests and other activities designed to boost ratings during measurement periods. (See Chapter 12 for a more detailed discussion of that problem.)

Arbitron Radio Samples

Arbitron provides audience estimates for three kinds of geographic units: area of dominant influence (ADI), total survey area (TSA), and metro survey area (MSA).

On the basis of return rates from previous surveys, Arbitron estimates the number of diaries it will have to distribute so it will get back enough usable diaries to meet its goal for each market. Its goals for in-tab (usable) diaries range from approximately 4,000 for the largest markets to 550 for the smallest ones.

Arbitron randomly selects an appropriate number of households from a list of telephone households. That sample is supplemented with a list that includes potentially unlisted homes. That list begins with all potential numbers, and all known telephone numbers are deleted from the list, so some of the remaining (unlisted) numbers could be working numbers. A sample is drawn from that list, which increases the likelihood that the final sample will include households with unlisted telephone numbers. The sample will not include any households that do not have telephones. The total sample is divided into equal-sized groups, one for each week of the survey period.

Selected households are contacted by letter and told they have been selected for the survey. They are also told that an interviewer will telephone them to request their cooperation. Interviewers make several attempts to reach each household.

Arbitron Radio Data Collection

Arbitron sends a diary to every person age 12 or older in each cooperating household. A few days before the survey period begins, interviewers telephone households to make sure that diaries have arrived and that participants understand how to use them. Interviewers call again in the middle of the survey week to ask about problems, to remind participants to return diaries as soon as possible after the survey, and to thank them for their participation. A small cash incentive is included with the diaries when they are mailed to the households. Arbitron employs additional cash incentives and other special procedures to encourage participation by African-Americans and Hispanics, including the use of Spanish-language diaries and interviewers.

Respondents are asked to record their personal radio listening in the diary for a seven-day period. Exhibit 15.4 shows a page from an Arbitron Radio Diary.

Exhibit 15.5 shows a portion of a page from an Arbitron Radio Report showing station audience estimates for persons age 18 to 49. Exhibit 15.6 shows trends in station audiences.

Arbitron Television

Arbitron also measures audiences of television stations in more than 200 local markets called Areas of Dominant Influence (ADIs). Diaries are used to gather data in all markets, and meters are used to supplement diary data in the fifteen or so largest markets. All markets are measured four times a year—in November, February, May, and July—and some larger markets are measured again in October, January, and March. (Chapter 17 describes a new Arbitron service, ScanAmerica®, which combines television audience measurement with household product purchase data in a concept called single-source research.)

Arbitron Television Diary Surveys

In each ADI, Arbitron establishes a goal for in-tab diaries—the number of completed diaries it must receive from viewers in that market. The minimum goal is 200 diaries, and it is higher in more populous markets. Based on return rates from previous surveys, Arbitron determines the number of households it must sample in an ADI to receive the appropriate number of completed diaries. Arbitron draws a separate sample for each of the four weeks of a diary survey period, using a procedure very similar to the one described in the earlier section on Arbitron radio samples.

Arbitron sends a letter to selected households to tell them they have been selected for the study. The letter says an interviewer will telephone to ask for their cooperation in the survey. Telephone interviewers make several attempts to reach the households.

Arbitron sends respondents one diary for each television set in the household. Telephone interviewers make two additional contacts with each household. The first call, on the second day of the survey period, is to make sure the diary has been received and that the family knows how to fill it out. The second call comes several days later and reminds the family to mail the diary back as soon as possible after it is completed.

Each family keeps a diary for one week. Bilingual (Spanish and English) diaries are sent to families that request them. For each television set, the family is supposed to record the station, program, time, and people watching. Cable programs and video-cassette recorder (VCR) usage are included. If the diary indicates the VCR was used

THURSDAY									
Time			**Station**			**Place**			
			Call letters or station name	*Check (✓) one*			*Check (✓) one*		
	Start	Stop	*Don't know? Use program name or dial setting.*	AM	FM	At Home	In a Car	At Work	Other Place
Early Morning (from 5 AM)									
Midday									
Late Afternoon									
Night (to 5 AM Friday)									

If you didn't hear a radio today, please check here. ☐

Exhibit 15.4 A page from an Arbitron Radio Diary. Reprinted by permission.

Target Audience
PERSONS 18-34

	MONDAY-FRIDAY 6AM-10AM				MONDAY-FRIDAY 10AM-3PM				MONDAY-FRIDAY 3PM-7PM				MONDAY-FRIDAY 7PM-MID				WEEKEND 10AM-7PM			
	AQH (00)	CUME (00)	AQH RTG	AQH SHR	AQH (00)	CUME (00)	AQH RTG	AQH SHR	AQH (00)	CUME (00)	AQH RTG	AQH SHR	AQH (00)	CUME (00)	AQH RTG	AQH SHR	AQH (00)	CUME (00)	AQH RTG	AQH SHR
KYW																				
METRO	150	1400	1.1	4.0	38	636	.3	1.0	52	588	.4	1.6	15	277	.1	1.0	13	243	.1	.6
TSA	159	1497			44	731			58	688			15	283			15	263		
WCAU																				
METRO	14	160	.1	.4	27	108	.2	.7	44	309	.3	1.4	30	369	.2	1.9	18	185	.1	.8
TSA	14	160			27	117			45	324			30	374			18	190		
WCOJ																				
METRO	2	45		.1	1	27			2	29		.1		16						
TSA	2	45			1	27			2	29				16						
WDAS																				
METRO	4	47		.1													4	49		.2
TSA	4	47															4	49		
WDAS-FM	①	②	③	④																
METRO	229	1205	1.7	6.1	229	1065	1.7	5.8	156	1075	1.2	4.8	95	781	.7	6.0	141	794	1.1	6.0
TSA	245	1359			266	1247			156	1194			99	859			142	802		
WEAZ																				
METRO	8	51	.1	.2	24	93	.2	.6	3	22		.1	5	35		.3	5	46		.2
TSA	8	67			25	114			3	27			5	35			7	62		
WEAZ-FM																				
METRO	151	980	1.1	4.0	254	1041	1.9	6.4	158	1084	1.2	4.9	36	535	.3	2.3	77	633	.6	3.3
TSA	180	1121			325	1215			207	1236			48	600			99	728		
A/F TOT																				
METRO	159	1019	1.2	4.2	278	1134	2.1	7.0	161	1106	1.2	4.9	41	569	.3	2.6	82	680	.6	3.5
TSA	188	1176			350	1329			210	1262			53	635			106	790		
WEGX																				
METRO	232	1739	1.8	6.2	253	1730	1.9	6.4	225	2148	1.7	6.9	109	1313	.8	6.9	175	1601	1.3	7.5
TSA	270	2039			301	2004			251	2536			114	1421			206	1881		

Exhibit 15.5 A portion of a page from an Arbitron Radio Report for the Philadelphia market in summer 1989. Reprinted by permission. All data are for persons age 18–34.
1. During an average quarter hour between 6:00 A.M. and 10:00 A.M., 22,900 persons listened to WDAS-FM for a minimum of five minutes.
2. During the 6:00 A.M. to 10:00 A.M. daypart, 120,500 different persons listened to WDAS-FM for a minimum of five minutes in a quarter hour.
3. During the average quarter hour in this daypart, 1.7 percent of all persons were listening to this station.
4. During the average quarter hour in this daypart, 6.1 percent of all persons who were listening to any radio station were listening to this station.

to record a program being telecast, the program is credited to the station identified in the entry. When the diary indicates the VCR was used to play back a program previously recorded from a station, the program is credited to that station — for the day and time of the original recording. When the diary indicates the VCR was used to play back something recorded before the current survey week (including rented movies), that entry is deleted from the diary.

• • • Arbitron Television Meter Surveys

In the very largest television markets, Arbitron also uses meters to supplement diary data. A double sampling procedure is used in those markets. Arbitron randomly draws what it calls a parent sample of households — many more households than it would use at any one time. Households in the parent sample are surveyed to determine their demographic characteristics and television usage. That information is used to categorize or stratify households in the parent sample. A stratified random sampling technique is used to develop a primary meter sample from the parent sample. Interviewers attempt to secure cooperation to place meters in those primary sample households. Households that refuse to cooperate are replaced by other households drawn from the parent sample.

Exhibit 15.7 shows a portion of an Arbitron Television Report.

Metro Audience Trends *
PERSONS 18-34

	MONDAY-FRIDAY 7PM-MID					WEEKEND 6AM-MID				
	SUMMER 88	FALL 88	WINTER 89	SPRING 89	SUMMER 89	SUMMER 88	FALL 88	WINTER 89	SPRING 89	SUMMER 89
KYW										
SHARE	1.0	1.7	2.1	1.2	1.0	2.1	1.8	1.7	2.0	1.1
AQH(00)	17	27	32	19	15	38	34	30	37	19
CUME RTG	2.1	2.2	3.2	2.8	2.1	6.3	6.1	5.5	7.2	4.5
WCAU										
SHARE	3.1	.6	1.5	2.3	1.9	1.1	.7	.8	.7	.7
AQH(00)	55	10	24	36	30	20	13	15	13	12
CUME RTG	2.8	1.7	1.2	2.1	2.8	2.4	2.6	1.7	1.5	2.3
WCOJ										
SHARE	*	*	.1	*	.1	*	*	.1	*	
AQH(00)	*	*	1	*		*	*	2	*	
CUME RTG	*	*	.1	*		*	*	.2	*	
WDAS										
SHARE	.2	.1	.1	.4		2.0	1.2	1.8	1.4	.2
AQH(00)	3	1	2	7		36	22	32	27	3
CUME RTG	.3	.3	.2	.4		2.5	2.0	2.6	2.0	.5
WDAS-FM										
SHARE	10.5	8.4	8.4	9.3	6.0	7.9	5.9	7.2	7.6	6.7
AQH(00)	185	130	130	145	95	144	110	129	144	121
CUME RTG	8.0	7.5	7.3	8.0	(1) 5.9	8.9	9.2	10.2	8.9	7.7
+WEAZ										
SHARE	.4	.3		.1	.3	.5	.2	.2	.1	.2
AQH(00)	7	5			5	9	4	3	2	3
CUME RTG	.6	.5			.3	1.0	.8	.3	.3	.3
WEAZ-FM										
SHARE	.5	2.8	3.0	2.5	2.3	1.0	2.7	2.6	2.8	3.3
AQH(00)	9	43	47	39	36	18	50	47	53	59
CUME RTG	1.0	2.7	3.3	3.1	4.0	1.4	4.7	4.7	4.9	6.3
WEGX										
SHARE	11.7	12.0	11.3	8.3	6.9	11.8	11.0	11.9	9.0	7.3
AQH(00)	206	185	175	129	109	216	206	214	170	131
CUME RTG	15.1	12.2	14.6	11.8	9.9	18.1	18.9	20.6	17.0	14.6

Exhibit 15.6 A portion of a page from an Arbitron Radio Report for the Philadelphia market in summer 1989 showing trends in station audiences. Reprinted by permission. All data are for persons age 18–34.

1. WDAS-FM's average quarter-hour share was 6.0, meaning 6 percent of all persons listening to the radio were listening to that station. That translated into 9,500 persons during the average quarter hour. During the 7:00 P.M. to midnight daypart, 5.9 percent of the age group listened to WDAS-FM for a minimum of five minutes in a quarter hour. All of those numbers were significantly lower than they were in the summer of 1988 (10.5, 18,500, and 8.0).

Time Period Estimates

DAY AND TIME / STATION PROGRAM	JAN 31 (1)	FEB 07 (2)	FEB 14 (3)	FEB 21 (4)	ADI TV HH RTG (5)	ADI TV HH SHR (6)	NOV 89 (59)	JUL 89 (60)	MAY 89 (61)	FEB 89 (62)	METRO RTG (8)	METRO SHR (9)	2+ (11)	18+ (12)	12-24 (13)	12-34 (14)	18-34 (15)	18-49 (16)	21-49 (17)	25-54 (18)	35+ (19)	35-64 (20)	50+ (21)	W 18+ (22)	W 12-24 (23)	W 18-34 (24)	W 18-49 (25)	W 21-49 (26)	W 25-49 (27)	W 25-54 (28)	W WW (29)	M 18+ (30)	M 18-34 (31)	M 18-49 (32)	M 21-49 (33)	M 25-49 (34)	M 25-54 (35)
RELATIVE STD-ERR THRESHOLDS (1σr) 25% / 50%	15 / 4	17 / 5	18 / 5	16 / 4	4 / 1						9 / 2		4 / 1	3 / 1	13 / 3	8 / 2	11 / 3	5 / 1	5 / 1	5 / 1	3 / 1	5 / 1	6 / 1	5 / 1	22 / 6	17 / 4	8 / 2	8 / 2	10 / 2	9 / 2	13 / 3	6 / 1	19 / 5	10 / 2	11 / 3	12 / 3	10 / 2
FRIDAY 7:30P– 8:00P																																					
WWAY JEOPARDY	13	20	20	14	17	29	25	38	34	28	22	38	10	13	4	4	4	6	6	8	18	13	26	16	3	5	7	8	8	9	8	10	5	5	5	4	6
WECT WHO BOSS–S	21	14	15	13	16	28	37	30	31	36	9	16	13	12	16	15	15	13	13	12	11	11	12	16	5	21	17	17	14	16	10	9	3	3	8	9	7
WJKA HARD COPY	1	1	2	5	4	7	4	1	1	1	8	7	3	2	2	4	5	4	4	4	3	3	2	4		5	5	4	3	3	5	3	3	3	4	4	4
WUNJ PTV	–	1	1	1	1	1	–	1	1	2	1	2	1	1							1		1	1		1											
HUT/PVT/TOT	54	56	53	61	56		56	46	50	66	57		43	43	38	35	37	36	37	36	47	42	58	50	48	46	43	44	39	42	42	35	27	28	30	27	30
8:00P– 8:30P																																					
WWAY FULL HOUSE	12	13	11	17	13	22	22	21	27	22	21	35	12	9	9	11	11	9	9	9	7	7	9	12	13	15	13	14	13	12	13	5	7	5	5	5	5
WECT BAYWATCH	19	19			19	32	22	21	27	22	14	22	13	12	16	10	7	10	10	9	7	7	6	14	16	9	13	13	12	12	11	16	5	8	8	5	9
TRUE BLUE			23		23	41							19	19	11	11			17	19	24		21	16													
WJKA DNT LK40BRWN				–	6	11	6	5			2	4	4	4		7		3	3	2	2	1	4	4		1	1	1	1	2	2	2		1	1		
SPC MV PRSNT					2	3	3	1			5	7	1	1		2		1	1	1	2	1	3	2		1	1	1	1		1	1		1	1	1	
BRADYS					2	4	4	2			7	6	1	2				1		1	1	1	2	2		1	1	1	1	2	1		2	1	1		
––4 WK AVG––		6			20	34			28	17			15	14	10	10	8	12	12	12	18	18	19	16	16	10	14	14	14	14	13	12	7	7	10	9	10
WUNJ PTV	3	1	4	2	2	2	6	5	1	8	2	4	4	3				1		2	4	3	4	4		1	1	1	1		2	2		1	1		
HUT/PVT/TOT	63	57		64	60		55	41	52	61	62		46	44	39	38	37	37	38	38	43	43	57	50	40	45	44	45	44	45	46	36	30	30	30	29	32
8:30P– 9:00P																																					
WWAY FMLY MATTERS	8	8		16	10	17	19	21	23	19	16	27	7	5	4	5	5	5	5	6	6	6	7	7	4	5	7	7	9	8	6	3	3	3	3	4	4
WECT BAYWATCH	23	17		20	20	34					14	23	14	13	16	11	9	11	12	11	15	6	16	14	14	11	13	13	13	13	13	9	8	9	10	8	9
TRUE BLUE		24			24	44							20	20					17	19	24	17	21	14	11							18		11	11		
––4 WK AVG––					24	44											10							11			15	15	14	15	14	13					
WJKA DNT LK40BRWN				–	9	18	7	5	9	9	2	5	5	5		10		5	6				6	6		3	2	2	2	2		2		1	1		
SPC MV PRSNT					2	3	3	3	3	2	5	8	1	1				1	1	1	1	1	3	3				1			1	1		1	1	1	
BRADYS					3	5	5	4	4	3	4	7	2	2				1	1	1	1	1	3	3		1	1	1	1	2	1		2	1	1		
––4 WK AVG––		9			21	37	31	28			15	26	15	15	11	11	10	13	13	13	18	18	19	16	14	11	11	15	14	15	14	13	9	11	11	9	11
WUNJ PTV	3	1	4	3	3	3	7	5	9	9	2	4	5	4				2		2	4	4	3	6	3	3	2	2	1	2	1	2	1	1	1		
HUT/PVT/TOT	59	48	54	64	56		53	44	52	59	57		42	42	35	34	34	35	36	37	46	43	55	46	32	39	40	41	40	42	41	36	30	30	30	29	32

Exhibit 15.7 A portion of a page from an Arbitron Television Report for the Wilmington, North Carolina, television market in February 1990. Reprinted by permission.

1. During the first week of the measurement period, WWAY had an ADI (Area of Dominant Influence) household rating of 13 between 7:30 P.M. and 8:00 P.M. That means 13 percent of all television households were watching that station. In the other three weeks of the measurement period, WWAY's ratings were 20, 20, and 14.
2. Its average rating was 17. Its average share (percentage of households watching television) was 29.
3. In November 1989, its average share was 25.
4. The station's ADI rating for women age 18–34 was 5.

Nielsen Station Index

Local television audiences are also measured by Nielsen Station Index (NSI), a service of Nielsen Media Research, which is owned by The Dun & Bradstreet Corporation. NSI measures audiences at least four times a year in most markets and up to seven times a year in larger markets. Nielsen calls these markets Designated Market Areas (DMAs), and they are equivalent to what Arbitron calls Areas of Dominant Influence (ADIs). The four-week measurements, known as "sweeps," are based on diaries. Meters are used in the largest markets as well.

NSI Samples

NSI sample sizes vary with the size and importance of the market; larger and more important markets have larger samples. NSI determines how many in-tab (completed) diaries it will need for each market and analyzes previous return rates for each market. That analysis determines how large the gross sample should be to achieve the desired net sample size.

NSI stratifies lists of telephone households by postal zip code and street address and adds possible unlisted numbers with the following procedure. First, all known telephone numbers are removed from a list of possible numbers; the remaining unlisted numbers are added to the list of telephone households. Second, a random sample is drawn from the combined list and divided into equal-sized groups, one for each of the four weeks of the survey.

NSI Data Collection

Interviewers telephone the households that are selected by the procedure just described to secure their cooperation and to verify that they have working television sets. Those telephone interviews are conducted in Spanish if necessary.

NSI sends the cooperating households a diary for each television set. It tries to get additional cooperation by sending diaries to households that initially refused to cooperate and to households that could not be contacted by telephone. NSI takes additional steps to try to increase cooperation among ethnic households. Spanish-speaking households receive special cover letters, Spanish-language diaries, and special incentives. African-American households receive increased incentives and reminder telephone calls during the survey period.

Exhibit 15.8 shows a portion of a page from an NSI report on the Chicago television market.

Nielsen Television Index

The only measurement of national television audience size is provided by Nielsen Media Research's Nielsen Television Index (NTI). Its people meters—electronic

METRO HH	THURSDAY 6.00PM– 7.30PM		DMA HH											DMA RATINGS																					
			RATINGS				MULTI-WEEK AVG.	SHARE TREND						PERSONS			WOMEN					FEM PER		MEN					TNS	CHILD					
R T G 1	S H R 2	STATION PROGRAM	WEEKS 1	2	3	4	RTG 7	SHR 8	NOV '88 10	MAY '88 11	JAN '88 12			2+ 14	18+ 15	12-34 16	18-34 17	18-49 18	25-49 19	25-54 20	18+ 21	12-34 22	12-24 23	18+ 24	18-34 25	18-49 26	25-49 27	25-54 28	2-17 29	6-11 30				
		R.S.E. THRESHOLDS 25•⅞ (1 S.E.) 4 WK AVG 50•⅞	2 LT	2 LT	2 LT	2 LT	1 LT							1 LT	1 LT	2 LT	1 LT	1 LT	1 LT	1 LT	3 LT	2 LT	2 LT	2 LT	5 LT	3 LT	4 LT	2 LT	2 LT	2 LT	4 LT	6 LT			
6.00PM																																			
8	14	WBBM CBS EVE NWS	9	8	8	6	8	14	15X	13	15			4	5	1	1	2	3	6	1	2	3	3	5	1	4	1	2	3	3			
<<		WCFC SING OUT AMER	<<	<<	<<	<<	<<		X	NR	NR																							
<<		WCIU AVG. ALL WKS	<<	<<	<<	1	<<			NR	NR																						1	
<<		PANCHTO&ARTURO			<<		<<																											
<<		SENORA		<<	<<	1	<<																					②				1	1
12	21	WFLD COSBY SHOW ①	12	13	11	12	12	21	18X	15	16			8	5	9	7	7	6	7	8	9	9	8	7	14	12	4	5	4	4	3	16	16	20
1	2	WGBO IT'S A LIVING	1	1	1	1	1	2	1X	2	2			1							1	1				1	1							1	2
10	17	WGN CHEERS	10	10	10	9	10	17	17X	20	16			6	6	7	8	6	6	6	7	5	7	6	6	8	6	5	6	6	4	2	1	2
14	24	WLS EYEWIT NWS-6	14	13	14	14	14	24	23	26	25			8	10	4	4	5	7	11	5	7	8	9	9	1	2	8	2	4	5	5	3	2	3
5	9	WMAQ AVG. ALL WKS	5	5	6	7	6	10	11	10	11			3	4	2	1	3	2	2	3	2	2	2	2	2	1	2	1	1	1				
4	8	USA TODAY	5				5	8						3	3	1	1	2	2	5	2	2	2	2	2	2	1	2	1	1	1				
6	10	INSIDE EDITION		5	6	7	6	10						3	4	2	1	3	2	2	3	3	3	3	4	2	1	3	3	3	2	3			
2	3	WPWR A TEAM	2	1	2	2	2	3	5	3	7			1	1	1	1	1	1	1	1	1	1	1	1	1	1	1	1	1	1				
2	4	WTTW MACNEIL&LEHRER	3	1	2	2	2	4	3X	3	3			1	1	1	1	1	1	1	1	1	1	1	1	1		1	1	1	1		1	2	1
<<		WYCC AVG. ALL WKS	<<	<<	<<		<<																											
<<		WOODWRIGHT SHP	<<	<<			<<																											
<<		BODYWATCH			<<	<<	<<																											
57		HUT/PUT/TOTALS *	58	53	59	58	57		54	46	59			36	37	28	28	30	32	42	31	35	37	38	38	28	28	32	25	26	26	29	34	39
6.30PM																																			
8	14	WBBM ENT TONIGHT 30	9	8	9	7	8	13	12	14	12			4	5	3	4	5	7	4	4	5	6	6	3	3	4	2	3	4	4	3	1	
<<		WCFC HEADLINE NWS	<<	<<	<<	<<	<<		X	NR	NR																							
<<		WCIU AVG. ALL WKS	<<	<<	<<	1	<<			NR	NR																						1	1
<<		PANCHTO&ARTURO		<<			<<																											
1	1	SENORA		<<	<<	1	1	1									1						1										1	
7	11	WFLD AVG. ALL WKS	6	7	6	6	6	10	11	9	10			4	3	5	4	4	3	4	4	4	4	3	6	6	3	4	4	3	3	8	4	5
6	10	BULLS BKBL	6		6		6	10						3	3	4	4	4	2	3	3	3	3	2	5	4	2	3	3	2	2	4	5	3
7	12	CURRENT AFFAIR		7		6	7	11						4	3	6	4	4	4	5	5	5	4	5	3	8	8	2	3	3	3	11	5	6
2	3	WGBO KATE & ALLIE	2	1	1	2	1	2	2X	3	2			1	1	2	2	2	1	1	1	1	2	1	1	1	1	1	1	1		4	3	2
13	22	WGN NIGHT COURT	14	13	14	13	13	22	20X	15	14			9	9	13	12	10	9	8	10	9	9	8	10	11	14	9	14	11	9	9	14	7	9
18	29	WLS WHEEL-FORTNE	16	18	20	18	18	30	29	36	36			11	13	6	6	8	10	16	8	10	12	12	12	6	5	10	4	5	6	7	6	6	3
6	9	WMAQ AVG. ALL WKS	8	5	6	4	6	9	11	8	10			3	3	1	2	3	3	4	2	2	2	2	2	2	2	2	1	2	2	1	6	3	3
9	13	FAMILY FEUD	8				8	13						5	4	3	3	4	4	4	4	5	4	4	5	2	3	2	2	2	1	1	3	1
5	8	USA TODAY		5	6	4	5	8						2	3	2	2	3	3	4	2	3	3	3	3	2	1	2	1	1	2	1	1	1	
2	3	WPWR A TEAM	2	1	2	3	2	3	4	3	7			1	1	1	1	1	1	1	1	1	1	1	1	1		2	1	1	1	1		2	
3	6	WTTW MACNEIL&LEHRER	4	3	3	3	3	5	5X	5	5			2	2			1	2	2	1	1	1	1	1			2	1	1	1	1	2	1	
<<		WYCC AVG. ALL WKS	<<		<<	<<	<<																											
<<		GROWING YEARS	<<				<<																											
<<		BSNSS-MANAG'MNT		<<		<<	<<																											
<<		PRNCP-ACCNT'NG			<<	<<	<<																											
61		HUT/PUT/TOTALS *	65	58	60	61	61		56	49	61			41	43	36	35	37	38	47	38	40	41	42	43	35	37	38	33	34	33	34	37	40

Exhibit 15.8 A portion of a page from a Nielsen Station Index Report on the Chicago television market, called a Designated Market Area (DMA). *Source:* Nielsen Media Research. Reprinted by permission.

1. The DMA household rating for the "Bill Cosby Show" (syndicated) was 12 (percent) the first week, 13 the second week, 11 the third week, and 12 the fourth week. Over the four-week period, its average rating was 12, and its average share of audience was 21 percent.
2. The show's rating among teenagers was 16, meaning it was viewed by 16 percent of the teenagers in the DMA.

devices that provide a minute-by-minute record of program viewing and audience demographics — in a national sample of television households provide fast and continuous estimates of national television audiences, including networks, independent stations, superstations, the Public Broadcasting Service (PBS), cable networks such as Music Television (MTV), and pay cable services such as Home Box Office (HBO). The people meter also measures television set usage for videocassette recorders, computers, and video games.

...NTI Sample

Nielsen uses a multistage random selection process to choose households for its sample, and every U.S. household has an equal chance of being selected. Although no single household in the sample can be said to represent all television households, the sample as a whole is representative of television households as a group. After sample households have been identified, Nielsen uses field surveyors to locate each one. (They have found some living quarters in railroad boxcars, beer trucks, caves, and trees.)

Specially trained representatives then contact the selected households to recruit them for the sample. Nielsen reports that 55 percent of households originally selected for the sample agree to participate. Households that do become part of the sample are replaced after twenty-four months, which means the sample is continuously changing to reflect changing demographic characteristics of the population and to combat co-operation fatigue. On a typical day, approximately 3,700 households provide data for NTI reports. Those households include approximately 8,500 persons age 2 and older, including approximately 700 teenagers and 1,400 children age 2 to 11.

... NTI Data Collection

Television set tuning and audience composition data are gathered by the Nielsen people meter. The meter automatically records the time the television set is turned on and the station it is tuned to. Each person in the household has an assigned number on the meter, which is programmed with demographic information about those view-ers. Guests who watch television in the household must provide their own demo-graphic data. As viewers enter the room, they are supposed to push their button to indicate the start of viewing; they are supposed to push the button again when they leave. In that way, Nielsen is able to report the demographic characteristics of televi-sion audiences.

Each people meter is connected by a special telephone line to the Nielsen computer in Florida. Every day at 3:00 A.M., the people meters "call" the Nielsen computer to report their data; that process is completed by 7:00 A.M. Data processing begins by 11:30, and reports are available for agencies and other subscribers to access them via computers and online connections.

... NTI Reports

In addition to data available from its computers, NTI also issues a variety of printed reports. Two of those reports are illustrated here. Exhibit 15.9 is a page from an NTI report showing household viewing, and Exhibit 15.10 is a page showing audi-ence demographics.

... TvQ

The broadcast audience research discussed thus far is based on actual or reported viewing behavior—*how many* people *watched* a particular program. In contrast, TvQ—a service of Marketing Evaluations, Inc.—measures the audience's *familiarity* with and *attitudes* toward network television programs, movies, and specials. In other words, TvQ is a *qualitative* instead of a quantitative measure of the audience. Such data are useful because of the assumption that the audience's attitudes toward a pro-gram are as important as the decision to watch the program.

Nielsen **NATIONAL TV AUDIENCE ESTIMATES**　　　　　　　　　　**EVE. THU. AUG. 10, 1989**

TIME	7:00	7:15	7:30	7:45	8:00	8:15	8:30	8:45	9:00	9:15	9:30	9:45	10:00	10:15	10:30	10:45		
HUT	43.7	44.9	45.4	47.0	46.9	49.2	50.4	52.5	53.5	54.8	55.0	55.3	53.0	52.7	52.2	50.7		

①

ABC TV

←A MAN CALLED HAWK→　←MISSION: IMPOSSIBLE→　←PRIMETIME LIVE→
　　　　(R)　　　　　　　　(R)(PAE)

AVERAGE AUDIENCE (Hhlds (000) & %) {	4,700				6,960				8,590			
	5.2	5.2	*	5.2	* 7.7	7.1	*	8.3	* 9.5	9.6	*	9.4 *
SHARE AUDIENCE %	10	11	*	10	14	13	*	15	* 18	18	*	18 *
AVG. AUD. BY 1/4 HR %	5.5	4.9	5.1	5.3	6.9	7.3	8.2	8.3	9.7	9.5	9.5	9.2

CBS TV

←—48 HOURS—→←EQUALIZER→　←BEST OF KNOTS LANDING→
BEHIND THE BADGE　　　(PAE)
　　　(R)

AVERAGE AUDIENCE (Hhlds (000) & %) {	8,770				7,500				6,780			
	9.7	9.3	*	10.1	* 8.3	7.9	*	8.7	* 7.5	7.3	*	7.7 *
SHARE AUDIENCE %	19	19	*	20	* 15	15	*	16	* 14	14	*	15 *
AVG. AUD. BY 1/4 HR %	9.1	9.5	10.2	9.9	7.7	8.1	8.8	8.6	7.3	7.4	7.7	7.8

NBC TV

BILL COSBY　A DIFFERENT　CHEERS　DEAR JOHN　←—L.A. LAW—→
SHOW　　WORLD　　(R)　　(R)　　(R)
(R)　　(R)

AVERAGE AUDIENCE (Hhlds (000) & %) {	② 13,020	13,830	16,090	13,920	11,660		
	14.4	15.3	17.8	15.4	12.9	12.8 *	13.0 *
SHARE AUDIENCE %	30	30	33	28	25	24 *	25 *
AVG. AUD. BY 1/4 HR %	13.2	15.7	14.8	15.9	17.5	18.0	15.4	15.4	12.9	12.6	12.9	13.1

INDEPENDENTS
(INCL. SUPERSTATIONS)

AVERAGE AUDIENCE	11.8	10.9	10.7	10.9	11.0	11.9	11.7	11.0
SHARE AUDIENCE %	27	24	22	21	20	22	22	21

SUPERSTATIONS

AVERAGE AUDIENCE	3.2	3.1	3.3	3.5	3.7	4.0	3.6	3.7
SHARE AUDIENCE %	7	7	7	7	7	7	7	7

PBS

AVERAGE AUDIENCE	1.3	2.3	2.5	2.9	2.4	2.4	1.9	1.6
SHARE AUDIENCE %	3	5	5	6	4	4	4	3

CABLE ORIG.

AVERAGE AUDIENCE	6.1	6.4	6.4	7.7	③ 7.5	8.5	8.6	7.6
SHARE AUDIENCE %	14	14	13	15	14	15	16	15

PAY SERVICES

AVERAGE AUDIENCE	1.7	2.4	3.2	3.6	4.8	4.8	5.4	5.2
SHARE AUDIENCE %	4	5	7	7	9	9	10	10

U.S. TV HOUSEHOLDS:　90,400,000　　　　　　　　For explanation of symbols, See page B.

Exhibit 15.9　A page from a Nielsen Television Index Report on national television audiences. *Source:* Nielsen Media Research. Reprinted by permission.

1. Between 8:00 and 8:15, 46.9 percent of all television households were watching television. That is known as Households Using Television, or the HUT level.
2. The "Bill Cosby Show" was viewed in 13,020,000 television households and had an average minute rating of 14.4 (percent). Its audience share was 30, meaning 30 percent of the households using television were watching that program. Its average audience rating was 13.2 for the first quarter hour and 15.7 for the second quarter hour.
3. Between 9:00 and 9:30, cable originated programming (on such cable networks as Cable News Network or Music Television) had a 7.5 rating (percent of TV households) and a 14 share (share of households using television).

TvQ data are based on mail questionnaires returned by approximately 1,700 individuals age 6 and older in a representative sample of U.S. television households. TvQ issues seven reports each television season—from late September through late July.

Respondents rate television programs on a six-point scale:

1. "It's one of my favorites."　　5. "It's poor."
2. "It's very good."　　　　　　　6. "I've never seen it before."
3. "It's good."
4. "It's fair."

DAY / TIME / NETWORK PROGRAM NAME	HOUSE- HOLDS	TOTAL PERS (2+)	WORKING WOMEN 18-49	LOH 18-49 W/CH <3	WOMEN TOTAL	18-34	18-49	25-54	35-64	55+	MEN TOTAL	18-34	18-49	25-54	35-64	55+	TEENS TOT 12-17	TEENS FEM 12-17	CHILDREN TOT 2-11	CHILDREN TOT 6-11
THURSDAY EVENING																				
6.00- 6.30PM TVU	42.5	24.6	20.3	18.1	22.7	27.9	19.4	20.3	22.3	27.2	42.8	22.7	15.5	16.2	18.3	23.2	39.0	23.8	25.0	21.1	21.5
6.30- 7.00PM TVU	43.9	25.7	23.3	21.1	25.2	29.9	21.5	22.5	24.4	29.0	44.3	24.2	16.5	17.8	20.1	25.3	39.9	22.3	23.1	19.9	19.9
7.00- 7.30PM TVU	44.3	26.1	25.5	23.4	23.8	31.0	21.8	23.4	25.4	30.5	45.7	25.5	18.0	19.6	21.9	27.0	39.8	18.3	19.4	19.2	19.7
7.30- 8.00PM TVU	46.2	28.3	28.4	26.1	26.8	33.0	24.4	25.8	28.0	32.5	47.0	27.7	21.2	22.6	24.7	28.4	40.7	19.6	22.1	21.9	22.9
8.00- 8.30PM TVU	48.0	29.8	30.7	28.4	28.6	34.6	25.7	27.6	30.3	35.1	47.5	29.7	21.9	24.3	26.8	31.2	44.0	21.0	23.4	22.0	23.5
A A MAN CALLED HAWK	5.2	2.9	2.8	2.4	3.0^	3.7	2.0	2.7	3.5	4.5	5.1	3.1	1.5	2.1	2.3	3.4	5.9	1.7^	1.5^	1.4	1.5^
C 48 HOURS	9.3	5.4	5.7	5.0	4.0^	7.0	3.3	4.6	5.6	7.6	11.7	5.8	3.3	3.9	4.3	6.3	10.3	2.2^	1.7^	2.0	2.2^
N BILL COSBY SHOW ①	14.4	8.8	10.4	10.6	11.1	10.4	10.7	9.9	9.5	9.0	11.8	6.6	6.8	6.1	6.5	5.8	8.2	10.1	14.9	8.8	10.0
8.30- 9.00PM TVU	51.4	32.2	33.3	31.4	30.6	36.9	28.9	30.4	32.9	37.3	48.6	32.7	25.0	27.4	30.3	34.4	46.7	21.8	25.4	24.3	26.2
A A MAN CALLED HAWK	5.2	3.0	2.8	2.3	2.4^	3.6	1.7	2.3	3.1	4.4	5.6	3.2	1.9	2.2	2.6	3.1	5.8	1.3^	.9^	1.8	1.8^
C 48 HOURS	10.1	6.0	6.0	5.4	5.8	7.5	4.1	5.4	6.4	8.1	11.3	6.6	4.5	4.9	5.6	7.3	10.5	2.5	1.4^	2.4	2.3
N A DIFFERENT WORLD	15.3	9.2	11.5	12.2	13.2	10.9	13.0	11.5	10.8	9.1	10.0	6.5	7.3	6.4	6.5	5.7	7.4	11.4	16.2	9.8	11.6
9.00- 9.30PM TVU	54.1	33.8	35.2	33.2	34.7	38.4	31.8	32.8	35.6	38.9	48.2	35.4	27.8	30.5	33.7	37.4	48.5	22.9	24.8	23.9	26.3
A MISSION: IMPOSSIBLE	7.1	4.0	3.5	3.2	3.1^	4.6	2.7	3.5	4.2	5.3	6.2	4.0	2.2	3.0	3.9	4.7	6.3	2.9	2.7^	3.2	3.8
C EQUALIZER	7.9	4.6	4.1	3.8	3.5^	5.7	3.3	4.1	4.5	5.9	9.1	4.9	2.6	3.2	3.9	5.5	9.1	2.0^	1.6^	2.1	1.8^
N CHEERS	17.8	10.6	13.3	13.6	15.6	12.6	14.2	12.7	12.7	10.7	12.4	9.5	9.8	9.3	9.7	8.9	10.7	9.3	10.3	8.4	10.0
9.30-10.00PM TVU	55.2	34.5	36.4	34.3	37.0	39.5	32.0	33.6	36.2	40.4	50.7	36.4	28.0	31.3	34.9	39.2	49.9	24.1	25.8	22.7	24.8
A ABC NEWSBRIEF-THU(SUS)>												②									

Exhibit 15.10 A page from a Nielsen Television Index Report on the demographic composition of national television audiences. *Source:* Nielsen Media Research. Reprinted by permission.
1. The "Bill Cosby Show" was viewed by 14.4 percent of all television households, 8.8 percent of all persons, and 10.4 percent of all adult women.
2. Its demographic rating for men age 18–34 was 6.8.

Based on those viewer evaluations, TvQ calculates and reports the following scores for each program:

- *Familiarity Score:* The percentage of respondents who have any opinion (No. 1 through No. 5). It is a measure of awareness of the show.
- *Favorite Score:* The percentage of respondents rating the show as one of their favorites (No. 1).
- *TvQ Score:* The percentage who rate a program as one of their favorites from among those who are familiar with it; the favorite score divided by the familiarity score.
- *Negative Q:* Total of the fair and poor scores divided by the familiarity score.

In addition to qualitative ratings for television programs, TvQ also measures and reports similar data about television performers, sports stars, and cartoon characters. Exhibit 15.11 shows a portion of a page from a TvQ report for the NBC network show "Cheers."

Summary

In terms of money and effort expended, audience measurement is the most extensive type of advertising research; millions of dollars are spent each year to measure or estimate the audiences of print and broadcast vehicles. Advertisers understandably want to know the size and composition of audiences of media vehicles in which

CHEERS
SITUATION COMEDY

	FAMILIARITY	NORMS		POSITIVE TvQ	NORMS		SCALE POINTS						NEGATIVE Q	NORMS	
	FAM	PGM TYPE	ALL PGMS	TVQ	PGM TYPE	ALL PGMS	FAVOR-ITE	VERY GOOD	GOOD	FAIR	POOR	NOT SEEN	NEG Q	PGM TYPE	ALL PGMS
TOTAL SAMPLE															
TOTAL INDIVIDUALS	78	① 50	45	35	② 29	29	26	14	21	10	5	24	19	26	25
6 - 11	63	52	41	36	50	44	23	8	22	7	3	37	16	14	18
12 - 17	86	64	52	35	40	38	30	20	18	11	7	14	20	18	20
18 - 34	87	60	52	39	26	25	34	16	24	10	3	13	16	28	27
35 - 49	80	48	48	31	23	24	25	16	18	12	9	20	26	31	28
50 AND OVER	58	37	38	31	25	25	18	10	19	8	3	42	19	30	25
18 - 49	85	55	50	36	25	26	30	16	22	11	6	15	20	29	27
18 AND OVER	78	49	48	35	25	26	26	14	21	10	5	24	19	29	27
TOTAL MALES															
6 AND OVER	72	47	43	42	28	27	30	14	17	8	3	28	16	27	26
18 - 34	84	54	48	44	24	23	38	16	19	9	2	16	14	30	29
35 - 49	80	44	42	39	23	23	31	17	18	6	8	20	17	31	29
50 AND OVER	54	32	35	38	21	26	21	11	12	9	1	46	19	30	24
18 - 49	82	50	47	42	24	23	35	16	19	8	4	18	15	30	29
18 AND OVER	74	43	43	42	23	24	31	15	17	8	3	26	16	30	28
TOTAL FEMALES															
6 AND OVER	77	55	47	28	30	30	22	14	24	11	6	23	22	26	25
18 - 34	89	66	54	34	27	28	30	15	28	11	5	11	17	25	25
35 - 49	80	54	49	24	23	25	19	15	18	18	10	20	35	31	27
50 AND OVER	61	41	40	26	27	30	16	9	25	7	4	39	19	30	28
18 - 49	86	61	53	30	26	26	26	15	24	14	7	14	24	27	26
18 AND OVER	77	53	47	28	26	26	22	13	25	11	8	23	22	28	26
25 - 54	83	58	52	28	25	25	23	14	25	13	8	17	25	29	26

Exhibit 15.11   A portion of a page from a TvQ report on the NBC network show "Cheers." Reprinted by permission of Marketing Evaluations, Inc.

1. The show's familiarity score is 76; it's the total of the scale point ratings — poor through favorite. The norm or average for all situation comedies is 50, so "Cheers" is much above average. The norm for all programs is 45.
2. The show's TvQ rating is 35 — the percentage who say it is their favorite divided by the percentage who are familiar with it. That is also higher than the norms for situation comedies and for all programs.

they place advertising. They assume that advertising messages cannot have an effect unless they are seen. It is important to remember that audience research provides estimates of the size and composition of the audience of a media vehicle and not of the audience of a specific advertisement. Nevertheless, audience estimates are useful because they indicate potential audiences for advertisements.

Audience data are collected in several ways, and the methods of data collection influence audience estimates. Diaries and interviews rely on respondents' memories and are subject to the errors of such memories. Both methods require a long time to process the data and to issue reports. Diaries are relatively inexpensive, and interviews give researchers more control. Electronic meters are not subject to memory problems (unless viewers forget to use the people meter buttons), but they cannot confirm if anyone was in the room or paying attention to the television set. Most methods rely on cooperation from respondents, and research companies are finding it increasingly difficult to get such cooperation.

RADAR® measures network radio audiences by using telephone interviews to ask respondents to recall their radio listening for the previous twenty-four hours. Birch Radio uses telephone interviews to measure local radio station audiences. Arbitron and Nielsen use diaries (and meters in the largest markets) to measure local television and radio station audiences, and Nielsen uses people meters to measure national television audiences. TvQ uses mail questionnaires to compile data for its qualitative measure of audience familiarity with and attitudes toward television programs (advertising vehicles).

Notes
● ● ●

1. Jeremy Gerard, "TV Networks Want Nielsen to Change Rating Methods," *New York Times*, December 14, 1989, p. 33(Y).
2. Bill Carter, "Networks Want Every Viewer to Count," *New York Times*, July 10, 1989, p. 35(Y).
3. Steve Sternberg, "Measuring VCR Playback," *Marketing and Media Decisions* (March 1988), 122–124.

Self-Test Questions
● ● ●

1. Discuss the strengths and weaknesses of diaries as data gathering methods in broadcast audience measurement. Do the same analysis for interviews (telephone and personal) and meters.
2. Name the sources (companies) of the following kinds of audience data: spot television, spot radio, network television, network radio.
3. Explain the essential differences between NTI and TvQ.
4. Discuss the techniques that companies like Arbitron and Nielsen use to increase the representativeness of their samples.
5. Explain the difference between an area of dominant influence (ADI) and a designated market area (DMA).

6. Explain why diaries are used to measure television station audiences in most markets.

7. Explain the method that RADAR® uses to gather data for its network radio audience measurement. Evaluate the procedure it follows when interviewers are unable to contact respondents for two or three days.

8. Discuss how the people meter has changed the way Nielsen measures network television audiences. Explain the problems associated with the people meter.

9. Discuss the concept of passive audience measurement systems. Explain the advantages a passive technique would have over current methods as well as its drawbacks.

10. Describe a common technique used by research companies to ensure that interviewers get a random (and thus a representative) division of male and female respondents.

11. Explain and evaluate the fundamental differences between the methodologies used by Birch Radio and Arbitron Radio.

12. Define the following terms as they apply to broadcast audience measurement: yesterday-listening, in-tab diaries, random-digit dialing, qualitative data, passive measurement systems.

13. Evaluate the way companies like Arbitron television treat videocassette usage.

14. Look at Exhibit 15.2. What was the average number of women age 18 to 49 that listened to the 9:00 news? [The answer is 385,000.]

15. Look at the Saturday-Sunday data in Exhibit 15.3. What was the average quarter-hour share for WBT? [The answer is 2.7.]

16. Look at the 6:30 data in Exhibit 15.8. Which station had the highest average share? [The answer is WLS.]

17. Look at Exhibit 15.9. If an advertiser placed a commercial in the final quarter hour of "Equalizer," what is the best estimate of the percent of households that saw the commercial? [The answer is 8.6. That's the rating for the final fifteen minutes. Of course, that is a rating for households tuned to the network. We don't know how many saw the commercial, but the program rating is the best estimate.]

• • • Suggestions for Additional Reading

Carter, B. "Are There Fewer Viewers? Networks Challenge Nielsen." *New York Times* (April 30, 1990), C7(Y).

Fannin, R., and J. Mandese. "Adding to the Vocabulary." *Marketing and Media Decisions* (October 1988), 69–73.

Haring, B. "Company Totes Up Popularity Quotients." *Billboard* (May 1989).

Hurley, D. "Those Hush-Hush Q Ratings — Fair or Foul?" *TV Guide* (December 10, 1988), 2–6.

Lipman, J. "Retired-Athlete Factor Emerges as a Plus." *Wall Street Journal* (March 14, 1989).

Mandese, J. "A Dream Come True?" *Marketing and Media Decisions* (July 1988), 30–37.

Tedesco, R. "TV to Go." *Marketing and Media Decisions* (November 1989), 43–46.

Walley, W. "Meters Set New TV Ground Rules." *Advertising Age* (October 30, 1989), 12.

Walley, W. "Nets to Chart Out-of-Home Viewers." *Advertising Age* (October 9, 1989), 59.

CHAPTER 16

Audience Research: Print

Advertisers use two kinds of print audience research data. *Primary audience* measurements include people who subscribe to or buy copies of newspapers or magazines. Primary audience research is essentially a measure of circulation or number of copies sold. Companies that conduct primary audience research use similar procedures — they require publications to file semiannual publishers' statements of circulation, and the companies inspect and audit publication records to verify the publishers' claims. The Audit Bureau of Circulations does that for publications that have paid circulation, and the Business Publications Audit of Circulation does the same for publications that have paid and unpaid circulation.

Total audience measurements include all people who read a publication, regardless of whether they buy it or read it in a library, doctor's office, barber shop, or other out-of-home locations. Companies that conduct total audience research interview samples of people and ask them to name publications they have read.

Compared to primary audience research, which is a measure of copies sold, total audience research is a measure of readers — based on what they say they have read. Because primary audience research is primarily concerned with counting copies of a publication, it is generally more accurate than total audience research, which is based on only samples and which is subject to readers' faulty memories. However, advertisers are usually more interested in an estimate of the total number of people who read a publication than in the number of copies sold, so they are more likely to want total audience estimates. Magazine audience research tends to concentrate on total audience estimates, and newspaper audience research tends to focus on circulation or primary audience research. Simmons Market Research Bureau, Mediamark Research, and Mendelsohn Media Research are sources of total audience estimates for publications.

••• Audit Bureau of Circulations

In the early 1900s, some newspaper and magazine publishers were making exaggerated claims about their circulations in attempts to attract more advertising. That made it difficult for advertisers to believe any circulation claims, so publishers, advertisers, and advertising agencies formed the cooperative and not-for-profit organization called the Audit Bureau of Circulations (ABC) in 1914.

ABC now establishes standards for reporting circulation, audits circulation data, and distributes that data about newspapers, consumer magazines, farm publications, and business magazines. ABC audits approximately three-fourths of all publications in the United States and Canada. Approximately 4,600 advertising agencies, advertisers, and publishers are ABC members.

The following descriptions of data collection and reporting are based on procedures for daily newspapers. ABC procedures are similar for other kinds of publications.

••• ABC Publisher's Statement

Publishers who belong to ABC must keep detailed and auditable records of circulation information. Although ABC does not require specific record-keeping procedures, it advises and assists publishers in setting up appropriate methods and records.

ABC does require a semiannual publisher's statement, so many publishers find it convenient to follow ABC recommendations about bookkeeping because of the required format of the publisher's statement. (See Exhibit 16.1.) Each statement covers a six-month period. ABC collects the statements, examines them for internal consistency and accuracy, and makes them available to ABC members who need information about a publication's circulation. ABC does not audit these statements, however.

Durham (Durham County), North Carolina
DURHAM MORNING HERALD (Morning & Sunday)
THE DURHAM SUN (Evening)

Newspaper
Publisher's Statement
For 6 Months Ended September 30, 1989

Audit Bureau of Circulations

Newspaper Publisher's Statement

Subject to audit by **Audit Bureau of Circulations**, 900 N. Meacham Road, Schaumburg, IL 60173-4968

FOR 6 MONTHS ENDED SEPTEMBER 30, 1989

DURHAM MORNING HERALD (Morning & Sunday)
THE DURHAM SUN (Evening)
Durham (Durham County), North Carolina

	Combined Daily	Morning		Evening	Sunday
1A. TOTAL AVERAGE PAID CIRCULATION (BY INDIVIDUALS AND FOR DESIGNATED RECIPIENTS):	66,843	47,785	①	19,058	64,751

1B. TOTAL AVERAGE PAID CIRCULATION (BY INDIVIDUALS AND FOR DESIGNATED RECIPIENTS) BY ZONES:
(See Par. 1E for description of area)

CITY ZONE

	Population	Occupied Households
1980 Census:	112,774	41,801
#12-31-88 Estimate:	123,000	52,400

	Combined Daily	Morning	Evening	Sunday
Carriers not filing lists with publisher	26,924	17,798	9,126	22,524
Single Copy Sales	6,599	3,109	3,490	8,549
Mail Subscriptions	71	56	15	35
School-Single Copy/Subscriptions, See Par. 11(b)	47	47		
Employee Copies, See Par. 11(c)	840	420	420	420
TOTAL CITY ZONE	**34,481**	**21,430** ②	**13,051**	**31,528**

RETAIL TRADING ZONE

	Population	Occupied Households
1980 Census:	385,924	134,338
#12-31-88 Estimate:	434,500	160,100

	Combined Daily	Morning	Evening	Sunday
Carriers not filing lists with publisher	21,534	21,534		26,479
Single Copy Sales	8,324	2,643	5,681	5,180
Mail Subscriptions	757	748	9	53
School-Single Copy/Subscriptions, See Par. 11(b)	178	178		3
TOTAL RETAIL TRADING ZONE	**30,793**	**25,103**	**5,690**	**31,715**
TOTAL CITY & RETAIL TRADING ZONES	**65,274**	**46,533**	**18,741**	**63,243**

	Population	Occupied Households
1980 Census:	498,698	176,139
#12-31-88 Estimate:	557,500	212,500

ALL OTHER

	Combined Daily	Morning	Evening	Sunday
Single Copy Sales and Carrier not filing lists with publisher	1,050	808	242	1,063
Mail Subscriptions	519	444	75	445
TOTAL ALL OTHER	**1,569**	**1,252**	**317**	**1,508**
TOTAL AVERAGE PAID CIRCULATION (BY INDIVIDUALS AND FOR DESIGNATED RECIPIENTS)	**66,843**	**47,785**	**19,058**	**64,751**

AVERAGE PAID CIRCULATION (BY INDIVIDUALS AND FOR DESIGNATED RECIPIENTS) BY QUARTERS:

	Combined Daily	Morning	Evening	Sunday
April 1 to June 30, 1989	66,840	47,749	19,091	64,645
July 1 to September 30, 1989	66,845	47,820	19,025	64,857

1C. THIRD PARTY (BULK) SALES:

	Combined Daily	Morning	Evening	Sunday
Hotels, Motels — Available for guests	80	69	11	89
TOTAL AVERAGE THIRD PARTY (BULK) SALES	**80**	**69**	**11**	**89**

#S&MM Estimate. See Par. 11(a).

651

Exhibit 16.1 The front page of an Audit Bureau of Circulations publisher's statement. Reprinted by permission. This information is provided by the newspaper and is distributed by ABC but is not audited.
1. The average paid circulation for the morning edition was 47,785.
2. The morning circulation in the city zone — the city limits and their immediate surrounding area — was 21,430.

...ABC Audit Report

Each year, ABC auditors visit ABC publications and inspect records and files: invoices for the purchase of newsprint, pressroom reports of the numbers of copies printed, transcripts of circulation records, carrier and mail subscription prices, policies for handling returns (unsold copies), analysis of carrier and subscription sales, policies for unpaid subscriptions, and a geographic breakdown of circulation sales.

ABC compares the audit information with the data on the publisher's statement and issues an annual audit report. The first page of a daily newspaper audit report is shown in Exhibit 16.2 The audit reports also include a map of the newspaper's market area, circulation breakdown by area, times of press runs, circulation-promotion contests, and policies about arrears (unpaid subscription bills).

...Other ABC Reports

ABC makes other information and services available to its members. Circulation data from all member newspapers are compiled into summary form in the FAS-FAX report illustrated in Exhibit 16.3. Other reports and services include Magazine Trend Reports, Canadian Newspaper Factbook, Daily Newspaper Rate Book, Magazine Market Coverage Reports, County Penetration Reports, Newspaper and Magazine Coupon Distribution Verification Services, and Audited ZIP/Postal Code Circulation Program. Another service, the Data Bank Service, provides computer-generated studies of circulation, markets, and costs available in printed copies, on computer diskettes, on magnetic tape, and through online services.

Business Publications Audit of Circulation

Like ABC, Business Publications Audit of Circulation (BPA) is a not-for-profit organization of publishers, advertisers, and advertising agencies. BPA audits and verifies the circulations of nearly 1,500 business publications and consumer magazines, including all-controlled (nonpaid), all-paid, or a combination of controlled and paid.

Publications audited by BPA are targeted at specific groups of readers in certain industries or professions. Publications whose readers do not pay for their subscriptions but usually receive them free are said to have *controlled circulation*, because the publishers control the subscriptions (circulation). Publishers do that so they can tell advertisers and media planners that their publications reach certain types of readers (target audiences) in specific job classifications.

...BPA Reports

BPA's procedures are similar to those of ABC. Publishers submit a semiannual publisher's statement, which is printed and distributed by BPA to members who

PRINTED AND RELEASED
BY ABC JANUARY, 1990

AUDIT REPORT: Newspaper

DURHAM MORNING HERALD
(Morning & Sunday)
THE DURHAM SUN (Evening)
Durham, (Durham County), North Carolina

Audit Bureau of Circulations

TOTAL AVERAGE PAID CIRCULATION FOR 12 MONTHS ENDED SEPTEMBER 30, 1989:

	Combined Daily	Morning	Evening	Sunday
1A. TOTAL AVERAGE PAID CIRCULATION (BY INDIVIDUALS AND FOR DESIGNATED RECIPIENTS):	67,128	47,818 ①	19,310	64,987

1B. TOTAL AVERAGE PAID CIRCULATION (BY INDIVIDUALS AND FOR DESIGNATED RECIPIENTS) BY ZONES:
(See Par. 1E for description of area)

CITY ZONE

	Population	Occupied Households
1980 Census:	112,774	41,801
#12-31-88 Estimate:	123,000	52,400

	Combined Daily	Morning	Evening	Sunday
Carriers not filing lists with publisher	27,547	18,077	9,470	22,911
Single Copy Sales	6,471	3,043	3,428	8,516
Mail Subscriptions	72	56	16	36
School-Single Copy/Subscriptions, See Par. 11(b)	70	70		
Employee Copies, See Par. 11(c)	840	420	420	420
TOTAL CITY ZONE	35,000	21,666	13,334	31,883

RETAIL TRADING ZONE

	Population	Occupied Households
1980 Census:	385,924	134,338
#12-31-88 Estimate:	434,500	160,100

	Combined Daily	Morning	Evening	Sunday
Carriers not filing lists with publisher	26,500	21,933	4,567	27,153
Single Copy Sales	3,131	2,053	1,078	4,452
Mail Subscriptions	749	740	9	55
School-Single Copy/Subscriptions, See Par. 11(b)	231	231		6
TOTAL RETAIL TRADING ZONE	30,611	24,957	5,654	31,666
TOTAL CITY & RETAIL TRADING ZONES..............	65,611	46,623	18,988	63,549

	Population	Occupied Households
1980 Census:	498,698	176,139
#12-31-88 Estimate:	557,500	212,500

ALL OTHER

	Combined Daily	Morning	Evening	Sunday
Single Copy Sales and Carriers not filing lists with publisher	969	726	243	980
Mail Subscriptions	548	469	79	458
TOTAL ALL OTHER	1,517	1,195	322	1,438
TOTAL AVERAGE PAID CIRCULATION (BY INDIVIDUALS AND FOR DESIGNATED RECIPIENTS) ...	67,128	47,818	19,310	64,987

1C. THIRD PARTY (BULK) SALES:

	Combined Daily	Morning	Evening	Sunday
Hotels, Motels — Available for guests	72	61	11	77
TOTAL AVERAGE THIRD PARTY (BULK) SALES........	72	61	11	77

#S&MM Estimate. See Par. 11(a).

Exhibit 16.2 The front page of an Audit Bureau of Circulations audit report. Reprinted by permission. The data are based on an audit of the newspaper's records.
1. For the twelve-month period—which is different from the period covered in the publisher's statement in Exhibit 16.1—the average paid circulation for the morning edition was 47,818.

NORTH CAROLINA	SPECIAL SERVICES		CZ OR NDM OH'S	CIRC	RATIO CIRC/OH'S %	RTZ OR NDM OH'S	CIRC	RATIO CIRC/OH'S %	TOTAL NDM OR CZ & RTZ OH'S	CIRC	TOTAL CIRCULATION AS OF 9/30/89	AS OF 9/30/88
KANNAPOLIS (CABARRUS CO.)			13,800			36,400			50,200			
INDEPENDENT	E (M-F)	Z		8,039	58.25		3,115	8.56		11,154	11,253	11,054
INDEPENDENT	SUN	Z		8,418	61.00		3,572	9.81		11,990	12,095	11,732
KINSTON (LENOIR CO.)			9,500			34,400			43,900			
FREE PRESS	E (M-F)	Z		6,838	71.98		6,987	20.31		13,825	14,241	14,257
FREE PRESS	SUN	Z		7,006	73.75		7,529	21.89		14,535	14,951	14,881
LENOIR (CALDWELL CO.)			7,100			15,500			22,600			
NEWS-TOPIC	E	Z		4,814	67.80		8,088	52.18		12,902	13,054*	12,773*
LEXINGTON (DAVIDSON CO.)			6,500			25,100			31,600			
DISPATCH	E			4,809	73.98		9,864	39.30		14,673	14,858	14,946
LUMBERTON (ROBESON CO.)			7,400			33,500			40,900			
ROBESONIAN	E (M-F)	Z		4,692	63.41		8,756	26.14		13,448	13,597	13,628
ROBESONIAN	SUN	Z		5,367	72.53		9,811	29.29		15,178	15,329	15,470
MONROE (UNION CO.)			7,300			21,600			28,900			
ENQUIRER-JOURNAL	E (M-F)	Z		3,236	44.33		8,954	41.45		12,190	13,128	12,628
ENQUIRER-JOURNAL	SUN	Z		3,777	51.74		9,409	43.56		13,186	14,163	13,562
MORGANTON (BURKE CO.)			6,000			23,300			29,300			
NEWS-HERALD	E (M-F)	Z		3,363	56.05		8,256	35.43		11,619	11,795	11,856
NEWS-HERALD	SUN	Z		3,109	51.82		8,057	34.58		11,166	11,343	11,341
NEW BERN (CRAVEN CO.)			37,400#						37,400			
SUN JOURNAL	E	#	15,624		41.78					15,624	15,925	15,271
RALEIGH (WAKE CO.)			75,700			262,500			338,200			
NEWS & OBSERVER, TIMES	CMB DLY	Z,C		54,146	71.53		63,578	24.22		117,724	162,556	164,375
NEWS & OBSERVER	M	Z,C		41,415	54.71		55,666 ①	21.21		97,081	141,800	139,978
TIMES	E (M-F)	Z,C		12,731	16.82		7,912	3.01		20,643	20,756	24,397
NEWS & OBSERVER	SUN	Z,C		52,773	69.71		78,520	29.91		131,293	186,881	185,562
ROANOKE RAPIDS (HALIFAX CO.)			6,200			14,500			20,700			
HERALD	E (M-F)			4,212	67.94		6,681	46.08		10,893	12,180	11,870
HERALD	SUN			4,783	77.15		6,768	46.68		11,551	12,835	12,546
ROCKINGHAM (RICHMOND CO.)			6,400			11,400			17,800			
RICHMOND COUNTY JOURNAL	E (M-F)			3,114	48.66		5,690	49.91		8,804	9,124	8,910

(‹ CITY OF PUBLICATION
#NEWSPAPER DESIGNATED MARKET
☆CHANGE IN PUBLISHING PLAN AND/OR FREQUENCY
*AVERAGE FOR 3 MONTHS

"Z" Provides ABC Audited
ZIP Code Analysis
"C" Participant, ABC Coupon
Distribution Verification Service

Exhibit 16.3 A portion of a page from an Audit Bureau of Circulations FAS-FAX report comparing circulations of several newspapers. Reprinted by permission.
1. The circulation of the morning *News & Observer* in the retail trading zone—a large area surrounding the city zone—was 55,666. That was slightly more than 21 percent of the households in the retail trading zone: the newspaper's coverage.

request it. BPA field auditors visit each publication annually to examine circulation records and to verify data on the publisher's statement. An essential part of a BPA audit is to verify that a magazine's readers are *qualified*, meaning they are engaged in the jobs claimed by the publisher. That verification is usually accomplished by a survey of a sample of subscribers. An important part of the publisher's statement, then, shows business and occupational data about the publication's readers.

If a publisher desires, or if an audit reveals discrepancies or inaccuracies, BPA issues an audit report that combines data from the two latest publisher's statements and the audit. In most cases, however, the publisher's statement is correct, so BPA does not issue an audit report. When BPA issues an audit report because of discrepancies, however, media buyers tend to rely on the audit report rather than the publisher's statement.

Exhibit 16.4 shows a portion of a BPA publisher's statement. Other parts of the report show a geographic analysis of circulation (region and state), subscription price (if any), length of subscriptions, sources of subscriptions, subscription incentives (if any), paid subscriptions that are past due, and subscription renewal rate.

PUBLISHER'S STATEMENT
FOR 6 MONTH PERIOD ENDING DECEMBER 1985

THE CRITERION

Criterion Publishing Company
360 Park Avenue South
New York, NY 10010
(212) 487-5200

Official Publication of: None
Established: 1931
Issues Per Year: 12

No attempt has been made to rank the information contained in this report in order of importance, since BPA believes this is a judgement which must be made by the user of the report.

BUSINESS PUBLICATIONS AUDIT
OF CIRCULATION, INC.
360 Park Avenue South
New York, NY 10010
(212) 532-6880

FIELD SERVED
THE CRITERION serves the field of data processing systems and procedures in manufacturing industries, service organizations, finance, insurance companies, government, utilities, retail and wholesale trade and transportation, communication, printing and publishing firms.

DEFINITION OF RECIPIENT QUALIFICATION
Qualified recipients are corporate officials, controllers, data processing and accounting personnel, purchasing and other management personnel in the above field. Also qualified are a limited number of library addressed copies.

AVERAGE NON-QUALIFIED CIRCULATION

	Copies
Advertiser and Agency	443
Non-Qualified Paid	28
Rotated or Occasional	26
Samples	122
All Other	242
TOTAL	**861**

* SEE PARAGRAPH 11

1. AVERAGE QUALIFIED CIRCULATION BREAKDOWN FOR PERIOD

	Qualified Non-Paid		Qualified Paid		Total Qualified	
	Copies	Percent	Copies	Percent	Copies	Percent
Single	7,007	34.1%	12,917	62.9%	19,924	97.0%
*Group	-	-	523	2.5	523	2.5
Association	-	-	-	-	-	-
*Bulk	-	-	100	0.5	100	0.5
TOTALS	**7,007**	**34.1%**	**13,540**	**65.9%**	**20,547**	**100.0%**

2. QUALIFIED CIRCULATION BY ISSUES WITH REMOVALS AND ADDITIONS FOR PERIOD

1985 Issue	Qualified Non-Paid	Qualified Paid	Total Qualified	Number Removed	Number Added	1985 Issue	Qualified Non-Paid	Qualified Paid	Total Qualified	Number Removed	Number Added
July	6,936	13,546	20,482	778	533	November	7,286	13,278	20,564	528	558
August	6,696	13,899	20,595	351	464	December	7,215	13,388	20,603	345	384
September	6,857	13,644	20,501	523	429						
October	7,049	13,485	20,534	651	684				**TOTALS**	3,176	3,052

Exhibit 16.4 Portions of a publisher's statement distributed by Business Publications Audit of Circulation. Reprinted by permission.

1. This magazine's average qualified circulation for the six-month period was 20,547. Of that, 34 percent was nonpaid and 66 percent was paid.

2. In November, the qualified circulation was 20,564. For that issue, the magazine removed 528 subscribers and added 558 new qualified subscribers.

Simmons Market Research Bureau

Simmons Market Research Bureau's annual Study of Media and Markets is a widely used source of data about magazine audiences. The Simmons study also measures exposure to other media and reports demographic and psychographic characteristics of product users (including heavy, medium, and light users) of more than 5,100 brands in more than 800 product categories.

... Simmons Sample

The Simmons Study of Media and Markets is based on a national probability sample of adults in 19,000 different households (no more than one adult from any household). Using a multistaged area probability sample design, Simmons selects geographic areas from U.S. Census Bureau files and sends investigators to each of the selected areas to list all housing units. Within each designated interviewing area, five households are randomly selected as starting points for interviewing; interviews are conducted in three to five preselected, consecutive dwelling units. No substitutions are permitted. For each selected household, one adult, predesignated by gender, is interviewed.

Simmons sends each designated adult a letter to introduce the company and the study and to stress the importance of getting information from a variety of people. The letter also illustrates the ten-dollar bill that respondents are to receive for completing the three-part interview process. (Respondents also receive a small gift at the first interview session.) The firm makes special efforts to secure the cooperation of reluctant sample members by means of personal letters, telephone calls, and an audiocassette explaining the purpose of the study in greater detail. Approximately 75 percent of the predesignated adults complete the first personal interview.

... Simmons Data Collection

Simmons uses an interviewing technique called *through-the-book* to measure respondents' exposure to magazines and thus to estimate total audiences. The first step (screening) is to give respondents a stack of cards that have magazine logos printed on them. (The logo is a color reproduction of the magazine's name as it appears on the cover.) Respondents are asked to select logos of the magazines they might have read or looked into during the previous six months. Interviewers then show respondents a skeletonized recent issue of each magazine they select. (*Skeletonized* means the advertisements and some editorial elements are removed. That is done to reduce the bulk of the magazines and to make it easier for interviewers to carry them.) Interviewers first ask respondents about their readership of articles in the issue; respondents are then asked if this was the first time they had seen the specific issue or whether they had seen it before. Respondents are counted as part of the magazine's audience if they are sure they have seen the issue before. Respondents are also asked to specify the place they read the magazine: their own (or someone else's) home, workplace, library, medical office, barbershop, or beauty parlor, or on public transportation.

Interviewers also secure data about respondents' exposure to other media. They ask if respondents read a newspaper the previous day—a technique called *yesterday-reading*. Radio listening is also measured by interviews—questions about radio listening the previous day. Television viewing is measured by two-week diaries maintained by the respondents.

Data collection takes place in three steps. (1) The first personal interview takes approximately forty-five minutes. Interviewers collect demographic data about respondents and obtain magazine and newspaper exposure data using through-the-book and yesterday-reading techniques. (2) At the end of the first interview, interviewers give respondents a self-administered questionnaire that asks about ownership, purchase, and usage of products and services in more than 800 categories. (3) At least four weeks after the first interview, interviewers return and repeat the magazine and newspaper exposure measurements. The two sets of audience data, one from each interview, are used by Simmons to determine average issue audience estimates, turnover, and accumulation. (*Turnover* represents the part of the average audience of one issue that will not be reached by a second issue. *Accumulation* refers to the number of people who will be reached by two issues.) They are also asked about radio listening in the second interview. A subsample provides data about television viewing using a two-week personal diary.

... Simmons Reports

Simmons issues an annual forty-three-volume report about product usage, publication audiences, and multimedia audiences. Exhibit 16.5 is a page from a Simmons product usage volume that shows demographic characteristics of regular cola users. Exhibit 16.6 is a portion of a page from one of the publication audience data books. Exhibit 16.7 is a portion of a page from a Simmons volume that reports estimated reach and frequency data for magazines.

... Mediamark

Mediamark Research uses a modified recent-reading technique to produce data about magazine total-audience estimates and other procedures to measure exposure to other media and product usage.

... Mediamark Sample

Mediamark's sample selection begins with a list of more than 70 million households obtained from a commercial direct mail company. Mediamark's sample consists of three parts: a sample of metropolitan areas, a sample of nonmetropolitan areas, and specific samples of ten individual markets. The individual markets are oversampled to provide enough respondents to allow Mediamark to prepare reports for each market.

Within each section, Mediamark randomly selects a single household address. Interviewers are instructed to attempt to interview the persons in that household as well as several households adjacent to it. Randomly selecting the starting household gives the sample geographic dispersion; using clusters reduces the time and expense

0116
P-18

REGULAR COLA DRINKS (CARBONATED, NOT DIET): USAGE IN LAST 7 DAYS
(FEMALES)

0116
P-18

	TOTAL U.S. '000	ALL USERS				HEAVY USERS SEVEN OR MORE				MEDIUM USERS THREE–SIX				LIGHT USERS TWO OR LESS			
		A '000	B % DOWN	C % ACROSS	D INDX	A '000	B % DOWN	C % ACROSS	D INDX	A '000	B % DOWN	C % ACROSS	D INDX	A '000	B % DOWN	C % ACROSS	D INDX
TOTAL FEMALES	93136	92137	100.0	56.0	100	18786	100.0	20.2	100	15545	100.0	16.7	100	17786	100.0	19.1	100
FEMALE HOMEMAKERS	89931	46778	89.7	54.7	98	16437	87.5	19.2	95	13712	88.1	16.0	96	16629	93.9	19.4	102
EMPLOYED MOTHERS	21125	13312	25.5	63.0	113	5390	28.5	25.3	126	3339	21.5	15.8	95	4623	26.0	21.9	115
18 – 24	13023	8790	16.9	67.6	121	3848	20.5	29.5	146	2753	17.7	21.1	126	2197	12.4	16.9	88
25 – 34	21913	14091	27.0	64.3	115	5457	29.0	24.9	123	3972	25.5	18.1	108	4662	26.2	21.3	111
35 – 44	17640	9969	19.1	56.4	101	4043	21.5	22.9	114	3548	16.4	14.6	86	3378	19.0	19.1	100
45 – 64	12297	6861	13.2	55.8	100	2119	11.3	17.2	85	2092	13.4	17.0	102	2650	14.9	21.5	113
55 – 64	11417	5636	10.8	49.4	88	1564	8.3	13.7	68	1907	12.3	16.7	100	2165	12.2	19.0	99
65 OR OLDER	16828	6782	13.0	40.3	72	1795	9.3	10.4	52	2293	14.7	13.6	82	2735	15.4	16.3	85
18 – 34	34936	22888	43.9	65.5	117	9304	49.5	26.6	132	6726	43.2	19.3	115	6859	38.6	19.6	103
18 – 49	58690	36260	69.5	61.8	110	14579	77.6	24.8	123	10138	65.1	17.3	103	11543	64.9	19.7	103
25 – 54	51869	30921	59.3	59.6	106	11619	61.8	22.4	111	8613	55.3	16.6	99	10689	60.1	20.6	108
35 – 49	23759	13372	25.6	56.3	101	5275	28.1	22.2	110	3412	21.9	14.4	86	4684	26.3	19.7	103
50 OR OLDER	34446	15877	30.9	46.1	82	4206	22.4	12.2	61	5427	34.9	15.8	94	6243	35.1	18.1	95
GRADUATED COLLEGE	14543	7625	14.6	52.4	94	2093	11.1	14.4	71	2202	14.1	15.1	91	3330	18.7	22.9	120
ATTENDED COLLEGE	17352	9576	18.4	55.2	99	3075	16.4	17.7	88	2811	18.1	16.2	97	3690	20.7	21.3	111
GRADUATED HIGH SCHOOL	39412	22683	43.5	57.6	103	8244	43.9	20.9	104	6849	44.0	17.4	104	7591	42.7	19.3	101
DID NOT GRADUATE HIGH SCHOOL	21831	12252	23.5	56.1	100	5373	28.6	24.6	122	3704	23.8	17.0	102	3175	17.9	14.5	76
EMPLOYED FULL-TIME	41060	23680	45.4	57.7	103	8881	47.3	21.6	107	6679	42.9	16.3	97	8119	45.6	19.8	104
EMPLOYED PART-TIME	8908	5200	10.0	58.4	104	1877	10.0	21.1	104	1330	8.5	14.9	89	1992	11.2	22.4	117
NOT EMPLOYED	43168	23258	44.6	53.9	96	8028	42.7	18.6	92	7556	48.5	17.5	105	7674	43.1	17.8	93
PROFESSIONAL/MANAGER	12976	7003	13.4	54.0	96	1888	10.1	14.5	72	2090	13.4	16.1	96	3026	17.0	23.3	122
TECH/CLERICAL/SALES	23489	13571	26.0	57.8	103	5082	27.1	21.6	107	3722	23.9	15.8	95	4768	26.8	20.3	106
PRECISION/CRAFT	1329	771	1.5	58.0	104	**285	1.5	21.4	106	**177	1.1	13.3	80	**308	1.7	23.2	121
OTHER EMPLOYED	12174	7534	14.5	61.9	111	3504	18.7	28.8	143	2020	13.0	16.6	99	2010	11.3	16.5	86
SINGLE	17043	10520	20.2	61.7	110	4204	22.4	24.7	122	3153	20.3	18.5	111	3163	17.8	18.6	97
MARRIED	53816	30320	58.2	56.3	101	10719	57.1	19.9	99	8798	56.5	16.3	98	10803	60.7	20.1	105
DIVORCED/SEPARATED/WIDOWED	22278	11296	21.7	50.7	91	3862	20.6	17.3	86	3615	23.2	16.2	97	3819	21.5	17.1	90
PARENTS	33507	21864	41.9	65.3	117	8789	46.8	26.2	130	6074	39.0	18.1	108	7001	39.4	20.9	109
WHITE	79569	43487	83.4	54.7	98	15189	80.9	19.1	95	12705	81.6	16.0	96	15592	87.7	19.6	103
BLACK	10996	7171	13.8	65.2	116	2951	15.7	26.8	133	2391	15.4	21.7	130	1829	10.3	16.6	87
OTHER	2572	1479	2.8	57.5	103	**646	3.4	25.1	125	**469	3.0	18.2	109	**364	2.0	14.2	74

Exhibit 16.5 A page from a Simmons product usage book showing demographic characteristics of regular cola users. *Source:* Simmons Market Research Bureau, Inc., "1989 Study of Media and Markets." Reprinted by permission.
1. An estimated 3,848,000 women age 18–24 are heavy users of regular cola.
2. That is an estimated 20.5 percent of adult female heavy users.
3. An estimated 29.5 percent of women age 18–24 are heavy users, compared to 20.2 percent of all women regardless of age.
4. The index number of 146 compares the usage of women age 18–24 to all adult women. It is derived by dividing 29.5 by 20.2 and multiplying by 100. It can be interpreted as follows: Women age 18–24 are 46 percent more likely to be heavy users of regular cola than the average adult woman.

of conducting interviews. If a household consists of all males or all females, a random procedure is used to select the adult to be interviewed. If both a male and a female are living in the household, interviewers use a predetermined procedure to select either the male or the female. That, plus the procedure for randomly selecting households, means the Mediamark sample actually consists of random samples of male and female respondents.

• • • Mediamark Data Collection

Chilton Research Services, a private research company that specializes in field interviews, conducts the interviews for Mediamark. The designated households are first notified by mail of their selection in the sample. The first step in the data collection process is a fifty-minute face-to-face interview to collect data about demographics and media exposure. Interviewers make up to six attempts to reach each household, and respondents are given small gifts during the first interview. Special interviewers are used in cases of language difficulty.

At the end of the first interview, field workers give respondents a self-completing product information questionnaire booklet that asks about usage of approximately

①　②　　③　　④⑤

	TOTAL U.S. '000	ADULTS A '000	B % DOWN	C % ACROSS	D INDX	MALES A '000	B % DOWN	C % ACROSS	D INDX	FEMALES A '000	B % DOWN	C % ACROSS	D INDX	FEMALE HOMEMAKERS A '000	B % DOWN	C % ACROSS	D INDX
TOTAL	178193	178193	100.0	100.0	100	85056	100.0	47.7	100	93136	100.0	52.3	100	85531	100.0	48.0	100
AMERICAN BABY	2277	2277	1.3	100.0	100	301	0.4	13.2	28	1976	2.1	86.8	166	1884	2.2	82.7	172
AMERICAN HEALTH	2648	2648	1.5	100.0	100	793	0.9	29.9	63	1856	2.0	70.1	134	1685	2.0	63.6	133
ARCHITECTURAL DIGEST	2142	2142	1.2	100.0	100	1226	1.4	57.2	120	916	1.0	42.8	82	873	1.0	40.8	85
BABY TALK	1726	1726	1.0	100.0	100	236	0.3	13.7	29	1490	1.6	86.3	165	1420	1.7	82.3	171
BARRON'S	1390	1390	1.3	100.0	100	1101	1.3	79.2	166	*289	0.3	20.8	40	*289	0.3	20.8	43
BETTER HOMES & GARDENS	22608	22608	12.7	100.0	100	4710	5.5	20.8	44	17899	19.2	79.2	151	17042	19.9	75.4	157
BON APPETIT	3585	3585	2.0	100.0	100	874	1.0	24.4	51	2711	2.9	75.6	145	2564	3.0	71.5	149
BRIDE'S	3174	3174	1.8	100.0	100	*272	0.3	8.6	18	2902	3.1	91.4	175	2211	2.6	69.7	145
BUSINESS WEEK	6568	6568	3.7	100.0	100	4804	5.6	73.1	153	1765	1.9	26.9	51	1694	2.0	25.8	54
CAR AND DRIVER	4817	4817	2.7	100.0	100	4324	5.1	89.8	188	493	0.5	10.2	20	361	0.4	7.5	16
CHANGING TIMES	2080	2080	1.2	100.0	100	1250	1.5	60.1	126	829	0.9	39.9	76	829	1.0	39.9	83
COLONIAL HOMES	1830	1830	1.0	100.0	100	485	0.6	26.5	56	1345	1.4	73.5	141	1244	1.5	68.0	142
CONDE NAST LIMITED (GROSS)	16775	16775	9.4	100.0	100	5350	6.3	31.9	67	11425	12.3	68.1	130	9772	11.4	58.3	121
CONDE NAST LIMITED PLUS(GRS)	19136	19136	10.7	100.0	100	6694	7.9	35.0	73	12442	13.4	65.0	124	10755	12.6	56.2	117
CONDE NAST PKG. WOMEN(GROSS)	23805	23805	13.4	100.0	100	1865	2.2	7.8	16	21940	23.6	92.2	176	17505	20.5	73.5	153
CONSUMERS DIGEST	3268	3268	1.8	100.0	100	1714	2.0	52.4	110	1554	1.7	47.6	91	1514	1.8	46.3	97
COSMOPOLITAN	11737	11737	6.6	100.0	100	1314	1.5	11.2	23	10423	11.2	88.8	170	8583	10.0	73.1	152
COUNTRY LIVING	6446	6446	3.6	100.0	100	1681	2.0	26.0	54	4785	5.1	74.0	142	4612	5.4	71.3	149
CREATIVE IDEAS FOR LIVING	2005	2005	1.1	100.0	100	340	0.4	17.0	36	1665	1.8	83.0	159	1574	1.8	78.5	164
CYCLE	2118	2118	1.2	100.0	100	1879	2.2	88.7	186	*239	0.3	11.3	22	*212	0.2	10.0	21
CYCLE WORLD	2034	2034	1.1	100.0	100	1783	2.1	87.7	184	*250	0.3	12.3	24	*224	0.3	11.0	23
DIAMANDIS MAG NETWORK(GROSS)	20100	20100	11.3	100.0	100	17158	20.2	85.4	179	2942	3.2	14.6	28	2627	3.1	13.1	27
DIAMANDIS MTRCYCL GRP(GROSS)	4152	4152	2.3	100.0	100	3663	4.3	88.2	185	489	0.5	11.8	23	436	0.5	10.5	22
DISCOVER	3901	3901	2.2	100.0	100	2367	2.8	60.7	127	1534	1.6	39.3	75	1398	1.6	35.8	75
EBONY	8719	8719	4.9	100.0	100	3610	4.2	41.4	87	5110	5.5	58.6	112	4340	5.1	49.8	104
ELLE	2122	2122	1.2	100.0	100	*326	0.4	15.4	32	1796	1.9	84.6	162	1422	1.7	67.0	140
ESQUIRE	2528	2528	1.4	100.0	100	1770	2.1	70.0	147	758	0.8	30.0	57	729	0.9	28.8	60
ESSENCE	4012	4012	2.3	100.0	100	1336	1.6	33.3	70	2676	2.9	66.7	128	2070	2.4	51.6	107
FAMILY CIRCLE	18140	18140	10.2	100.0	100	2139	2.5	11.8	25	16001	17.2	88.2	169	15046	17.6	82.9	173
THE FAMILY HANDYMAN	3349	3349	1.9	100.0	100	2297	2.7	68.6	144	1052	1.1	31.4	60	1052	1.2	31.4	65

Exhibit 16.6 A portion of a page from a publication audience data volume in a Simmons report. *Source:* Simmons Market Research Bureau, Inc., "1989 Study of Media and Markets." Reprinted by permission.

1. The average issue audience of *Better Homes and Gardens* is estimated to be 22,608,000 adults.
2. That is 12.7 percent of the 178,193,000 adults in the United States.
3. Its average issue audience includes 4,710,000 men—5.5 percent of all adult men.
4. Approximately 21 percent of the magazine's audience are men. However, men comprise only 47.7 percent of the population.
5. The index number of 44 compares the male composition of the magazine's audience with the male composition of the U.S. population. It can be interpreted as follows: The male composition of the readers of the magazine is 56 percent less than the male composition of the population.

5,700 brands in 450 product categories. They promise the respondents a ten-dollar gift if they complete the questionnaire, which is picked up by the interviewer a few days later. The Mediamark sample consists of more than 20,000 adults who complete the interview process.

Mediamark uses the *recent-reading* technique to measure the total audiences of more than 250 consumer magazines. In that technique, respondents are given a deck of magazine logo cards and are asked to select the logos of the magazines they are sure they have read within the previous publication interval for each magazine—that is, the last thirty days for monthlies and the last seven days for weeklies. (The logos are the magazines' nameplates as they appear on their covers.) Only those respondents who are certain they have read or looked into a particular magazine are counted as part of its total audience. Respondents are asked other questions about magazine readership, including how frequently they read particular magazines, where they read them, the number of days on which the magazines were read, and the amount of time spent reading each magazine.

TOTAL ADULTS
REACH AND FREQUENCY

(IN THOUSANDS)

	U.S. TOTAL	AVERAGE AUDIENCE	RATING	TURNOVER RATE	REACH				FREQUENCY DISTRIBUTION			
					ONE	TWO	THREE	FOUR	1 OF 4	2 OF 4	3 OF 4	4 OF 4
AMERICAN BABY	178193	2277	1.3	.468	2277	3341	4035	4548	2053	1079	766	650
AMERICAN HEALTH	178193	2648	1.5	.496	2648	3963	4835	5487	2607	1323	888	669
ARCHITECTURAL DIGEST	178193	2143	1.2	.950	2143	3321	4133	4751	2472	1161	696	422
BABY TALK	178193	1726	1.0	.522	1726	2627	3235	3694	1836	897	572	390
BARRON'S	178193	1390	0.8	.466	1390	2039	2461	2774	1252	656	467	399
BETTER HOMES & GARDENS	178193	22609	12.7	.423	22609	32179	38107	42352	16977	10103	7836	7436
BON APPETIT	178193	3585	2.0	.424	3585	5106	6069	6771	2811	1558	1197	1205
BRIDE'S	178193	3174	1.8	.601	3174	9082	6442	7496	4218	1832	971	474
BUSINESS WEEK	178193	6568	3.7	.902	6568	9868	12057	13689	6528	3340	2216	1604
CAR AND DRIVER	178193	4817	2.7	.419	4817	6837	8109	9036	3707	2073	1608	1648
CHANGING TIMES	178193	2080	1.2	.546	2080	3214	3992	4584	2367	1119	678	419
COLONIAL HOMES	178193	1830	1.0	.476	1830	2701	3272	3696	1694	880	615	505
CONDE NAST LIMITED (NET)	178193	14196	8.0	.452	14196	20610	24693	27667	11897	6455	4882	4233
CONDE NAST LIMITED PLUS(NET)	178193	15831	8.9	.461	15831	22814	27223	30419	12784	7276	5448	4911
CONDE NAST PKG. WOMEN(NET)	178193	17114	9.6	.390	17114	23796	27881	30800	11676	6993	5728	6402
CONSUMERS DIGEST	178193	3268	1.8	.479	3268	4833	5858	6619	3045	1584	1101	889
COSMOPOLITAN	178193	11737	6.6	.420	11737	16669	19757	21992	8941	5114	3970	3968
COUNTRY LIVING	178193	6466	3.6	.461	6466	9449	11377	12795	5676	3049	2192	1878
CREATIVE IDEAS FOR LIVING	178193	2005	1.1	.570	2005	3147	3944	4556	2446	1114	638	358
CYCLE	178193	2118	1.2	.433	2118	3034	3618	4046	1711	935	708	692
CYCLE WORLD	178193	2034	1.1	.445	2034	2939	3520	3947	1710	921	682	634
DIAMANDIS MAG NETWORK(NET)	178193	13804	7.7	.350	13804	18633	21526	23579	8213	5033	4394	5939
DIAMANDIS MTRCYCL GRP(NET)	178193	3145	1.8	.379	3145	4336	5068	5597	2113	1225	1016	1242
DISCOVER	178193	3901	2.2	.437	3901	5607	6694	7491	3187	1744	1310	1250
EBONY	178193	8719	4.9	.328	8719	11581	13281	14487	4823	2967	2669	4029
ELLE	178193	2122	1.2	.514	2122	3213	3946	4497	2203	1090	706	497
ESQUIRE	178193	2528	1.4	.560	2528	3944	4925	5674	2998	1389	814	474
ESSENCE	178193	4012	2.3	.386	4012	5561	6517	7208	2763	1594	1307	1544
FAMILY CIRCLE	178193	18140	10.2	.442	18140	26164	31220	34877	14627	8395	6276	5578
THE FAMILY HANDYMAN	178193	3350	1.9	.460	3350	4889	5885	6620	2941	1565	1129	985

Exhibit 16.7 A portion of a page from a Simmons report showing reach and frequency estimates for magazines. *Source:* Simmons Market Research Bureau, Inc., "1989 Study of Media and Markets." Reprinted by permission.
1. Two issues of *Better Homes and Gardens* will reach 32,179,000 different adults.
2. The turnover rate tells what portion of the average issue audience will not be reached by a second issue. If the magazine's two-issue reach were 45,218,000 (22,609,000 times 2 issues), its turnover rate would be 100 percent.
3. This says 10,103,000 adults will see two issues out of the average four published.

Mediamark measures newspaper readership with a yesterday-reading technique similar to the recent-reading method used for magazines. Interviewers give respondents a list of the newspapers circulated in the respondents' cities and ask them to indicate the newspapers they read the previous day or previous Sunday. Interviewers obtain radio audience data by asking respondents about the stations they listened to the previous day or previous weekend. Similar methods are used to measure audiences for television and cable.

. . . Mediamark Reports

The data about media audiences and product usage are published in a twenty-four-volume report each spring. Users can also access the data through online databases or computer diskettes. Exhibits 16.8 and 16.9 show portions of Mediamark reports about women drinkers of regular cola drinks.

. . . Mendelsohn

Mendelsohn's Survey of Adults and Markets of Affluence differs from Simmons and Mediamark in one important regard: It is a measure of media habits — including

		ALL				HEAVY MORE THAN 7				MEDIUM 3 - 7				LIGHT LESS THAN 3			
BASE: WOMEN	TOTAL U.S. '000	A '000	B % DOWN	C % ACROSS	D INDEX	A '000	B % DOWN	C % ACROSS	D INDEX	A '000	B % DOWN	C % ACROSS	D INDEX	A '000	B % DOWN	C % ACROSS	D INDEX
ALL WOMEN	93246	52998	100.0	56.8	100	13047	100.0	14.0	100	19083	100.0	20.5	100	20868	100.0	22.4	100
HOUSEHOLD HEADS	29963	16068	30.3	53.6	94	3694	28.3	12.3	88	6084	31.9	20.3	99	6290	30.1	21.0	94
HOMEMAKERS	81513	45405	85.7	55.7	98	10954	84.0	13.4	96	16777	87.9	20.6	101	17674	84.7	21.7	97
GRADUATED COLLEGE	13785	6888	13.0	50.0	88	1046	8.0	7.6	54	2235	11.7	16.2	79	3606	17.3	26.2	117
ATTENDED COLLEGE	16801	9292	17.5	55.3	97	2165	16.6	12.9	92	3078	16.1	18.3	90	4050	19.4	24.1	108
GRADUATED HIGH SCHOOL	38857	22970	43.3	59.1	104	6112	46.8	15.7	112	8477	44.4	21.8	107	8380	40.2	21.6	96
DID NOT GRADUATE HIGH SCHOOL	23802	13848	26.1	58.2	102	3725	28.6	15.6	112	5292	27.7	22.2	109	4831	23.2	20.3	91
18-24	13210	9588	18.1	72.6	128	2915	22.3	22.1	158	3146	16.5	23.8	116	3528	16.9	26.7	119
25-34	21916	13904	26.2	63.4	112	3907	29.9	17.8	127	5031	26.4	23.0	112	4966	23.8	22.7	101
35-44	17438	10635	20.1	61.0	107	2815	21.6	16.1	115	3838	20.1	22.0	108	3982	19.1	22.8	102
45-54	12206	6602	12.5	54.1	95	1428	10.9	11.7	83	2256	11.8	18.5	90	2920	14.0	23.9	107
55-64	11966	5562	10.5	46.5	82	969	7.4	8.1	58	2257	11.8	18.9	92	2336	11.2	19.5	87
65 OR OVER	16509	6706	12.7	40.6	71	1015	7.8	6.1	44	2555	13.4	15.5	76	3136	15.0	19.0	85
18-34	35126	23493	44.3	66.9	118	6822	52.3	19.4	139	8177	42.8	23.3	114	8494	40.7	24.2	108
18-49	58799	37661	71.1	64.1	113	10368	79.5	17.6	126	13295	69.7	22.6	110	13998	67.1	23.8	106
25-54	51561	31141	58.8	60.4	106	8147	62.4	15.8	113	11125	58.3	21.6	105	11868	56.9	23.0	103
EMPLOYED FULL TIME	41858	24858	46.9	59.4	104	6699	51.3	16.0	114	8855	46.4	21.2	103	9304	44.6	22.2	99
PART-TIME	8622	4731	8.9	54.9	97	1062	8.1	12.3	88	1869	9.8	21.7	106	1799	8.6	20.9	93
SOLE WAGE EARNER	11678	8625	12.5	56.7	100	1630	12.5	14.0	100	2654	13.9	22.7	111	2342	11.2	20.1	90
NOT EMPLOYED	42766	23409	44.2	54.7	96	5286	40.5	12.4	88	8358	43.8	19.5	95	9765	46.8	22.8	102
PROFESSIONAL	7603	4004	7.6	52.7	93	622	4.8	8.2	58	1420	7.4	18.7	91	1962	9.4	25.8	115
EXECUTIVE/ADMIN./MANAGERIAL	5711	3032	5.7	53.1	93	628	4.8	11.0	79	1054	5.5	18.5	90	1350	6.5	23.6	106
CLERICAL/SALES/TECHNICAL	21870	12588	23.8	57.6	101	3288	25.2	15.0	107	4728	24.8	21.6	106	4572	21.9	20.9	93
PRECISION/CRAFTS/REPAIR	1232	795	1.5	64.5	114	*227	1.7	18.4	132	*288	1.5	23.4	114	*280	1.3	22.7	102
OTHER EMPLOYED	14064	9170	17.3	65.2	115	2996	23.0	21.3	152	3234	16.9	23.0	112	2939	14.1	20.9	93
H/D INCOME $60,000 OR MORE	11224	5413	10.2	48.2	85	939	7.2	8.4	60	1784	9.3	15.9	78	2691	12.9	24.0	107
$50,000 - 59,999	8080	4559	8.6	56.4	99	954	7.3	11.8	85	1544	8.1	19.1	93	2058	9.9	25.5	114
$35,000 - 49,999	18837	11273	21.3	59.8	105	2067	22.0	15.2	109	3858	20.2	20.5	100	4547	21.8	24.1	108
$25,000 - 34,999	15901	9314	17.6	58.6	103	2338	17.9	14.7	105	3188	16.7	20.0	98	3788	18.2	23.8	106
$15,000 - 24,999	17273	10282	19.4	59.5	105	2719	20.8	15.7	113	3803	19.9	22.0	108	3760	18.0	21.8	97
LESS THAN $15,000	21930	12156	22.9	55.4	98	3228	24.7	14.7	105	4906	25.7	22.4	109	4023	19.3	18.3	82

Exhibit 16.8 A portion of a page from a Mediamark report showing demographics of cola drinkers. © Mediamark Research, Inc. All rights reserved. Reprinted by permission.

1. An estimated 2,915,000 women age 18–24 are heavy users of cola drinks (consume more than seven glasses per week).
2. That is an estimated 22 percent of all female heavy users.
3. An estimated 22 percent of women age 18–24 are heavy users, compared to 14 percent for all women regardless of age.
4. The index number of 158 compares the usage of women age 18–24 with all women. It is derived by dividing 22.1 by 14 and multiplying by 100. It can be interpreted as follows: The usage level of women 18 to 24 is 58 percent higher than the usage level of all women (the average).

magazine reading—and product consumption of affluent Americans, those whose household incomes are $60,000 or higher. Those 31 million adults make up nearly 20 percent of the U.S. population.

... Mendelsohn Sample

A company called Survey Sampling, Inc., selects the names of 28,500 adults from a computer file of more than 84 million names and addresses furnished by a company called Donnelley Marketing. Donnelley constructs its database from telephone directories and automobile registration records. The names are randomly selected from a subgroup of households that are predicted to have incomes greater than $60,000. (The Donnelley file does not report household income, but the company is able to predict it based on other data, including Census Bureau information.)

Mendelsohn mails a sixteen-page questionnaire to each of the 28,500 adults. The letters are individually addressed, have postage stamps affixed by hand, and include a

BASE: WOMEN	TOTAL U.S. '000	① A '000	② B % DOWN	ALL C % ACROSS	③④ D INDEX	HEAVY MORE THAN 7 A '000	B % DOWN	C % ACROSS	D INDEX	MEDIUM 3-7 A '000	B % DOWN	C % ACROSS	D INDEX	LIGHT LESS THAN 3 A '000	B % DOWN	C % ACROSS	D INDEX
ALL WOMEN	93246	52998	100.0	56.8	100	13047	100.0	14.0	100	19083	100.0	20.5	100	20868	100.0	22.4	100
AMERICAN BABY	2811	1903	3.6	67.7	119	*551	4.2	19.6	140	722	3.8	25.7	126	631	3.0	22.4	100
AMERICAN HEALTH	2849	1670	3.2	58.6	103	*526	4.0	18.5	132	498	2.6	17.5	85	647	3.1	22.7	101
AMERICAN WAY	*374	*163	.3	-	-	*32	.2	-	-	*13	.1	-	-	*117	.6	-	-
ARCHITECTURAL DIGEST	1979	1058	2.0	53.5	94	*183	1.4	9.2	66	*290	1.5	14.7	72	*230	1.1	28.0	125
AUDUBON	820	*415	.8	50.6	89	*63	.5	7.7	55	*122	.6	14.9	73	*371	1.8	19.3	86
BABY TALK	1925	1180	2.2	61.3	108	*386	3.0	20.1	143	*423	2.2	22.0	107	*88	.4		
BARRON'S	*272	*152	.3			*19	.1			*45	.2			*103	.5		
BASSMASTER	*552	*364	.7			*62	.5			*198	1.0			5417	26.0	22.6	101
BETTER HOMES & GARDENS	23999	-13418	-25.3	55.9	98	3341	25.6	13.9	99	4661	24.4	19.4	95	9275	44.4	22.8	102
BHG/LHJ COMBO (GR)	40646	23018	43.4	56.6	100	5710	43.8	14.0	100	8034	42.1	19.8	97	*271	1.3	31.0	139
BLACK ENTERPRISE	874	638	1.2	73.0	128	*236	1.8	27.0	193	*131	.7	15.0	73	992	4.8	25.6	114
BON APPETIT	3874	1928	3.6	49.7	87	*457	3.5	11.8	84	477	2.5	12.3	60	763	3.7	21.3	95
BRIDE'S MAGAZINE	3585	2147	4.1	59.9	105	*595	4.6	16.6	119	789	4.1	22.0	108	372	1.8	24.8	111
BUSINESS WEEK	1503	851	1.6	56.6	100	*140	1.1	9.3	67	*338	1.8	22.5	110	1378	6.6	19.1	85
THE CABLE GUIDE	7215	4226	8.0	58.6	103	1227	9.4	17.0	122	1621	8.5	22.5	110	*260	1.2		
CAR & DRIVER	*573	*398	.8			*23	.2			*115	.6			*96	.5		
CAR CRAFT	*357	*221	.4			*92	.7			*33	.2			*326	1.6	21.0	94
CHANGING TIMES	1549	815	1.5	52.6	93	*165	1.3	10.7	76	*324	1.7	20.9	102	255	1.2	18.6	83
CHICAGO TRIBUNE MAGAZINE	1371	671	1.3	48.9	86	*156	1.2	11.4	81	260	1.4	19.0	93	440	2.1	29.4	131
COLONIAL HOMES	1499	858	1.6	57.2	101	*174	1.3	11.6	83	*245	1.3	16.3	80	4177	20.0	26.7	119
CONDE NAST LIMITED (GR)	15666	9045	17.1	57.7	102	2165	16.6	13.8	99	2702	14.2	17.2	84	5814	27.9	21.5	96
CONDE NAST WOMEN (GR)	27093	15447	29.1	57.0	100	4608	35.3	17.0	122	5027	26.3	18.6	91	704	3.4	30.1	135
CONSUMERS DIGEST	2337	1323	2.5	56.6	100	*154	1.2	6.6	47	*466	2.4	19.9	97	2549	12.2	23.6	105
COSMOPOLITAN	10799	6450	12.2	59.7	105	1729	13.3	16.0	114	2172	11.4	20.1	98	990	4.7	26.2	117
COUNTRY HOME	3774	2169	4.1	57.5	101	*550	4.2	14.6	104	628	3.3	16.6	81	*159	.8	16.3	73
COUNTRY JOURNAL	978	568	1.1	58.1	102	*173	1.3	17.7	126	*236	1.2	24.1	118	1513	7.3	25.3	113
COUNTRY LIVING	5972	3340	6.3	55.9	98	862	6.6	14.4	103	985	5.1	16.2	79	656	3.1	29.4	131
CREATIVE IDEAS FOR LIVING	2230	1292	2.4	57.9	102	*208	1.6	9.3	67	*427	2.2	19.1	94	*75	.4	17.5	78
DELTA SKY (AIR GROUP ONE)	428	*222	.4	51.9	91	*80	.5	14.0	100	*87	.5	20.3	99	1184	5.7	32.0	143
DIAMANDIS MAGAZINE NTWK (GR)	3698	2323	4.4	62.8	111	*408	3.1	11.0	78	735	3.9	19.9	97	*402	1.9	23.6	105
DISCOVER	1704	1020	1.9	59.9	105	*257	2.0	15.1	108	*360	1.9	21.1	103	817	3.9	22.2	99
DISNEY CHANNEL MAGAZINE	3683	2344	4.4	63.6	112	827	6.3	22.5	160	700	3.7	19.0	93	*77	.4		
DUCKS UNLIMITED	*556	*267	.5			*59	.5			*132	.7			599	2.9	25.6	114
EAST/WEST NETWORK (GR)	2343	1126	2.1	48.1	85	*288	2.0	11.4	81	*262	1.4	11.2	55	1164	5.6	21.9	98
EBONY	5314	3651	6.9	68.7	121	1054	8.1	19.8	142	1433	7.5	27.0	132	564	2.7	24.7	110
ELLE	2282	1184	2.2	51.9	91	*289	2.2	12.7	91	*332	1.7	14.5	71				

Exhibit 16.9 Portion of a page from a Mediamark report showing magazine readership of female users of regular (not diet) cola drinks. © Mediamark Research, Inc. All rights reserved. Reprinted by permission.

1. An estimated 13,418,000 female cola drinkers read *Better Homes and Gardens*.
2. That is equivalent to 25.3 percent of all female cola drinkers.
3. Approximately 56 percent of the magazine's female audience are cola drinkers.
4. The index number is derived by dividing 55.9 by 56.8—the percent of all women who are regular cola drinkers—and multiplying by 100. It can be interpreted as follows: The typical female reader of *Better Homes and Gardens* is somewhat less likely than the average woman to be a regular cola drinker.

new five-dollar bill as an incentive. The original mailing and three follow-ups generated a 65 percent response rate in the 1989 survey.

. . . Mendelsohn Data Collection

The sixteen-page questionnaire asks respondents about their radio listening and television viewing (amount of time on average days), publication readership (number of issues seen recently), and cable television viewing. It also asks about travel (destinations, hotels, airlines, car rental companies, and travelers' checks), automobile and boat ownership, credit card usage, amount of money spent on major household furnishings, appliances, artwork, jewelry, cosmetics, alcoholic beverages, value of home, insurance, and investments. Exhibit 16.10 is a portion of a page from the 1989 Mendelsohn Survey of Adults and Markets of Affluence.

TABLE 1
VOLUME I: TOTAL ADULTS WITH HOUSEHOLD INCOMES OF **$60,000 OR MORE**
SEX AND AGE
AVERAGE ISSUE AUDIENCES
(IN THOUSANDS)

	TOTAL AFFLUENT ADULTS	AMERICAN HERITAGE	ARCHITECTURAL DIGEST	ART & ANTIQUES	ARTNEWS	THE ATLANTIC MONTHLY	BARRON'S	BETTER HOMES & GARDENS	BON APPETIT	BUSINESS MONTH	BUSINESS WEEK	CFO	COLONIAL HOMES
TOTAL													
PERCENT COVERAGE	① 30800 / 100.0	476 / 1.5	2783 / 9.0	551 / 1.8	238 / .8	422 / 1.4	808 / 2.6	8990 / 29.2	2873 / 9.3	432 / 1.4	② 2478 / 8.0	256 / .8	1004 / 3.3
ADULT MALES	15357	266	1076	203	124	243	550	2773	762	326	1646	201	298
PERCENT COMPOSITION	49.9	55.8	38.7	36.8	51.9	57.4	68.1	30.8	26.5	75.4	66.4	78.5	29.7
PERCENT COVERAGE	100.0	1.7	7.0	1.3	1.8	1.6	3.6	18.1	5.0	2.1	③ 10.7	1.3	1.9
ADULT FEMALES	15443	210	1707	348	115	180	258	6217	2111	106	832	55	706
PERCENT COMPOSITION	50.1	44.2	61.3	63.2	48.1	42.6	31.9	69.2	73.5	24.6	33.6	21.5	70.3
PERCENT COVERAGE	100.0	1.4	11.1	2.3	.7	1.2	1.7	40.3	13.7	.7	5.4	.4	4.6
AGE													
18 TO 24 YEARS	821	31	86	35	15	2	7	129	20	7	20		31
PERCENT COMPOSITION	2.7	6.4	3.1	6.3	6.1	.6	.9	1.4	.7	1.5	.8		3.1
PERCENT COVERAGE	100.0	3.7	10.4	4.2	1.8	.3	.8	15.7	2.4	.8	2.4		3.7
25 TO 29 YEARS	1473	12	145	34	15	19	93	371	159	33	105	11	44
PERCENT COMPOSITION	4.8	2.5	5.2	6.1	6.2	4.6	11.5	4.1	5.5	7.7	4.2	4.2	4.4
PERCENT COVERAGE	100.0	.8	9.9	2.3	1.0	1.3	6.3	25.2	10.8	2.3	7.1	.7	3.0
30 TO 34 YEARS	3831	34	282	44	25	42	75	1258	351	45	273	55	109
PERCENT COMPOSITION	12.4	7.1	10.1	7.9	10.3	9.9	9.3	14.0	12.2	10.4	11.0	21.5	10.8
PERCENT COVERAGE	100.0	.9	7.4	1.1	.6	1.1	2.0	32.8	9.2	1.2	7.1	1.4	2.8
35 TO 39 YEARS	5864	52	457	82	20	82	115	1783	574	61	351	49	205
PERCENT COMPOSITION	19.0	10.9	16.4	14.8	8.5	19.4	14.3	19.8	20.0	14.1	14.2	19.3	20.5
PERCENT COVERAGE	100.0	.9	7.8	1.4	.3	1.4	2.0	30.4	9.8	1.0	6.0	.8	3.5

Exhibit 16.10 Portion of a page from the 1989 Mendelsohn Survey of Adults and Markets of Affluence. Reprinted by permission.

1. Mendelsohn estimates that there are 30,800,000 adults with household incomes of $60,000 or more.
2. *Business Week's* audience includes 2,478,000 readers with incomes of $60,000 or more. That is 8 percent of all affluent adults.
3. *Business Week's* audience includes 1,646,000 adult males; its affluent audience is 66 percent male and 34 percent female. *Business Week* reaches 10.7 percent of the 15,357,000 adult males in the United States.

Summary

Primary audience research measures circulation or number of copies sold. Companies that conduct primary audience research use similar procedures — they require publications to file semiannual publishers' statements of circulation, and the companies inspect and audit publication records to verify the publishers' claims. The Audit Bureau of Circulations does that for publications that have paid circulation, and the Business Publications Audit of Circulation does the same for publications that have paid and unpaid circulation.

Total audience research measurements include all people who read a publication, regardless of whether they buy it or read it in a library, doctor's office, barbershop, or other out-of-home locations. Companies that conduct total audience research interview samples of people and ask them to name publications they have read. The recent-reading technique asks respondents to name the magazines they have read or looked into recently. The through-the-book method is a more rigorous measure of audiences because it counts only those respondents who can recall reading several articles in recent issues of magazines. Magazine audience research tends to concentrate on total audience estimates, and newspaper audience research tends to focus on circulation or primary audience research. Simmons Market Research Bureau, Mediamark Research, and Mendelsohn Media Research are sources of total audience estimates for consumer magazines.

Because primary audience research is primarily concerned with counting copies of a publication, it is generally more accurate than secondary audience research, which is based on only samples and which is subject to readers' faulty memories. However, advertisers are usually more interested in an estimate of the total number of people who read a publication than in the number of copies sold, so they are more likely to want total audience estimates.

Self-Test Questions

1. Define and explain the following terms as they apply to print-audience measurement: primary audience, total audience, through-the-book, recent-reading, publisher's statement, audit report, FAS-FAX, controlled circulation, qualified circulation, logo cards.
2. Explain the basic difference between primary audience data and total audience data. Without regard to specific research companies, explain differences in how primary and total audience data are collected.
3. Name two sources of primary audience data for publications. Name two sources of total audience data.
4. Describe an important difference in the ways Simmons Market Research Bureau and Mediamark gather magazine readership data. Explain how Mendelsohn is different from the other two.

5. Look at Exhibit 16.1. What is the total evening circulation in the retail trading zone? [The answer is 5,690.]
6. Look at Exhibit 16.3. What is the *News & Observer's* (morning) penetration percentage in the city zone? [The answer is 54.71.]
7. Look at Exhibit 16.5. What percent of heavy users are college graduates? [The answer is 11.1.] What percent of single females are heavy users? [The answer is 24.7.]
8. Look at Exhibit 16.6. What percent of the readers of *Cycle World* are female? [The answer is 12.3.]

• • • Suggestions for Additional Reading

Carmody, D. "Magazine Circulation Rules Altered." *New York Times*, May 17, 1990, p. C1(Y).

CHAPTER 17

Other Syndicated Research

Two other types of syndicated research used by advertisers are discussed in this chapter. *Competitive activity research* measures and reports advertising expenditures by companies and brands in various media. When advertisers and agencies plan advertising and media campaigns, they find it useful to know how much money their competitors spent on advertising and how they spent it. That includes the amount spent in each medium and vehicle, and when and where it was spent. *Single-source research* is a relatively new concept in research. It measures the media and advertising exposure for a sample of households and also measures those households' product purchases. Single-source research thus enables advertisers to see direct and immediate consequences (purchases) of their advertising and promotion efforts.

Competitive Activity Research

A section of Chapter 12 discusses limitations of competitive activity research, and you should review that section. Here is a summary of those limitations.

1. For some media categories, all networks or vehicles are measured, and data from those measurements are probably more accurate than data based only on samples of stations, publications, or outdoor companies.
2. For some media categories, all time periods are measured (meaning all year), and data from such measurements are probably more accurate than data from only samples of time periods.
3. In most cases, data are gathered by monitors (employees or electronic devices) employed by the syndicated research companies, and data from such sources are probably more reliable than self-reported data from media owners or managers.
4. Estimates of media expenditures are usually derived from rate information supplied by networks, stations, and publications. In other words, the research companies measure the number of full-page ads or the number of thirty-second network television commercials. The companies use rate cards from the media to estimate expenditures. Advertisers do not report what they spend for those advertisements. The prices that advertisers actually pay could vary because of discounts and negotiations.

Despite some shortcomings, competitive media activity data are important for advertising decision makers. Decision makers who use such data must remember the shortcomings and treat the data as estimates and not as absolute measures.

Several firms provide competitive media activity data. Broadcast Advertisers Reports measures and reports expenditures in broadcast and cable media. Leading National Advertisers measures and reports expenditures in newspapers, magazines, and outdoor advertising and also publishes multimedia reports, and Radio Expenditure Reports does the same for spot radio.

... Broadcast Advertisers Reports

As noted, Broadcast Advertisers Reports (BAR) — a service of the Arbitron Company since 1987 — compiles and publishes data about advertising expenditures in network and spot television, network radio, syndicated television, and cable television. Data are collected by monitoring the output of stations, networks, and syndicated programs. Expenditures are estimated from rate information provided by stations, networks, and agencies. That rate information is used to assign an estimated rate to each daypart or program; BAR assumes that all advertisers within that daypart or program pay the same rate.

BAR Network Television

BAR continuously monitors and makes recordings of the three commercial broadcast television networks (ABC, CBS, and NBC). BAR editors examine the recordings and note details about every commercial—network, program, sponsoring company, brand, and length. Using rate information provided by the networks and other industry sources, BAR estimates the cost of each commercial and tabulates totals for all brands. The information is published in weekly reports and monthly and quarterly summaries.

Exhibits 17.1 and 17.2 show portions of pages from a BAR quarterly summary for network television.

BAR Spot Television

It would be prohibitively expensive to monitor spot television advertising on the more than 1,100 commercial stations in the more than 200 television markets in the United States. Consequently, BAR monitors a sample of approximately 350 stations in the seventy-five largest television markets, where approximately 85 percent of all national television advertising dollars are spent. It would be impractical to monitor even those 350 stations all the time, so BAR limits its continuous, daily monitoring to stations in the seventeen largest markets. Stations in the remaining fifty-eight markets are monitored one random week per month, and BAR projects the weekly totals to four-week estimates. In all the markets, telecasts are recorded on audio- and videotape, which is analyzed on a system that uses both BAR personnel and a computerized recognition system.

Exhibit 17.3 is a portion of a page from a BAR spot television report showing advertiser expenditures by company.

Other BAR Reports

BAR monitors and records seventeen major radio networks on a continuous, daily basis for its network radio reports. (See Exhibit 17.4.) It does the same for syndicated television programming—original programs produced and sold to individual stations, as in the case of "Jeopardy." Those programs are transmitted from the producer to the stations via earth satellite, and BAR monitors the programming as it is transmitted to the satellite. (See Exhibit 17.5.) BAR provides a similar report for cable television networks, based on its off-the-satellite monitoring of Cable News Network (CNN), Entertainment and Sports Programming Network (ESPN), The Family Channel, Music Television (MTV), WTBS, and the USA Network. (See Exhibit 17.6.)

• • • Leading National Advertisers

Leading National Advertisers (LNA) compiles and publishes data about advertising expenditures in magazines, outdoor advertising, and newspapers. It also combines those data with data compiled by Broadcast Advertisers Reports and distributes them as part of the LNA/Arbitron Multi-Media quarterly service. LNA also measures and reports advertising expenditures in the *Wall Street Journal*, *USA Today*, and other publications.

SECTION 4 BRAND DETAIL WITHIN PRODUCT CLASS

Exhibit 17.1 A portion of a page from a Broadcast Advertisers Reports network television report showing brand detail within product class. Reprinted by permission.

1. Levi Apparel spent $623,500 for six network commercials for men's jeans in the current (second) quarter. It had spent $376,200 in the first quarter.
2. In the current quarter, it spent $560,500 for three prime time commercials. Its year-to-date (YTD) prime time expenditures are $815,300.

SECTION 2 BRAND DETAIL WITHIN PARENT COMPANY

PARENT COMPANY BRAND/PRODUCT PROGRAM	NETWORK AND DAY	CLASS CODE & TIME	MONTH 1		MONTH 2		MONTH 3		QTR & YEAR TO DATE	
			NO OF MINUTES/COMM SECONDS	DOLLAR EST '000	NO OF MINUTES/COMM SECONDS	DOLLAR EST '000	NO OF MINUTES/COMM SECONDS	DOLLAR EST '000	NO OF MINUTES/COMM SECONDS	DOLLAR EST '000
3M COMPANY										
BUF PUF PDTS-CLEANSING SPONGE										
HEALTH SHOW-SUN	A SUN	0132 930A	2 :45	6.9					2 :45	6.9
S/S DAYTIME TOTALS			2 :45	6.9					2 :45	6.9
PRODUCT TOTALS										
PRODUCT TOTALS YTD									31 13:30	295.5
BUF PUF PDTS-DAILY CLEANSER		D111								
PRODUCT TOTALS YTD									40 15:30	882.3
POST-IT NOTE PADS		B321								
ABC WORLD NEWS TONIGHT	A M-F	630P	2 1:00	121.0	2 1:00	114.4			4 2:00	235.4
CBS EVENING NEWS	C M-F	630P	3 1:30	153.3	2 1:00	101.8			5 2:30	255.1
E/L FRINGES TOTALS			5 2:30	274.3	4 2:00	216.2			9 4:30	490.5
PRODUCT TOTALS YTD									19 9:30	890.5
SCOTCHGARD PDTS-FABRIC PROTECTOR		M433								
ALL MY CHILDREN	A M-F	100P	3 1:00	42.9	2 :45	30.6	1 :45		5 :45	73.5
GENERAL HOSPITAL -NAT-	A WED	300P			1 :30	20.7 ①			1 :30	20.7
GENERAL HOSPITAL -REG-	A FRI	300P					1 :30			
HOME-M/F PAINS-M-F	A M-F	1200N	2 1:00	18.3	5 :45	19.2	4 2:30	14.3 ②	4 2:30	28.8
ONE LIFE TO LIVE	A FRI	1100A	1 :30	20.8	3 1:30	6.2			3 1:15	26.0
AS THE WORLD TURNS	A MON	200P	1 :15	6.6			1 :15		1 :15	6.6
FAMILY FEUD-M-F	C WED	200P	1 :30	4.3	2 :30	4.4			3 1:00	8.7
NOW YOU SEE IT	C M-F	1000A			2 :30	4.4			2 :30	4.4
PRICE IS RIGHT	C M-F	1030A	3 1:00	32.8	2 1:00	30.0	2 1:00		6 3:00	63.2
YOUNG AND THE RESTLESS	C FRI	123P	1 :30	10.5	1 :30	5.7			2 1:00	20.9
ANOTHER WORLD	N M-F	1030A			1 :30	5.7			1 :30	5.7
CLASSIC CONCENTRATION	N WED	101P			1 :30	3.7			2 :30	3.7
DAYS OF OUR LIVES	N M-F					14.8				14.8
GENERATIONS	N THU		3 1:15	8.5	4 1:30	9.1	7 1:00		7 :30	17.6
SANTA BARBARA	N M-F	1231P			1 1:00	13.2			2 1:00	13.2
SCRABBLE	N WED	301P							1 :30	
WHEEL OF FORTUNE-NBC	N MON	1001A								
PAT SAJAK SHOW	C M-F	1130P	19 7:30	158.2	33 11:45	244.5	53 20:00	14.3	53 20:00	416.8
M/F DAYTIME TOTALS			5 1:45	74.2	6 1:45	77.0	1 3:30		11 3:30	151.2
E/L FRINGES TOTALS			24 9:30	232.2	39 13:30	321.5	63 23:30		64 23:30	553.7
PRODUCT TOTALS-NAT							:30	14.3	12 46:00	14.3
PRODUCT TOTALS-REG							:30	14.3	64 23:30	566.0
PRODUCT TOTALS YTD			2 5:30	232.2	3 13:30	321.5				
PARENT CO. M/F DAYTIME TOTALS			19 7:45	158.0	33 11:45	244.5	53 20:00	14.3	53 20:00	416.8
PARENT CO. S/S DAYTIME TOTALS			2 :45				1 :45		20 8:30	6.9
PARENT CO. E/L FRINGES TOTALS			10 4:15	348.5	10 2:45	293.2	1 :30		75 28:45	641.0
PARENT CO. TOTALS			31 12:45	513.4	43 15:30	637.7				
= PARENT CO. M/F PRIME TIME YTD									12 46:00	1065.4
= PARENT CO. M/F DAYTIME YTD									53 20:00	562.4
= PARENT CO. S/S DAYTIME YTD									20 8:45	128.4
= PARENT CO. E/L FRINGES YTD									29 12:00	1044.6
= PARENT CO. TOTALS YTD									162 62:00	2553.0
900 USA										

Exhibit 17.2 A portion of a page from a Broadcast Advertisers Reports network television report showing brand detail within parent company. Reprinted by permission.

1. Scotchgard spent $20,700 for a thirty-second commercial on "General Hospital" in the second month of the quarter.
2. Scotchgard spent $28,300 for seven commercials on "Growing Pains" in the quarter.

SECTION 2 ADVERTISER EXPENDITURES BY COMPANY

CLASS CODE	PAGE INDEX SEC. 3	NATIONAL COMPANY OR AFFILIATION / ADVERTISER OR BRAND/PRODUCT	ESTIMATED EXPENDITURES (000)					NUMBER OF MARKETS				% U.S. TV HOMES			
			MONTH 1	MONTH 2	MONTH 3	QTR	YTD	M1	M2	M3	O	MO1	MO2	MO3	QTR
	316	WOOLWORTH F W CO	259.1	421.8	260.3	941.2	941.2	5	6	6	6	9	8	9	8
V313	320	ANDERSON LITTLE CTHG STR													
V313	320	ATHLETIC SHOE FACTORY													
V235	194	ATHLETIC X-PRESS SHOE ST													
V235	320	CHAMPS SPORTING GOODS			139.6	139.6	286.8								
V313	321	FOOT LOCKER SHOE STORE	646.9	1455.5	50.5	2153.0	4572 ①	24	24	31	45	47	0.22.8 ②	5	③
V313	318	KINNEY SHOE STORE					522.7								
V313		RICHMAN BROTHERS CLTH ST	146.0	331.5	84.9	562.4	562.4	4	4	4	8	8	8	8	8
V323	349	WOOLWORTH EXPRESS-DETAILS SEC 3		26.3	26.3	26.3	92.0								
V323	360	WOOLWORTH VARIETY-DETAILS SEC 3		175.2	64.1	239.2	824.1								
		NATIONAL COMPANY TOTALS	1052.0	2410.3	599.4	4061.7	7806.9								
V211	68	WORTHEN BANKING CORP													
		WORTHEN BK7/LITTLE ROCK		4	39.4	39.8	76.1	1			1	5	5	5	5
V232	141	WORTHINGTON MOTEL													
		WORTHINGTON MOTEL-&FAIRMONT			6	6	6	1			1	9	1	9	9
V311	316	YOLANDA'S FSHN BOUTIQUE					7.3				1				3
V111	40	YUGO AUTO DLR-LISTED IN SECTION 3	8.6	2.6	6.0	17.2	70.5	2			2				5
V339	376	YUM YUM TREE INTERNATL					6.6				1				6
		YUM YUM TREE CANDY STRS													
V319	322	Z & M UNIFORMS	21.4		21.4	21.4	43.9	2		2	2	4	2		4
V334	375	ZACK'S FROZEN YOGURT													
V334	375	ZACK3 FAMOUS YOGURT STR	22.1	12.6	5.4	40.1	40.1	1	1	1	7	7	7	7	7
		ZAYRE CORP													
V311	316	HIT OR MISS CLOTHING STR	71.0	84.0	21.0	176.1	217.2	2	2	2	7	2	1	2	5
V345	417	HOME CLUB WRHS MMBRSHP	1877.9	1693.5	1245.0	4816.9	7148.4	9	9	10	13	13	13	13	14
V311	316	T J MAXX CLOTHING STORE	335.3	926.7	1209.6	2471.7	4195.8	13	14	18	22	22	22	22	27
		NATIONAL COMPANY TOTALS	2283.8	2704.2	2475.6	7463.8	11564.5								
V217	81	ZENITH ELECTRONICS CORP					16.2				1				4
		HEATH ZENITH COMPUTER ST													
V190	56	ZIEBART INTERNATL CORP													
		ZIEBART AUTO SERVICES	46.7	39.3	25.5	3.9	3.9	7	8	7	5	5	4	5	8
V345	417	ZIEGLER LUMBER CO													
		ZIEGLER BUILDING SUPPLY	18.4	13.6	13.5	46.5	137.8	1	1	1	3	7	2	7	5
V321	345	ZCMI DEPT-DETAILS SEC. 3	33.3	62.3	114.2	209.8	376.8	1	1	1	1	4	4	4	4
V311	68	ZIONS CO-OP MERCANTILE INST													
		ZIONS UTAH BANCORPORATION													
V211		ZIONS FIRST NAT'L/SALT LK					6.4				1				1
		ZOOLOGICAL SOCIETY OF SAN DIEGO													
V239	214	SAN DIEGO WILD ANIMAL PK			82.9	82.9	82.9	1		1	1			6.2	6.9
V239	214	SAN DIEGO ZOO		227.1	227.1	227.1	265.1	2		2	2			6.2	6.2
		NATIONAL COMPANY TOTALS	310.0	227.1	310.0	310.0	365.0								

Exhibit 17.3 A portion of a page from a Broadcast Advertisers Reports spot television report showing expenditures by company. Reprinted by permission.
1. The F. W. Woolworth Company spent $4,572,300 in the year to date to advertise its Foot Locker shoe stores.
2. In the current quarter, it advertised in thirty-one markets.
3. Those thirty-one markets included nearly 52 percent of U.S. television homes.

SECTION 3 BRAND DETAIL WITHIN PRODUCT CLASS

CLASS CODE	PRODUCT CLASSIFICATION BRAND/PRODUCT	QTR YTD	NETWORK AND MO	TOTAL* NO. OF COMM.	TOTAL* DOLLAR EST. (000)	M-F DRIVE TIME NO. OF COMM.	M-F DRIVE TIME DOLLAR EST. (000)	M-F MIDDAY NO. OF COMM.	M-F MIDDAY DOLLAR EST. (000)	S/S DAYTIME NO. OF COMM.	S/S DAYTIME DOLLAR EST. (000)	M-S EVENING NO. OF COMM.	M-S EVENING DOLLAR EST. (000)
A117	MULTIPLE APPAREL, MFRS & MISC / BOBBY JONES APPRL-MENS SPORTSW	QTR	MO1	6	5.1					4	3.1	2	2.1
			MO2	6	6.2					6	6.2	2	2.1
			MRN	9	9.4					7	7.4		
			NRN	3	1.1					3	1.3		
		QTR	TOT	12	11.3					10	9.3	2	2.1
		YTD	TOT	12	11.3					10	9.3	2	2.1
A131	REGULAR, CASUAL & SPORT FOOTWE / BRITISH KNIGHT SHOES	QTR	TOT	36	87.4	3	6.5	9	18.9	18	52.8	5	7.2
			MO1	13	26.00		2.1	1	2.1	8	17.40	1	2.4
			ACR	4	14.4	1	2.1	1	2.1	6	15.00	1	1.2
			AFR	8	26.0		2.1	1	2.1	6	17.2	2	2.4
		QTR	TOT	13	26.0							7	
		YTD	TOT	49	113.4	4	8.6	10	21.0	26	70.2	7	9.6
	RED WING SHOES & BOOTS	QTR	TOT	1	20.4	1	20.4	4	40.7	1	20.4		
			MO1	4	122.1	2	61.7	6	162.8			5	7.2
			MO2	5	203.5	1	40.7	6	40.7	2	40.7	2	2.4
			MO3	4	122.1	5	142.5	9	244.2	2	61.1		
			AER	13	447.7	6	142.5			2	61.1	1	1.2
			AFR	13	447.7	6	142.8	1	40.7	2	61.1	2	2.4
		QTR	TOT	14	468.1	6	162.8					7	9.6
		YTD	TOT										
	A131 CLASS TOTALS	QTR	TOT	37	107.2	4	26.9	9	18.9	18	52.8	5	7.2
		QTR	MO1	17	148.1	3	63.2	2	42.8	8	37.8	2	2.4
			MO2	5	122.0	1	40.7	4	162.8	9			
			MO3	4		2		1	40.7	1	40.7		
			ACR							1	5.0	1	1.2
			AER	13	447.7	5	142.5	6	244.2	2	61.2	1	2.4
			AFR	4	14.6		2.1	1	2.1	6	11.2	2	9.6
			ARR	2	2.4					10	78.5	7	
		QTR	TOT	26	473.7	6	144.6	7	246.3	10	131.3		
		YTD	TOT	63	581.5	10	171.4	16	265.2	28			
A141	APPAREL ACCESSORIES / WELLS LAMONT-GLOVES	QTR	TOT	12	447.7	3	81.4	7	284.9	2	81.4		
		YTD	TOT	12	447.7	3	81.4	7	284.9	2	81.4		
A142	NOTIONS / E-Z QUIT IMITATION CIG	QTR	MO1	153	61.3	23	74.8	4	8.6	14	13.4	229	118.1
			MO2	264	118.7	4	6.2	2	1.6	5	4.8	48	20.2
			MO3	249	116.7							6	24.7
			ACR	125	93.4					1	.5	1	4.5
			ADR	68	24.0								
			AER	62	37.2								
			AFR	126	22.3	3	2.4	4	3.2	3	1.5	24	2.4
			MRN	204	97.7							8	6.9
			NRN	99	22.9	3	5.4			2	1.8		
			SMN	24	13.1	1	2.4			1	2.0	20	14.0
		QTR	TRN	828	386.00 ②	27	10.2	4	3.2	6	5.3	55	25.4
		YTD	TOT	1881	996.3 ①	29	82.0	8	11.2	20	24.7	284	143.1

Exhibit 17.4 A portion of a page from a Broadcast Advertisers Reports network radio report showing brand detail within product class. Reprinted by permission.
1. E-Z Quit imitation cigarettes spent $386,000 for 828 commercials in the quarter.
2. It placed 126 of those commercials — at an estimated cost of $25,200 — on the ABC-FM Radio Network.

SECTION 2 BRAND DETAIL WITHIN PARENT COMPANY

PARENT COMPANY BRAND/PRODUCT PROGRAM	MONTH 4			MONTH 5			MONTH 6			QUARTER			YEAR TO DATE		
	NO OF COMM	NO OF MINUTES	ESTIMATED DOLLARS (000)	NO OF COMM	NO OF MINUTES	ESTIMATED DOLLARS (000)	NO OF COMM	NO OF MINUTES	ESTIMATED DOLLARS (000)	NO OF COMM	NO OF MINUTES	ESTIMATED DOLLARS (000)	NO OF COMM	NO OF MINUTES	ESTIMATED DOLLARS (000)
3M COMPANY															
BUF PUF PDTS															
CLEANSING SPONGE															
21 JUMP STREET	1	:30	53.4 ①							1	:30	53.4	3	1:00	98.3
AMERICAS MOST WANTED													1	:05	28.3
DONAHUE													1	:15	7.8
DUET													2	:30	25.9
OPRAH WINFREY SHOW	2	1:00	48.8							2	1:00	48.8	4	1:00	32.0
REPORTERS													1	:30	71.0
SALLY JESSY RAPHAEL													2	1:00	5.2
SWEETHEARTS													1	:30	11.2
TOTAL BRAND/PRODUCT	3	1:30	102.2							3	1:30	102.2	15	5:30	280.4
BUF PUF PDTS-															
DAILY CLEANSER															
DONAHUE													4	1:00	88.6
DUET													10	3:00	103.4
LIVE/REGIS&KATHIE LEE													1	:15	13.4
OPRAH WINFREY SHOW													2	1:00	18.2
REPORTERS													9	3:00	66.1
SALLY JESSY RAPHAEL													13	4:45	39.8
SWEETHEARTS													4	1:30	50.4
TELEVISION ACDMY HLL FM													2	:30	23.7
TRACEY ULLMAN SHOW													7	1:45	23.3
TOTAL BRAND/PRODUCT													52	16:45	448.8
SCOTCHGARD PDTS-															
FABRIC PROTECTOR															
DONAHUE	2	:45	23.3	3	1:15	37.0				5	2:00	60.3	5	2:00	50.3
SALLY JESSY RAPHAEL				3	1:00	12.0				3	1:00	12.0	3	1:00	12.0
SWEETHEARTS	2	1:00	10.8	6	1:45	18.6				8	2:45	29.4	8	2:45	29.4
TOTAL BRAND/PRODUCT	4	1:45	34.1	12	4:00	67.6				16	5:45	101.6	16	5:45	101.6
PARENT COMPANY TOTAL-															
21 JUMP STREET	1	:30	53.4							1	:30	53.4	7	2:15	186.9
AMERICAS MOST WANTED													1	:05	28.3
DONAHUE	2	:45	23.3	3	1:15	37.0				5	2:00	60.3	16	5:45	171.5
LIVE/REGIS&KATHIE LEE													3	:45	38.4
OPRAH WINFREY SHOW	2	1:00	48.8							2	1:00	48.8	6	2:00	18.9
REPORTERS													10	3:30	64.2
SALLY JESSY RAPHAEL				3	1:00	12.0				3	1:00	12.0	18	6:45	57.7
SWEETHEARTS	2	1:00	10.8	6	1:45	18.6				8	2:45	29.4	13	4:00	90.7
TELEVISION ACDMY HLL FM													2	:30	23.7
TRACEY ULLMAN SHOW													7	1:45	13.3
TOTAL PARENT COMPANY	7	3:15	136.3	12	4:00	67.6				19	7:15	203.8	83	28:00	830.7

Exhibit 17.5 A portion of a page from a Broadcast Advertisers Reports national syndicated television report showing brand detail within parent company. Reprinted by permission.

1. In month 4, the 3M Company spent $53,400 for a commercial about Buf Puf cleansing sponges on "21 Jump Street."

SECTION 4 BRAND DETAIL WITHIN PRODUCT CLASS

CLASS CODE	PRODUCT CLASSIFICATION BRAND/PRODUCT	NET-WORK AND MONTH	QTR YTD	TOTAL NO. OF COMM.	TOTAL ESTIMATED DOLLARS	M-F DAYTIME NO. OF COMM.	M-F DAYTIME ESTIMATED DOLLARS	S/S DAYTIME NO. OF COMM.	S/S DAYTIME ESTIMATED DOLLARS	NIGHTTIME NO. OF COMM.	NIGHTTIME ESTIMATED DOLLARS	LATE NIGHT NO. OF COMM.	LATE NIGHT ESTIMATED DOLLARS
A112	COATS, SUITS, DRESSES & RAINWEAR *****												
	MTV TOUR JACKET OFFER	TOT	QTR	2	5294	2	5294						
		TOT	YTD	2	5294	2	5294						
A115	SPORTSWEAR TOPS *****												
	AMERICAN MUSCLE SHIRT	TOT	QTR	4	7329	1	668			3	6661		
		MON1	QTR	1	862			1	862			1	555
		MON2	QTR	3	3698	1	555	1	862	1	2588	1	555
		ESPN	QTR	4	4560	1	555	1	862	1	2588	1	555
		TOT	YTD	8	11889	2	1123	1	862	4	9249	1	555
	BODIES/MOTION APPRL	TOT	QTR	184	134358	184	134358						
		MON1	QTR	59	29171	59	29171						
		MON2	QTR	15	11095	15	11095						
		MON3	QTR	6	6258	6	6258						
		ESPN	QTR	80	46524	80	46524						
		TOT	YTD	264	180682 ①	264	180682						
	BODIES/MOTION APPRL - 2BSC TRNG APPRL	MON2	QTR	48	53232	48	53232						
		MON3	QTR	48	50064	48	50064						
		ESPN	QTR	96	103296	96	103296						
		TOT	YTD	96	103296	96	103296						
	SHAH SAFARI SHIRT	TOT	QTR	26	43888	14	23632			9	15192	1	1688
		MTV	QTR	6	5838			2	3376	3	2919		
		MTV1	QTR	6	5838			3	2919	3	2919		
		TOT	YTD	32	49726	14	23632	5	6295	12	18211	1	1688
	WARNER BROS T SHIRT OFFR	MON2	QTR	3	176	3	176						
		FAM	QTR	1	56	1	56						
		TBS	QTR	1	120	1	120						
		TOT	YTD	3	176	3	176						
A116	SPORTSWEAR BOTTOMS *****												
	BRANDER APPRL - CHILDRENS JEANS	TOT	QTR	2	2972	2	738			1	2972		
		MON1	QTR	1	555	1	555						
		MON2	QTR	1	2434					1	2434		
		MON3	QTR	1	2434					1	2434		
		ESPN	QTR	4	3727					2	5406		
		TOT	YTD	5	6699								
	BRANDER APPRL - MENS JEANS	TOT	QTR	5	4553	2	1707			2	2434	1	1772
		MON1	QTR	1	555	1	555						
		MON2	QTR	2	3143	1	1662			1	4157	1	2523
		ESPN	QTR	8	10130	4	2667			2	6089	2	2588
		TOT	YTD	13	19296	6				4	10246	3	
	BRANDER APPRL MENS&CHILDRENS JEANS	TOT	QTR	2	3640	1	668	1	555	1	2972	1	4311
		MON1	QTR	1	2092	1	369	1	555	2	4157	2	4311
		ESPN	QTR	1	2555			1	555	4	10246	3	6083
		TOT	YTD	3	2647			1	555			1	2972
		TOT	QTR	5	6287	2	1037	1	555			2	1723
	BUGLE BOY APPRL - MENS JEANS	MON2	QTR	72	236224	19	24529	3	3873	38	141804	12	67958
		MON3	QTR	31	34173	8	8560	5	5600	1	14531	1	5022
		CNN	QTR	9	8233					30	5531	6	8524
		MTV	QTR	72	94011	27	33489	8	9473	30	42525	6	61854
		TBS	QTR	105	176317					18	114463	6	72980
		TOT	YTD	105	278561	27	33489	8	9473	51	162619	19	72980

Exhibit 17.6 A portion of a page from a Broadcast Advertisers Reports cable television report showing brand detail within product class. Reprinted by permission.

1. Sportswear Tops spent an estimated $46,524 to advertise Bodies/Motion apparel. All eighty of its commercials were on ESPN, and its year-to-date total is $180,882.

PIB/LNA Magazine Analysis Service

LNA gathers data about advertising expenditures in more than 180 consumer magazines that belong to Publishers Information Bureau (PIB), a trade association of magazine publishers. PIB members mark the paid ads in issues of their magazines and send them to LNA, where coders record information about each advertisement—advertiser, brand, product class, size, and whether the ad was national or regional.

LNA uses the one-time open (noncontract) rate on the rate card for each magazine to estimate costs of the advertisements. The rates used for the estimates are one-time rates, which means they do not reflect possible discounts because of a particular brand's volume of advertising. The information is processed, printed, and distributed to PIB members and to advertisers and agencies that purchase it from LNA.

Exhibit 17.7 shows a portion of a page from a PIB/LNA magazine report.

LNA Newspaper Measurement

LNA measures and reports advertising space and expenditures in approximately ninety newspapers in seventy markets. (The newspapers pay for the service.) Coders measure and record information about advertisements in every issue: newspaper's name, advertiser's name, and ad size. LNA uses the newspapers' open (nondiscounted) rate to estimate the cost of the advertisements. Estimated expenditures from those newspapers in seventy markets are projected to provide estimates for the top 125 markets.

Exhibit 17.8 shows a portion of a page from an LNA report on newspaper advertising expenditures. Exhibit 17.9 shows a portion of a page from LNA's *Wall Street Journal* report, and Exhibit 17.10 shows a portion of a page from LNA's *USA Today* report.

LNA Outdoor Report

LNA cooperates with the Outdoor Advertising Association of America (OAAA) to gather data about expenditures in outdoor advertising. Plant operators, the companies that own or lease the billboard structures in more than 250 markets of at least 100,000 population, send data to LNA about expenditures by national brands. LNA compiles the information and publishes it in a quarterly report.

Exhibit 17.11 shows a portion of a page from an LNA outdoor advertising report.

LNA/Arbitron Multi-Media Service

Leading National Advertisers and Arbitron combine data in special reports that show advertising expenditures in nine media categories. Although the reports do not provide the details of the separate reports for individual media, they are convenient because they combine estimates from nine sources into one.

Three reports are available. The Ad Dollar Summary (Exhibit 17.12) reports total expenditures for the nine media categories but does not give subtotals for individual categories. The Company/Brand Dollar report (Exhibit 17.13) shows expenditures by individual media category, with listings arranged by parent companies and their brands. The Class/Brand Dollar report (Exhibit 17.14) is more convenient because it reports brand expenditures by product category.

TRANSPORTATION - AGRICULTURE

CHRYSLER CORP DETROIT, MI 48288
AUTOMOTIVE SALES DIVISION
CHRYSLER HIGHLAND PARK, MI 48203
CHRYSLER-PLYMOUTH CARS & WAGONS
T111 (1988 YTD:) $0.0

CHRYSLER CORP DETROIT, MI 48288
AUTOMOTIVE SALES DIVISION
CHRYSLER HIGHLAND PARK, MI 48203
CHRYSLER-PLYMOUTH GENERAL PROMOTION
T111-B (1988 YTD:) $0.0

CHRYSLER CORP DETROIT, MI 48288
AUTOMOTIVE SALES DIVISION
CHRYSLER HIGHLAND PARK, MI 48203
CHRYSLER-PLYMOUTH PASSENGER CARS
T111 (1988 YTD:) $926.0

Exhibit 17.7 A portion of a page from a Publishers Information Bureau/Leading National Advertisers report on advertising expenditures in magazines. Reprinted by permission.

1. Chrysler Corporation placed twelve pages of advertising for Chrysler-Plymouth passenger cars in *Newsweek* at an estimated cost of $997,700.
2. One of those was a black and white ad in the August issue which cost an estimated $59,800.

LNA/MEDIA RECORDS
BRAND DETAIL
JANUARY - JUNE 1989

EXPENDITURES

CLASS/PARENT/ BRAND/CITY	NEWS PAPER	APR	MAY	JUN	QTR	YTD
** F117 SAUCES, GRAVIES, DIPS						
CAMPBELL SOUP CO/PREGO SPAGHETTI SAUCE (CONTINUED)						
DALLAS	N M		1409		1409	1409
DALLAS	TH AD					33270
DENVER	P M		832		832	832
FRAMINGHAM	N E			317	317	636
GRNWCH STF	A E		335		335	335
GRNWCH STF	T E		337		337	337
HARTFORD	C M			1301 ①	1301	2609
HOUSTON	P AD	2202			2202	2202
HOUSTON	C AD	2127	2007		4134	4134
INDIANAPLS	N E		590		590	590
INDIANAPLS	S M		590		590	590
LONG ILAND	N E		1844		1844	1844
NEW BRUNSW	HN E		544		544	544
NEW YORK	N M		2890		2890	2890
NEWARK	SL M		1876		1876	1876
PHOENIX	AR M	816			816	816
PHOENIX	G E	816			816	816
SAN JOSE	MN AD		2211		2211	2211
ST LOUIS	PD M	901			901	901
ST LOUIS	PD S					3015
WASH SBRN	FJ M			147	147	147
WASHINGTON	P M			1635	1635	1635
WSTCH RCKL	RD E		375	375	375	375
TOTAL NEWSPAPERS		6862	18572	7347	32781 ②	73062
TOTAL BRAND EXP.					32781	73062
NEWSPAPERS PROJ. 125 MKTS.					49013	125748

EXPENDITURES

CLASS/PARENT/ BRAND/CITY	NEWS PAPER	APR	MAY	JUN	QTR	YTD
CPC INTERNATIONAL INC/HELLMANNS REAL & LIGHT MAYONNAISE (CONTINUED)						
TOTAL SUNDAY MAGS.			80289		80289	80289
TOTAL BRAND EXP.					80289	80289
SUNDAY MAGS. PROJ. 125 MKTS.					80289	80289
PHILIP MORRIS COMPANIES INC/GOOD SEASONS SALAD DRESSINGS MIX						
PARADE		330726			330726	330726
TOTAL SUNDAY MAGS.		330726			330726	330726
TOTAL BRAND EXP.					330726	330726
SUNDAY MAGS. PROJ. 125 MKTS.					330726	330726
PHILIP MORRIS COMPANIES INC/KRAFT LOW CALORIE SALAD DRESSING						
PARADE		280800			280800	280800
TOTAL SUNDAY MAGS.		280800			280800	280800
TOTAL BRAND EXP.					280800	280800
SUNDAY MAGS. PROJ. 125 MKTS.					280800	280800
PHILIP MORRIS COMPANIES INC/ KRAFT MIRACLE WHIP & MIRACLE WHIP LIGHT						
PARADE				189700	189700	189700
TOTAL SUNDAY MAGS.				189700	189700	189700
TOTAL BRAND EXP.					189700	189700
SUNDAY MAGS. PROJ. 125 MKTS.					189700	189700
PHILIP MORRIS COMPANIES INC/KRAFT MIRACLE WHIP SALAD DRESSING						
PARADE					189700	189700
TOTAL SUNDAY MAGS.					189700	189700
TOTAL BRAND EXP.					189700	189700
SUNDAY MAGS. PROJ. 125 MKTS.					189700	189700

Exhibit 17.8 A portion of a page from a Leading National Advertisers report of newspaper advertising expenditures. Reprinted by permission.

1. Prego Spaghetti Sauce spent $1,301 for newspaper advertising in the Hartford *Courant* in June. That was its only advertising in that newspaper in the second quarter. The total for the first six months (year-to-date or YTD) in that newspaper is $2,609.
2. In the measured newspapers, the total YTD measured expenditures for Prego was $73,062. Projecting that total gives an estimate of $125,748 in the top 125 markets.

WALL ST. JOURNAL ADVERTISING REPORT
BRAND DETAIL
JANUARY – OCTOBER 1989

WSJ EDITION	JANUARY		FEBRUARY		MARCH		APRIL		MAY		JUNE		1ST HALF	
	LINES	DOLLARS	LINES	DOLLARS	LINES	DOLLARS	LINES	DOLLARS	LINES	DOLLARS	LINES	DOLLARS	LINES	DOLLARS
NATIONAL	*PAINE WEBBER GROUP INC*		*PAINE WEBBER GROUP INC*		*TOMBSTONE ADV, SECURITY & TENDER OFFERS*		*PAINE WEBBER DEVELOPMENT CORP SEC OFF*				*B157 (CON'T)* / *B157-0*		0	0
NATIONAL	*PAINE WEBBER GROUP INC*		491	26,421			*PAINE WEBBER INC ANNOUNCEMENT*		163	8,825	100 *B157-8*	5,381	754	40,627
NATIONAL	517	27,819	*PAINE WEBBER GROUP INC* 117	6,710			*PAINE WEBBER INC MER/ACQ ANNOUNCEMENT*		126	6,780	*B157-8* 309	16,613	1,009	54,322
EASTERN	169	9,666			57	3,110			57	3,284			343	19,660
WESTERN	28	1,690											28	1,690
TOTAL	714	39,175	117	6,710	57	3,110			183	10,064	309	16,613	1,380	75,672
NATIONAL	588	31,625	*PAINE WEBBER GROUP INC* 555	29,866	142	7,641	*PAINE WEBBER INC SECURITY OFFERING* 1,163	62,634	2,046	110,150	1,802	97,019	6,296	338,935
EASTERN	243	13,888	256	14,592	294	16,821	206	11,753	57	3,284	59	3,378	1,115	63,716
MIDWEST			113	6,956	121	7,417	131	8,031			40	2,455	405	24,859
SOUTHWEST			37	2,453	34	2,267	41	2,721					112	7,441
WESTERN			76	4,615	72	4,350	89	5,372					237	16,337
TOTAL	831	45,513	1,037	58,482	663	38,496	1,630	90,511	2,103	113,434	1,901	102,852	8,165	449,288 ②

Exhibit 17.9 A portion of a page from a Leading National Advertisers *Wall Street Journal* advertising report. Reprinted by permission.

1. Paine Webber spent an estimated $31,625 for 588 agate lines of advertising in the national edition in January. (An agate line is a space measure for newspaper advertising. One column inch equals 14 agate lines, so that was 42 column inches.)
2. The company spent an estimated $449,288 for 8,165 lines in the first half of the year.

USA TODAY
USA TODAY

CLASS/COMPANY/BRAND SECTION
January – September 1989

CLASS/COMPANY/BRAND	CLASS CODE	TOTAL ADVERTISING				NATIONAL ADV.				REG./DEMO ADV.				# OF INS.
		PAGES	% OF MAG	DOLLARS	% OF MAG	PAGES	% OF MAG	DOLLARS	% OF MAG	PAGES	% OF MAG	DOLLARS	% OF MAG	
BRIDGESTONE CORPORATION														
BRIDGESTONE (USA) INC TV PROGRAM	T1418	1.00	0.0	67.945	0.0	1.00	0.0	67.945	0.0	0.00	0.0	0	0.0	1
BRIDGESTONE TIRES CAR	T1410	3.00	0.1	201.768	0.1	3.00	0.1	201.768	0.1	0.00	0.0	0	0.0	3
DAYTON TIRES CAR	T1410	2.00	0.1	127.028	0.1	2.00	0.1	127.028	0.1	0.00	0.0	0	0.0	2
FIRESTONE MASTER CARE CAR CARE SERVICE	T1540	4.00	0.1	264.101	0.2	4.00	0.1	264.101	0.2	0.00	0.0	0	0.0	4
FIRESTONE TIRES CARS	T1410	3.00	0.1	192.774	0.1	3.00	0.1	192.774	0.1	0.00	0.0	0	0.0	3
TOTAL		13.00	0.4	853.616	0.5	13.00	0.5	853.616	0.5	0.00	0.0	0	0.0	13
BRITISH AEROSPACE PLC														
STERLING 825	T1120	3.00	0.1	136.344	0.1	3.00	0.1	136.344	0.1	0.00	0.0	0	0.0	3
STERLING 827	T1120	3.44	0.1	205.844	0.1	3.44	0.1	205.844	0.1	0.00	0.0	0	0.0	5
STERLING PASSENGER CARS	T1120	3.00	0.1	175.074	0.1	3.00	0.1	175.074	0.1	0.00	0.0	0	0.0	3
TOTAL		9.44	0.3	517.262	0.3	9.44	0.3	517.262	0.3	0.00	0.0	0	0.0	11
CHRYSLER CORP														
CHRYSLER CORP AUTOMOTIVE GP	T1118	1.00	0.0	52.265	0.0	1.00	0.0	52.265	0.0	0.00	0.0	0	0.0	1
CHRYSLER CORP SPORTING EVENTS	T1118	8.00	0.3	570.740	0.3	8.00	0.3	570.740	0.3	0.00	0.0	0	0.0	4
CHRYSLER LEBARON	T1110	2.00	0.1	118.166	0.1	2.00	0.1	118.166	0.1	0.00	0.0	0	0.0	2
CHRYSLER PASSENGER CARS & LIGHT TRUCKS	T1110	2.00	0.1	124.370	0.1	2.00	0.1	124.370	0.1	0.00	0.0	0	0.0	1
CHRYSLER-PLYMOUTH CARS & WAGONS	T1110	1.00	0.0	47.834	0.0	1.00	0.0	47.834	0.0	0.00	0.0	0	0.0	1
CHRYSLER-PLYMOUTH PASSENGER CARS	T1110	33.00	1.1	1,665.976	1.0	33.00	1.2	1,665.976	1.2	0.00	0.0	0	0.0	23
DODGE LIGHT TRUCKS	T1210	7.00	0.2	347.792	0.2	7.00	0.2	347.792	0.2	0.00	0.0	0	0.0	4
DODGE OMNI	T1210	2.00	0.1	130.130	0.1	2.00	0.1	130.130	0.1	0.00	0.0	0	0.0	2
DODGE PASSENGER CARS	T1110	6.00	0.2	322.886	0.2	6.00	0.2	322.886	0.2	0.00	0.0	0	0.0	4
DODGE PASSENGER CARS & LIGHT TRUCKS	T1110	15.00	0.5	787.864	0.5	15.00	0.5	787.864	0.5	0.00	0.0	0	0.0	8
DODGE RAM	T1210	0.49	0.0	17.458	0.0	0.49	0.0	17.458	0.0	0.00	0.0	0	0.0	1
DODGE SPIRIT	T1110	3.00	0.1	179.293	0.1	3.00	0.1	179.293	0.1	0.00	0.0	0	0.0	3
EAGLE PASSENGER CARS	T1110	1.00	0.0	49.993	0.0	1.00	0.0	49.993	0.0	0.00	0.0	0	0.0	1
EAGLE PREMIER & SUMMIT	T1110	1.00	0.0	52.265	0.0	1.00	0.0	52.265	0.0	0.00	0.0	0	0.0	1
JEEP LIGHT TRUCKS	T1210	5.00	0.2	239.170	0.2	5.00	0.2	239.170	0.2	0.00	0.0	0	0.0	5
JEEP WRANGLER	T1210	2.00	0.1	118.166	0.1	2.00	0.1	118.166	0.1	0.00	0.0	0	0.0	2
PLYMOUTH ACCLAIM	T1110	2.00	0.1	109.757	0.1	2.00	0.1	109.757	0.1	0.00	0.0	0	0.0	2
PLYMOUTH VOYAGER	T1210	1.00	0.0	47.834	0.0	1.00	0.0	47.834	0.0	0.00	0.0	0	0.0	1
TOTAL		92.49	3.2	4,981.959	3.0	92.49	3.3	4,981.959	3.1	0.00	0.0	0	0.0	66

①

Exhibit 17.10 A portion of a page from a Leading National Advertisers *USA Today* Report. Reprinted by permission.

1. Chrysler Corporation spent an estimated $1,665,976 for thirty-three pages of advertising for passenger cars between January and September. That represented 1.1 percent of all advertising in *USA Today* in that period.

OUTDOOR ADVERTISING SERVICE
BRAND DETAIL
January - September 1989

CLASS
  COMPANY
    BRAND
      STATE - MARKET
	CURRENT QUARTER $ (000)			YEAR-TO-DATE $ (000)		

	TOTAL	POSTER	PAINT	TOTAL	POSTER	PAINT
G111 CIGARETTES (CON'T)						
RJR NABISCO INC (CON'T)						
SALEM FILTER CIGARETTES (G1110)						
MEMPHIS	16.0	2.2	13.8	16.0	2.2	13.8
NASHVILLE-DAVIDSON	86.3	24.6	61.7	178.8	76.8	102.0
TX AUSTIN	55.5	7.5	48.0	55.5	7.5	48.0
BEAUMONT-PORT ARTHUR-ORANGE	1.7	1.7	0.0	8.4	8.4	0.0
BROWNSVILLE-HARLINGEN-SAN BENIT	0.0	0.0	0.0	22.9	20.5	2.4
CORPUS CHRISTI	0.0	0.0	0.0	29.7	14.0	15.7
DALLAS-FT WORTH	17.3	8.9	8.4	17.3	8.9	8.4
HOUSTON	210.8	① 139.6	71.3	433.7	215.1	218.7
SAN ANTONIO	35.3	18.1	17.2	35.3	18.1	17.2
VICTORIA	0.0	0.0	0.0	4.3	4.3	0.0
WICHITA FALLS	0.8	0.8	0.0	0.8	0.8	0.0
VA DANVILLE-MARTINSVILLE-COLLINSVILLE	3.2	3.2	0.0	9.2	9.2	0.0
RICHMOND	3.8	3.8	0.0	15.1	11.7	3.4
ROANOKE	5.2	3.6	1.6	12.0	5.5	6.5
WA BREMERTON	1.9	1.9	0.0	7.6	7.6	0.0
SEATTLE & TACOMA	95.0	62.6	32.3	213.0	117.1	95.8
SPOKANE	0.0	0.0	0.0	1.9	1.9	0.0
WI MILWAUKEE	40.5	21.1	19.4	143.2	62.5	80.8
WV HUNTINGTON-ASHLAND	2.3	2.3	0.0	5.9	5.9	0.0
WHEELING-STEUBENVILLE-WEIRTON	9.2	5.6	3.6	18.2	12.3	5.9
BRAND TOTAL	3,208.4	1,248.6	1,959.7	7,749.2	3,219.1	4,530.1
SALEM LIGHTS MENTHOL FILTER KING CIG (G1110)						
LA NEW ORLEANS	0.0	0.0	0.0	192.9	0.0	192.9
VANTAGE KING CIG RG FL (G1110)						
CA LOS ANGELES METRO MARKET	0.0	0.0	0.0	72.9	29.0	43.9
SAN DIEGO	19.3	0.9	18.4	19.3	0.9	18.4
SAN FRANCISCO-OAKLAND-SAN JOSE METRO	0.0	0.0	0.0	30.6	15.4	15.2
IL ROCKFORD	0.0	0.0	0.0	2.5	0.9	1.6
NC GREENSBORO-WINSTON-SALEM-HIGH POINT	0.0	0.0	0.0	2.2	0.0	2.2
OH COLUMBUS OH	15.5	0.0	15.5	120.3	56.6	63.6
BRAND TOTAL	34.8	0.9	33.9	247.8	102.8	144.9

Exhibit 17.11 A portion of a page from a Leading National Advertisers outdoor advertising report. Reprinted by permission.
1. RJR Nabisco spent $210,800 to advertise Salem filters in Houston in the current quarter. That included $139,600 in poster panels (printed signs attached to the billboard structure) and $71,300 for painted bulletins (advertising painted on panels).

• • • Radio Expenditure Reports

Estimates of advertising expenditures in spot radio are reported by Radio Expenditure Reports (RER). The estimates are based on data supplied to RER by national station representative firms and on data obtained by surveys of stations. The data are for nearly 2,500 radio stations in more than 200 markets in the United States and are projected to an adjusted national gross estimate.

Exhibits 17.15 and 17.16 show portions of pages from an RER report.

LNA/ARBITRON MULTI-MEDIA SERVICE

AD $ SUMMARY BRAND INDEX

January – September 1989

BRAND / PARENT COMPANY	CLASS CODE	9-MEDIA YTD $ (000)	MEDIA USED
CALDOR JEWELRY / MAY DEPARTMENT STORES CO	G722	193.8	M
CALDOR SPORT TOY HOBBY / MAY DEPARTMENT STORES CO	G727	1,095.9	M
CALDWELL COLLEGE (RES) / CALDWELL COLLEGE	B133	69.2	M
CALENDAR CONSTRUCTION / COMPANY UNKNOWN	B111	76.4	M
CALERA TRUESCAN SYSTEMS / CALERA RECOGNITION SYSTEMS INC	B311	37.4	M
CALGARY BEER / CENTURY IMPORTERS INC	F310	27.7	O
CALGON AFTER BATH LOTION / SMITHKLINE BEECHAM PLC	D131	(1) 603.5	MNSYC
CALGON BATH PRODUCTS / SMITHKLINE BEECHAM PLC	D131	229.4	NSYC
CALGON FOAMING MILK BATH / SMITHKLINE BEECHAM PLC	D131	411.3	NSYC
CALGON MOISTURIZING FOAM BATH / SMITHKLINE BEECHAM PLC	D131	604.9	NSYC
CALGON WATER CONDITIONER / SMITHKLINE BEECHAM PLC	H411	861.5	NSY
CALHOUNS COLLECTORS SOCIETY / CALHOUNS COLLECTORS SOCIETY INC	B189	6.2	M
CALICO CORNERS (HOUSEHOLD) / EVERFAST INC	G714	625.1	PWS
CALIF CAR CRASH COVERAGE / COMPANY UNKNOWN	B222	33.3	S
CALIF COOLER WINE BEVERAGE / BROWN-FORMAN CO	F320	1,404.0	NSY
CALIF GOLD BOOK / ADVANCE PUBLICATIONS	B410	10.3	S

BRAND / PARENT COMPANY	CLASS CODE	9-MEDIA YTD $ (000)	MEDIA USED
CALIFORNIA MILK ADVISORY BD DAIRY PROMO / CALIFORNIA MILK ADVISORY BOARD	F139-9	144.0	O
CALIFORNIA MILK ADVISORY BD MILK PROMOTN / CALIFORNIA MILK ADVISORY BOARD	F131-9	87.8	O
CALIFORNIA MILK ADVISORY BOARD BUTTER PR / CALIFORNIA MILK ADVISORY BOARD	F131-9	275.5	M
CALIFORNIA MILK ADVISORY BOARD PROMO / CALIFORNIA MILK ADVISORY BOARD	F131-9	410.3	O
CALIFORNIA MINI TRUCK INC AUTO (MISC) / CALIFORNIA MINI TRUCK INC	G619	37.0	M
CALIFORNIA MUSEUM OF SCIENCE & INDUSTRY / CALIFORNIA MUSEUM OF SCIENCE & INDUSTRY	G321	69.4	M
CALIFORNIA MUSIC THEATRE / COMPANY UNKNOWN	G321	74.6	M
CALIFORNIA NECTARINE PROMOTION / CALIFORNIA TREE FRUIT AGREEMENT	F142-9	729.9	NR
CALIFORNIA OLIVE IND & PARTICIPATING COS / OLIVE ADMINISTRATION COMMITTEE	F116-9	95.1	M
CALIFORNIA OLIVE INDUSTRY / OLIVE ADMINISTRATION COMMITTEE	F116-9	447.2	M
CALIFORNIA PEACHES PROMOTION / CALIFORNIA TREE FRUIT AGREEMENT	F142-9	360.1	NR
CALIFORNIA PERFUME / REVLON GROUP INC	D113	3,096.2	MNSY
CALIFORNIA PLUMS PROMO / CALIFORNIA TREE FRUIT AGREEMENT	F142-9	352.8	NR
CALIFORNIA POOLS & SPAS HOME / CALIFORNIA POOLS & SPAS	H529-5	170.9	PO
CALIFORNIA PRUNES / CALIFORNIA PRUNES ADVISORY BOARD	F142-9	2,808.4	MNS
CALIFORNIA RAISIN ADVISORY BOARD / CALIFORNIA RAISINS ADVISORY BOARD	F142-9	5,928.3	MNSYC

Exhibit 17.12 A portion of a page from a Leading National Advertisers/Arbitron Multi-Media Service showing total advertising expenditures and media used. Reprinted by permission.

1. SmithKline Beecham spent $603,500 to advertise Calgon After Bath lotion in magazines (M), network television (N), spot television (S), syndicated television (Y), and cable (C). Other media designated on the page are Sunday magazines (W), newspapers (P), outdoor (O), and network radio (R).

COMPANY/BRAND $

LNA/ARBITRON MULTI-MEDIA SERVICE
January - September 1989
YEAR-TO-DATE ADVERTISING DOLLARS (000)

PARENT COMPANY/BRAND	CLASS CODE	9-MEDIA TOTAL	MAGAZINES	SUNDAY MAGAZINES	NEWSPAPERS	OUTDOOR	NETWORK TELEVISION	SPOT TELEVISION	SYNDICATED TELEVISION	CABLE TV NETWORKS	NETWORK RADIO
RJR NABISCO INC (CONTINUED)											
MILK-BONE DOG BISCUITS	G511	9,144.4 [1]	816.5				7,031.1	24.2	274.3	998.3	
MILK-BONE DOG TREATS	G511	784.9					705.5	1.1		78.3	
MORE 120S FILTER CIGARETTES	G111	5,015.7	3,492.5			1,523.2					
MORE 120S MENTHOL FILTER CIGARETTES	G111	3,808.5	3,808.5								
MORE FILTER CIGARETTES	G111	1,762.9				1,762.9					
MORE LIGHT 100S & 120S MENTHOL FIL CIG	G111	2.6				2.6					
MORE LIGHT FILTER CIGARETTES	G111	570.6				570.6					
MORE LT 120 CIG RG & MN FL	G111	246.9				246.9					
MORE WHITE LTS 120 CIG MN FL	G111	1,886.4	1,886.4								
MORE WHITE LTS 120 RG FL	G111	1,453.9	1,453.9								
NABISCO 100% BRAN	F122	421.0	421.0								
NABISCO BAKERS OWN COOKIES	F163	1,070.1			30.7		1,069.4	0.7			
NABISCO BRANDS INC GENERAL PROMOTION	F190-8	6,335.5					6,294.5	1.4		39.6	
NABISCO BRANDS INC SPORTING EVENTS	F122	1,214.1	1,214.1								
NABISCO CEREALS	F122	50.1	17.7		32.4						
NABISCO CHEWY CHIPS AHOY COOKIES	F163	7.5						1.3	3.9	2.3	
NABISCO CHIPS AHOY	F163	2,379.3					1,606.4	189.0	381.5	202.4	
NABISCO CHIPS AHOY COOKIES	F163	3,815.1	22.5				3,219.5	99.8	165.8	307.5	
NABISCO COOKIES	F190-8	69.2	69.2								
NABISCO DINAH SHORE INV GLF TORNT TV PRG	F163	43.2					43.2				
NABISCO DOUBLE STUFF OREOS	F163	111.4					75.0	13.5	5.6	17.3	
NABISCO FIG NEWTONS	F163	3,550.5					3,013.3	23.1	238.0	276.1	
NABISCO FOOD PRODUCTS	F190	1,192.4	1,036.8		135.8			0.2		19.6	
NABISCO FROSTED WHEAT SQUARES CEREAL	F122	2,388.1	2,123.4	201.7	63.0						
NABISCO FRUIT WHEATS	F122	1,249.6	1,249.6								

Exhibit 17.13 A portion of a Leading National Advertisers/Arbitron Company Brand Dollar report. Reprinted by permission.

1. RJR Nabisco spent an estimated $9,144,400 to advertise Milk-Bone dog biscuits in the first nine months, including $7,031,100 in network television, $24,200 in spot television, $274,300 in syndicated television, and $998,300 in cable television networks.

CLASS/BRAND $

LNA/ARBITRON MULTI-MEDIA SERVICE
January - September 1989
QUARTERLY AND YEAR-TO-DATE ADVERTISING DOLLARS (000)

CLASS/COMPANY/BRAND		CLASS CODE	9 MEDIA TOTAL	MAGAZINES	SUNDAY MAGAZINES	NEWSPAPERS	OUTDOOR	NETWORK TELEVISION	SPOT TELEVISION	SYNDICATED TELEVISION	CABLE TV NETWORKS	NETWORK RADIO
G111 CIGARETTES							*CONTINUED*					
RJR NABISCO INC												
WINSTON FILTER CIGARETTES (CONTINUED)												
WINSTON KING SIZE FILTER CIGARETTES	88 YTD	G111	10,945.9	37.7	198.3	374.9	10,335.0	--	--	--	--	--
	Q1		517.8	460.0	57.8	--	--	--	--	--	--	--
	Q2		2,470.5	2,464.2	--	.4	6.3	--	--	--	--	--
	Q3		2,784.4	2,784.4	--	--	--	--	--	--	--	--
	89 YTD		5,772.7 ①	5,708.6	57.8	--	6.3	--	--	--	--	--
	88 YTD		3,795.3	3,740.5	--	--	54.8	--	--	--	--	--
WINSTON LIGHTS KING SIZE CIGARETTES	89 YTD	G111	92.9	--	--	92.9	--	--	--	--	--	--
	89 YTD		92.9	--	--	92.9	--	--	--	--	--	--
	88 YTD		3,754.7	3,295.5	--	200.0	259.2	--	--	--	--	--
WINSTON LIGHTS COMPETITION MENTHOL	89 YTD	G111	58.1	--	58.1	--	--	--	--	--	--	--
	89 YTD		58.1	--	58.1	--	--	--	--	--	--	--
WINSTON ULTRA LIGHTS REGULAR	89 YTD	G111	86.3	--	--	86.3	--	--	--	--	--	--
	89 YTD		86.3	--	--	86.3	--	--	--	--	--	--
YVES SAINT LAURENT RITZ 100 CIG BOX FIL	Q1	G111	303.2	303.2	--	--	--	--	--	--	--	--
	Q2		121.2	121.2	--	--	--	--	--	--	--	--
	Q3		35.9	35.9	--	--	--	--	--	--	--	--
	89 YTD		460.3	460.3	--	--	--	--	--	--	--	--
	88 YTD		387.1	266.0	--	21.9	99.2	--	--	--	--	--
COMPANY TOTAL	Q1		49,674.8	32,121.8	1,705.3	1,607.1	14,239.6	--	--	--	--	--
	Q2		44,815.4	29,809.6	824.2	1,829.2	12,152.4	--	--	--	--	--
	Q3		40,854.2	28,059.9	500.3	634.8	11,617.3	--	--	--	--	--
	89 YTD		135,144.4	89,991.3	3,030.8	4,071.1	38,009.3	--	--	--	--	--
	88 YTD		111,704.6	61,430.5	5,157.1	2,211.0	42,892.8	--	--	13.2	--	--
ROTHMANS INTERNATIONAL PLC												
DUNHILL INTERNATIONAL CIGARETTES	Q2	G111	87.9	87.9	--	--	--	--	--	--	--	--
	Q3		45.3	45.3	--	--	--	--	--	--	--	--
	89 YTD		133.2	133.2	--	--	--	--	--	--	--	--
	88 YTD		116.7	116.7	--	--	--	--	--	--	--	--
DUNHILL INTERNAL SUPERIOR MILD FIL CIG	Q1	G111	27.0	27.0	--	--	--	41.9	--	--	--	--
	Q3		59.2	59.2	--	--	--	41.9	--	--	--	--
	89 YTD		35.9	35.9	--	--	--	--	--	--	--	--
	89 YTD		122.1	122.1	--	--	--	--	--	--	--	--
	88 YTD		56.0	56.0	--	--	--	--	--	--	--	--

Exhibit 17.14 A portion of a page from a Leading National Advertisers/Arbitron Class Brand Dollar report. Reprinted by permission.
1. RJR Nabisco spent an estimated $5,772,700 on advertising for Winston king size filters in the first nine months of 1989, compared with $3,795,300 for the same period in 1988.

ALL ADVERTISERS REPORT
(BY CATEGORY)

PARENT PRODUCT / BRAND	JANUARY	FEBRUARY	MARCH	FIRST QTR	YTD
AGRICULTURAL					
CONSUMER LAWN PRODUCTS					
BIO LAB INC.					
BIOGUARD LAWN CARE			31,640	31,640	31,640
CHEVRON USA INC.					
ORTHO	236	470	2,044	2,750	2,750
ORTHO RAPID GRO			360	360	360
PARENT TOTAL	236 *	470 *	2,404 *	3,110 *	3,110 *
HYGRADE					
NU LIFE FERTILIZER		10,560	5,280 (1)	15,840	15,840
LAWN DOCTOR			3,680	3,680	3,680
MICHIGAN PEAT CO.					
BACCTO PEAT LITE		1,000	2,000	3,000	3,000
PRO GRASS LAWN SERVICE			6,480	6,480	6,480
RINGER CORP. LAWN RESTORER			104,798	104,798	104,798
SCOTT, O.M. & SONS CO.					
SCOTT FERTILIZER	900-	17,720	621,210	638,930	638,930
SCOTT FOUR STEP	900-	30,210	223,460	252,770	252,770
PARENT TOTAL	900- *	47,930 *	844,670 *	891,700 *	891,700 *
SECURITY CHACON LAWN & GARDEN		2,300	27,780	30,080	30,080
TRUE GREEN			15,220	15,220	15,220
** TOTAL $	664-	62,260	1,043,952	1,105,548	1,105,548

Exhibit 17.15 A portion of a page from Radio Expenditure Reports showing estimates of spot radio advertising. Reprinted by permission.
1. Hygrade spent an estimated $10,560 in February and $5,280 in March to advertise Nu Life fertilizer.

```
     (A)                                    (B)                     (C) PAGE     167
COMMUNICATIONS                   TELECOMMUNICATION COMPANIES    FIRST QUARTER  1989

                                          (E)
                             BARNSTABLE/HYANNIS   (MA)                  960
                             BURLINGTON   (VT)                          180
                             MANCHESTER   (NH)                        9,150
                             PORTLAND   (ME)                         13,520
                             PORTSMOUTH/DOVER   (NH)                  3,710
                             PROVIDENCE/WARWICK   (RI)               12,495
                             SPRINGFIELD   (MA)                       6,410
                             WORCESTER   (MA)                         9,800
                                                                ------------
              (D)                    TOTAL                           57,209  ***
     NYNEX CORP.
       NEW ENGLAND TELEPHONE DAYTIME
                             BANGOR/PRESQUE ISLE   (ME)              2,158
                             BURLINGTON   (VT)                       4,090
                             PORTLAND   (ME)                ①        2,070
                             PROVIDENCE/WARWICK   (RI)              13,305
                             SPRINGFIELD   (MA)                      9,201
                                                                ------------
                                     TOTAL                          30,824  ***
     NYNEX CORP.
       NEW ENGLAND TELEPHONE MEASURED
                             MONTPELIER   (VT)                         468
                                                                ------------
                                     TOTAL                             468  ***
```

Exhibit 17.16 A portion of a page from Radio Expenditure Reports showing spot radio expenditures by market. Reprinted by permission.

1. Nynex Corporation spent an estimated $2,070 to advertise its New England Telephone daytime service in Portland in the first quarter.

Single-Source Research

Single-source research is a relatively new and important development in advertising and marketing. To understand the significance of single-source research, one must consider the more traditional way of doing research on the relationship between advertising and sales. What advertisers really want to know about advertising, of course, is its effect on consumer purchase behavior. That relationship is difficult to ascertain because so many factors other than advertising—such as price, distribution, and the competition—can affect sales. It has also been difficult to determine advertising's effect on sales because research about advertising exposure and product purchase has usually been conducted with different groups or samples of people.

Traditional Measures of Product Consumption and Media Exposure

Advertisers have long had research sources to tell them about the products and brands people buy and consume. Syndicated services such as Nielsen Food Index, Nielsen Drug Index, or Sales Area Marketing, Inc., use a technique called *store audits* to measure product movement in retail grocery stores and drugstores. That information is an important source for determining brands' share of market, but it does not tell anything about the people who purchase those products.

Such information can be provided by national consumer panel studies in which selected households maintain diaries of product and brand purchases. Typically, those studies do not provide any information about media exposure of people in those households.

Several sources tell advertisers about television audiences: Nielsen Media Research, Arbitron, Simmons Market Research Bureau, and Mediamark. All of those sources can also provide information about the demographics of viewers. Simmons and Arbitron can even tell advertisers about the users of specific products and the media they are exposed to. However, those measures are self-reports of what people say they *use*, not the specific items they *purchase*. In other words, we can ascertain the demographic characteristics of people who say they use canned soup, and we can find out what television programs they say they watch. But those facts are not the same as knowing about the programs that are watched by people whom we know purchased canned soup during the same week they watched television programs featuring soup commercials.

Until recently, information about media exposure and information about consumer purchases came from different sources, and advertisers had to make inferences about the connections between advertising exposure and product sales. Single-source research makes it easier to measure that connection, at least with regard to television advertising. A single source, one group of households, provides data about television exposure and product purchases. A people meter, similar to the one described in Chapter 15, measures the households' television program exposure, while an electronic scanner records their store purchases. The data can be combined to show the products and brands that are purchased by viewers of specific programs.

Two measures of single-source research data are discussed in this chapter: Arbitron's ScanAmerica and Nielsen's Scantrack®.

• • • Arbitron's ScanAmerica®

One of the new single-source research services is ScanAmerica® from Arbitron. It now operates with a representative sample of 600 households in Denver, Colorado. Approximately 60 percent of designated households agreed to participate, and approximately 90 percent of the participating households provide viewing and purchasing data each week. Nearly 70 percent of the households have been in the sample for more than nine months. Arbitron planned to launch a national ScanAmerica® service with 1,000 households in late 1990 and to expand to 2,000 households in late 1991. By late 1993, it plans to reach 5,000 households. Arbitron also plans to convert other local market measures to ScanAmerica® by 1995.

ScanAmerica® Data Collection
Television viewing data are provided by people meters attached to television sets in the sample households. The meter records when the set is on and the channel

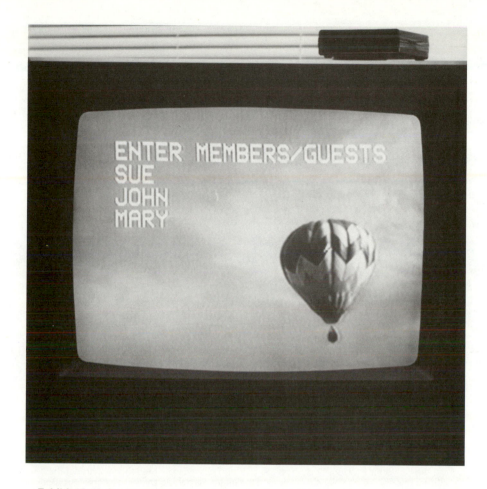

Exhibit 17.17 ScanAmerica's® on-screen prompt reminds viewers to log on to the meter by pushing their preassigned button. This photograph shows that Sue, John, and Mary are logged on. Reprinted by permission of Arbitron Ratings Co.

it is tuned to, including cable channels and videocassette recorder usage. To indicate who is watching the set, each household member presses a preassigned button on a remote hand-held keypad. A prompt appears on the television screen periodically to remind viewers to log on to the meter. Exhibit 17.17 illustrates how the on-screen prompt reminds viewers to log on.

Households provide product purchase data by using a portable Universal Product Code (UPC) scanning wand to record the bar codes printed on products. This is not like some other systems that require sample members to make all of their purchases at one store. Using the scanning wand also makes it possible to record purchases at any kind of store. (See Exhibit 17.18.) Sample households also complete a detailed questionnaire about their store preferences, purchases of durable goods (such as au-

Exhibit 17.18 ScanAmerica® families record their purchases by waving the data scan wand over the Universal Product Code. The wand is then placed in its holder, which transfers the product codes from the wand's memory to the meter. Reprinted by permission of Arbitron Ratings Co.

tomobiles, cameras, or stereo equipment), services (banks, for example), and the newspapers they read.

ScanAmerica® Reports

ScanAmerica® combines data from television viewing measures and product purchase measures to produce reports that show what ScanAmerica® calls Buyer-Graphics® of individual programs. Exhibits 17.19 and 17.20 illustrate BuyerGraphics®.

• • • Nielsen Scantrack

Nielsen Marketing Research's single-source research service is called Scan-track®. A national probability sample of 15,000 households records product purchases

DAY AND TIME / STATION PROGRAM	ADI TV HH RATINGS BY WEEKS				ADI RATINGS				CANNED SOUP TV HH				
	1 JAN 03	2 JAN 10	3 JAN 17	4 JAN 24	ADI TVHH	PERS 25-54	WOM 25-54	MEN 25-54	TOTAL	LIGHT	MEDIUM	HEAVY	NON-USERS
RELATIVE STD-ERR 25% THRESHOLDS (1σ) 50%	3 –	3 –	3 –	3 –	1 –	1 –	2 –	2 –					
THURSDAY													
10:00P-10:15P													
KWGN HL STRT BLUS	3	2	2	2	2	1	2	1	2	2	2	2	4
KCNC NEWS 4 LT ED	17	18	17	16	17	13	15	11	17	14	15	23	15
KMGH 7 NEWS AT 10	6	5	6	7	6	4	4	3	6	5	7	5	6
KUSA NINE NWS 10	13	15	14	18	15	11	11	11	16	16	17	14	10
KTVD NUGGETS BKBL	4				4	2	1	4	4	1	4	6	3
NEW T ZONE		1	1	2	2	1	1	1	1	2	2	1	2
--4 WK AVG--					2	1	1	2	2	2	2	2	2
KDVR NGHT COURT-S	3	2	4	2	3	2	1	2	3	2	2	3	4
KRMA PTV	1	1	1	1	1	1		1	1	1	1	1	
KBDI PTV	1	–	–	–								1	
HUT/TOTAL	53	51	54	56	54	39	40	38	54	52	52	59	48
10:15P-10:30P													
KWGN HL STRT BLUS	3	2	2	2	2	1	2	1	2	3	2	2	3
KCNC NEWS 4 LT ED	14	14	16	14	14	11	13	9	14	12	12	19	14
KMGH 7 NEWS AT 10	4	5	5	6	5	3	3	3	5	4	6	5	4
KUSA NINE NWS 10	13	13	15	18	15	10	10	11	15	15	17	14	12
KTVD NUGGETS BKBL	3				3	2	1	3	4	1	3	7	1
NEW T ZONE		2	1	2	1	1	1	1	1	2	1	1	1
--4 WK AVG--					2	1	1	2	2	2	2	3	1
KDVR NGHT COURT-S	3	2	4	3	3	2	2	2	3	3	2	3	4
KRMA PTV	1	1	–	–	1			1	1	1	1		1
KBDI PTV	1	–											
HUT/TOTAL	47	46	51	52	49	35	36	35	50	48	47	54	44
10:30P-10:45P													
KWGN HL STRT BLUS	4	2	3	3	3	2	2	1	3	3	2	3	4
KCNC TONIGHT SHOW	10	13			11	6	8	5	11	10	9	15	13
BRONCOS UPDT			12	13	13	8	9	8	13	11	12	16	11
--4 WK AVG--					12	7	8	7	12	10	10	16	12
KMGH INSIDE EDITN	4	6	5		5	3	3	3	5	5	5	6	3
SPR BWL UPDT				5	5	2	3	1	5	3	6	5	3
--4 WK AVG--					5	3	3	2	5	5	5	5	3
KUSA CHEERS-S	14	14	13		14	10	11	9	14	15	14	13	10
NINE NWS 10				14	14	8	7	9	14	8	19	14	14
--4 WK AVG--					14	10	10	9	14	13	15	14	11
KTVD NUGGETS BKBL	3				3	2	1	3	3	1	3	6	1
ALL IN FAMLY		1	1	1	1	1	1		1	1		2	
--4 WK AVG--					1	1	1	1	2	1	1	3	1
KDVR NEWHART-S	2	2	2	2	2	1	1	1	2	2	2	2	2
KRMA PTV	1	1	–	–	1	1	1		1	1	1	1	
KBDI PTV	–	1	1	–					1			1	
HUT/TOTAL	42	42	42	47	43	29	29	28	44	41	43	47	39
10:45P-11:00P													

Exhibit 17.19 A portion of a page from an Arbitron BuyerGraphics® report on the Denver market. Reprinted by permission.

1. KCNC's news program had a household rating of 17 percent, meaning it was viewed in 17 percent of all the households.
2. Its BuyerGraphics® rating for heavy purchasers of canned soup was 23, meaning that 23 percent of the heavy purchasers watched that newscast. Note how much higher it is than comparable ratings for light, medium, or nonpurchasers.

from all types of stores by using portable scanning wands. A subsample of 5,000 households in more than twenty major markets provides television viewing data by means of people meters. Using a system developed by Nielsen Media Research, Scantrack identifies individual commercials and matches the programs that consumers watch to the advertisements they are exposed to. Linking that exposure information to data about purchases enables advertisers to evaluate the effectiveness of television advertising—to tell what kind of people buy products and whether they saw advertising for those products.

Time Period Estimates

① ②

DAY AND TIME / STATION PROGRAM	ADI RTG		INCOME TV HH				HOME TVHH		NEWSPAPERS TVHH				AUTOMOBILE OWNERSHIP PERSONS 25-54																		SHOP AT DEPT STORES PERSONS 25-54									
	ADI TVHH	PERS 25-54	$0K-19K	$20K-34K	$35K-49K	$50K+	OWN	RENT	POST-WKDY	POST-SUN	RMN-WKDY	RMN-SUN	BUICK	CHEVY	CRYS/PLYM	DODGE	FORD	HONDA	MERCURY	NISSAN	OLDS	SUBARU	TOYOTA	VOLKSW	USD 1-3 YRS	USD 3-5 YRS	FSHN BAR	JOSLIN'S	MAY D&F	MERVYN'S	SEARS	TARGET	K-MART	WAL-MART
RELATIVE STD-ERR ▲ THRESHOLDS (1σ) 25% 50%	1 1	1 1																																
THURSDAY 6:30P- 7:00P																																		
KWGN CHRLS N CHRG	6	3	6	7	5	5	6	7	6	5	5	5	2	3	6	3	3	2	3	4	9	5	5	1	1	3	2	3	1	1	4	2	4	2
KCNC COLO EVE NWS	9	5	11	9	9	8	10	8	9	9	11	11	5	7	6	6	5	5	8	8	11	10	8	2	5	5	6	6	7	6	3	6	5	4
KMGH WHEEL OF FOR	10	5	15	11	10	9	13	9	13	12	13	15	7	5	8	6	6	5	2	3	7	4	2	3	4	5	3	8	6	4	4	5	4	6
KUSA USA TODAY	7	6	8	12	7	8	8	9	11	13	11	8	4	4	7	6	3	10	6	3	6	12	3	7	6	7	6	7	7	3	7	6	6	9
ENTRTNMT TON	9	6	7	7	6	7	9	9	13	13	11	9	4	4	8	6	5	10	4	5	5	6	5	5	6	6	6	9	7	8	6	6	9	8
--4 WK AVG--	1	1	1	1	1	13	1	1	3	3	1	1	1	3	2	7	4	1	6	4	6	2	4	2	5	6	2	3	7	7	7	4	6	9
KTVD TOO CLS CMFT	1	1	1	2	6	12	1	1	1	1	1	1	1	1	1	1	1	1	4	10	5	7	2	1	5	4	2	9	7	1	6	4	6	8
KDVR NGHT COURT-S	6	2	7	7	6	1	5	8	4	3	7	3	1	3	2	1	1	1	6	3	3	8	3	2	1	1	2	3	7	7	5	4	1	3
KRMA PTV	1	1	2	2	6	3	1	1	3	1	1	1	1	1	1	5	1	1	1	1	3	2	2	5	5	4	2	1	2	4	5	1	1	3
KBDI PTV	1	1	2	1	3	3	3	3					1	1	1	1	1	1	1	1	3	1	2	2	1	1	2	1	2	1	1	1	1	
HUT/TOTAL	53	31	58	55	49	51	56	50	56	54	55	56	27	29	31	33	30	29	28	32	41	33	30	23	29	31	22	36	30	32	30	30	32	30
7:00P- 7:30P																																		
KWGN HLY CHRS PAR	4	2	6	5	3	1	4	4	6	5	4	3	2	3	4	2	2		2	1	1		2	3	2	2	1	1	1	1	2	2	2	2
THR IS SANTA	3	1	7	5	3		7	1	5	4	4	6	1	1	2	1	1	1	1	1	1	1	1	1	1	1	1	1	1	1	2	2	1	1
CINEMA 2	3	1	5	3	2	4	3	4	4	4	3	4	1	1	2	5	1	1	6	1	1	18	1	18	16	3	15	17	16	15	12	14	15	13
--4 WK AVG--	23	15	23	22	26	26	24	24	22	25	26	26	17	15	22	15	13	14	16	21	13	18	13	18	16	10	3	3	7	12	10	8	11	5
KCNC BILL COSBY	6	3	8	6	6	6	12	7	11	12	10	7	3	7	5	4	10	12	8	8	14	9	4	5	11	10	8	8	7	6	8	8	10	10
KMGH 48 HOURS	13	10	14	10	15	14	10	6	9	11	10	8	2	3	1	10	6	10	4	4	12	8	4	4	3	5	4	4	3	7	4	5	10	6
KUSA GRFLD CHR SP	8	8	10	8	11	8	8	10	8	9	8	8	7	4	1	6	4	6	3	4	6	4	4	6	4	5	4	5	6	6	6	5	5	6
--4 WK AVG--	7	4	6	7	6	6	6	5	9	10	11	9	3	3	5	2	7	10	3	7	11	8	5	6	3	6	3	3	3	3	5	5	5	7
KUSA MISN IMPSBLE	10	9	12	10	10	9	10	13	12	14	11	10	3	4	4	6	5	4	3	4	6	5	6	5	4	5	8	4	6	10	5	5	5	6
SCRT FLS HVR	9	6	10	10	3	8	9	9	12	10	11	9	5	5	3	2	6	7	3	7	11	5	6	2	4	6	4	6	6	7	6	5	5	5
PSYCHC DTCTV	8	5	8	10	12	8	9	9	10	10	11	8	4	5	3	1	1	8	2	5	6	1	5	1	2	2	3	8	3	6	7	5	5	6
--4 WK AVG--	8	5	8	8	8	8	9	9	10	10	10	9	2	2	3	1	1	1	4	4	6	1	5	1	1	1	3	6	5	3	6	5	5	6
KTVD AIRWOLF	5	2	3	4	5	5	1	1	3	3	3	2	2	2	3	3	2	1	4	7	6	1	2	3	3	4	1	2	2	1	6	5	5	1
KDVR FILM FESTVAL	3	1	3	3	3	1	2	5	3	3	3	4	2	1	1	1	1	1	2	5	1	1	1	1	5	5	1	1	6	2	1	1	1	1
KRMA PTV	2	1	1	3	4	3	1		1	1	1	2	1	2	1	3	2	1	1	2	2		2	2	2	2	1	2	2	1	2	2	2	1
KBDI PTV	1	1	1	2	1	1	3	5	1	1	1	1	2	1	3	3	1	1	4	1	1	1	1	1	2	1	1	1	1	1	1	1	1	1
HUT/TOTAL	56	35	59	56	52	59	58	52	57	58	57	59	29	32	35	32	33	41	24	38	49	38	33	27	36	35	28	36	35	36	35	33	35	32

Exhibit 17.20 A portion of a page from a ScanAmerica® BuyerGraphics® report on the Denver market. Reprinted by permission.
1. "The Bill Cosby Show" had a television household rating of 23, meaning it was viewed in 23 percent of the households.
2. The BuyerGraphics® rating for owners of Mercury automobiles was 6, meaning only 6 percent of Mercury owners watched the program. Note how much lower that is than the comparable ratings for other owners, particularly owners of Chrysler-Plymouth cars.

Nielsen Market Research also has scanning systems in a sample of more than 3,000 carefully selected stores. Those scanning systems enable Scantrack® to report brand sales and prices paid. Scantrack also monitors and reports retailer advertising support (retailers who feature a manufacturer's products in newspaper advertising), retailer display activity (special store displays and promotions), and retailer coupon support. In addition, it can report the extent of national and spot television advertising support delivered to individual markets.

... Summary

Because advertisers' media strategies are often influenced by their competitors' strategies, advertisers find it useful to know the competition's media expenditures. Such information is gathered, compiled, and distributed to advertisers and advertising agencies by several syndicated research companies. For some media, those estimates are based on tabulations of all advertisements in all vehicles throughout the year. For other media, estimates are based on samples of time periods (only certain periods per month) and samples of vehicles (samples of stations).

Broadcast Advertisers Reports (BAR) compiles information about advertising expenditures on network radio, network television, spot television, cable television, and syndicated television. Leading National Advertisers (LNA) reports advertising expenditures in newspapers, magazines, and outdoor advertising. LNA also combines its data with that of BAR and issues LNA/Arbitron Multi-Media reports on expenditures in nine media categories.

Single-source research measures the media and advertising exposure for a sample of households and also measures those households' product purchases. Single-source research thus enables advertisers to see direct and immediate consequences (purchases) of their advertising and promotion efforts. Arbitron's ScanAmerica® and Nielsen's Scantrack® measure television audiences with people meters and measure household purchases by having family members use a scanning wand to record purchases.

... Self-Test Questions

1. Define and explain the following terms: Universal Product Code, open rate, and people meter.
2. Review the four concerns about competitive activity data discussed in Chapter 12. Derive a list of questions from that discussion and use it to evaluate the sources described in this chapter.
3. Explain the essential difference in the methodology used for BAR network television estimates and BAR spot television estimates.
4. Name the companies that provide competitive activity data for the following: newspapers, magazines, outdoor, television, network radio, spot radio.

5. Explain how most companies described in Chapter 17 determine their estimates of the cost of the advertising they measure.

6. Explain the fundamental premise or concept behind the idea of single-source research. Discuss why it is better than traditional forms of research.

7. Look at Exhibit 17.1. What dayparts did Bugle Boy use? [The answer is Saturday-Sunday daytime and early or late fringe.]

8. Look at Exhibit 17.2. How many commercials did Scotchgard place on "The Young and the Restless" in the quarter? [The answer is 6.]

9. Look at Exhibit 17.3. What were the total national expenditures for the F.W. Woolworth Company in the quarter? [The answer is $4,061,700.]

10. Look at Chrysler-Plymouth general promotion data in Exhibit 17.7. What were its total estimated expenditures in June? [The answer is $595,900.]

11. Look at Philip Morris expenditure data for Good Seasons salad dressing in Exhibit 17.8. What publication(s) did it use? [The answer is *Parade*.]

12. Look at Exhibit 17.12. What media did Brown-Forman use to advertise California Coolers? [The answer is network television, spot television, and syndicated television.]

13. Look at data for Nabisco Fig Newtons in Exhibit 17.13. In which medium did it spend its largest share of dollars? [The answer is network television.]

14. Look at Exhibit 17.15. How much did Scott fertilizer spend on spot radio in the quarter? [The answer is $638,930.]

15. Look at data for the 10:15 to 10:30 segment in Exhibit 17.19. Which station had the highest BuyerGraphics® rating for heavy canned soup purchasers? [The answer is KCNC.]

··· Suggestions for Additional Reading

Buck, S. and A. Yates. "Television Viewing, Consumer Purchasing, and Single-Source Research." *European Research*, 15 (1987), 34–39.

Carlin, I. "Single-Source: Sorry, Toto, We're Still in Kansas." *Marketing and Media Decisions*, (December 1988), 115–116.

Curry, D. J. "Single-Source Systems: Retail Management Present and Future." *Journal of Retailing*, 65 (1989), 1–20.

Fannin, R. "Marketing and Media Research: Learning the Terms." *Marketing and Media Decisions*, (October 1988), 78–82.

Fannin, R., and J. Mandese. "Marketing and Media Research: Adding to the Vocabulary." *Marketing and Media Decisions*, (October 1988), 69–76.

Gay, V. "Arbitron Joins Rivals: Will Roll Out National Ratings Service." *Advertising Age*, (June 27, 1988), 112.

Kamin, H. "The Age of Single Source." *Review of Business*, (Summer 1989), 23–26.

Larson, J. "Farewell to Coupons?" *American Demographics*, (February 1990), 14–17.

Riche, M. F. "Look Before Leaping." *American Demographics*, (February 1990), 18–20.

Schwartz, J. "Back to the Source." *American Demographics*, (January 1989), 22–26.

Teinowitz, J. "Arbitron, Nielsen Set to Track TV Ads." *Advertising Age*, (July 17, 1989), 46.

Wood, W. "Update: Single Source." *Marketing and Media Decisions*, (September 1989), 116–117.

PART FOUR

The Outlook for Advertising Research

I t is safe to predict that advertising research will change as the media and other technologies change. Cable television, the continuing growth in use of the videocassette recorder, changes in magazine and newspaper publishing, and changes in marketing practices have already altered the nature of advertising; and they will continue to influence changes in the conduct of advertising research.

As the changes continue, trained and creative researchers will be needed. In this concluding chapter, we speculate about new challenges for advertising research, review some of the persisting issues, and look at career opportunities in advertising research. ■

CHAPTER 18

Looking Ahead

"What will be, is." *Austin O'Malley*

"Prediction is very difficult, especially about the future." *Niels Bohr*

Have you ever heard of the proposal, made in the 1800s, that the U.S. Patent Office be closed, because everything that could be invented had been invented? Or what of the predictions in the middle of the twentieth century that in the early 1980s American society would enjoy unparalleled prosperity, fueled by low-cost energy? What of the predictions, made in the early days of television, that movies would become a thing of the past, and that radio was doomed? And what of more recent predictions about the prevalence of home computers, interactive cable television systems, videotape recorders, and other sophisticated products? Some of the predictions were found to be conservative; others were found to be overly optimistic.

Although predicting the future is risky, it seems reasonable to speculate on the direction advertising research is likely to take in the next few years. In the marketplace, entrepreneurs do it all the time to keep a step ahead of the industry and the competition.

Levels of Technological Change

The study of technological change occurs on three levels. The first is the description of the changes themselves—their attributes and capabilities. Compared to the other two stages, this is fairly easy because we have a good understanding of the technology involved. We know about integrated circuits and large-scale integration, and we understand many of their capabilities. The technologies discussed in this chapter have passed this initial stage. We need not speculate about the potential for videorecording equipment for the home, or the applications of personal computers in the home, or the potential for increased use of shop-at-home services. All of this technology has been available for several years. We are fairly certain about the capabilities of these technologies.

In contrast, we are less certain about the second stage of technological change—the diffusion of the technologies throughout society and the extensions of their initial capabilities into unforeseen activities. We are not certain how many consumers will buy high-definition television sets. We are not certain how many of them will buy digital audio disc players to go with their stereo systems. We are not certain how many consumers will buy home computers and actually use them.

We are even less certain about the third stage in our study of technological change—the impact of technological change on our society. To what extent will American consumers become increasingly independent of the major television networks for their viewing? Will any of the superstations, such as WTBS or TNT, soon take over as the ratings leader? To what extent will television viewers zip and zap to be able to watch television on their own schedules rather than those of the networks? Will time-shifting completely change the notion of a network television schedule? The implications of these questions for advertising researchers are very important.

New Media Technologies

When television was new, and later, when color television came along, some consumers were hesitant to buy right away, preferring to wait "until they get it perfected." In marketing parlance, they were the laggards, the consumers who are always last in their neighborhood to adopt a new product idea. In recent times, technological change has come faster than it once did. Consumers are accustomed to advances in all kinds of technology; and although laggards still exist, many consumers have come to expect fast change in applications of technology.

One area of change concerns the rapidly increasing number of media choices that consumers have, especially with their television sets. Nearly 60 percent of all television households subscribe to cable television, and many have access to more than thirty cable channels. For consumers in rural areas and in other areas not served by cable, and for viewers who want independence from cable, satellite reception provides access to a large number of viewing options. And the satellite antenna technology is becoming more affordable and practical. In early 1990, a group of communications companies announced plans for Sky Cable, a satellite system capable of transmitting television signals from an orbiting satellite to an eighteen-square-inch antenna in viewers' homes. The satellite's 108-channel capacity has led some observers to predict that such systems might eventually replace cable television. Companies such as Procter and Gamble, General Foods, General Mills, or General Motors could even lease entire channels for commercial programming.[1]

Videotex is another media technology that may catch on with consumers and hence with advertisers in the 1990s. Videotex systems are commercial databases accessible to consumers with a personal computer and a modem, a device that connects the computer to the database. In addition to giving subscribers access to up-to-the-minute news and financial information, videotex systems can also include the ability to make banking transactions and to order merchandise. Several videotex ventures failed in the 1980s, primarily because of a lack of consumer interest. A few bold companies are banking on more user-friendly technology and more sophisticated consumers to make videotex successful in the 1990s. Those systems are likely to include some form of advertising messages.

Exciting new technologies are not limited to the electronic media. Some magazine publishers have the technology (called selective binding) to enable them to tailor copies of magazines with specific articles and even advertisements for individual viewers. In other words, the articles and advertisements in your copy of a magazine would be different from those in a copy going to a neighbor or friend—because of different demographic characteristics or because of different preferences.

••• Implications for Advertising Research

Advertisers have traditionally been cautious about new media vehicles, such as new magazines and new television stations. They were cautious about cable television at first, but as they saw cable's increasing growth and saw opportunities to reach specialized cable networks, they began to use cable television as an advertising medium.

Advertisers have also been less cautious about using new and specialized magazines for their advertising campaigns. Magazines serve just about any area of human endeavor that one can name. At the consumer level, general consumer magazines compete with magazines that specialize in narrow areas. Many cities now have their metropolitan magazine, a local business publication, a local entertainment guide, a home and garden magazine, and other highly specialized publications. The number of business publications is also staggering, as demonstrated by any recent edition of *Standard Rate and Data Service—Business Publications*. Most of these publications depend heavily, if not completely, on the sale of advertising space for revenue.

Advertisers are always looking for new ways to deliver messages to target markets. In addition to cable television and specialized publications, they have begun to try advertising on rental videotapes and have caused a minor controversy by running advertisements before feature films in movie theaters. They have tried motion picture product placement—that is, arranging to have their products prominently displayed in motion pictures. In the movie *E.T.*, Reese's Pieces candy appeared in a supporting role, and Coor's beer was also an identifiable brand.

Even yellow pages telephone directories, long a medium that received almost no attention in the advertising trade press, have become a contender for advertising dollars. Advertisers have more directory options now, including the silver pages for the senior citizen market and numerous local and specialized directories.

Direct marketing has also become increasingly sophisticated in recent years, and advertisers have responded by spending much more in that medium. Through all types of direct advertising, including television, mail, and other methods, advertisers are finding ways of targeting their markets with increased precision. Americans' penchant for shopping by mail, which is not a new idea because Grandmother did it all the time if she lived in rural America, has opened new opportunities for marketers to identify their customers and to return to them again and again with advertising for products they are most likely to buy.

Advertisers' improved abilities to identify their markets and to target them with greater accuracy has not gone unnoticed by people outside the advertising industry. Witness the furor in 1990 over the targeting of African-American consumers and "virile" women in marketing plans for certain brands of cigarettes. The brand Uptown, test marketed to African-American smokers, and the brand Dakota, targeted to young, blue-collar women, both created an uproar among government officials, critics of smoking, and observers of social trends.

All of those changes have important implications for advertising research. For while they provide advertisers with increased potential for advertising effectively, they also make for greater difficulty in gauging results. One researcher said, "We are faced with a new challenge in some of [the] nontraditional media, whether it's billboards or subway signs or videocassettes. That's going to be a real challenge in the future because almost all advertisers are testing some of those services, and, quite frankly, the statistics of measuring them are a little skimpy right now."[2] Another researcher, commenting on the need for research in yellow pages, said, "Syndicated research services are vitally needed. Our clients have a lot of trouble accepting or believing publisher-generated research."[3]

Advertising research will be affected by technology, too. In Chapter 17, we described the relatively new concept of single-source research, in which companies can measure television exposure and product purchases—electronically from the same group of households. In addition to relying on people meters to record television viewing, those companies use portable scanning wands that read the Universal Product Code bar codes on grocery products. The ability to infer a more direct relationship between exposure to advertising and subsequent purchases has already changed some conceptions of how advertising works and is likely to continue to affect advertising and advertising research in the 1990s. Theoretically, there is no reason that single-source methods cannot be expanded to cover all media usage. The problems are coordination—obtaining cooperation of participants and maintaining it—and avoiding the biasing effects that could arise when the method becomes too intrusive to participants. Cost is also a major problem; such systems are very expensive and will require support from a large number of major subscribers.

Audience Research

Associated with the growth of media availabilities — cable channels, VCRs, specialized magazines, videotex, and satellite broadcasts — comes a serious problem for advertising researchers. The fragmentation that results from increased media availabilities produces smaller audiences. That can be very advantageous for an advertiser trying to target a narrow audience, but for other advertisers it means buying time and space in a large number of vehicles to reach a large and diversified market. Fragmented media buys can be expensive, and they lead advertisers to ask for better evidence of audience size and composition.

To the researcher, the new media availabilities mean difficulty in conducting the kind of research that advertisers want. Take, for example, an imaginary city that has only two television stations and no cable system. With a small sample of television set owners, estimating the relative popularity of two competing programs that are aired at 8:00 on Monday night is simple. In contrast, a typical metropolitan area may have, for example, three major network affiliates, two independent stations, a low-power station, and a public broadcasting station. Add to those availabilities a local cable television system that provides an additional thirty or more channels. Then add the fact that most families own two or more television sets, all of which may be connected to the cable system. It is clear that evaluating audience sizes in this common situation can be very difficult.

The effect of this fractionalization is that the sample of respondents selected for a ratings sweep must include sufficient numbers of people in each demographic segment who watch each channel; otherwise the statistical reliability is diminished. Suppose, for example, that a carefully drawn sample for a thirty-five-channel cable system includes only fifty men age 25–34. Each man represents two percentage points for that segment; and if all of them are watching television at the same time (highly unlikely), their viewing is spread across the thirty-five channels, and the estimates for the channels are highly unreliable. The solution is to increase the sample size, which is very expensive.

With the increase in channel availabilities, what will be the effect on channel hopping or grazing — switching from one station to another during commercial breaks? It has long been known that the rating for a program is not necessarily the rating for the commercials appearing during the program. R. D. Percy & Company has reported that ratings for network in-program commercials are approximately 13 percent below the ratings of the programs in which they appear.[4] A. C. Nielsen is working on an improved people meter that will answer the question of ratings for commercials.[5]

Commercial avoidance varies by program and by commercial, a situation that calls for additional research. In a recent Grammy music awards program, the average commercial was avoided by 10 percent of the average program audience, ". . . but Pepsi commercials featuring Michael Jackson were zapped by only one percent."[6] As advertisers employ techniques that make advertisements look like programs, measurement will probably become increasingly difficult, especially if advertisers want to know exactly how viewers responded to their commercials. A recent Ragu foods spot was designed to look and sound like a TV situation comedy, with a laugh track and applause. Other advertisers are using vignettes, in which programlike content is wrapped around an otherwise ordinary ad.

Message Research

As consumers become accustomed to being bombarded from all directions by advertising messages, how adept do they become at tuning out those messages that are aimed at them? Clutter is a serious problem because it means numerous advertisers are calling for consumers' attention in all the media and could, at a minimum, drive them not to pay attention. Just getting a commercial into a program that reaches a desired target audience is not enough.

As advertising rates escalate in the media, advertisers increasingly turn to smaller units of purchase. Television was once a sixty-second medium but became a thirty-second medium many years ago. And now that the networks are accepting fifteen-second spots, advertisers have still another format to use. This message fragmentation combines with audience fragmentation to make the research effort increasingly difficult.

The potential impact of single-source data on message research is great. Referring to the difference between what a person thinks about an advertisement and that person's actual purchasing decision, Edward Tauber asks, "Who needs recall when you have behavior?"[7]

Competitive Activity Research

Advertisers continue to want to know how other advertisers use the media—how much they spend in each medium and the scheduling they use. It's a little like a card player looking at the opponent's hand, except that in this case the opponent can also look back. The desire of advertisers to obtain complete competitive information was what led Broadcast Advertiser Reports to begin measuring cable usage by advertisers. It is what will lead other research firms to provide data on other kinds of competitive activity.

As cable television and related media become more widespread, advertisers will use them more and more and will want more research. That research will have problems, and solving those problems will be expensive. It could be that advertising research will become so expensive that judgment will become increasingly important.[8]

Research with Long-Term Implications

For the most part this book has focused on applied research, and, in Part Three, on applied research in syndicated form. But you will recall that in Chapter 1 we spent some time discussing theoretical research, or basic research. We pointed out that this research has long-term implications, not day-to-day implications, and that some companies don't like to spend money on this kind of research because it does not provide instant, usable results.

Developments in the media and in the techniques of marketing increasingly put pressure on advertising research professionals to conduct research that shows the relative performance of several advertisements or media schedules. As conducting such research becomes increasingly difficult, it is easy to understand why basic research is left largely to the academic community, the Advertising Research Foundation, and others sufficiently interested to conduct it. But certainly advertising research and advertising itself will be more effective if researchers can build theory of how advertising works.

One researcher has pointed out the danger that some researchers will become so concerned with the potential problems with the newer media that they lose sight of current problems and unanswered questions. Even today, advertising research has failed to answer many basic questions about how advertising works in the traditional media. If those questions remain unanswered, and if advertiser concern and money shift to newer forms of media, the money and effort may be wasted. The researcher lamented the tendency to emphasize short-run problems and neglect problems that could lead to more productive advertising. He conceded that new research technology can be productive for some advertisers who know what they are doing, but he said that for most "the new technology means little more than that they will have to work harder to waste ad budgets than they did before."[9]

... Current Research Issues Likely to Continue

Many of the problems that faced researchers many years ago continue to face them. Some issues never die.

Research directors know the need for improved communication between the research department and company management. They cite the need for researchers who are also marketers and who understand the marketing significance of their research projects. Research directors cite the continuing search for researchers who can write well enough to communicate the results of their research to the decision makers. They also cite the desirability of a researcher's ability to make effective oral presentations and, very important, to participate in the marketing decision-making process. Said one research director, "I'm always impressed when someone in my department is invited to a meeting where research is not the subject, but they're being asked to be there because their business judgment is respected. And I think that's the future of enhancing the function."[10]

Research directors point to the opportunity to gather more information than in the past and the responsibility to use the data wisely. One researcher said, "I've never been in a position where I wasn't inundated with more data than I could look at. Now it's getting worse, but I think the tools to deal with that are getting better all the time.

But the problem 30 years ago and the problem today and the problem 20 years from now is trying to decide what you're going to look at, what kind of answers do I need out of that data."[11]

Researchers point to the lack of standards by which research should be conducted. Comparability of data continues to be a problem, as highlighted in the controversies surrounding audience measurement and copy testing.

Researchers point to the increasing problem of obtaining cooperation from potential respondents. This has brought greater use of the telephone, especially with Wide-Area Telecommunications Service (WATS) lines. Heavier use of computer tabulation is also standard.

In addition, researchers point to what they consider to be excess concern for cutting research costs at the expense of quality. This becomes an increasingly important problem as research costs escalate.

Finally, there is a problem that may never go away. It is the gap that exists between the advertising researcher and the rest of the advertising business. Especially in the creative function of advertising, research is often viewed with skepticism. A 1989 study reported that many advertising managers of companies that use advertising agencies believe agencies are not as up to date on research methods as they are on creative trends. Most of the managers surveyed believed that research reduced risk, but they did not think that research ensured the success of an advertising campaign.[12]

"Creatives are right-brain, nonnumeric artists. Researchers are left-brain, linear, number-crunchers who depend on science, not art," said one researcher.[13] Researchers, he said, are a threat. They conduct what he called "disaster checks," research that implies recklessness of creative people. They use day-after recall, which can be a pass-fail test for a creative execution.

● ● ● Careers in Advertising Research

For the person wanting to make a career in research, this discussion has some important implications. The specific training necessary for persons entering research will depend on the type of research the person wants to conduct. But certain qualifications are nearly always desirable or necessary. Writing skills are very important if the researcher is to be able to communicate to nonresearchers. One cannot depend on a secretary to correct mistakes or rewrite poorly written documents.

Oral communication is important to making effective presentations to clients or management.

The ability to analyze data and see relevant relationships is basic, although extensive training in quantitative methods is not a universal requirement. Understanding problems and being able to recommend and implement research designs are important abilities.

Depending on the situation, management skills may be important. The ability to deal with clients is important.

Professional appearance is also important.

In formal education, some researchers say that a master of business administration degree (MBA) is almost mandatory for a job in corporate research. Graduate training is generally likely to become more important in the future, and doctoral degrees are important for high level research positions.

What about the rift between the research department and other departments? How should an entry-level employee approach a career that seems likely to suffer from built-in tension? There may be hope. About more forward-looking researchers, one industry spokesman said,

> Researchers and creatives can be viewed as more similar than dissimilar since research can be creative, too. In fact, researchers who customize each design and survey instrument need to be just as creative as the people who design each advertising concept and copy. The challenge for both crafts is to escape standardization and strive to meet the business objectives, which create the need for their inspirations.[14]

••• Summary

Throughout this book we have emphasized that advertising research is a technique designed to reduce risk in advertising decision making. That will continue to be true of advertising research in the future. With better-trained researchers, development of improved techniques, and better application of techniques, research will take on an increasingly important role in the marketing and advertising of goods and services.

••• Notes

1. Wayne Walley, "Advertiser Channels on Sky Cable?", *Advertising Age* (March 5, 1990), 17.
2. "Is Marketing Research Doing Its Job?" *Advertising Age* (March 17, 1986), 47.
3. Judith Graham, "Yellow Pages Execs Seek Outside Ratings," *Advertising Age* (November 28, 1988), 24.
4. "To Have and To Hold," *Marketing and Media Decisions* (July 1988), 36.
5. Wayne Walley, "Nielsen's New Meter May Give Ratings for Ads," *Advertising Age* (June 5, 1989), 1.
6. "To Have and To Hold," 36.
7. Edward M. Tauber, "Agency Research Department: 1990," *Journal of Advertising Research* (April/May 1987), 6.
8. William A. Claggett, "Marketing and Advertising in the 1980's," *Advertising Age Yearbook 1981* (Chicago: Crain Books, 1981), 3–15.
9. Gus Priemer, "How, When, Why?", *Marketing and Media Decisions* (November 1981), 111–112.
10. "Is Marketing Research Doing Its Job?", 35.
11. "Is Marketing Research Doing Its Job?", 36.

12. Alice Gagnard and James E. Swartz, "Top American Advertising Managers View Agencies and Research," *Journal of Advertising Research*, Vol. 28 (December 1988/January 1989), 35–40.

13. Robert S. Duboff, "Can Research and Creative Co-Exist?", *Advertising Age* (March 17, 1986), 22.

14. "Can Research and Creative Co-Exist?", 22.

• • • Suggestions for Additional Reading

Conhaim, W. W. "Videotex: Beneficial for the Elderly." *Information Today*, (1989), 26–28.

Gagnard, A., and J. E. Swartz. "Top American Advertising Managers View Agencies and Research." *Journal of Advertising Research*, 28 (1988/1989), 35–40.

Grover, V., and R. Sabherwal. "Poor Performance of Videotex Systems." *Journal of Systems Management*, 40 (1989), 31–37.

Honomichl, J. J. "British, U.S. Researchers Ponder Their Differences." *Advertising Age*, (August 28, 1989), 42.

McClure, B. S. "Electronic Marketing — Learning from America's Largest Retailer." *Supermarket Business*, (October 1988), 13–15.

Murray, P. C. "Alternative Publishing: CD-ROM and Other New Technologies Take Off." *Electronic Publishing and Printing*, 4 (1989), 44–51.

Stewart, D. W. "Measures, Methods, and Models in Advertising Research." *Journal of Advertising Research*, 29 (1989), 54–60.

Truet, B., and M. Hermann. "A Skeptic's View of Videotex." *Telephony*, (July 10, 1989), 26–27.

"Videotex in France: High-Wired Society." *Economist*, August 19, 1989, p. 55.

APPENDIX A

Table of Random Numbers

• • • • • • • •

Tables of random numbers are generated by computers. No relationship exists between one number and the next. To use such a table, you select a starting point and proceed vertically or horizontally. Select the starting point by closing your eyes and pointing to a number on one of the pages.

Suppose you want to draw a sample of 100 persons from a numbered list of 5,000 people. Because your list of people is numbered from 1 to 5,000, the random numbers you draw will also have to be between 1 and 5,000. Suppose your starting point is at column 4 and line 3. The first number there is a 9, which you cannot use because you must have four-digit numbers between 1 and 5,000. The next number, 7, is useless also. But next comes a 2, which can be used. Your first respondent for the sample will be person numbered 2,657 — the 7 is from the next column. As you continue to read left to right, your next number will be 3,936. Continue reading to the right across the page, drop down to the next line, and continue until you have your sample.

You could also use this table for random-digit dialing. First randomly select a regular telephone number from the directory. Keep the three-number prefix but replace the last four numbers with a four-digit number from this table.

Table A.1 Five-Digit Random Numbers*

Line	(1)	(2)	(3)	(4)	(5)	(6)	(7)	(8)	(9)	(10)	(11)	(12)	(13)	(14)
1	10480	15011	01536	02011	81647	91646	69179	14194	62590	36207	20969	99570	91291	90700
2	22368	46573	25595	85393	30995	89198	27982	53402	93965	34095	52666	19174	39615	99505
3	24130	48360	22527	97265	76393	64809	15179	24830	49340	32081	30680	19655	63348	58629
4	42167	93093	06243	61680	07856	16376	39440	53537	71341	57004	00849	74917	97758	16379
5	37570	39975	81837	16656	06121	91782	60468	81305	49684	60672	14110	06927	01263	54613
6	77921	06907	11008	42751	27756	53498	18602	70659	90655	15053	21916	81825	44394	42880
7	99562	72905	56420	69994	98872	31016	71194	18738	44013	48840	63213	21069	10634	12952
8	96301	91977	05463	07972	18876	20922	94595	56869	69014	60045	18425	84903	42508	32307
9	89579	14342	63661	10281	17453	18103	57740	84378	25331	12566	58678	44947	05585	56941
10	85475	36857	53342	53988	53060	59533	38867	62300	08158	17983	16439	11458	18593	64952
11	28918	69578	88231	33276	70997	79936	56865	05859	90106	31595	01547	85590	91610	78188
12	63553	40961	48235	03427	49626	69445	18663	72695	52180	20847	12234	90511	33703	90322
13	09429	93969	52636	92737	88974	33488	36320	17617	30015	08272	84115	27156	30613	74952
14	10365	61129	87529	85689	48237	52267	67689	93394	01511	26358	85104	20285	29975	89868
15	07119	97336	71048	08178	77233	13916	47564	81056	97735	85977	29372	74461	28551	90707
16	51085	12765	51821	51259	77452	16308	60756	92144	49442	53900	70960	63990	75601	40719
17	02368	21382	52404	60268	89368	19885	55322	44819	01188	65255	64835	44919	05944	55157
18	01011	54092	33362	94904	31273	04146	18594	29852	71585	85030	51132	01915	92747	64951
19	52162	53916	46369	58586	23216	14513	83149	98736	23495	64350	94738	17752	35156	35749
20	07056	97628	33787	09998	42698	06691	76988	13602	51851	46104	88916	19509	25625	58104
21	48663	91245	85828	14346	09172	30168	90229	04734	59193	22178	30421	61666	99904	32812
22	54164	58492	22421	74103	47070	25306	76468	26384	58151	06646	21524	15227	96909	44592
23	32639	32363	05597	24200	13363	38005	94342	28728	35806	06912	17012	64161	18296	22851
24	29334	27001	87637	87308	58731	00256	45834	15398	46557	41135	10367	07684	36188	18510
25	02488	33062	28834	07351	19731	92420	60952	61280	50001	67658	32586	86679	50720	94953

*Includes first three pages of *Table of 105,000 Random Decimal Digits*, Bureau of Transport Economics and Statistics, Statement No. 4914 (Washington, D.C.: U.S. Interstate Commerce Commission, 1949).

Table A.1 (continued)

Line	Col. (1)	(2)	(3)	(4)	(5)	(6)	(7)	(8)	(9)	(10)	(11)	(12)	(13)	(14)
26	81525	72295	04839	96423	24878	82651	66566	14778	76797	14780	13300	87074	79666	95725
27	29676	20591	68086	26432	46901	20849	89768	81536	86645	12659	92259	57102	80428	25280
28	00742	57392	39064	66432	84673	40027	32832	61362	98947	96067	64760	64584	96096	98253
29	05366	04213	25669	26422	44407	44048	37937	63904	45766	66134	75470	66520	34693	90449
30	91921	26418	64117	94305	26766	25940	39972	22209	71500	64568	91402	42416	07844	69618
31	00582	04711	87917	77341	42206	35126	74087	99547	81817	42607	43808	76655	62028	76630
32	00725	69884	62797	56170	86324	88072	76222	36086	84637	93161	76038	65855	77919	88006
33	69011	65795	95876	55293	13988	27354	26575	08625	40801	59920	29841	30150	12777	48501
34	25976	57948	29888	88604	67917	48708	18912	82271	65424	69774	33611	54262	85963	03547
35	09763	83473	73577	12903	30883	18317	28290	35797	05998	41688	34952	37888	38917	88050
36	91567	42595	27958	30134	04024	86385	29880	99730	55536	84855	29080	09250	79656	73211
37	17955	56349	90999	49127	20044	59931	06115	20542	18059	02008	73708	83517	36103	42791
38	46503	18584	18845	49618	02304	51038	20655	58727	28168	15475	56942	53389	20562	87338
39	92157	89634	94824	78171	84610	82834	09922	25417	44137	48413	25555	21246	35509	20468
40	14577	62765	35605	81263	39667	47358	56873	56307	61607	49518	89656	20130	77490	18062
41	98427	07523	33362	64270	01638	92477	66969	98420	04880	45585	46565	04102	46880	45709
42	34914	63976	88720	82765	34476	17032	87589	40836	32427	70002	70663	88863	77775	69348
43	70060	28277	39475	46473	23219	53416	94970	25832	69975	94884	19661	72828	00102	66794
44	53976	54914	06990	67245	68350	82948	11398	42878	80287	88267	47363	46634	06541	97809
45	76072	29515	40980	07391	58745	25774	22987	80059	39911	96189	41151	14222	60697	59583
46	90725	52210	83974	29992	65831	38857	50490	83765	55657	14361	31720	57375	56228	41546
47	64364	67412	33339	31926	14883	24413	59744	92351	97473	89286	35931	04110	23726	51900
48	08962	00358	31662	25388	61642	34072	81249	35648	56891	69352	48373	45578	78547	81788
49	95012	68379	93526	70765	10592	04542	76463	54328	02349	17247	28865	14777	62730	92277
50	15664	10493	20492	38391	91132	21999	59516	81652	27195	48223	46751	22923	32261	85653

Table A.1 (continued)

Line	Col. (1)	(2)	(3)	(4)	(5)	(6)	(7)	(8)	(9)	(10)	(11)	(12)	(13)	(14)
51	16408	81899	04153	53381	79401	21438	83035	92350	36693	31238	59649	91754	72772	02338
52	18629	81953	05520	91962	04739	13092	97662	24822	94730	06496	35090	04822	86774	98289
53	73115	35101	47498	87637	99016	71060	88824	71013	18735	20286	23153	72924	35165	43040
54	57491	16703	23167	49323	45021	33132	12544	41035	80780	45393	44812	12515	98931	91202
55	30405	83946	23792	14422	15059	45799	22716	19792	09983	74353	68668	30429	70735	25499
56	16631	35006	85900	98275	32388	52390	16815	69298	82732	38480	73817	32523	41961	44437
57	96773	20206	42559	78985	05300	22164	24369	54224	35083	19687	11052	91491	60383	19746
58	38935	64202	14349	82674	66523	44133	00697	35552	35970	19124	63318	29686	03387	59846
59	31624	76384	17403	53363	44167	64486	64758	75366	76554	31601	12614	33072	60332	92325
60	78919	19474	23632	27889	47914	02584	37680	20801	72152	39339	34806	08930	85001	87820
61	03931	33309	57047	74211	63445	17361	62825	39908	05607	91284	68833	25570	38818	46920
62	74426	33278	43972	10119	89917	15665	52872	73823	73144	88662	88970	74492	51805	99378
63	09066	00903	20795	95452	92648	45454	09552	88815	16553	51125	79375	97596	16296	66092
64	42238	12426	87025	14267	20979	04508	64535	31355	86064	29472	47689	05974	52468	16834
65	16153	08002	26504	41744	81959	65642	74240	56302	00033	67107	77510	70625	28725	34191
66	21457	40742	29820	96783	29400	21840	15035	34537	33310	06116	95240	15957	16572	06004
67	21581	57802	02050	89728	17937	37621	47075	42080	97403	48626	68995	43805	33386	21597
68	55612	78095	83197	33732	05810	24813	86902	60397	16489	03264	88525	42786	05269	92532
69	44657	66999	99324	51281	84463	60563	79312	93454	68876	25471	93911	25650	12682	73572
70	91340	84979	46949	81973	37949	61023	43997	15263	80644	43942	89203	71795	99533	50501
71	91227	21199	31935	27022	84067	05462	35216	14486	29891	68607	41867	14951	91696	85065
72	50001	38140	66321	19924	72163	09538	12151	06878	91903	18749	34405	56087	82790	70925
73	65390	05224	72958	28609	81406	39147	25549	48542	42627	45233	57202	94617	23772	07896
74	27504	96131	83944	41575	10573	08619	64482	73923	36152	05184	94142	25299	84387	34925
75	37169	94851	39117	89632	00959	16487	65536	49071	39782	17095	02330	74301	00275	48280

Line	Col. (1)	(2)	(3)	(4)	(5)	(6)	(7)	(8)	(9)	(10)	(11)	(12)	(13)	(14)
76	11508	70225	51111	38351	19444	66499	71945	05422	13442	78675	84081	66938	93654	59894
77	37449	30362	06694	54690	04052	53115	62757	95348	78662	11163	81651	50245	34971	52924
78	46515	70331	85922	38329	57015	15765	97161	17869	45349	61796	66345	81073	49106	79860
79	30986	81223	42416	58353	21532	30502	32305	86482	05174	07901	54339	58861	74818	46942
80	63798	64995	46583	09785	44160	78128	83991	42865	92520	83531	80377	35909	81250	54238
81	82486	84846	99254	67632	43218	50076	21361	64816	51202	88124	41870	52689	51275	83556
82	21885	32906	92431	09060	64297	51674	64126	62570	26123	05155	59194	52799	28225	85762
83	60336	98782	07408	53458	13564	59089	26445	29789	85205	41001	12535	12133	14645	23541
84	43937	46891	24010	25560	86355	33941	25786	54990	71899	15475	95434	98227	21824	19585
85	97656	63175	89303	16275	07100	92063	21942	18611	47348	20203	18534	03862	78095	50136
86	03299	01221	05418	38982	55758	92237	26759	86367	21216	98442	08303	56613	91511	75928
87	79626	06486	03574	17668	07785	76020	79924	25651	83325	88428	85076	72811	22717	50585
88	85636	68335	47539	03129	65651	11977	02510	26113	99447	68645	34327	15152	55230	93448
89	18039	14367	61337	06177	12143	46609	32989	74014	64708	00533	35398	58408	13261	47908
90	08362	15656	60627	36478	65648	16764	53412	09013	07832	41574	17639	82163	60859	75567
91	79556	29068	04142	16268	15387	12856	66227	38358	22478	73373	88732	09443	82558	05250
92	92608	82674	27072	32534	17075	27698	98204	63863	11951	34648	88022	56148	34925	57031
93	23982	25835	40055	67006	12293	02753	14827	23235	35071	99704	37543	11601	35503	85171
94	09915	96306	05908	97901	28395	14186	00821	80703	70426	75647	76310	88717	37890	40129
95	59037	33300	26695	62247	69927	76123	50842	43834	86654	70959	79725	93872	28117	19233
96	42488	78077	69882	61657	34136	79180	97526	43092	04098	73571	80799	76536	71255	64239
97	46764	86273	63003	93017	31204	36692	40202	35275	57306	55543	53203	18098	47625	88684
98	03237	45430	55417	63282	90816	17349	88298	90183	36600	78406	06216	95787	42579	90730
99	86591	81482	52667	61582	14972	90053	89534	76036	49199	43716	97548	04379	46370	28672
100	38534	01715	94964	87288	65680	43772	39560	12918	86537	62738	19636	51132	25739	56947

Table A.1 (continued)

Line	Col. (1)	(2)	(3)	(4)	(5)	(6)	(7)	(8)	(9)	(10)	(11)	(12)	(13)	(14)
101	13284	16834	74151	92027	24670	36665	00770	22878	02179	51602	07270	76517	97275	45960
102	21224	00370	30420	03883	94648	89428	41583	17564	27395	63904	41548	49197	82277	24120
103	99052	47887	81085	64933	66279	80432	65793	83287	34142	13241	30590	97760	35848	91983
104	00199	50993	98603	38452	87890	94624	69721	57484	67501	77638	44331	11257	71131	11059
105	60578	06483	28733	37867	07936	98710	98539	27186	31237	80612	44488	97819	70401	95419
106	91240	18312	17441	01929	18163	69201	31211	54288	39296	37318	65724	90401	79017	62077
107	97458	14229	12063	59611	32249	90466	33216	19358	02591	54263	88449	01912	07436	50813
108	35249	38646	34475	72417	60514	69257	12489	51924	86871	92446	36607	11458	30440	52639
109	38980	46600	11759	11900	46743	27860	77940	39298	97838	95145	32378	68038	89351	37005
110	10750	52745	38749	87365	58959	53731	89295	59062	39404	13198	59960	70408	29812	83126
111	36247	27850	73958	20673	37800	63835	71051	84724	52492	22342	78071	17456	96104	18327
112	70994	66986	99744	72438	01174	42159	11392	20724	54322	36923	70009	23233	65438	59685
113	99638	94702	11463	18148	81386	80431	90628	52506	02016	85151	88598	47821	00265	82525
114	72055	15774	43857	99805	10419	76939	25993	03544	21560	83471	43989	90770	22965	44247
115	24038	65541	85788	55835	38835	59399	13790	35112	01324	39520	76210	22467	83275	32286
116	74976	14631	35908	28221	39470	91548	12854	30166	09073	75887	36782	00268	97121	57676
117	35553	71628	70189	26436	63407	91178	90348	55359	80392	41012	36270	77786	89578	21059
118	35676	12797	51434	82976	42010	26344	92920	92155	58807	54644	58581	95331	78629	73344
119	74815	67523	72985	23183	02446	63594	98924	20633	58842	85961	07648	70164	34994	67662
120	45246	88048	65173	50989	91060	89894	36036	32819	68559	99221	49475	50558	34698	71800
121	76509	47069	86378	41797	11910	49672	88575	97966	32466	10083	54728	81972	58975	30761
122	19689	90332	04315	21358	97248	11188	39062	63312	52496	07349	79178	33692	57352	27862
123	42751	35318	97513	61537	54955	08159	00337	80778	27507	95478	21252	12746	37554	97775
124	11946	22681	45045	13964	57517	59419	58045	44067	58716	58840	45557	96345	33271	53464
125	96518	48688	20996	11090	48396	57177	83867	86464	14342	21545	46717	72364	86954	55580

Research Companies and Information Sources

Advertising Age
740 Rush St.
Chicago, IL 60611

Advertising Research Foundation
3 E. 45th St.
New York, NY 10022

Advertising Slogans of America
See The Scarecrow Press, Inc.

Adweek
A/S/M Communications, Inc.
6 Piedmont Center
3525 Piedmont Rd.
Atlanta, GA 30305

American Academy of Advertising
Dr. Robert L. King, Executive Secretary
School of Business
University of Richmond
Richmond, VA 23173

American Advertising Federation
1400 K St., N.W., Suite 100
Washington, DC 20005

American Association of Advertising
Agencies
666 Third Ave., 13th Floor
New York, NY 10017

American Demographics
108 N. Cayuga St.
Ithaca, NY 14850

American Statistics Index
See Congressional Information Service

The Arbitron Company
142 W. 57th St.
New York, NY 10019

ASI Market Research, Inc.
79 Fifth Ave.
New York, NY 10003

Association of National Advertisers
155 E. 44th St.
New York, NY 10017

Audit Bureau of Circulations
900 N. Meacham Rd.
Schaumburg, IL 60173-4968

Ayer Directory of Publications
See IMS Press

Birch/Scarborough Research
12350 NW 39th St.
Coral Springs, FL 33065-2404

BPA
360 Park Ave. South
New York, NY 10010

Broadcast Advertisers Reports
800 Second Ave.
New York, NY 10017

Broadcasting/Cablecasting Yearbook
Broadcasting Publications, Inc.
1735 DeSales St., N.W.
Washington, DC 20036

Business Periodicals Index
See H. W. Wilson Company

Business and Economics Databases Online
See Libraries Unlimited

Buyer's Guide to Outdoor Advertising
Institute of Outdoor Advertising
342 Madison Ave.
New York, NY 10173

Cable Advertising Directory
National Cable Television Association
1724 Massachusetts Ave., N.W.
Washington, DC 20036

CD-ROM Source Disk
Diversified Data Resources, Inc.
6609 Rosecroft Pl.
Falls Church, VA 22043-1828

Census Catalog and Guide
See U.S. Government Printing Office

CIS Annual Index to Congressional
Publications and Public Laws
See Congressional Information Service

City and County Data Book
See U.S. Government Printing Office

Commerce Publications Update
See U.S. Government Printing Office

Commercial Atlas and Marketing Guide
Rand McNally & Co.
P.O. Box 127
Skokie, IL 60676-9809

Compact Disclosure
The Public Company Information Source
5161 River Rd.
Bethesda, MD 20816

Congressional Information Service
4520 East-West Highway, Suite 800
Bethesda, MD 20814

Consumer Electronics Annual Review
Electronic Industries Association
2001 Eye St., N.W.
Washington, DC 20006

D & B Donnelley Demographics
Donnelley Marketing Information Services
P.O.Box 10250
Stamford, CT 06904

Data Sources for Business and Market Analysis
See The Scarecrow Press, Inc.

Dictionary of Advertising Terms
Crain Books
740 Rush St.
Chicago, IL 60601

Dictionary of Advertising and Direct Mail Terms
Barron's Educational Series, Inc.
250 Wireless Blvd.
Hauppauge, NY 11788

Dictionary of Marketing, Advertising and Public Relations
International Textbook Co., Ltd.
Furnival House, 14-18 High Holburn
London, England

Direct Marketing Association
6 E. 43rd St.
New York, NY 10017

Directory of Directories
See Gale Research Company

Dissertation Abstracts
University Microfilms
300 N. Zeeb Rd.
Ann Arbor, MI 48106

Dow Jones News/Retrieval
P.O. Box 300
Princeton, NJ 08540

Editor & Publisher International Yearbook
Editor & Publisher Market Guide
11 W. 19th St.
New York, NY 10011

The Effective Echo: A Dictionary of Advertising Slogans
Special Libraries Association
1700 18th St., N.W.
Washington, DC 20009

Effective Frequency
See Association of National Advertisers

Electronic Media Rating Council
420 Lexington Ave.
New York, NY 10017

Encyclopedia of Associations
See Gale Research Company

Encyclopedia of Business Information Sources
See Gale Research Company

ERIC
Educational Resources Information Center
Office of Educational Research & Improvement
U.S. Department of Education
555 New Jersey Ave.
Washington, DC 20208
For CD-ROM version, see SilverPlatter Information, Inc.

Evaluating Advertising: A Bibliography of the Communications Process
See Advertising Research Foundation

Gale Research Company
Book Tower
Detroit, MI 48226

Gallup & Robinson, Inc.
P.O. Box 525, Research Park
Princeton, NJ 08540

GPO on SilverPlatter
See SilverPlatter Information, Inc.

Guide to Reference Books
American Library Association
50 E. Huron St.
Chicago, IL 60611

Handbook of Business Information
See Libraries Unlimited

Harvey Research Organization
1400 Temple Building
Rochester, NY 14604-1581

IMS Press
426 Pennsylvania Ave.
Fort Washington, PA 19034

Index to U.S. Government Periodicals
Infodata International, Inc.
175 E. Delaware Pl.
Chicago, IL 60611

Information Sources in Advertising History
Greenwood Press
P.O. Box 5000
Westport, CT 06880

InfoTrac
Information Access Co.
362 Lakeside Dr.
Foster City, CA 94404

Journal of Advertising
See American Academy of Advertising

Journal of Advertising Research
See Advertising Research Foundation

Journal of Marketing
Journal of Marketing Research
American Marketing Association
250 S. Wacker Dr., Suite 200
Chicago, IL 60606

Leading National Advertisers, Inc.
136 Madison Ave.
New York, NY 10016

Libraries Unlimited
P.O. Box 263
Littleton, CO 80160-0263

Macmillan Dictionary of Marketing and Advertising
Nichols Publishing Co.
P.O. Box 96
New York, NY 10024

Madison Avenue
750 Third Ave.
New York, NY 10017

Madison Avenue Handbook
Peter Glenn Publications
17 E. 48th St.
New York, NY 10017

Magazine Article Summaries
P.O. Box 325
Topsfield, MA 01983

Magazine Publishers Association
575 Lexington Ave.
New York, NY 10022

Marketing and Media Decisions
401 Park Avenue South
New York, NY 10016

Media Cost Guide
ad forum, inc.
18 E. 53rd St.
New York, NY 10022

Media Market Guide
Bethlehem Publishing, Inc.
P.O. Box 119
Bethlehem, NY 03574

Mediamark Research, Inc.
708 Third Ave.
New York, NY 10017

Mendelsohn Media Research
841 Broadway
New York, NY 10003-4704

Monthly Catalog of U.S. Government Publications
See U.S. Government Printing Office

National Register of Advertising Headlines and Slogans
Asher-Gallant Press
201 Montrose Rd.
Westbury, CT 11590

National Register Publishing Co.
3004 Glenview Rd.
Wilmette, IL 60091

Newspaper Advertising Bureau
1180 Avenue of the Americas
New York, NY 11036

Nexis
MeadDataCentral
P.O. Box 933-TD
Dayton, OH 45401

Nielsen Media Research
Nielsen Plaza
Northbrook, IL 60062

Outdoor Advertising Association of America
1899 L St., N.W., Suite 403
Washington, DC 20036

Psychological Abstracts
American Psychological Association
1200 17th St., N.W.
Washington, DC 20036

PsycLit
American Psychological Association
1400 N. Uhle St.
Arlington, VA 22201
For CD-ROM version,
see SilverPlatter Information, Inc.

Public Affairs Information Service
11 W. 40th St.
New York, NY 10018

RADAR®
Statistical Research, Inc.
111 Prospect St.
Westfield, NJ 07090

Radio Advertising Bureau
304 Park Avenue South
New York, NY 10010

Radio Expenditure Reports
740 W. Boston Post Rd.
Mamaroneck, NY 10543

Reader's Guide to Periodical Literature
See H. W. Wilson Company

Readex
140 Quail St.
St. Paul, MN 55115

The Scarecrow Press, Inc.
P.O. Box 656
Metuchen, NJ 08840

Search Strategies in Mass Communication
Longman, Inc.
95 Church St.
White Plains, NY 10601

SilverPlatter Information, Inc.
37 Walnut St.
Wellesley Hills, MA 02181

Simmons Market Research Bureau
380 Madison Ave.
New York, NY 10017

Slogans
See Gale Research Company

Slogans in Print
DDB-Needham
437 Madison Ave.
New York, NY 10022

Social Sciences Index
See H. W. Wilson Company

Standard Directory of Advertisers
Standard Directory of Advertising Agencies
See National Register Publishing Co.

Standard Periodical Directory
Oxbridge Communications, Inc.
150 Fifth Ave., Suite 301
New York, NY 10011

Standard Rate and Data Service
See National Register Publishing Co.

Starch INRA Hooper
566 E. Boston Post Road
Mamaroneck, NY 10543

Survey of Buying Power Data Service
Sales and Marketing Management
633 Third Ave.
New York, NY 10017

Survey of Current Business
See U.S. Government Printing Office

Survey of World Advertising Expenditures
See Starch INRA Hooper

Television Bureau of Advertising
477 Madison Ave.
New York, NY 10022

Television and Cable Fact Book
1836 Jefferson Pl., N.W.
Washington, DC 20036

TVQ
Marketing Evaluations, Inc.
14 Vanderventer Ave.
Port Washington, NY 11050

Ulrich's International Periodicals Directory
R. R. Bowker Company
205 E. 42nd St.
New York, NY 10017

U.S. Bureau of the Census
See U.S. Government Printing Office

U.S. Department of Commerce
See U.S. Government Printing Office

U.S. Government Printing Office
710 N. Capitol St.
Washington, DC 20416

U.S. Industrial Outlook
See U.S. Government Printing Office

VU/TEXT
VU/TEXT Information Services, Inc.
1211 Chestnut St.
Philadelphia, PA 19107

Who's Who in Advertising
Redfield Publishing Co.
P.O. Box 325
Monroe, NY 10950

H. W. Wilson Company
950 University Ave.
Bronx, NY 10452

Working Press of the Nation
The National Research Bureau
310 S. Michigan Ave.
Chicago, IL 60604

World Chamber of Commerce Directory
P.O. Box 1029
Loveland, CO 80539

Index